International dimensions in family law

MANCHESTER
1824
Manchester University Press

International dimensions in family law

John Murphy

Published by Manchester University Press
Oxford Road, Manchester M13 9NR, UK
and Room 400, 175 Fifth Avenue, New York, NY 10010, USA
www.manchesteruniversitypress.co.uk

Distributed exclusively in the USA by
Palgrave, 175 Fifth Avenue, New York,
NY 10010, USA

Distributed exclusively in Canada by
UBC Press, University of British Columbia, 2029 West Mall,
Vancouver, BC, Canada V6T 1Z2

British Library Cataloguing-in-Publication Data
A catalogue record for this book is available from the British Library

Library of Congress Cataloging-in-Publication Data applied for

ISBN 0 7190 6842 8 *hardback*
EAN 978 0 7190 6842 3

First published 2005

14 13 12 11 10 09 08 07 06 05 10 9 8 7 6 5 4 3 2 1

Typeset in 10/12pt Times
by Graphicraft Limited, Hong Kong
Printed in Great Britain
by CPI, Bath

Contents

Preface

Over recent decades, English family law has acquired an increasingly important international dimension. This book endeavours to explore the reasons for, and the extent of, this process of internationalisation. It covers ground that has hitherto been more familiar to public and private international lawyers and to EC lawyers than to domestic family lawyers. The aim is not merely to bring together in one book the various strands of this rather diffuse material, but also to approach this substantial body of law from the perspective of a domestic family lawyer.

Taken as a whole, the book offers a sustained, critical account of the most significant international dimensions in English family law and implicit in its title is the idea that there is now a sizeable corpus of law that may be referred to as 'international family law'. There may be those who balk at such labelling. They may well see its contents not so much as a discrete body of law, but rather as a somewhat selective grouping of various European, public and private international law issues. To those readers, I pose this question: in what way is this any different from the way in which we have traditionally defined the parameters of domestic family law? What matters most is that we begin to grapple in a much more systematic way with the range of issues considered in this book, for the growth in their significance can hardly be denied.

In making my own foray into thinking about these matters I have incurred many debts. The Universities of Copenhagen, Stockholm and Helsinki were all good enough over a period of three years to welcome me to visiting professorships where I learned much about Scandinavian family law and policy. Further afield – at Brigham Young University, Provo, Utah and at Queen's University, Ontario – I was fortunate enough to test out some of my ideas on the way in which English law ought to approach that most topical of juridical phenomena, the same-sex family. Lynn Wardle and Nick Bala were instrumental in enabling me to present and discuss my ideas at these locations and I am grateful to them.

Others to whom I owe a debt of gratitude include Hugh Bevan, Christian Witting, Jane Fortin and Nigel Lowe. The first two helped to engineer it so that I could spend some time researching this book at the Universities of Cambridge and Melbourne, respectively. Jane Fortin was kind enough to provide me with some rather obscure materials that I was unable to get from my own university library, while Nigel Lowe helped me to grapple with the inter-relationship between certain Conventions and various European Regulations. If I have failed to appreciate all the niceties of that inter-relationship, it is in no way his fault.

Quite independently, I must also record my gratitude to the British Academy for generously providing me with financial assistance in connection with this project.

Finally, the biggest thanks of all must go to my family, Anne and Lukas. They showed patience and understanding beyond what could reasonably be asked of them. And it is unfortunate that this small acknowledgement cannot properly repay their love and support.

I have attempted to present the material on the basis of those materials available to as of July 2004. These include the Brussels IIA Regulation which, though not in force at the time of writing, came into force on 1 March 2005. The text of this book was, however, finished and submitted well before the enactment of the Civil Partnership Act 2004. I have tried to amend the contents of chapters 3 and 4 so far as possible at proof stage to take account of its last-minute enactment in late 2004.

John Murphy
Cambridge, July 2004

Introduction

Over the past few decades, we have witnessed a rapid growth in the availability of speedier, cheaper, international travel and fewer, less rigid restrictions on immigration. Young people now travel further and more regularly than in the past, and they also stay away longer. The year abroad, either before or after University, is now rather commonplace; and for company employees, too, there is now more scope than ever before for international secondments and relocations. Within the now expanded Europe Union, the principle of free mobility of labour is an absolutely central value,[1] and this has accounted for a significant increase in intra-European migration.[2] At the same time, globalisation and the growth in the number of multinational corporations has contributed to the number of internationally mobile professionals who move abroad in pursuit of job opportunities and new experiences. One way or another, many more young persons now find themselves migrating and becoming integrated into new, foreign patterns of living. Not uncommonly, such cross-border relocation can lead, in time, to the formation of what we might conveniently call 'international relationships' and the establishment (later) of 'international families'. It can also be the source of family breakdown.[3]

This change in living patterns is not, however, the only reason why family life – and thus family law – has tended to acquire an international dimension. At least as important is the fact that, during the same period, there has been

[1] For details of the free movement provisions, see L. Woods, 'Family Rights in the EU – Disadvantaging the Disadvantaged' [1999] *Child and Family Law Quarterly* 17.

[2] In 2001, 60 per cent of the vastly increased overseas-born population came from European countries: see Census 2001 (available online at www.statistics.gov.uk.cci/nugget.asp?id=767).

[3] See I.M. Ellman, 'Divorce in the United States' in S.N. Katz, J. Eekelaar & M. Maclean (eds), *Cross Currents – Family Law and Policy in the United States and England* (Oxford: Oxford University Press, 2000).

a steady growth in the number of international Conventions and other instruments that are specifically related to family matters and which, to a greater or lesser extent, have a bearing on the content of family law in this country.[4] Finally, the plight of the world's many child refugees and orphans has increasingly become the concern of the developed states. And the explosion in intercountry adoption that this concern provoked from about 1990 onwards has helped to force that topic onto the mainstream family law agenda.

In short, English family law has had to broaden its horizons in recent years to deal adequately with the myriad of novel issues raised by migrant single adults, migrant families and migrant children.[5] Indeed, there can be no doubt that for a significant minority of people either resident or domiciled in this country, the traditional boundaries of family law (at least so far is it is generally taught in English law schools) fail to accommodate or give adequate emphasis to what are now crucial international dimensions. According to the 2001 Census, approximately one in twelve persons living in this country was born abroad,[6] with 7.9 per cent of the total population being people from non-white ethnic minorities.[7] For many such people, the

[4] See L. Silberman, 'The Hague Children's Conventions: The Internationalization of Child Law' in Katz *et al*, *op cit*, n 3. Beyond the Hague Conventions (and several European instruments) there is a wide range of other international instruments that have a negligible, minimal or merely tangential bearing on domestic family law. These have neither been given the force of law in this country, nor look likely to receive it. As such, they are not dealt with in this book. Similarly excluded from detailed consideration are certain family law Conventions that have been ratified by this country – eg, the European Convention on Adoption 1967 and the European Convention on the Legal Status of Children Born out of Wedlock 1975 – but which, again, have not yet been given, and look unlikely to receive, the force of law. For most of these instruments, see the rigorous analysis supplied in G. Douglas, 'The Significance of International Law for the Development of Family Law in England and Wales' in C. Bridge (ed), *Family Law Towards the Millennium: Essays for P.M. Bromley* (London: Butterworths, 1997). And for discussion of one further instrument – the European Convention on the Exercise of Children's Rights 1995 – that looks unlikely even to be signed (let alone ratified) by this country, see J. Fortin, *Children's Rights and the Developing Law* (London: Butterworths, 2003) pp 199–201.

[5] The interests of children – whether they are the adoptees or the birth children of a migrating family – are not necessarily congruent with those of their parents or would-be parents: see H.L. Ackers, 'From "Best Interests" to Participatory Rights – Children's Involvement in Family Migration Decisions' [2000] *Child and Family Law Quarterly* 167; H.L. Ackers, 'Children, Migration and Citizenship in the European Union: Intra-Country Mobility and the Status of Children in EC Law' (1999) 21 *Children and Youth Services Review* 987; P. Hayes, 'Giving Due Consideration to Ethnicity in Adoption Placements – A Principled Approach' [2003] *Child and Family Law Quarterly* 255; E. Bartholet, 'Where do Black Children Belong? The Politics of Race-Matching in Adoption' (1991) 139 *University of Pennsylvania Law Review* 1163.

[6] Census 2001 (available online at www.statistics.gov.uk.cci/nugget.asp?id=767).

[7] *Loc cit* (at www.statistics.gov.uk.cci/nugget.asp?id=767).

traditional boundaries and rules of family law – closely associated as they are with Christian religious values[8] – are simply out of touch with their own cultural traditions and expectations.

As was said in the Preface, this book is intended to reflect the increasing internationalisation of family life and family law, and it endeavours to provide detailed coverage of the major international elements in this area that are, at best, only partially dealt with in existing books on family law or international law.[9] To take but one example, it contains a good deal of private international law that is nearly always overlooked by traditional family law texts and courses. Yet this body of law would seem nowadays to be of much greater practical significance than topics such as nullity of marriage that continue to receive detailed and lengthy consideration in most traditional texts.[10] And there is arguably an element of irony here, for if we leave to one side the highly political and topical transsexual marriage cases, the three most important cases concerning nullity of marriage over the last decade or so have all contained an important foreign element that has been largely overlooked.[11] Given the centrality in political terms of immigration and citizenship issues, it seems wholly appropriate that we should now place greater emphasis on the rules concerning the recognition of 'strange' family forms (such as polygamous marriages and heterosexual and same-sex civil partnerships) upon which such migration rights may turn.

Much of the conflicts of law material is, of course, to be found in specialist works on private international law. Yet the present submission is that the treatment there often lacks the insights of a specialist family lawyer. The

[8] See, eg, D. Bradley, 'Comparative Law, Family Law and Common Law' (2003) 23 *Oxford Journal of Legal Studies* 127, at 130–131; Church of England Report, *The Church and the Law of Nullity of Marriage* (London: SPCK, 1955).

[9] Most standard family law texts pay little regard to matters such as the recognition of foreign marriages and divorces and intercountry adoption. The exceptional topic that does generally get discussed is that of international child abduction. There are some specialist books dealing with international aspects of family law, but these tend to be aimed primarily at practitioners and not the academy: see, eg, N. Lowe, M. Everall & M. Nicholls, *International Movement of Children: Law, Practice and Procedure* (Bristol: Jordan Publishing, 2004). Others are rather narrow in their scope, dealing with just one aspect of the law: see, eg, G. Van Bueren, *The International Law on the Rights of the Child* (Dordrecht: Martinus Nijhoff, 1995); S. Detrick and P. Vlaardingerbroek (eds), *Globalization of Child Law – The Role of the Hague Conventions* (Dordrecht: Martinus Nijhoff, 1999); P. Beaumont & P. McEleavy, *The Hague Convention on International Child Abduction* (Oxford: Oxford University Press, 1999).

[10] N. Lowe & G. Douglas, *Bromley's Family Law* (London: Butterworths, 1998) pp 76–105; S. Cretney, J.M. Masson & R. Bailey-Harris, *Principles of Family Law* (London: Sweet & Maxwell, 2003) pp 35–68; J. Herring, *Family Law* (Harlow: Longman, 2001) pp 34–56.

[11] See *Militante v Ogunwomoju* [1994] *Family Law* 17; *Gereis v Yagoub* [1997] 1 FLR 854; *A-M v A-M (Divorce: Jurisdiction: Validity of Marriage)* [2001] 2 FLR 6.

style is often highly technocratic with the concerns of such lawyers being predominantly the narrow, legalistic questions of jurisdiction, applicable law and the recognition and enforcement of foreign judgments. While it would be wrong to suggest that such matters are unimportant in family law conflicts cases – they clearly are not – it is nonetheless true that policy ought also to play an important part in shaping the relevant rules of private international family law. Put contrariwise, it would be naïve to assume that applying technocratic conflicts rules in a policy vacuum to family law disputes will always (or even regularly) deliver just outcomes.[12] Yet this seems to be the conflicts tradition. As John Collier readily concedes in his conflicts textbook, a policy-driven approach to private international law has enjoyed 'limited appeal on this side of the Atlantic'.[13] And when policy does rear its head, it does so usually under the guise of comity and *forum non conveniens* principles which are, in essence, more concerned with respect for particular Nation States and their courts than with respect for, or concern about, the interests and needs of individual family members.

A similar kind of criticism can be made of European Community forays into the field of family law.[14] For while it is true that the Council of the European Union has begun steadily to produce European legislation with a direct bearing on English family law, it has done so for reasons other than respect for families and family life (albeit that such respect is required by Article 8 of the European Convention on Human Rights). Clare McGlynn has captured the essence of the early European initiatives thus:

> EU family law is being developed as part of a package of measures to promote integration, enhance judicial co-operation, give substance to the concept of EU citizenship and ensure the sound operation of the single market. Thus, the project is in fact highly political, being premised on a particular vision of a deeply integrated Europe, with little reference made to the principles, policies and theoretical bases . . . appropriate for a transnational family law.[15]

The danger, of course, is that these European initiatives will be evaluated according to their furtherance of the broader European integration project. This is not to suggest that all those who specialise in EU law will necessarily fail to appreciate the human element associated with *EU family law*; and it would be misleading to give the impression that this element has gone

[12] For the intimate and inevitable relationship between family law and policy, see J. Eekelaar, *Family Law and Social Policy* (London: Weidenfeld & Nicolson, 1978).

[13] J.G. Collier, *Conflict of Laws* (Cambridge: Cambridge University Press, 2001) p 383.

[14] See, eg, P. McEleavy, 'The Brussels II Regulation: How the European Community has Moved into Family Law' (2002) 51 *International and Comparative Law Quarterly* 883.

[15] C. McGlynn, 'The Europeanisation of Family Law' [2001] *Child and Family Law Quarterly* 35, at 35.

unnoticed in such circles. Tamara Hervey, for example, has been critical in the context of the free movement rights of family members, that the law is not so much concerned with the rights and interests of family members *per se*, but 'with the economic function of family members, [and] in particular the function of support of movement of workers'.[16]

The point here, then, is that, as the EU makes bolder and bolder incursions into the realm of family law regulation,[17] it will be increasingly important to evaluate these steps according to the relevant kinds of yardstick that are generally applied by family law specialists within the study of municipal family law. After all, there would seem to be the distinct possibility in the future of not merely a unified private international family law, but also of a harmonised system of European family law more generally.[18] Such prospects, it is submitted, ought not to be ignored by domestic family lawyers even if they may be somewhat distant at present.[19] Nor should such lawyers assume a passive position in relation to all of this. Instead, English family lawyers must inform themselves of the present position and the outstanding issues that look likely to be addressed. They must also be prepared to contribute in a meaningful and constructive way to the inevitable policy debates

[16] T. Hervey, 'A Gendered Perspective on the Right to Family Life in European Community Law' in N. Neuwahl & A. Rosas (eds), *The EU and Human Rights* (The Hague: Martinus Nijhoff, 1995). See also I. Moebius & E. Szyszczak, 'Of Raising Pigs and Children' (1998) 18 *Yearbook of European Law* 125.

[17] The original Brussels Convention had no relevance to family law matters outside of its application to maintenance agreements. Brussels II went further. It dealt with jurisdiction in cases of divorce, annulment and separation as well as with disputes about parental responsibility between *spouses* (see ch 5), while Brussels IIA went further still by impacting significantly on the law and practice associated with child abduction (see ch 8). The proposed Brussels III and IV Regulations will see yet more regulation of family law matters when they commence their regulation of succession and matrimonial (and analogous) property matters.

[18] In relation to the Convention that formed the template for the Brussels II Regulation, the European Commission commented that, 'family law . . . has to be faced as part of the phenomenon of European integration': European Commission, *Explanatory Report on the Convention on Jurisdiction and the Recognition and Enforcement of Judgments in Matrimonial Matters* OJ C 221/27, 16 July 1998, para 1. See also the arguments that the harmonisation of conflicts rules often serves as a prelude to harmonisation of substantive private law in T.M. de Boer, 'The Relation Between Uniform Substantive Law and Private International Law' in A.S. Hartkamp *et al* (eds), *Towards a European Civil Code* (Dordrecht: Kluwer, 1994), H. Koch, 'Private International Law: A "Soft" Alternative to the Harmonisation of Private Law?' (1995) 3 *European Review of Private Law* 329 and McGlynn, *op cit* n 15.

[19] The European Convention on Contact Concerning Children (considered in ch 10) seeks to impose certain substantive rules of law, but this is yet to enter into force. See also, D. Martiny, 'Is Unification of Family Law Feasible or Even Desirable?' in A.S. Hartkamp *et al* (eds), *Towards a European Civil Code* (Dordrecht: Kluwer, 2nd ed, 1998).

that lie ahead. EU involvement in family law matters must clearly be informed on wider bases than merely the 'economic role of the family'.[20] We can only expect disappointment if the family continues to be perceived as a mere 'part of the economic sector'[21] and as a 'unit of consumption'.[22] We ought, in short, to be concerned by Clare McGlynn's observation that the current understanding of a proper European family policy is as 'a means by which to achieve the economic and political goals of the EU'.[23]

This book comprises an attempt to broaden traditional family law horizons. It is divided into five Parts which, to be clear from the outset, are not intended to represent watertight subdivisions. There is no doubt that there exists considerable overlap between them. But this categorisation does serve to provide a loosely thematic arrangement of the various chapters. Part I of the book is introductory and scene-setting. Chapter 1 considers the various ways in which family law has become increasingly internationalised and the extent to which the international dimensions within family law have in practical terms overtaken more traditional topics, such as nullity of marriage and legitimacy. Chapter 2 provides an introductory account of the various kinds of international instrument that have a bearing on English family law and it seeks to categorise these instruments according to whether they are prescriptive in nature, whether they seek to inculcate international co-operation on a certain matters, or whether they aim to harmonise international standards. It assesses critically the varying degrees to which such instruments provide enforceable rights and obligations, together with the necessary machinery to secure such enforcement.

Part II of the book addresses the main legal issues affecting adults that arise in consequence of the formation and termination (whether by death or dissolution) of 'international familial relationships'. Important issues of citizenship, inheritance rights and immigration rights are closely bound up with the formation and breakdown of such families. It is thus vital to consider the way in which English law (including English private international law) deals with such matters. In chapter 3, we consider the rules governing the recognition of foreign marriages, and, somewhat speculatively, the rules that *might* be applied to the recognition of foreign registered partnerships (including same-sex partnerships). Chapter 4 supplies highly critical consideration of the discretionary bases upon which recognition of such marriages and partnerships can be denied. In particular the focus is upon the dubious

[20] Conclusions of the Council and of the Ministers Responsible for Family Affairs, OJ 1989 C 2777/2, 31 October 1989.

[21] These terms were used in a Communication from the Commission on Family Policies quoted in McGlynn, *op cit* n 15, at 37.

[22] *Loc cit.*

[23] *Loc cit*, at 45.

nature of the policy factors that have, from time to time, been invoked to deny recognition to a marriage that otherwise complies with the two chief requirements of formal and essential validity. The chapter also considers in depth the way in which the English courts may have to address the tricky, but seemingly inevitable, question of whether they *ought* to recognise a foreign registered partnership.

In chapter 5 the focus shifts to the recognition of foreign divorces, annulments and legal separations. In chapter 6 attention is devoted to the various proprietary and financial consequences of marriage (and partnership) formation: namely, rights of succession, rights to financial maintenance and proprietary entitlements according to various systems of community of property and ante-nuptial agreements.

Part III of the book is concerned with child-centred issues. In chapter 7 the law in relation to intercountry adoptions (that is, the adoption by English adults of foreign children) is considered. In chapter 8, we address the now astoundingly complex area of international child abduction. There is full discussion of both the Hague and the European Conventions together with detailed, critical analysis of the way in which (post-Brussels IIA) the applicability and operation of these Conventions will vary dramatically depending on which two States are involved in an abduction dispute.

Part IV of the book provides critical analysis of three further international instruments that are of present or (seemingly) prospective importance for English family law. The first of these, the United Nations Convention on the Rights of the Child, is discussed in chapter 9. This Convention has now been around for a long time and does not look destined to be made a part of English domestic law in the same formal way that the Hague Adoption and Abduction Conventions have been. Nonetheless, it has been extremely widely ratified and for that reason manages to exert some degree of influence over municipal family law. Furthermore, the fact that it has not been given the force of domestic law does not change the fact that, upon the United Kingdom's ratification of it, it became operative at the level of public (as opposed to private) international law, setting international standards and imposing obligations on individual Nation States. In chapter 10 we consider two additional Conventions that look set to have some bearing on English family law in the none-too-distant future. They are the Hague Child Protection Convention 1996 and the European Convention on Contact Concerning Children 2003.

Chapter 11 forms Part V of the book. It offers a series of reflections on the various international dimensions in family law that are currently in existence and on those that may well emerge in the future. The chapter also assesses the kinds of policies and politics that so markedly shape their content and, where appropriate, suggests ways in which these aspects of English family might be remoulded or refined in the future. But for those only concerned with particular areas of the law, rather than the international picture as a whole, each substantive chapter has been concluded with a critique of the current law. I have offered these critiques recognising fully that the whole of the book may not yet strike all domestic family lawyers as essential reading. Nonetheless, the book was not primarily designed to be read in this somewhat specious way. Rather, it is intended *as a whole* to bring to the attention of such lawyers the significance and the extent of the various international strands in municipal family law. Thus, while it is my hope that readers will engage with the whole and share my view that complex matters of private international law, hitherto tangential matters of community law and unenforceable elements of public international law ought no longer to be ignored, side-lined or downgraded, I have also endeavoured to bring a consistent, personal, 'family lawyer's' perspective to each of the substantive topics. Doubtless my comments and observations will not be the final word on all or any or these issues. But if they at least provoke debate and dialogue between domestic academic family lawyers they will have served a useful function.

Part I

Introductory matters

1

The internationalisation of family law

Despite any impression to the contrary, this book is mainly concerned with domestic family law: that is, with the rules of law that apply within the jurisdiction of England and Wales.[1] What the title is intended to convey, and indeed the very premise upon which the book is written, is that municipal family law ought no longer to be thought of as a body of rules that reflects, shapes and reinforces jurisdictionally specific and culturally homogeneous values and norms.[2] Rather, it is intended to convey that the focus of this work is on the fact that modern municipal family law bears a number of important, if somewhat diffuse, international dimensions. Furthermore, the central contention is that these international dimensions cannot continue to be dismissed as peripheral or irrelevant merely because they have not so far been systematically analysed in the way that this book attempts to deal with them. Practitioners are no longer 'in denial' in this regard and specialist practitioner-oriented literature has already begun to emerge.[3] Indeed, as one solicitor has cautioned, '[a]ll family lawyers will [nowadays] come across a

[1] Part IV of the book is the exception in that it deals with several international Conventions that have not formally been incorporated into English law. Nonetheless, as the relevant chapters make clear, these Conventions are either already very influential so as to have a noteworthy indirect effect on the content of English domestic law, or they look set be to be given the force of law within the foreseeable future.

[2] For the dynamic relationship between law and norms, see J. Eekelaar, 'Uncovering Social Obligations: Family Law and the Responsible Citizen' in M. Maclean (ed), *Making Law for Families* (Oxford: Hart Publishing, 2000) p 16.

[3] See, eg, the practitioner journal *International Family Law* (which began in 1997). See also N. Lowe, M. Everall & M. Nicholls, *International Movement of Children: Law, Practice and Procedure* (Bristol: Jordan Publishing, 2004); G. Van Bueren, *The International Law on the Rights of the Child* (Dordrecht: Martinus Nijhoff, 1995); S. Detrick & P. Vlaardingerbroek (eds), *Globalization of Child Law – The Role of the Hague Conventions* (Dordrecht: Martinus Nijhoff, 1999).

case with an international element' and mistakes in dealing with such a case 'could have a devastating effect on your client, as well as giving the client the right to bring a negligence action'.[4]

At the time of writing, it is Europe that is spearheading the way to yet further internationalisation.[5] The EC Regulation generally known as Brussels IIA[6] has had a profound impact not only on the jurisdiction rules in relation to divorces involving a foreign element but also upon the law and practice of child abduction within Europe. Furthermore, other such Regulations look to be more or less imminent. Brussels III and IV will, once their texts have been finalised, serve to harmonise the private international law rules among EU States with respect to matrimonial (and analogous) property on the one hand, and succession on the other.[7]

European initiatives are not, however, the only source of English family law's internationalisation. In fact, the process has been gaining momentum more generally for close on half a century (although admittedly some international dimensions have been present within English law for a lot longer than that). This chapter seeks both to explain the various factors that have contributed to this process of internationalisation and to elaborate upon the central premise of the book that these international aspects are destined to become more prominent and more challenging in the years to come.

The internationalisation of English family law

There appear to be four main sources from which English law has become increasingly internationalised over recent decades. Each is considered in turn.

Binding conventions and other international instruments

A number of international instruments have either been consciously incorporated into English law by virtue of domestic legislation, or have become operative without the need for any action on the part of Parliament. Either way, the rights and obligations embodied in these various instruments have become enforceable before the English courts. As regards those instruments

[4] A. Thomas, 'Family Law in Europe – The Way Ahead' [2004] *Eurojuris* (available on the internet at www.eurojuris.net/eng/article-detail.asp?ArticleId=195).

[5] See C. McGlynn, 'The Europeanisation of Family Law' [2001] *Child and Family Law Quarterly* 35.

[6] Council Regulation (EC) No 2201/2003 (repealing but, so far as divorce law is concerned, almost precisely re-enacting, parts of Council Regulation (EC) No 1347/2000 – generally called 'Brussels II').

[7] See C.M.V. Clarkson, 'Brussels III – Matrimonial Property European Style' [2002] *Family Law* 683.

that have been electively incorporated into English law, the most important for present purposes are the Hague Convention on the Civil Aspects of International Child Abduction 1980,[8] the European Convention on Recognition and Enforcement of Decisions Concerning Custody of Children and on Restoration of Custody of Children 1980,[9] the Hague Convention on Protection of Children and Co-operation in Respect of Intercountry Adoption 1993[10] and the European Convention on Human Rights. (The last-named Convention is not specifically a family law instrument[11] but it has still had a profound effect upon the way in which family law litigation is conducted and the way in which substantive family law now develops in this country.[12]) In turn, these various Conventions were given the force of law in this country by virtue of the Child Abduction and Custody Act 1985,[13] the Adoption (Intercountry Aspects) Act 1999[14] and the Human Rights Act 1998.[15] Others that appear likely candidates to be similarly incorporated in the future are the Hague Child Protection Convention 1996 and the European Convention on Contact Concerning Children 2003.

Turning to those international instruments that have become directly effective in this country (that is, with no need for parliamentary action), the

[8] For detailed discussion, see ch 8.

[9] See *ibid.*

[10] For detailed discussion, see ch 7.

[11] For this reason, it does not receive independent consideration in this book. Discussion of its impact specifically on family law is already legion, and little can be added here. See, eg, H. Swindells, '"Crossing the Rubicon" – Family Law Post the Human Rights Act 1998' in S. Cretney (ed), *Family Law: Essays for the New Millennium* (Bristol: Jordan Publishing, 2000); J. Fortin, *Children's Rights and the Developing Law* (London: Butterworths, 2003) p 31; *id*, 'Rights Brought Home for Children' (1999) 62 *Modern Law Review* 350; *id*, 'Children's Rights and the Impact of Two International Conventions: The UNCRC and the ECHR' in The Rt Hon LJ Thorpe & C. Cowton (eds), *Delight and Dole: The Children Act 10 Years on* (Bristol: Jordan Publishing, 2002); J. Murphy, 'Aids, Human Rights and Family Law' (forthcoming in M. Brazier, J. McHale & J. Harrington (eds), *AIDS, Europe and Human Rights* (Oxford: Oxford University Press, 2005)).

[12] Most profoundly, in *Bellinger v Bellinger* [2003] 1 FLR 1043, the House of Lords issued a declaration under s 4 of the HRA 1998 that s 11(c) of the Matrimonial Causes Act 1973 is now incompatible with the European Human Rights Convention insofar as it denies persons of the same sex the right to marry one another. See also *Ghaidan v Godin-Mendoza* [2004] UKHL 30 in which the House of Lords held that domestic landlord and tenant legislation, when read so as to be compatible with the Human Rights Convention, could be seen to confer a right to succeed to a tenancy on a same-sex partner although the legislation makes reference to those living together as 'man and wife'. The same-sex partners in this case were, according to their Lordships, living in a suitably 'marriage-like' relationship.

[13] Section 1(1).

[14] This was brought into force only on 1 June 2003 by virtue of the Adoption (Intercountry Aspects) Act 1999 (Commencement No 8) Order (SI 2003, No 189).

[15] Section 1.

most important to date is the Brussels IIA Regulation.[16] There are, however, others on the horizon – namely, Brussels III and Brussels IV (dealing with matrimonial (and analogous) property, and with succession). These instruments will undoubtedly have a marked impact upon upon a good deal of the law discussed in chapter 6. But since the text of these instruments was not finalised, or even close to being finalised, at the time of writing, it was not possible to analyse them in any depth.

Sources of international influence

With rather more subtlety, English family law has also to some extent been internationalised by virtue of various forms of external influence. The first of these influences is substantive international law. For whether in the form of Treaties or the decisions of international tribunals, public international law will sometimes have the capacity to embody an international consensus on certain principles and norms that are suitable for adoption at the level of domestic private law. The United Nations Convention on the Rights of the Child provides a prime example in this context. In itself, it is neither directly effective so as to create enforceable rights on the part of individual citizens, nor has it ever formally been given the force of law in the United Kingdom. But it has nonetheless constituted an important and persuasive consideration in the context of a number of court decisions, and it exerts on States Parties a certain amount of politico-legal pressure to adapt domestic law in line with agreed international norms. Thus, as Maher has remarked (albeit in relation to Hague, not United Nations, Conventions):

> It may be . . . noted that the use of a Hague Convention as a source of ideas and principles for more general application is to be found not only in statute but also in the reasoning of the courts. [Thus] [i]n a number of decisions the courts have held that they can apply the 'philosophy' underlying the Hague Convention on Child Abduction to cases concerning . . . countries which are not signatories to the Convention.[17]

Influence within this first category is by no means limited to the politico-legal will to comply with the spirit, if not the letter, of Hague and United Nations Conventions. Regional Treaties, too, are capable of exerting such influence. Thus, for example, the right to respect for one's private and family life contained in Article 8 of the European Convention on Human Rights featured prominently in English case law concerning the rights of unmarried fathers (and their biological children) for quite some time prior to the formal incorporation of that Convention into English law. In similar vein, EC law

[16] For detailed discussion of its impact on in the areas of divorce and international child abduction, see chs 5 and 8, respectively.

[17] G. Maher, 'Implementation of Hague Conventions in Domestic Law: The United Kingdom Approach' [1995] *Civil Justice Quarterly* 21, at 36–37.

can be shown to be influential in shaping the concepts critical to delimiting the boundaries of family law.[18] Thus, after the European Court of Justice had effectively limited the concept of 'family' to those units based on heterosexual matrimony[19] the English court felt able to run with that concept and deny the application of the Equal Treatment Directive to same-sex couples on the basis that there could not be, by definition, sexual orientation discrimination against a same-sex family.[20]

More progressively, the House of Lords has recently followed the lead set by the European Court of Human Rights in holding that a domestic rule of law that prohibits transsexuals from marrying according to their new sex is inconsistent with the right to marry and found a family contained in Article 12 of the Human Rights Convention.[21] In so doing, the House or Lords was effectively moving on from dated domestic authority[22] and related Strasbourg jurisprudence[23] that had been produced prior to the vastly liberalised marriage and civil partnership laws that have proliferated throughout Europe in the interim.[24]

A second, more localised, form of international influence can be traced to legal developments in other jurisdictions. And while in the past this kind of influence was largely confined to the courts of this country seeking guidance from the related jurisprudence of fellow common law jurisdictions in novel and hard cases, more recent times have revealed a similar willingness to follow foreign leads on the part of the legislature. A prime example is the Child Support Act 1991 which replaced judicial discretion with the administrative application of a fixed formula as the basis upon which a non-resident parent's financial support obligations towards his or her children should be calculated. This was largely inspired by, and modelled upon, Australian and American legislation from some years earlier.[25]

[18] See, C. McGlynn, 'A Family Law for the EU' in J. Shaw (ed), *Social Law and Policy in an Evolving EU* (Oxford: Hart Publishing, 2000); T. Hervey, 'A Gendered Perspective on the Right to Family Life in European Community Law' in N. Neuwahl & A. Rosas (eds), *The EU and Human Rights* (Dordrecht: Kluwer, 1995); L. Woods, 'Family Rights in the EU – Disadvantaging the Disadvantaged' [1999] *Child and Family Law Quarterly* 17.

[19] *Netherlands v Reed* [1986] ECR 1283.

[20] *Grant v South West Trains Ltd* [1998] 1 FLR 839.

[21] *Bellinger v Bellinger* [2003] 1 FLR 1043.

[22] *Corbett v Corbett* [1971] P 83.

[23] *Rees v UK* [1987] 2 FLR 111; *Cossey v UK* [1991] 2 FLR 492; *Sheffield and Horsham v UK* [1998] 2 FLR 928.

[24] See the change in tack in *Goodwin v UK* [2002] 2 FLR 487 and *I v UK* [2002] 2 FLR 518.

[25] See M. Maclean & J. Eekelaar, 'Child Support: The British Solution' (1993) 7 *International Journal of Law and the Family* 205. Since its enactment, the formula used to calculate child support has been revised a number of times and nowadays bears rather less resemblance to those models that initially inspired it: see, N. Wikely, 'Child Support: The New Formula' [2000] *Family Law* 820.

More recently still, as the cultural and societal similarities between this country and her western European neighbours has grown, and as those between the UK and other common law jurisdictions (most notably the United States) has waned to some extent,[26] the focus has shifted from what other common law judges do, to what other European States do. A good example of such European influence was what became an overwhelming case for the introduction of Civil Partnership legislation along the lines of that first produced by the Danes[27] and now widely replicated around Europe.[28] Several Private Members' attempts to introduce such legislation were made, but at last the case has won government support and an Act of Parliament to legalise registered partnerships between homosexual couples was finally enacted as the Civil Partnership Act 2004 in November 2004.[29]

Another example of European family law exerting influence over the content of English family law can be seen in the changing attitudes of the English courts to ante-nuptial agreements that are widely recognised and used throughout Europe and elsewhere, but which are not currently regarded as valid in this country. As recently as 1995, a leading Family Division judge was resolutely against the enforcement of ante-nuptial agreements that purported to determine spouses' respective rights and obligations on the occasion of divorce. He said:

> The rights and responsibilities of those whose financial affairs are regulated by statute cannot be much influenced by contractual terms which were devised for the control and limitation of standards that are intended to be of universal application throughout our society.[30]

[26] For examples of these cultural connections and distinctions, see G. Douglas, 'The Significance of International Law for the Development of Family Law in England and Wales' in C. Bridge (ed), *Family Law Towards the Millennium: Essays for P.M. Bromley* (London: Butterworths, 1997) pp 87–88. On Anglo-American comparisons, see S.N. Katz, J. Eekelaar & M. Maclean (eds), *Cross Currents – Family Law and Policy in the United States and England* (Oxford: Oxford University Press, 2000) and D. Bradley, 'Comparative Law, Family Law and Common Law' (2003) 23 *Oxford Journal of Legal Studies* 127.

[27] Act 372 (1989), s 5(2). For commentary and analysis, see M.P. Broberg, 'The Registered Partnership for Same-Sex Couples in Denmark' [1996] *Child and Family Law Quarterly* 149, esp at 152–153; I. Lund-Andersen, 'Cohabitation and Registered Partnership in Scandinavia: The Legal Position of Homosexuals' in J. Eekelaar & T. Nhalpo (eds), *The Changing Family – Family Forms and Family Law* (Oxford: Hart Publishing, 1998) pp 399–401; L. Nielsen, 'Family Rights and the "Registered Partnership" in Denmark' (1990) 4 *International Journal of Law and the Family* 297.

[28] They exist, in one form or another, in Belgium, France, Denmark, Hungary, The Netherlands, Norway, Sweden and certain Autonomias in Spain.

[29] This Act was passed after the completion of the manuscript for this book and there was very limited opportunity at proof stage to do more than note its enactment.

[30] *F v F (Ancillary Relief: Substantial Assets)* [1995] 2 FLR 45, at 66 *per* Thorpe J.

By 2002, the idea that such contracts are also contrary to public policy in so far as they contemplate divorce and therefore undermine the idea that marriage is a life-long union had all but been abandoned. As Connell J said: '[t]he public policy objection to such agreements, namely that they tend to diminish the importance of the marriage contract, seems to me to be of less importance now that divorce is so commonplace.'[31] In addition, even though the divorce courts cannot shift wholesale from the position that Parliament has conferred upon them to regulate the financial affairs of divorcing spouses, they may nonetheless take into account the terms of any putative ante-nuptial agreement insofar as it is indicative of relevant conduct of the parties or of general background circumstances. For both of these concerns form relevant desiderata for the judges in their exercise of the statutory discretion in maintenance matters on divorce.[32] In a telling recent dictum, Wilson J openly divulged the reason for this change of approach: the influence of foreign systems of family law. He said this: 'Where other jurisdictions . . . have been persuaded that there are cases where justice can only be served by confining the parties to their rights under prenuptial agreements, we should be cautious about too categorically asserting the contrary.'[33]

In the light of these decisions, it may well be that English law will follow the Australian lead and abandon the present stance according to which ante-nuptial contracts are treated as invalid *per se*. Certainly, the courts have signalled a willingness to give effect to ante-nuptial settlements, for these can be distinguished from ante-nuptial agreements on the basis that they regulate the parties' financial affairs *during the subsistence of a marriage* and therefore do not purport to undermine the statutory powers of the divorce court.[34] And even more radically, some English family law academics have now begun to discuss the merits and disadvantages of foreign community of property systems.[35]

[31] *M v M (Prenuptial Agreement)* [2002] 1 FLR 654, at 661. See the similar conclusion reached by a current Law Lord in B. Hale, 'The Family Law Act 1996 – The Death of Marriage?' in C. Bridge (ed), *Family Law Towards the Millennium: Essays for P.M. Bromley* (London: Butterworths, 1997) and S. Poulter, 'The Definition of Marriage in English Law' (1979) 42 *Modern Law Review* 409.

[32] See Matrimonial Causes Act 1973, s 25(1), (2)(g). In *M v M (Prenuptial Agreement)* [2002] 1 FLR 654, Connell J said (at 661): 'In my view it matters not whether the court bears such an agreement in mind as part of the circumstances of the case (a very important factor) or as an aspect of the parties' conduct. Under either approach the court should look at any such agreement and decide in the particular circumstances what weight should, in justice, be attached to it.' See also *K v K (Ancillary Relief: Prenuptial Agreement)* [2003] 1 FLR 120 where the terms of an ante-nuptial contract were considered relevant to the court's decision on financial relief.

[33] *S v S (Divorce: Staying Proceedings)* [1997] 2 FLR 100, at 103.

[34] *N v N (Jurisdiction: Prenuptial Agreement)* [1999] 2 FLR 745, at 752 *per* Wall J.

[35] See A. Barlow, T. Callus & E. Cooke 'Community of Property – A Study for England and Wales' (2004) 37 *Family Law* 47.

Finally, Chapter II of the 2003 European Convention on Contact Concerning Children – although it is yet to receive the force of law – contains provisions that form substantive rules of domestic law.[36] This willingness to harmonise rules of substantive law (and not merely conflicts rules) marks an arguably most portentous development.

Changing patterns of family life

There are at least two notable bi-products of the increase in the willingness to migrate of families and family members. The first concerns a comparable increase in the number of divorces with an international element. The second concerns international child abduction. So far as the treatment of divorces with a foreign element is concerned, the English courts were at one time only occasionally required to consider the cultural and religious aspects with which many such divorces are bound up. But as the number of people now requesting such dissolutions has increased – particularly women habitually resident in this country – domestic law has had to adapt in order to strike the appropriate balance between cultural pluralism and fundamental conceptions of equality. Indeed, as the Lord Chancellor of the day remarked in relation to the provisions of the Family Law Act 1986 dealing with foreign divorces obtained otherwise than by means of proceedings:

> There are public policy elements here. Such divorces are informal, arbitrary and usually unilateral . . . In addition, these divorces are almost exclusively obtained by men and therefore discriminate against women . . . [Thus] one of the aims is to give greater protection to wives resident in the UK whose husbands have obtained an informal divorce abroad.[37]

Hand in hand with the dissolution of international marriages goes that of international child abduction. In fact, this topic now seems to figure in the law reports at least as much as any other, and certainly more than most. Where a mother originating from overseas suffers the breakdown of her marriage in this country, she will not infrequently seek to return to her country of origin surreptitiously taking any children of the family with her. Of course, it can also work in reverse and the removing parent need not be the mother. In any event, whichever parent removes the children, and whether the abduction is incoming or outgoing, it is equally clear that the problem is not confined to situations involving the breakdown of marriage; abductions may just as well occur following the break-up of long-term cohabitational relationships. Indeed, unmarried mothers may feel somehow more at liberty to remove their children without the father's consent; and in

[36] For details, see ch 10.

[37] HL Debates, vol 473, Col 1082. For further discussion of the policy issues at stake, see ch 5.

such cases there might well be legal complications associated with disputed parental responsibility and custody rights on the part of the unmarried father.

The short point is that changing family forms and family living patterns demand a new legal order – increasingly one that reflects the growing internationalisation of family life. In relation to child abduction alone, it is noteworthy that there was a 79 per cent growth in the number of reported cases during the latter part of the 1990s.[38]

Globalisation

Globalisation describes the phenomenon by which corporations, non-governmental organisations and host of other entities have come to exist within a supra- or transanational commercial or legal world. Given the importance in world terms of these various international entities, it follows that domestic equivalents, confined as they are within specific national borders, are now of less significance in terms of commercial power and international influence. So far as the commercial world is concerned, globalisation has caused a great deal of convergence in political norms that arguably undermine the independence and sovereignty of the Nation State.[39] But as Ewoud Hondius has argued, such convergence does not stop there. Instead, he contends that globalisation has also produced an increased commonality of cultural and social values so that, in turn, family law has become a viable candidate for greater harmonisation.[40] A similar view is taken by Koens, who suggests that these influences make it 'obvious that a merely national point of view will no longer suffice for a good understanding of current and future persons and family law'.[41]

Migration patterns and population change

As statistics taken from the Government's Official National Statistics Website reveal: '[m]igration into this country increased from 265,000 in 1993 to 513,000 in 2002' and '[o]ut-migration also increased over the period . . . from

[38] Lowe *et al*, *op cit* n 3, p 561.

[39] See M. Loughlin, *Sword & Scales: An Examination of the Relationship Between Law and Politics* (Oxford: Oxford University Press, 2000) pp 144–147.

[40] See E.H. Hondius, 'Naar een Europees personen – En Familierecht' in H. Franken & J. de Ruiter (eds), *Drie Treden: Over Politiek, Beleid en Recht* (Zwolle, W.E.J. Tjeenk Willink, 1995) pp 173–181 (quoted in K. Boele-Woelki, 'The Road Towards a European Family Law' [1997] Electronic Journal of Comparative Law, available at www.ejcl.org/11/art11-1.html#h3).

[41] M.J.C. Koens, *Het Hedendaagse Personen – En Familierecht* (Zwolle: W.E.J. Tjeenk Willink, 1995) p 13 (quoted in Boele-Woelki, *op cit* n 40).

266,000 in 1993 to 359,000 in 2002'.[42] What these figures illustrate is the significant growth in, and current scale of, migration affecting modern Britain. Perhaps even more importantly, however, these statistics also reveal the fact that the number of inward migrants consistently outstrips the number of outward migrants. This means (given a relatively stable overall population) that there is growing minority of persons in this country for whom the cultural traditions and social values that once arguably characterised quintessential Englishness are to some extent alien.[43] Accordingly, those aspects of family law that reflect and buttress these often outmoded norms and values find themselves inevitably tested from time to time; and with 8.3 per cent of the current population having been born abroad,[44] this should come as no surprise. But when such challenges arise, it is critical that English family law judges respond in a suitably pluralistic and broadminded manner. It would, for example, be thoroughly unacceptable if the validity of a foreign marriage were nowadays to be judged according to the outmoded yardstick of whether it resembled a marriage 'as understood in Christendom'.[45]

Even beyond those laws premised upon a particular set of religious or cultural values, there is a host of other legal problems that naturally flow from these population dynamics. The most obvious example, of course, is that of international child abduction, which is remarkably common in the modern era, there being cases reported in virtually every issue of the specialist periodical *Family Law* as well as in the Family Law Reports.

Conclusion and critique

There is a very active private international law community that has produced (and continues to produce) a sizeable number of Conventions that, to varying degrees, have the potential to impact significantly upon English family law. Unfortunately, the principles underpinning these Conventions are not always consistent with one another, and there is therefore the danger that the United Kingdom will become Party to a number of conflicting Conventions. It is a danger that has accounted for the delay in ratifying the

[42] www.statistics.gov.uk.cci/nugget/as?id=767.

[43] These differences are generally less pronounced in relation to European immigrants – who accounted for some 89,000 of the incoming population in 2002: www.statistics.gov.uk.cci/nugget/as?id=767 – but even here (especially in relation to matrimonial property and civil partnership rules) the differences can be quite pronounced. See further, chs 4 and 6.

[44] www.statistics.gov.uk.cci/nugget/as?id=766. In just one decade ending with 2002, '3.9 million people entered the country as migrants': *loc cit.*

[45] *Hyde v Hyde* (1866) LR 1P & D 130, at 133 *per* Lord Penzance.

1996 Child Protection Convention, and it is still more pronounced in relation to the various international instruments that relate to child abduction. One scholar has even described the problem as being one of 'too many cooks',[46] while others have suggested that we seem to be moving from an era in which it was apt to speak of the 'conflict of laws' to one in which the more appropriate appellation would be the 'conflict of Conventions'.[47]

In the light of these observations, what appears necessary is a fuller participation in the negotiation and drafting of important future Conventions. Professor Chris Clarkson has conducted sterling work in relation to the imminent Brussels III Regulation (which will be directly effective, and enforceable under the jurisdiction of the Court of Justice). But such preliminary involvement is not only unusual, it is also not without its consequences. For as Droz and Dyer have noted, there are certain international Conventions that can never meaningfully be ratified by this country for the simple reason that they have been drafted in terms that are alien to the common law.[48] Such observations merely emphasise the importance associated with coming to terms with, and participating more fully in, the internationalisation of English family law. This is not something that has escaped the attention of EU Law specialists. Thus, as McGlynn suggests:

> development must not be left to those debating the need for greater legitimacy of the European projects of citizenship, judicial co-operation and the single market. [Rather] [i]f family laws are to be adopted at the EU level, they must only be so if . . . those with a knowledge of the development of family laws at national level engage with the European debate.[49]

Participation in the drafting of international Conventions is one thing. But giving optimal effect to them domestically can sometimes be quite another. This therefore raises the question of which way is the best when it comes to implementing international Conventions. There are several options (all illustrated in chapter 2), but on balance, incorporating the original text into the Schedule of an Act of Parliament seems the most appropriate method. Doing so avoids any potential conflict between the terms of a Convention and any statute that might have been drafted separately in order to give effect to

[46] P.M. North, 'Hague Conventions and Reform of English Conflict of Laws' (1981) 6 *Dalhousie Law Journal* 417, at 438.

[47] Lowe *et al*, *op cit* n 3, p *vii*.

[48] G.A.L. Droz & A. Dyer, 'The Hague Conference and the Main Issues of Private International Law for the Eighties' (1981) 3 *Northwestern Journal of International Law and Business* 155, at 162. For a concrete example of such a Convention, see the Hague Convention Concerning the Powers of Authorities and the Law Applicable in Respect of the Protection of Infants 1961. See also, Maher, *op cit* n 17, at 28–29.

[49] McGlynn, *op cit* n 5, at 49.

the 'spirit of the Convention'. While this has the possible disadvantage[50] of allowing ambiguous Conventions to remain unaltered, it does avoid the arguably perverse situation in which a conflict between a domestic statute and an original Convention would be resolved with the terms of the statute prevailing.[51]

In short, then, given that modern Britain is now a multi-racial, multi-faith society with a number of firm commitments within the European Union, it seems wholly inappropriate for the courts and Parliament to continue to set the parameters of domestic family law according to vague notions of what are proper English family values. Our existing rules of private international law face new and important challenges arising from novel family forms and foreign, culturally imbued systems of family law. In meeting these challenges (as well as those arising in purely domestic matters) the English courts must display genuine pluralism with both eyes open, not just to English legal authority, but also to international and foreign norms and standards evident in international Conventions, foreign judicial decisions and foreign systems of municipal law.

[50] The argument that directly incorporating the vague terms of a Convention will inevitably lead to interpretational problems can easily be met by the fact that there is nothing to stop the statutory draftsmen from elaborating upon these uncertain or skeletal provisions. This in fact was done in relation to the Hague Intercountry Adoption Convention 1993 (alongside which a fair amount of primary and secondary legislation must be read) see ch 7.

[51] But even scheduling cannot guarantee perfect harmonisation of law and practice since many Conventions, out of necessary compromise, provide the facility to make certain reservations (see, eg, Art 26 of the Hague Child Abduction Convention which enables States (and one such State is the United Kingdom) to make a reservation as to the extent of the provision of legal aid).

2

The nature and import of international instruments concerning family law

Until relatively recently there was little need for domestic family lawyers to pay much regard to the content of international Treaties concerning family law. This is because, as Maher explains, 'the United Kingdom's constitutional principle [is] that international conventions do not in general terms take effect as part of domestic law unless and until legislation has been enacted to make appropriate alterations to domestic law'.[1] The most widely recognised exception to the general rule that international Conventions were typically unimportant was the Hague Convention on the Civil Aspects of International Child Abduction 1980 which, by virtue of the Child Abduction and Custody Act 1985, was directly incorporated into English law. Since then, of course, the EC Regulation known as Brussels IIA has forced itself into the conscience of domestic family lawyers (albeit more because of its impact on Child Abduction law than because of its rules in relation to divorces with a foreign element). But besides these two instruments, there is, as was explained in the chapter 1, a range of other instruments (extant or prospective) that have the capacity to affect the content of English family law.

Not all international instruments are similar in kind, however. And as such, this chapter seeks to elucidate two key factors upon which their actual or potential influence over domestic family law is contingent.[2] The first and most important of these is the enforceability of any given instrument. For at the risk of seeming overly Austinian, it can be argued that international

[1] G. Maher, 'Implementation of Hague Conventions in Domestic Law: The United Kingdom Approach' [1995] *Civil Justice Quarterly* 21, at 25–26.

[2] The two factors adopted here owe much to the classification of international instruments adopted in G. Douglas, 'The Significance of International Law for the Development of Family Law in England and Wales' in C. Bridge (ed), *Family Law Towards the Millenium: Essays for P.M. Bromley* (London: Butterworths, 1997). However, whereas Douglas' analysis is undertaken (at p 89) '[w]ithout ascribing any particular order of priority', the discussion here *is intended* to reflect the relative significance of the different classifications.

obligations that do not carry with them a meaningful system of enforceability count for very little. The second method of classification refers to the three main objectives of international instruments. As will be seen, however, only relatively loose observations can be made in connection with this method of classification. This is because individual instruments often seek to pursue more than one of these objectives at any one time and, as such, little can be concluded about the significance of any particular instrument on the strength of just one of these objectives.

Enforceability

Where international Conventions – such as the Hague and European Abduction Conventions, and the Hague Intercountry Adoption Convention – have been given the force of law by virtue of an Act of Parliament, they naturally take effect in just the same way as any other primary legislation. Yet, on the other hand, it is important to look closely at the nature of the duties in these Conventions. For not always will they create individual rights that are enforceable by private law actions. Instead, many of the obligations will relate to public bodies, especially the Central Authorities created under these Conventions and broadly speaking charged with securing their objectives. It therefore follows that any complaint that relates to the non-fulfilment of these obligations will have to be dealt with as a matter of public law. This means that judicial review, with all its contingencies concerning *locus standi*, etc, will have to be sought in order to ensure compliance with the Convention.

By contrast, some international instruments may be enforced at a specifically created international tribunal (or other forum) whose function is to adjudicate over litigation arising in connection with provisions contained in those instruments. A good example of this kind of forum is the European Court of Human Rights which has been engaged on a number of occasions in relation to the Convention's two family-centred rights – the right to respect for one's family life, and the right to marry and found a family.[3] Of course, since the formal entry into force of the Human Rights Convention via the Human Rights Act 1998, recourse may be had directly to the English courts in respect of breaches of Convention rights. But this does not detract from the importance of the Strasbourg court: it remains the ultimate arbiter on Convention Rights. Furthermore, its decisions are statutorily designated as being relevant (although not binding) in the context of subsequent litigation conducted before the English courts.[4]

[3] These rights are contained in Arts 8 and 12 of the Convention, respectively.

[4] Human Rights Act 1998, s 2. For discussion of the extent to which the English courts are bound by Strasbourg jurisprudence, see J. Murphy, 'Same-Sex Marriage – A Human Rights Approach' [2004] *Child and Family Law Quarterly* 245.

A second international tribunal of note in this context is the European Court of Justice, for this court possesses jurisdiction to hear cases involving provisions contained in European Regulations. This means for present purposes that the specific European family law initiatives embodied in the (extant and prospective) Brussels IIA, III and IV Regulations are referable to, and enforceable at, this forum. But as with the Abduction Conventions and the Intercountry Adoption Convention, most of the provisions contained in these essentially harmonising instruments create public law duties rather than private law rights.[5] As such, the fact that the European Court of Justice possesses jurisdiction to adjudicate matters arising from these instruments must be seen in its somewhat limited context.

A third, notably weaker, mechanism of enforcement relies upon a system of periodic monitoring by some specially created international body. The only example of this system of enforcement that is pertinent to this book[6] is the function fulfilled by the Committee on the Rights of the Child created under Article 43 of the United Nations Convention on the Rights of the Child. The efficacy of this system is somewhat questionable for reasons discussed fully in chapter 9. But it may be noted here that there are at present probably too few personnel on this Committee to consider promptly and comment properly on the lengthy reports produced by over 180 States that are Parties to the Convention.

Finally, an international instrument may rely on political pressure from other Contracting Parties in order to ensure compliance. This is the weakest form of enforceability; indeed it is probably inapt to describe political pressure as an enforceability mechanism at all. Conventions and Declarations that purport to have universal (or near-universal effect) are especially likely to rely on political pressure as the only means of securing compliance. And again the most pertinent example for present purposes is the United Nations Convention on the Rights of the Child in relation to which political pressure is supposed to operate in tandem with the monitoring system discussed above. Bernadette Walsh has even gone so far as to suggest that the Convention was specifically 'designed to pressurize governments into observing

[5] There are exceptions. For example, Brussels IIA, Arts 23(d) and 36(2) grant individuals a limited right to challenge, respectively, the otherwise automatic recognition of a foreign judgment on parental responsibility, and a right to seek partial recognition of a foreign judgment that relates to several matters not all of which are enforceable.

[6] There are other international instruments – such as the Optional Protocol to the United Nations International Covenant on Civil and Political Rights – which not only rely on such a system of enforcement, but which also contain one or two articles that are of *potential* relevance to family law. However, given the structure of this book – and in particular the election to focus on international instruments that are wholly or primarily family law oriented – these instruments are not discussed here. For a useful account, however, see G. Douglas, *op cit* n 2.

certain common standards'.[7] Yet analysis by both academics,[8] and the United Nations Committee on the Rights of the Child in its comments on the United Kingdom's second periodic report[9] tell a rather disappointing story in this respect – at least so far as this country is concerned. What their comments reveal is that any supposed political pressure in this context is rather more illusory rather than real, and for that reason of negligible effect.

Functions

Although this chapter is intended to be only very brief and introductory, it is worth including here a concise sketch of the three broad functions that international instruments endeavour to serve. But before considering them, two general points must be made. The first is that although three apparently distinct functions – harmonisation, co-operation and standard-fixing – can be identified, the dividing line between them is often so elusive as to render any attempt to classify rigidly the various instruments considered in this book according to this scheme a largely fruitless exercise.[10] (Examples of why this is so will be supplied in the following paragraphs.) The second prefatory point, however, is that a brief account of these various functions does at least provide some insight into what is generally thought to be achievable or desirable at a global (or, sometimes, only regional) level. As such, notwithstanding their unsuitability as a general taxonomical basis for classifying international instruments, a short account of each of these functions is provided.

Harmonisation

The first function that international instruments sometimes attempt to fulfil is the harmonisation of domestic laws. Because of the vast cultural differences that generally exist between the Developed Nations and the Developing

[7] B. Walsh, 'The United Nations Convention on the Rights of the Child: A British View' (1991) 5 *International Journal of Law and the Family* 170, at 171.

[8] See, eg, Douglas, *op cit* n 2, p 110; J. Fortin, *Children's Rights and the Developing Law* (London: Butterworths, 2003) p 48; C. Lyon, 'Children and the Law – Towards 2000 and Beyond: An Essay in Human Rights, Social Policy and the Law' in Bridge, *op cit* n 2, pp 34–45; N.V. Lowe, 'The Meaning and Allocation of Parental Responsibility – A Common Lawyer's Perspective' (1997) 11 *International Journal of Law, Policy and the Family* 192, at 202.

[9] Committee on the Rights of the Child, *Concluding Observations of the Committee on the Rights of the Child: United Kingdom of Great Britain and Northern Ireland* CRC/C/15 188 (Geneva: Centre for Human Rights, 2002) para 4. These observations are available at www.crights.org.uk/pdfs/UNCRC_conc_obs_2002.pdf.

[10] Cf the attempt made by Douglas (*op cit* n 2) in relation to a wider category of instruments than is considered in this work.

Nations, and because of the close relationship between cultural norms and family law, endeavours to harmonise family law rules work better where they are undertaken on a regional rather than a global basis. Furthermore, because there are also sometimes significant cultural differences between States located in the same region of the world, endeavours are usually confined to the harmonisation of private international law rules rather than substantive rules of family law.[11] The extant Brussels IIA, and the looming Brussels III and IV, are almost classic examples of such instruments. Their principle aim is to harmonise the rules relating to jurisdiction and the recognition and enforcement of judgments. But implicit within the ideal of uniform recognition and enforcement rules is the requirement of co-operation between Member States. Thus, where country X recognises and enforces judgments pronounced in the courts of country Y against persons now resident within X, country X is basically assisting the courts in country Y to pass *effective* judgment against those persons. It is therefore apparent that these Regulations are in practice as much about co-operation as they are about harmonisation. The same comment could be made with respect to the Hague Child Protection Convention 1996 which lays down common rules on jurisdiction and applicable law,[12] but which also works according to a heavily emphasised system of co-operation.[13]

Notwithstanding the fact that attempts at harmonisation possibly work better at a regional rather than a global level, it is nonetheless the case that the United Nations Convention on the Rights of the Child lays down many standards that are intended to be of universal application.[14] But here, it should be noted, the objective of harmonising rules of substantive law becomes inseparable from that of fixing general norms since many of the Convention's provisions bear an ineluctably normative quality. As such, it becomes difficult to say whether the Convention is primarily concerned with setting normative standards or with harmonising substantive rules.[15]

[11] But note that there is a vigorous debate about whether substantive harmonisation will and ought to follow. See C. McGlynn, 'The Europeanisation of Family Law' [2001] *Child and Family Law Quarterly* 35; D. Martiny, 'Is Unification of Family Law Feasible or Even Desirable?' in A.S. Hartkamp *et al* (eds), *Towards a European Civil Code* (Dordrecht: Kluwer, 2nd ed, 1998). And see more generally, T.M. de Boer, 'The Relation Between Uniform Substantive Law and Private International Law' in A.S. Hartkamp *et al* (eds), *Towards a European Civil Code* (Dordrecht, Kluwer, 1st ed, 1994); H. Koch, 'Private International Law: A "Soft" Alternative to the Harmonisation of Private Law?' (1995) 3 *European Review of Private Law* 329.

[12] It also puts in place common substantive rules concerning the acquisition and loss of parental responsibility: see Arts 16–18.

[13] See ch 10.

[14] See ch 9.

[15] It might on the one hand be argued that the Convention is more concerned with fixing norms than with achieving harmonisation since some of the rights contained

Co-operation

As already observed, the various (extant and prospective) Brussels Regulations pertaining to family law are intimately concerned with the co-operation ideal in that they require the courts in all Member States presumptively to recognise and enforce any judgment obtained in a fellow Member State. The Hague International Child Abduction Convention is also fundamentally concerned to achieve co-operation. For a start, all Contracting States are expected to rely upon one another to ensure the smooth return of abducted children. Equally, the requirement of co-operation is even more evident in the substantial set of Convention rules that spell out the way in which its day-to-day administration is to be conducted on a collaborative basis. But the Convention should not be seen as being wholly concerned with co-operation. It also contains a normative element which is evident, for example, in the somewhat vaguely drafted provision that grants sufficiently mature abductees the right be heard on the matter of whether or not they shall be returned.[16] Nor is the Convention devoid of harmonising features. To the contrary, it contains a number of fixed rules – most notably those governing the circumstances in which a child's return may be refused[17] – which render it equally susceptible to description as a harmonising instrument.

The Hague Child Protection and Intercountry Adoption Conventions are both equally capable of being construed in terms of their harmonising effect and their reliance upon a system of co-operation operated largely through the obligations placed upon Central Authorities.

Standard-fixing

The final function that is often served by international instruments (including those pertaining to family law) is that of setting human rights standards. Often these are somewhat vague or aspirational, and the United Nations Convention on the Rights of the Child provides many examples of both. Indeed, as Gillian Douglas has rightly pointed out, these are sometimes 'expressed at such a level of generality as to be worthless or meaningless'.[18] The problem here, however, is not simply one of vagueness. For as Douglas

in the Convention are couched in such vague language that there are bound to be differences in interpretation between States in which case exact uniformity cannot be expected (see ch 9). On the other hand, however, it could be argued that, since the Convention is largely unenforceable in real terms, it is illusory to perceive the Convention as a genuinely norm-setting instrument and that its most notable feature is that it has been so widely ratified that it is better seen as an emblem of global willingness to co-operate with respect to children's rights.

[16] Hague Abduction Convention, Art 13.

[17] *Ibid.*

[18] Douglas, *op cit* n 2, pp 89–90.

goes on to point out, too high a level of specificity is likely to dissuade certain States from ratifying any given Convention. If standards are fixed rigidly at what is perceived to be too high a level – that is, one to which they cannot presently or prospectively hope to aspire – they will simply decline to ratify the instrument.

Conclusion and critique

Of the three functions that international instruments may seek to fulfil, the greatest success seems currently to be associated with the co-operation and harmonisation objectives rather than the goal of norm-fixing. Yet if the analysis is left there, it conveys a very misleading message about what is achievable and, more importantly, desirable in international instruments concerning family law. The fact that the United Nations Convention appears to be highly aspirational yet relatively toothless is no reason to give up on norm-setting instruments. Instead, the better observation is that such Conventions count for little without some more solid accountability mechanism to ensure compliance than the rather flimsy Committee on the Rights of the Child. Either formal incorporation into domestic law, or the creation of a specialist tribunal to hear complaints about abrogations seems to do much to achieve this. And proof, as if it were needed, is abundant in the form of the European Convention on Human Rights both before and since its formal incorporation into English law. Other options in relation extant Conventions include the production of Optional Protocols that permit individual petitions to be lodged with a specially constituted Committee that has the power to conduct an investigation into the complaint lodged,[19] and the introduction of an inter-State complaints procedure.[20]

Not only is there nothing necessarily weak or ineffectual about norm-setting instruments, neither is there anything necessarily good – at least in the family law context – about those instruments that are designed to harmonise rules on jurisdiction. Take, for example, the inflexible jurisdiction rules of Brussels IIA. Here we find a worrying absence of any scope for a voluntary stay of jurisdiction regarding divorce on the ground that one forum is clearly more suitable than another for reasons of the strong personal connection between *both* parties and a particular Member State.

[19] See G. Van Bueren, *The International Law on the Rights of the Child* (Dordrecht: Martinus Nijhoff, 1995) pp 410–411.

[20] One such procedure exists in relation to the International Covenant on Civil and Political Rights and the Optional Protocol to that Covenant. For discussion, see D. McGoldrick, *The Human Rights Committee: Its Role in the Development of the International Covenant on Civil and Political Rights* (Oxford: Oxford University Press, 1991) ch 3.

Equally, the fact that the State first seised will have exclusive jurisdiction can generate a race to what, for one party – perhaps driven by a desire to minimise post-divorce support payments – is the most advantageous forum.[21] Such a race may well come at the cost of the parties giving up on any idea of reconciliation or, failing that, conciliation and mediation. The short point is that what works in the sphere of commercial law – where certainty and speed count for a great deal – does not necessarily work so well in the realm of family law. As such it is fair to conclude that harmonised jurisdiction rules *may* be a good thing, but a good deal of thought needs to go into the precise content of those rules. Harmonisation must create practical, not just emblematic, benefits. And one good idea, as is evident from the 1996 Hague Child Protection Convention, is that there should be an agreed hierarchy of jurisdictional bases.[22]

When we turn to co-operation, however, things are rather different. Indeed, there are those – such as Professor de Boer – who believe that in an age of ever greater European integration and closer international co-operation, the most valuable international conventions are 'the ones that promote judicial and administrative co-operation'.[23] There is everything to be said for initiatives whereby judges come together at international gatherings and learn something each other's legal culture and rules. In this way, handling domestic cases involving immigrants with the necessary degree of pluralism and understanding can be greatly facilitated. And in the chapters that follow, it will be seen that a recurring theme is that English family law is at the dawn of new age in this respect (evidenced in some notable decisions of the superior courts). That said, it will be equally apparent that there remain some areas – principally those concerning the recognition of foreign marriages and divorces – in which there are still a number of retrograde, culturally imperialistic principles at play.

[21] See N. Mostyn, 'Brussels II – The Impact on Forum Disputes' [2001] *Family Law* 359, at 363–365; P. McEleavy, 'The Brussels II Regulation: How the European Community has Moved into Family Law' (2002) 51 *International and Comparative Law Quarterly* 883, at 887; I. Karsten, 'Brussels II – An English Perspective' [1998] *International Family Law* 75.

[22] See ch 10. Although Brussels II has now been replaced by Brussels IIA, Lowe's comment in relation to the former that 'it is a surely matter of regret that a choice of jurisdictional rules is laid down without a hierarchy' remains valid in respect of the latter instrument: see N.V. Lowe, 'New International Conventions Affecting the Law Relating to Children – A Cause for Concern?' [2001] *International Family Law* 171, at 174.

[23] T.M. de Boer, 'The Hague Conference and Dutch Choice of Law: Some Criticisms and a Suggestion' (1993) 40 *Netherlands International Law Review* 1, at 13.

Part II

Formation and breakdown of international families

3

The recognition of foreign marriages and registered partnerships

In recent decades, adults in many countries have become increasingly able and willing to travel abroad in pursuit of work, study and lengthy foreign holidays. One consequence of this has been a growth in the number of men and women from this country who take foreign spouses abroad. In time, many of these married couples decide to settle in this country. In so doing, they commonly raise questions about immigration rights for the foreign spouses concerned.[1] Similar questions also arise where, for example, neither party is an English domiciliary but one of the parties to a foreign marriage has been offered employment in this country. Given the current climate in which immigration has become a highly politicised issue, the validity of such foreign marriages has correspondingly grown in significance, for it is frequently the validity of an overseas marriage that determines the immigration rights of a foreign spouse.[2]

In deciding whether a foreign marriage should be recognised as valid according to the English rules of private international law, the courts must consider a range of legal, cultural, moral, religious and social values that are held in high esteem both by the foreign spouse or spouses concerned, and by the relevant authorities in the country in which the marriage was celebrated.

[1] Law Com No 42, *Family Law: Report on Polygamous Marriages* (London: HMSO, 1971) paras 23–24, shows that between 1985 and 1995, some 175, 630 persons were permitted to settle in this country having migrated from India, Iran, Iraq and Saudi Arabia. Naturally, many of these people were Muslims for whom polygamous marriage would be seen as acceptable, and perhaps even desirable.

[2] See, eg, *R v Secretary of State for the Home Dept, ex p Ullah* [2003] EWCA Civ 1366 and *R (K) v London Borough of Lambeth* [2003] 2 FLR 1217. The significance of immigration following a foreign marriage was expressly recognised at the Hague Conference on Private International Law. Yet the Convention that followed – the Hague Convention on Celebration and Recognition of the Validity of Marriages 1978 – was thought unacceptable by the United Kingdom, and ratification was withheld.

Furthermore, the very fact of large-scale immigration to this country during the twentieth century has influenced the actual content of the relevant conflicts rules. In the modern, multicultural and pluralistic Britain of today, there is simply no room for a system of private international law that reflects the values of a bygone age when staunch Christian values held sway.[3] Gone are the days in which, as once was the case, it would have been possible to decide a case concerning the recognition of a foreign marriage on the basis of whether or not it resembled 'marriage as understood in Christendom'.[4] Family law has become more secular.

Immigration rights, however, are merely one concern of the English courts when deciding whether or not to recognise certain foreign marriages. Another is the fact that the ability to entertain divorces can sometimes be contingent on the existence of a valid foreign marriage; for without a valid marriage there can be no divorce. Accordingly, in such cases, the court may have to consider the validity of the marriage as a preliminary issue.[5] Similarly, succession rights, or perhaps even entitlements under life assurance policies or pension schemes, may also turn on the validity of a foreign marriage. So, too, among other things, may the rights of a spouse or former spouse to certain social security benefits,[6] the criminal law of bigamy, the applicability of certain rules of evidence, the remedies available for domestic violence,[7] contractual capacity, and the responsibility for children[8] turn on marital status.

In short, a wide range of legal and other issues may centre on, and thus require a proper system of law to recognise, the validity of foreign marriages. Even in the absence of legal proceedings instituted to test the validity of a foreign marriage, the marital status of the parties will, of course, be a matter of interest and importance to the husband and wife involved, and perhaps also to the community to which they belong. In this chapter, therefore, we consider the English conflicts rules in relation to the recognition of

[3] As one learned scholar has noted, the private international law rules had to respond to 'a decline in Christianity, the transformation of the British Empire into a Commonwealth of many different faiths and peoples and, and the emergence of a multi-racial Britain': see, S. Poulter, '*Hyde v Hyde* – A Reappraisal' (1976) 25 *International and Comparative Law Quarterly* 475, 508.

[4] *Hyde v Hyde* (1866) LR 1P & D 130, at 133 *per* Lord Penzance.

[5] See, eg, *A-M v A-M (Divorce: Jurisdiction: Validity of Marriage)* [2001] 2 FLR 6.

[6] See, eg, *R (K) v London Borough of Lambeth* [2003] 2 FLR 1217. See also N. Lowe & G. Douglas, *Bromley's Family Law* (London: Butterworths, 1998) pp 721–727.

[7] Part IV of the Family Law Act 1996 differentiates between married applicants and mere cohabitants: see further, J. Murphy, 'Domestic Violence – the New Law' (1996) 59 *Modern Law Review* 845.

[8] Under s 2(1) of the Children Act 1989, only married fathers automatically acquire parental responsibility in relation to their children.

foreign marriages. We also consider the related question of how the English courts *might* approach the question of whether to recognise a foreign registered civil partnership.

Before analysing these issues, however, we must first clarify the meaning of the term 'foreign marriage' as it is used in this chapter. It is important to do this because the phrase could in fact be used to describe three types of marriage that need to be distinguished. First, it could be used to describe marriages celebrated in this country according to some kind of foreign rites or custom. These marriages are of course 'foreign' in the sense that their form is alien to the laws of this country. Yet the validity of such a marriage – so long as it is contracted by *English domiciliaries* – is determined purely as a question of domestic matrimonial law.[9] Thus, for example, a marriage in England that is foreign only in the sense that it was celebrated according to, say, Romany custom is treated as invalid *ab initio* as a matter of English law.[10] And where a marriage according to Muslim rites follows an earlier civil ceremony, it is only the civil ceremony that domestic English law recognises.[11] The validity of such marriages is a relatively straightforward matter and is not a concern of this chapter.

The second way in which the term 'foreign marriage' can be used relates to marriages that are foreign in the sense that they were actually celebrated on foreign soil.[12] It is marriages of this kind with which we are principally concerned here. But we must also consider a third type of 'foreign' marriage. This last category comprises those marriages that take place in this country where at least one of the spouses is a foreign domiciliary.[13] Just as with the second category, these marriages require the application of certain rules of private international law – the rules relating to capacity.

[9] *Warrender v Warrender* (1835) 2 Cl & Fin 488; *Berthiaume v Dastous* [1930] AC 79; *R v Bham* [1966] 1 QB 159; *A-M v A-M (Divorce: Jurisdiction: Validity of Marriage)* [2001] 2 FLR 6. The forms of marriage permitted under English law are strictly limited in the Marriage Act 1949, Part V. For details, see S.M. Cretney, J.M. Masson & R. Bailey-Harris, *Principles of Family Law* (London: Sweet & Maxwell, 2003) pp 22–29. For discussion of the question of whether English law should accommodate a wider range of matrimonial forms than it currently does – in particular marriages associated with certain ethnic and religious minorities – see S. Poulter, *English Law and Ethnic Minority Customs* (London: Butterworths, 1986) ch 2.

[10] National Insurance Decision No R (S) 4/59.

[11] See, eg, *Qureshi v Qureshi* [1972] Fam 173, at 186 *per* Sir Jocelyn Simon P.

[12] There are two types of marriage to which this categorisation may only contentiously be applied: proxy marriages (where one party may be domiciled and resident in country X, but married by proxy in country Y), and marriages that take place in foreign consulates and embassies (where it may be argued that the extra-territoriality principle should apply).

[13] See, eg, *Simonin v Mallac* (1860) 2 Sw & Tr 67 (marriage in England between a French man and French woman); *Ogden v Ogden* [1908] P 46 (marriage in England between a French man and an English woman).

Under English private international law, the recognition of foreign marriages is dealt with almost exclusively as a matter of common law[14] which generally requires the courts to consider three questions. The first of these is whether the marriage satisfies the test of formal validity. For in terms of formalities, '[e]very marriage must be tried according to the law of the country in which it took place'.[15] Secondly, and in accordance with the decision of the House of Lords in *Brook v Brook*,[16] the marriage must also meet the test of essential validity. To do this, it is generally thought that the parties must have had the capacity to marry one another according to the respective laws of their ante-nuptial domicile. But even where the marriage satisfies these twin tests of formal and essential validity, it is important to note that, thirdly, recognition may still be refused at the discretion of the court on grounds of public policy. We shall deal here with only the first two aspects of foreign marriage recognition. The next chapter considers the court's discretion to refuse recognition on the basis of public policy.

Formal validity

The question of whether a marriage is formally valid needs to be analysed in various stages, each of which reflects a potentially problematic issue that may arise. First, there is the rather obvious and fundamental question of which matters relate to formal (as opposed to essential) validity. Next, there is the issue of whether disputes about the content of the foreign law governing the formalities for marriage should be treated by the English courts as questions of law or fact. Thirdly, we must consider what happens where the relevant foreign law regarding formalities changes between the date of the marriage, and the date on which recognition is sought. Fourthly, we must address the related problems of what approach to take to proxy marriages and those that take place within foreign embassies and consulates. Fifthly, we must consider the application of the *renvoi* doctrine in this context. And

[14] Some statutory provisions contained in the Marriage (Enabling) Act 1960 and the Foreign Marriage Act 1892 (as amended) apply in this context, but they are of very limited scope (see below). Work undertaken by the Law Commission in the 1980s with a view to proposing codification of the law in this area (see Working Paper No 89, *Private International Law: Choice of Law Rules in Marriage*, London: HMSO, 1985) resulted in the Commission recommending that the common law should be retained while the law was still developing rapidly: see Law Com No 165, *Choice of Law Rules in Marriage* (London: HMSO, 1987).

[15] *Herbert (Lady) v Herbert (Lord)* (1819) 3 Phillim 58, at 63 *per* Sir William Scott. This rule was established in *Scrimshire v Scrimshire* (1752) 2 Hagg Con 395. It has been reiterated many times since: see, eg, *Berthiaume v Dastous* [1930] AC 79, *Apt v Apt* [1948] P 83 and *McCabe v McCabe* [1994] 1 FLR 410.

[16] (1861) 9 HL Cas 193.

finally we must examine the several well-established exceptions to the general rule concerning formal validity.

The meaning of formal validity

In the early part of the twentieth century, Viscount Dunedin expressed the general rule that '[i]f a marriage is good by the laws of the country where it is effected, it is good the world over'; and this was so 'no matter whether the proceedings or ceremony which constituted marriage according to the law of the place would or would not constitute marriage in the country of the domicile of one or other of the parties'.[17] Thus, in the case before him, the marriage in France between two Catholics was denied recognition because it failed to comply with the French requirement of a civil ceremony.

Notwithstanding the ease with which Viscount Dunedin's rule may generally be applied, it is noteworthy that it omits any guidance as to just what constitute matters of formal validity. That said, it is uncontroversial that the requirements as to the kind of marriage ceremony (whether civil or religious), and the requirements as to witnesses, marriage hours, place of marriage, publicity and registration all concern formal validity. More difficult, however, is how to classify the requirement of consent to marriage (whether this entails the consent of the parties themselves, or that of their parents in appropriate cases). It may equally be argued to be both a matter of formal and essential validity because, on the one hand, the local law will almost certainly require that a marriage be consensual;[18] yet at the same time the domiciliary law will have an interest in a determining a person's capacity to consent to marry. Unfortunately, the common law rules of private international law fail to provide any clear guidance as to how consent should be treated.

Under English domestic law, the requirement of *parental* consent has historically been treated as a formal issue. The requirement was first introduced under Lord Hardwicke's Act,[19] which had no application in Scotland. It was the fact that Scotland historically permitted marriages without this formal requirement that led to many couples eloping in order to marry at a place called Gretna Green which lies just on the Scottish side of the England/Scotland border. In *Compton v Bearcroft*,[20] where the validity of such a marriage was tested judicially, the court found the marriage to be valid. And while it is true that at the time the courts did not distinguish between matters of form and capacity, it is nonetheless noteworthy that when that

[17] *Berthiaume v Dastous* [1930] AC 79, at 83.

[18] Note that the principle of 'free and full consent' to marriage is embodied in the Universal Declaration of Human Rights, Art 16(2).

[19] The Clandestine Marriages Act 1753.

[20] (1769) 2 Hagg Con 444.

distinction was introduced, the Gretna Green cases were readily categorised as centring on formal validity.[21]

The principle that parental consent is a marriage formality continues under the modern law of England and Wales, but these days only in relation to persons who marry below the age of eighteen years.[22] The absence of such consent does not affect the validity of the marriage;[23] it is only an express parental objection to the marriage that has this effect.[24] Even so, the fact that English domestic law regards parental consent as a marriage formality does not necessarily imply that the courts are bound to treat foreign laws concerning parental consent as a question of formality, too. Properly understood, the status of the parental consent requirement is a matter for the local law to determine. Thus, if foreign municipal law prescribes that parental consent is a capacity issue, the English courts should respect that prescription. Perhaps surprisingly, however, the case law reveals a rather different approach.

The most instructive cases clearly suggest that despite the local law's categorisation of parental consent as a capacity issue, the English courts will nonetheless treat it as a marriage formality. In *Ogden v Ogden*,[25] for example, despite a provision in the French Civil Code that made parental consent an absolute requirement in respect of the capacity of a man to marry below the age of twenty-five,[26] the Court of Appeal was happy to treat it as a formality. Despite defying logic and appearing somewhat imperialistic, the decision has since been followed[27] and seems fairly well settled.

In relation to the consent of the parties themselves, the English conflicts of law approach is no less controversial. This is mainly because of its unnecessary complexity, its inconsistency and its dubious inherent values. Under English domestic law, the classification of the *parties'* consent is clear: it is a matter of capacity. By legislation, a marriage is voidable if the consent of one of the parties was invalidated in one of the prescribed ways.[28] Yet in *Apt v Apt* – a case concerning a proxy marriage in Argentina – Cohen LJ, delivering the judgment of court, adopted a bifurcated approach to consent. He emphasised that only 'the method of giving consent as distinct from the fact of consent is essentially a matter for the *lex loci celebrationis*'.[29]

[21] *Brook v Brook* (1861) 9 HL Cas 193, at 216 *per* Lord Campbell LC.

[22] Marriage Act 1949, s 3.

[23] *Ibid*, s 48.

[24] *Ibid*, s 25.

[25] [1908] P 46.

[26] Art 148. The man in question in this case was just nineteen years of age.

[27] *Lodge v Lodge* (1963) 107 *Sol Jo* 437. See also the decision of the Court of Appeal in *Vervaeke v Smith* [1981] 1 All ER 55, at 87 *per* Arnold P (but the point was not considered on appeal: [1983] 1 AC 145).

[28] Under the Matrimonial Causes Act 1973, ss 12(c), 13(3) imperfect consent caused by duress, mistake, mental incapacity, ignorance of the other spouse's pregnancy by another will render the marriage voidable.

[29] [1948] P 83, at 88.

According to this approach, the local law is engaged only in relation to the question of whether an effective consent has been supplied. The actual test as to whether or not that consent is effective is to be referred to the law of the parties' domicile and is dealt with as matter of essential validity. While there is nothing in the private international law case law that contradicts this approach, nor is there anything there to give it any great support, either. This is an important point since the status of the proposition enunciated in *Apt v Apt* is itself unclear. The case strictly concerned only the narrow (though related) question of whether proxy marriages raised questions of formal or essential validity. Matters are further complicated by the fact that no clear rule can be ascertained from the subsequent case law. This is partly because of a marked inconsistency between the cases – English domestic law being applied either alone or in conjunction with the law of domicile[30] – and partly because of the coincidence between the law of the parties' antenuptial domicile and the local law.[31] Even so, the question of how to treat the consent requirement is an important matter because the rules on what constitutes a valid consent vary from one country to another. Forced marriages, for example, would fall foul of the English duress principle, but might nonetheless be regarded as acceptable in certain Asian countries.[32]

McClean has suggested a rationalisation of the case law along the lines that the problematic rule in *Sottomayor v De Barros (No 2)*[33] 'applies to [the] consent of [the] parties as it applies to [their] capacity to marry'.[34] But while this may explain the seemingly inconsistent case law, it does involve adopting an approach that, for complex reasons, affords special treatment to English male domiciliaries. This is something that McClean rightly considers to be objectionable elsewhere in his book.[35]

In the face of the legal uncertainty surrounding the question of whether the parties' consent should be treated as a matter of form or one of essence, it is suggested here that the preferable approach is to treat it as a matter of essence. In the first place, it involves some measure of inconsistency (if not also disingenuity) on the part of the English courts to treat the parties' consent as a matter of essence in the context of domestic marriages, yet at least potentially as a matter of form in the context of foreign marriages. Furthermore, there is less of a danger in this approach offending the English

[30] *Silver v Silver* [1955] 2 All ER 614; *Kassim v Kassim* [1962] P 224; *H v H* [1954] P 258. See also P.R.H. Webb, '"Shot-gun" Marriages and the Conflict of Laws' (1959) 22 *Modern Law Review* 198.

[31] See, eg, *Kenward v Kenward* [1951] P 124; *Szechter v Szechter* [1971] P 286.

[32] See Poulter, *op cit* n 9, pp 22–24.

[33] (1879) 5 PD 94.

[34] D. McClean, *Morris: The Conflict of Laws* (London: Sweet & Maxwell, 2000) p 209.

[35] *Ibid*, p 98. Cf the view expressed in T.C. Hartley, 'The Policy Basis of the English Conflict of Laws of Marriage' (1972) 35 *Modern Law Review* 571, 578.

consent principle than might at first be supposed. For the courts possess a residual discretion to refuse to recognise marriages that offend English public policy.[36] Adopting this approach would have the fourfold advantage of clarifying the law, injecting a degree of harmony between the domestic law and conflicts rules, still maintaining protection to persons bullied or tricked into marriage in appropriate cases, and achieving a degree of consistency with various international instruments that enunciate the essential character of the parties' consent.[37]

The status of foreign formalities rules in the English courts

When the question of whether to recognise a foreign marriage arises, a foreign system of rules will often be in issue since the local law governs the formal validity of a marriage.[38] This begs the question of what happens when the content of a foreign law is disputed in the context of English conflicts proceedings. It cannot, of course, be expected that any given English judge will be sufficiently expert in the relevant foreign law to deal with such disputes with his or her accustomed authority. Indeed, it is well settled that any such knowledge *must not* be imputed to the judge.[39] So how should such disputes be resolved, as questions of law (applying the usual interpretive and deductive techniques of an English judge), or as a question of fact, proven on the balance of probabilities?

Of course, disputes over the content of a foreign legal system's rules are as apt to engage matters of principle as any domestic legal disputes. But as the Court of Appeal made clear in *McCabe v McCabe*,[40] the content of a foreign system's matrimonial law is to be treated as a question of fact, not law. This approach was certainly in accord with the general private international law principle whereby the court must not seek to apply its own interpretation of a foreign rule in line with what it considers appropriate or just.[41] Instead, it

[36] See J. Murphy, 'Rationality and Cultural Pluralism in the Non-Recognition of Foreign Marriages' (2000) 49 *International and Comparative Law Quarterly* 643.

[37] Multilateral Convention on Consent to Marriage 1964, Art 1(1); Universal Declaration of Human Rights, Art 16(2).

[38] Foreign legal rules governing the capacity of one or both of the parties may also be in issue; and what is said here in relation to the status of foreign rules on formality applies equally to foreign rules concerning capacity.

[39] *Nelson v Bridport* (1846) 8 Beav 547.

[40] [1994] 1 FLR 410.

[41] *Buerger v New York Life Assurance Co* (1927) 96 LJKB 930. For fuller discussion of the status and proof of foreign law, see R. Fentiman, *Foreign Law in English Courts* (Oxford: Oxford University Press, 1998), P.M. North & J.J. Fawcett, *Cheshire and North's Private International Law* (London: Butterworths, 1999) ch 7, and T.C. Hartley, 'Pleading and Proof of Foreign Law: The Major European Systems Compared' (1996) 45 *International and Comparative Law Quarterly* 271.

must apply that interpretation which, on the preponderance of the expert evidence, seems to be the correct *local* understanding of the rule in question.[42] So doing can occasionally produce outcomes that may ostensibly appear somewhat surprising, perhaps even abhorrent. Take, for example, *McCabe* itself where a man domiciled in Eire married a woman domiciled in Ghana. At the time of the marriage, the parties were both resident in London and never in fact left London, nor even sent proxies to attend their wedding, which was celebrated in Ghana according to customary rites of the Akan people. The ceremony seemed to involve little more than the wife's relatives enjoying the gift of a bottle of gin and receiving some money provided by the groom by way of *Aseda*. There was minimal publicity given to the wedding.

Yet despite the lack of formality associated with the marriage, and regardless of how surprising it may appear to many non-Ghanaians, it was held to be valid on the balance of the conflicting expert evidence presented to the court. Butler-Sloss LJ noted that, '[t]here was considerable evidence provided to [the first instance judge] . . . as to the essential requirements of the customary marriage [which] . . . was not altogether easy to follow'.[43] Nonetheless, she stuck resolutely to her task and followed the preponderance of expert evidence which suggested that the marriage valid according to Akan custom.[44]

Changes in the foreign law

As we have seen, the general rule is that a marriage which is formally valid by the local law is valid the world over. However, this rule makes no mention of the critical time at which this validity is to be judged. This can be important because the local law on formalities may change over time such that a marriage that was invalid at its inception may later become valid by virtue of subsequent legislation that has retrospective effect. The converse, of course, is equally true. Accordingly, a question arises concerning the crucial date at which the formal validity of the marriage is to be tested. Is it to be judged on the basis of the law in operation at the time when the marriage was celebrated, or is it to be judged by reference to the local law operative when the validity of the foreign marriage falls to be determined by the English courts? The relevant and somewhat controversial law in this context is to be

[42] *Beatty v Beatty* [1924] 1 KB 807, at 816 *per* Scrutton LJ (evidence accepted from a local New York lawyer as to the finality of an order for alimony payments in that jurisdiction).

[43] *Ibid*, at 412–413.

[44] One among several regrettable features of the case, however, was the lack of argument about the place of celebration (given the absence of proxies). See further, J. Murphy, 'The Recognition of Overseas Marriages and Divorces: Some Opportunities Missed?' (1995) 46 *Northern Ireland Legal Quarterly* 35.

gleaned from the House of Lords decision in *Starkowski v A-G.*[45] There it was held that a marriage void at the time of celebration could retrospectively be validated by a change in the local law.

The case concerned a husband and wife, both of Polish domicile, who were married in Austria in May 1945. Under Austrian law, the marriage was void because the marriage occurred in a Roman Catholic Church without the civil ceremony at that time required under Austrian law. Several weeks after the ceremony, Austrian law changed so that such marriages could be validated retrospectively so long as they were duly registered in a public register. By 1949 the couple had moved to England where they had both acquired an English domicile. They then registered their marriage in Austria with the effect that, by Austrian law, their marriage was now valid. But in 1950 the couple separated and the woman purported to marry another man in England with whom she had a son. In recognising the retrospectively validated Austrian marriage, and in holding the second marriage to be void for bigamy, the House of Lords were able to settle the question in point: whether the son was illegitimate or not.

This decision has been criticised as being unsatisfactory on a number of levels.[46] To begin with, it is regrettable that the House of Lords left open the question of what would have been the position had the English marriage preceded the late registration of the first marriage in Austria. The Canadian authority of *Ambrose v Ambrose*[47] suggests that in such a case the second marriage should be treated as valid, since to do otherwise would be to allow a change in foreign law to affect the marital status of a marriage contracted between two English domiciliaries. Yet while such an approach would be in harmony with the accepted view that contingently validated foreign marriages remain invalid until the contingency is met,[48] it nonetheless hints at a second deficiency in *Starkowski*. This is that, if it is once accepted that changes in foreign law should not affect the marital status of English domiciliaries – and this seems to be the thrust of *Ambrose* – then it is difficult to see how the decision in *Starkowski* itself could be justified given that the parties had both acquired an English domicile before the date of retrospective validation.[49]

[45] [1954] AC 155. For critical analysis see D. Mendes da Costa, 'The Formalities of Marriage in the Conflict of Laws' (1958) 7 *International and Comparative Law Quarterly* 217.

[46] See North & Fawcett, *op cit* n 41, pp 707–708.

[47] (1961) 25 DLR (2d) 1 Canadian conflicts rules in this context are very similar to the English conflicts rules.

[48] *Pilinski v Pilinska* [1955] 1 All ER 631.

[49] The House of Lords attempted to justify its approach on the basis that the Austrian law dealt with formalities rather than status; but it is by no means clear that this was the case. Indeed, the amending legislation was concerned precisely with effecting changes in marital status rather than with amending Austrian formalities for marriage, and it was the effect of this legislation that was in issue in *Starkowski.*

Furthermore, parties to a marriage that is void at its inception could feel compelled to remain in a marital limbo for fear that their marriage would retrospectively be validated rendering any interim marriage a criminal, bigamous union. Given these considerations, it is surprising that the Law Commission recommended that there should be no change to the private international law rules in this area when it reported on the matter in 1987.[50]

Proxy marriages and marriages in foreign consulates and embassies

Where a marriage takes place in a foreign consulate or embassy, or where a marriage is contracted by proxy, the question of which country should be treated as being the place of celebration arises. In the case of proxy marriages, the problem stems from the fact that one or both contracting spouses remain resident in one country while the marriage ceremony takes place in another. In such circumstances, is the local law that of the country in which the ceremony occurs, or is it that of the country where consent was given? According to the Court of Appeal in *Apt v Apt*[51] – a case involving a woman who was resident and domiciled in England marrying by proxy a man resident and domiciled in Argentina – the applicable law governing formalities should be that of the country where the actual ceremony takes place, not the country of the wife's residence, albeit that consent was provided there. This decision can be justified in a number of ways. First, it is consistent with the general rule on formal validity which is in fact premised on the assumption that the relevant choice of law will be the law in operation at the place of celebration. Equally, it neatly avoids the difficulties that would otherwise arise if a marriage were to be celebrated by proxy in Country A on behalf of spouses resident respectively in Countries B and C.

On the other hand, however, there are at least two potential problems associated with the recognition of proxy marriages. To begin with, there is the danger that they could be used disingenuously to circumvent immigration rules by those keen to have close friends come and live with them in this country, where those persons would otherwise not be entitled so to do. Aware that these 'prostitute marriages' might lend themselves to such abuse, the judge at first instance in *Apt* nonetheless felt bound to afford recognition to the marriage in question. Deflecting the potential problem in the direction of the legislature, he said: '[t]here is nothing whatever to prevent Parliament from enacting in relation to domiciled British subjects generally that proxy marriages shall not be recognised in this country wherever celebrated'.[52] It is submitted, however, that the court's residual discretion to veto foreign marriages on the basis of public policy could be invoked in

[50] Law Commission, *op cit* n 14, para 2.13.
[51] [1948] P 83.
[52] [1947] P 127, at 139 *per* Lord Merriman P (*affd* [1948] P 83).

suitable cases thus avoiding any need for legislation.[53] A second possible objection to proxy marriages centres on the simple lack of solemnity that is sometimes associated with them. In *McCabe v McCabe*,[54] for example, it was far from clear that a proxy had been formally and consensually appointed on behalf of either the husband or the wife. And some of the expert evidence adduced in the case revealed that no ceremony at all was required according to Akan custom. But again, it is suggested that the best way to deal with cases in which there is a strong suggestion that the marriage is a sham is for the court to wield its discretion to veto recognition. The alternative – refusing recognition to *all* proxy marriages – is open to the twin criticisms of being both culturally imperialistic and unnecessarily heavy-handed.

In the case of a marriage celebrated in a foreign embassy or consulate, the difficulty from a private international law perspective lies in determining whether the embassy or consulate of Country X, situated in Country Y, should be taken to be the territory of Country X, or that of Country Y. The English courts were forced to address this issue head-on in the factually elaborate case of *Radwan v Radwan (No 2)*.[55] There, the husband who was domiciled in Egypt married his first wife in polygamous form in 1951. The following year he married his second wife, an English domiciliary, in the Egyptian consulate in Paris. This second marriage was also in polygamous form. In 1953, he pronounced a *talaq* (explained in chapter 5) in order to divorce his first wife. Three years later, the husband accompanied by his second wife moved to England and he acquired an English domicile. In 1970, in the Egyptian consulate in London, he pronounced a second *talaq* in order to divorce his second wife.

The case raised many questions including the validity of the *talaq* divorces. But in relation to the question of the formal validity of the second marriage in Paris, it was held that the Egyptian consulate was to be treated as French, not Egyptian, territory. The case thus makes it clear that a marriage that takes place *abroad* in a foreign embassy or consulate must comply with the formalities required by the State in which the building is located. But it cannot be taken to support the rather different proposition that the law of the territory in which foreign diplomatic premises are located will *always* be the relevant law against which to test the formal validity of a marriage. This is because the relevant formalities for a marriage celebrated in a foreign consulate or embassy situated *in England* between two domiciliaries of the foreign State have been declared judicially to be those applicable under the foreign law.[56] Arguments in favour of applying the extra-territoriality

[53] Indeed, it was a possibility canvassed by Lord Merriman in *Apt* itself: see [1947] P 127, at 141. See also ch 4 on the use of this discretion.

[54] [1994] 1 FLR 410.

[55] [1973] Fam 35.

[56] *Bailet v Bailet* (1901) 17 TLR 317.

principle that seems to operate on English soil can be countered with equal and opposite arguments in favour of the *Radwan* approach. As such, either approach could be acceptable. What is not acceptable, however, is a split approach, favouring neither one set of arguments nor the other, and which thus devoid of any consistent principle.

Renvoi

The *renvoi* doctrine is both complex and controversial.[57] It has its origins in the fact that there is no universal system of private international law that produces an internationally harmonised approach to choice of law questions. Complications therefore arise where the system of private international law in Country X alights on Country Y for the choice of law, but because of the different conflicts rules in operation in Country Y, an alternative choice of law would be selected. In the present context, the *renvoi* doctrine can complicate matters in the following way. Suppose a marriage takes place in Country A between two nationals of Country B. Suppose further that, when later domiciled in England, the married couple have occasion to test the validity of their marriage. The English court would of course begin by identifying the law in Country A as the applicable local law for formality. But if the private international law rules in Country A dictate that formal validity is to be judged according to the law of the parties' nationality, the choice of law might then be deflected to Country B. Everything would ultimately turn on whether the English court applied the *renvoi* doctrine and, in so doing, alighted upon a choice of law by application of the relevant rule of private international law in operation in Country A rather than simply applying the formalities rules that operate in Country A in respect of marriages between two nationals of that country. At bottom, the *renvoi* doctrine is concerned with the choice of a foreign law by reference not merely to the usual internal law of that country, but also by reference to any of its applicable rules of private international law.

In relation to the recognition of foreign marriages, it is far from clear whether the *renvoi* doctrine applies. This has repercussions for the certainty with which the formal validity of a foreign marriage may be assessed. When the Law Commission first considered the matter and published a Working Paper in 1985, it generally favoured the application of the *renvoi* doctrine in this context.[58] Yet those who responded to the Commission's working paper appeared to have been divided in their views when the Commission published its recommendations two years later.[59] The upshot has been that no

[57] For explanation and sustained critique of the two versions of the doctrine, see North & Fawcett, *op cit* n 41, ch 5.

[58] Law Commission (1985), *op cit* n 14, paras 2.39, 3.39.

[59] Law Commission (1987), *op cit* n 14, paras 2.5–2.6.

legislation has ensued and the existing case law continues to lack clarity. In *Taczanowska v Taczanowski*,[60] two Polish domiciliaries moved to England the year after they married in Italy according to a ceremony that did not comply with the formalities required by Italian law. Yet in considering the validity of the marriage, the English court took account of the fact that, under Italian private international law, the formal validity of the marriage would be judged according to Polish law because the spouses were both of Polish nationality. In the event, the court discovered that the marriage would not have been valid under Polish law and consequently refused recognition *on this basis*.[61]

While the case cannot be taken as firm authority that the English courts definitely will apply the *renvoi* doctrine, it nonetheless seems to support the contention that they might be prepared to do so. If the court in that case had been totally unwilling to apply the Italian choice of law rule, why would it have taken cognisance of it in the first place, and why did it consider whether the marriage would have been valid under Polish law?

Further apparent support for the English courts' preparedness to apply the *renvoi* doctrine to the question of formal validity can be seen in the slightly later case of *Hooper v Hooper*.[62] There, the English court applied the Iraqi private international law rule that required the formal validity of the marriage of two British nationals in Baghdad to be judged according to English formalities. Yet neither *Hooper* nor *Taczanowska* answer the question of what the English courts would do in this context[63] if faced with a marriage invalid by the law of the parties' common domicile, yet valid according to the formal requirements of the place of celebration? On the one hand, to afford recognition would be a rule of some convenience, giving effect to what the parties had (presumably) hoped was a valid marriage at the time of celebration. On the other hand, however, it would mean that English law would treat as valid a marriage that was invalid in the place of celebration, and thus militate against the general rule laid down in *Berthiaume v Dastous*.[64]

Exceptions to the general rule

This section began by considering the general rule according to which the formal validity of a marriage contracted abroad is judged for the purposes

[60] [1957] 2 All ER 563.

[61] In fact, the marriage was ultimately recognised as valid, but only according to an established exception to the general rule which is discussed below.

[62] [1959] 2 All ER 575.

[63] That is, where the local law refers the question of formal validity to the law of the parties' domicile.

[64] [1930] AC 79, at 83 *per* Viscount Dunedin.

of English private international law. At this point, however, it is necessary to identify the negative proposition to which this rule also lends itself: that marriages that are invalid by the local law are also invalid in England. The rule must be recast in this way because it is only in relation to the rule thus stated that the following (limited) exceptions exist. That is to say, while there are no occasions when a marriage which complies with the formalities prescribed by the local law will be invalid under the English conflicts rules, there are a few instances – of limited scope and limited practical significance – in which a marriage that does not comply with the local law will nonetheless be regarded as formally valid in England.

1 Marriages under the Foreign Marriage Act 1892

There are two classes of marriage dealt with by the Foreign Marriage Act 1892 that form exceptions to the general rule: consular marriages and those involving members of Her Majesty's Forces serving overseas. The first of these is probably of very limited practical significance nowadays; and the majority of the provisions that relate to such 'consular marriages'[65] are of an administrative or procedural nature.[66] They deal, for example, with matters such as the posting and filing of notice, and with registration.[67] These consular marriages appear ostensibly to constitute a facility whereby at least one UK national[68] may marry abroad without concerning himself with the particularities as to form prescribed by the local law. But the foreign system of law is not totally irrelevant to such marriages. This is because it is also prescribed that the person solemnising the marriage, or overseeing its solemnisation, must first be satisfied that the local authorities will not object to the marriage, and that insufficient facilities exist for the parties to marry under the law of the country concerned.[69] Equally – although the meaning of this is unclear – the Act grants the marriage officer the discretion to refuse to solemnise a marriage that in his opinion would be inconsistent with

[65] By s 8 of the Act, such 'consular marriages' may be solemnised only by, or in the presence of, a 'marriage officer', at that officer's official house, and with the parties making certain prescribed utterances as to the absence of impediments in the presence of two or more witnesses. Marriage officers are British consuls or ambassadors, or members of their diplomatic staff holding a marriage warrant from the Secretary of State: *ibid*, s 11.

[66] The failure to abide by these requirements does not affect the validity of the marriage: *Collett v Collett* [1968] P 482.

[67] See, eg, Foreign Marriage Act 1892, ss 2–4, 9. For further details see North & Fawcett, *op cit* n 41, pp 711–712.

[68] It is provided by regulation that at least one of the parties must be a UK national for the Act to apply: Foreign Marriage Order 1970 (SI 1970, No 1539) (as amended by the Foreign Marriage (Amendment) Order 1990 (SI 1990, No 598)). UK nationals are defined in the Foreign Marriage Act 1892, s 1(2).

[69] Foreign Marriage Order 1970 (SI 1970, No 1539); Foreign Marriage (Amendment) Order 1990 (SI 1990, No 598).

international law or the comity of nations.[70] Bearing these factors in mind, it is probably best to view consular marriages as only a quasi-exception to the general rule, and of little advantage in terms of avoiding the dictates of the local formalities. On the other hand, however, upon a return to England, there may be significant evidential value attached to having had one's marriage solemnised and registered in this way.

The second statutory exception centres on members of the British Forces serving abroad. Given the substantial number of British servicemen presently stationed around the world on various peace-keeping and humanitarian duties, it would seem that this second class of marriages provided for by the 1892 statute is currently of more potential present-day significance than that of consular marriages. Section 22 of the Act creates a facility for overseas marriages between persons at least one of whom is either a member of Her Majesty's Forces serving in a foreign territory,[71] or such other person employed in a capacity as specified by Order in Council.[72] Unlike the consular marriages for which the Act also provides, marriages involving members of the British Forces are valid for all purposes, as if they had been solemnised in the United Kingdom with due observance of the law.[73] Furthermore, and again in contrast to consular marriages, there is no requirement that the person solemnising the marriage[74] in the foreign territory must pay any heed to the formal requirements laid down by the local law. It is equally notable that a section 22 marriage may take place whether during, following or in the complete absence of any hostilities; and that the facility extends not just to British citizens, but also to those of other nations (so long as they are suitably connected to the British military[75]), and their children.[76]

2 Common law marriages

Long before the statutory regulation of marriage formalities in England, a marriage could be contracted with formal validity on the simple common

[70] Foreign Marriage Act 1892, s 19.

[71] Foreign territory for the purposes of the Act does not include the Commonwealth: s 22(2). It does, however, include a ship in foreign waters: s 22(3).

[72] Foreign Marriages (Armed Forces) Order 1964 (SI 1964, No 1000) (as amended by SI 1965, No 137 and SI 1990, No 599).

[73] Foreign Marriage Act 1892, s 22(1).

[74] Section 22(1) of the Foreign Marriage Act 1892 Act prescribes that such marriages may be solemnised by 'a chaplain serving with any part of the naval, military, or air forces . . . serving in that territory . . . [or] by a person authorised . . . by the commanding officer of any part of those forces'.

[75] In *Taczanowska v Taczanowski* [1957] 2 All ER 563, considered in the previous section, the marriage between a Polish officer serving with the British Army in Italy would have fallen into this exception had the Polish priest who performed the ceremony been acting under the directions of the British commanding officer.

[76] Foreign Marriage Act 1892, s 22(1A)(a)(ii) (as inserted by the Foreign Marriage Act 1947 and amended by the Foreign Marriage (Amendment) Act 1988).

law basis of reciprocated pledges in the present tense to take one another as man and wife.[77] The House of Lords later added a dubious qualification to this rule in *R v Millis*,[78] whereby the ceremony had to be performed by an episcopally ordained priest of either the Anglican or Roman Catholic Church.[79] And although long since superseded as a means by which to marry in this country, the form of such common law marriages continues to be relevant in certain circumstances to marriages contracted abroad. Indeed, there are three well-established circumstances in which marriages in accordance with the common law will be recognised as valid by the English courts.

First, a marriage that takes place in a country in which the common law of England applies will be treated as formally valid if it complies with the requirements just set out. The only uncertainty in this context is whether the *R v Millis* requirement that an episcopally ordained priest must perform the ceremony ever applies.[80] For while it is well established that the rule in *R v Millis* is inapplicable where no such priest is available,[81] it has never been formally established whether the rule applies where such a priest can be obtained.[82] In practical terms, the question is probably academic nowadays.[83] The days of the British Empire and Colonies are long since over, and the reach of the English common law beyond British shores is very limited. In any event, it can be argued that this is merely an example of the general rule (rather than an exception to it); for the local law is in fact the English common law.

By contrast, the second instance in which a common law marriage will be treated as valid *is* a genuine exception to the general rule; for it applies to

[77] For details, see Cretney *et al*, *op cit* n 9, p 9.

[78] (1844) 10 Cl & Fin 534. (Rule reiterated by the House of Lords in *Beamish v Beamish* (1861) 9 HLC 274.)

[79] Doubting the *Millis* qualification in *Merker v Merker* [1963] P 283, Sir Jocelyn Simon P said (at 293–294) that: '[t]his, though of course binding law, is now agreed to have been historically erroneous.' For further criticism of *Millis*, see P. Lucas, 'Common Law Marriage' [1990] *Cambridge Law Journal* 117.

[80] For doubt as to the correctness of this decision, see J. Jackson, *The Formation and Annulment of Marriage* (London: Butterworths, 1969) pp 18–19.

[81] *Catterall v Catterall* (1847) 1 Rob Eccl 580 (marriage ceremony performed by a Presbyterian minister in Australia prior to the proper establishment of the church there); *Wolfenden v Wolfenden* [1945] 2 All ER 539 (marriage celebrated by a minister of the Church of Scotland in China following a treaty giving the King jurisdiction in that country); *Penhas v Tan Soo Eng* [1953] AC 304 (marriage performed by layperson in Singapore: Jewish husband observing Jewish custom; Chinese wife following Chinese rites; *but* the essential element of reciprocal present tense pledges was present).

[82] There is an *obiter* suggestion in *Taczanowska v Taczanowski* [1957] 2 All ER 563 that in such circumstances an episcopally ordained priest must perform the ceremony.

[83] See McClean, *op cit* n 34, p 187.

marriages that take place in a foreign country that is not subject to the English common law. The precondition for the validity of such marriages is that the parties were faced with some insuperable difficulty as regards compliance with the formalities required by the local law. If this is the case, their common law marriage will be treated as formally valid in England.[84] Nonetheless, a sense of perspective is required here since there can be but a very few countries in which the need to invoke this exception will arise. Indeed, notwithstanding the fact that it may also apply to certain marriages on board *merchant* ships,[85] it is unquestionably of very limited practical significance. The major hurdle in this context is the opaque requirement that there be an 'insuperable difficulty' associated with compliance with the local law. It has been suggested judicially that either 'legal or religious difficulties' may suffice to trigger the operation of the exception.[86] Yet this is an unhelpful reformulation that merely begs the question of the requisite degree of legal or religious difficulty. Does it mean that compliance with the local law would result in criminal sanctions, or would a civil wrong suffice? And in any event, where could one envisage that compliance with the local law in Country X would amount to a criminal or civil wrong in Country Y?[87] Similarly, would a troubled conscience about conforming to a marriage that was markedly different to one's religious ideal suffice in this context; or would the local formalities actually need to be proscribed by the particular religious canon?[88]

An even more fundamental objection to recasting the original test of insuperable difficulty in terms of religious or legal difficulty is its capacity to undermine its (presumably) intended strictness. The phrase 'insuperable difficulty' would normally suggest the impossibility of compliance with the

[84] *Kent v Burgess* (1840) Sim 361.

[85] There is no direct authority on whether a common law marriage on a merchant ship lying in a foreign port, or on the high seas, would be treated as valid. However, extrapolating from *Culling v Culling* [1896] P 116 – where a marriage on a warship was treated as valid prior to such marriages being regulated by the 1892 Act (as amended in 1947 and 1988) – it is probable that such marriages would be recognised so long as (i) the ship was registered in England and (ii) there was an insuperable problem with marrying ashore (in the case of a ship in a foreign port), or of waiting until a suitable port was reached (in the case of a ship on the high seas).

[86] *Ruding v Smith* (1821) 2 Hag Con 371, at 373 *per* Lord Stowell.

[87] It may reasonably be assumed that the kinds of legal difficulty envisaged by Lord Stowell in *Ruding v Smith* would not arise in the country of celebration, for this would entail the ludicrous situation in which there was a legal sanction attached to compliance with the marriage laws of the country in question.

[88] In *Kochanski v Kochanska* [1958] P 147 Sachs J suggested *obiter* (at 152) that it may fall within this exception to show merely that 'conformity would go contrary to conscience'. But cf *Kent v Burgess* (1840) Sim 361 where a sense of annoyance and inconvenience caused by the local law's insistence upon a minimum period of residence in Belgium was held to fall short of an insuperable difficulty.

local law,[89] whereas the reformulation seems far less strict. At least one other writer seems as undecided as the courts. McClean, the current editor of *Morris: The Conflict of Laws*,[90] deals with this question under the heading 'Use of the local form impossible' (which appears consistent with the orthodoxy of *insuperable* difficulty). He then, however, queries whether the test 'might also involve an examination of the question as to whether the parties could travel to a neighbouring and more accommodating jurisdiction'.[91] Inherent in such an enquiry is the suggestion that there may be scope for a test based on impracticability rather than impossibility.

It is submitted that McLean's hypothetical might be considered inapposite for two reasons. First, it seems inappropriate because the exception in question is centred on what is required under the local law of the country concerned, not the law of a neighbouring country. Secondly, and more importantly, it also seems inapt because its inherent suggestion goes too far in undermining the abiding principle of *locus regit actum.* This is important because few rules of private international law are so firmly entrenched as that of *locus regit actum* in relation to the formal validity of foreign marriages. The exceptions to it should, in the interests of comity, be kept limited both in number and in scope. It is for this very reason that, in the context of consular marriages under the Foreign Marriage Act 1892, the marriage officer is both granted a discretion to refuse to solemnise a marriage that in his opinion would be inconsistent with international law or the comity of nations,[92] *and* required to assure himself that the local authorities will not object to the marriage and that insufficient facilities exist for the parties to marry under the local law.[93]

The third and final common law exception relates to marriages in countries under belligerent occupation. In such circumstances, compliance with the local law may be considered unreasonable or repugnant. The exception is perhaps most likely to be invoked when the military forces of State A occupy the territory of State B and the members of those forces consider it wholly inappropriate to marry according the law of State B. On the other hand – and this was very common during the latter part of the Second World War when the Nazis occupied much of Europe – it is also possible that nationals of State C may find it unreasonable or anathema to abide by the form of

[89] There is judicial support for such a strict interpretation in the case law: see *Preston v Preston* [1963] P 411, at 432 *per* Russell LJ. See also the Australian case of *Savenis v Savenis* [1950] SASR 309 where it was held that the complete absence of available register offices and registrars fell within the exception.

[90] McClean, *op cit* n 34, p 187.

[91] *Loc cit.*

[92] Foreign Marriage Act 1892, s 19.

[93] Foreign Marriage Order 1970 (SI 1970, No 1539); Foreign Marriage (Amendment) Order 1990 (SI 1990, No 598).

marriage imposed by the occupying forces of State D. Indeed the leading case of *Taczanowska v Taczanowski*,[94] which we have already considered, arose out of that very period. There, it will be recalled, the marriage was invalid by the local law of Italy, invalid by the law of the parties' domicile,[95] and invalid under the Foreign Marriage Act 1892.[96] Nonetheless, after the parties had moved to this country in 1947, the Court of Appeal held the marriage to be valid by virtue of its compliance with English common law.

While the operation of the exception has since been endorsed in relation to marriages involving the members of occupying forces,[97] the scope of its application to marriages involving non-military persons is slightly less clear. It is well established that it applies to former or escaped prisoners of war,[98] but whether it also applies to ordinary civilians has never been made clear. In *Merker v Merker* Sir Jocelyn Simon P made the *obiter* suggestion that it should be confined to:

> [m]arriages within the lines of a foreign army of occupation (which constitute, so to speak, an enclave within which it is reasonable to hold that the local law has no application), or of persons in a strictly analogous situation to the members of such an army, such as members of an organised body of escaped prisoners of war.[99]

On the one hand, the exception seems rooted in the moral or philosophical opposition of the spouses to the system of local law. In this case it is arguable that the exception should be extended to those ordinary civilians who also find unacceptable the law imposed by the occupying forces. On the other hand, however, it could be argued such an extension comes rather too close to the discredited[100] (and narrowly confined[101]) theory that compliance with the local law depends ultimately on voluntary submission to that law. The problem with this approach is that it gives rise to great uncertainty. As a former President of the Family Division once explained: to allow an exception based on the willingness of the parties to submit to the local law 'would be to leave the rule in *Berthiaume v Dastous* in tatters and to introduce anarchy in a field where order and comity are particularly required'.[102] It is submitted that this is the more compelling of the competing arguments.

[94] [1957] 2 All ER 563.
[95] To which the Italian rules of private international law pointed.
[96] The marriage failed under s 22 of that Act since the Polish chaplain who performed the marriage was not acting under the direction of the British commanding officer.
[97] *Merker v Merker* [1963] P 283.
[98] *Kochanski v Kochanska* [1958] P 147; *Preston v Preston* [1963] P 411.
[99] *Merker v Merker* [1963] P 283, at 295 *per* Sir Jocelyn Simon P.
[100] For discussion, see North & Fawcett, *op cit* n 41, pp 717–719.
[101] *Lazarewicz v Lazarewicz* [1962] P 171.
[102] *Merker v Merker* [1963] P 283, at 295 *per* Sir Jocelyn Simon P.

As such, while civilians who have been imprisoned by occupying forces may legitimately be caught by the exception, it would probably create more problems than it would solve to extend the exception to ordinary civilians who simply find the occupying forces inconvenient or objectionable. And while the injustice that could be caused by the rigidity of this rule can be readily envisaged, two things must be borne in mind: first, that the number of marriages that fall within this exception is likely to be small,[103] and, secondly, that the comity of nations remains of central importance in this sphere.

Essential validity

The second prerequisite for the recognition of a foreign marriage is its essential validity. This turns on the capacity of the parties to marry one another. Just as with formal validity, choice of law is crucial in this context. For as the rules governing capacity to marry vary widely from country to country, it follows that the courts must first know the appropriate law governing the capacity of the parties before they can decide the question of essential validity. However, unlike formal validity, there is no general rule governing choice of law in this context. Instead, the question of essential validity is both complex and controversial. For a start, it is not exclusively a legal issue.[104] And, secondly, the rules governing choice of law can vary according to the different kinds of impediment in issue. (While these two factors certainly complicate the law, they also provide it with the necessary flexibility to accommodate a number of the various (sometimes competing) policy objectives that arise in this context.) Thirdly, and perhaps most significantly, choice of law with respect to capacity is also complicated by the fact that there are a number of conflicting theoretical approaches.[105] The

[103] The exception enjoyed its heyday during the last weeks of the Second World War when thousands of marriages took place in Italy and Germany between Jews and Roman Catholics domiciled in Poland and other Eastern European States.

[104] Essential validity tends to centre on issues such as child marriage, previous marriage, marriage to a person of the same gender and marriage within prohibited degrees of consanguinity and affinity. These are all matters affecting legal capacity; but physical incapacity may also be an essential validity issue, and this is clearly a question of fact.

[105] For further discussion of the far less well supported tests, see R. Fentiman, 'The Validity of Marriage and the Proper Law' [1985] *Cambridge Law Journal* 256 and *Vervaeke v Smith* [1983] 1 AC 145, at 166 *per* Lord Simon *obiter* ('real and substantial connection test'); A.J.E. Jaffey, 'The Essential Validity of Marriage in the English Conflict of Laws' (1978) 41 *Modern Law Review* 38 ('alternative reference test'); Hartley, *op cit* n 35 ('elective dual domicile test'). See also Law Commission Working Paper No 89, *op cit* n 14 and R. Fentiman, 'Activity in the Law of Status: Domicile, Marriage and the Law Commission' (1986) 6 *Oxford Journal of Legal Studies* 353.

two main contenders (in terms of both academic and judicial support) are associated with the rival 'dual domicile' and the 'intended matrimonial home' tests. These are considered first in order to provide a suitable theoretical background against which to consider the current rules on essential validity.

The dual domicile and intended matrimonial home tests

1 The tests critically examined

The orthodox explanatory account of choice of law in relation to essential validity is the dual domicile theory according to which the parties' capacity to marry is governed by the law of their ante-nuptial domicile. On this view, a marriage should be regarded as invalid if either party lacked capacity under the law of his or her ante-nuptial domicile.[106] By contrast, the rival intended matrimonial home theory posits that capacity is presumptively governed by the law of the husband's domicile at the time of the marriage, but that this presumption is rebutted if at the time of the marriage it could be inferred that the parties intended to establish their home in another country and they did in fact establish it there within a reasonable time. At the time this latter account was first propounded, it was usual for the parties to establish their matrimonial home in the country of the husband's domicile. As such, whether operating according to the presumption or its rebuttal, this theory was designed to alight upon a choice of law reflecting the country in which the parties had elected to establish their matrimonial home.

The main practical difference between the two approaches lies in the fact that while the intended matrimonial home test invariably refers the question of capacity to a single system of law, the dual domicile test may require that a second such system be taken into account. This is because capacity is assessed according to the law of the domiciles of *both parties*. It follows from this that there is generally greater scope for the marriage to be invalidated according the dual domicile test.[107] However, given the fact that during the last hundred years or so capacity to marry has been gradually extended in many countries, it is also important to recognise that this practical difference between the two approaches is of much less significance than in former times.

By contrast, there are several very significant theoretical differences between the two tests. The chief justification for the intended matrimonial home test is that it seeks to ensure compliance with the law in the community

[106] It makes no difference whether the incapacity is absolute (ie, prohibitive of marriage generally) or relative (ie, prohibitive of marriage to a fixed set of individuals such as specific relations).

[107] This is not, however, ineluctably the case: see, eg, *Schwebel v Ungar* (1964) 48 DLR (2d) 644.

where the couple intend to live. In so doing, it ensures that the marriage does not offend against the religious, moral and social (including eugenic) principles that form the basis of the capacity rules in the State in which the couple intend make their home. It can also render irrelevant the corresponding principles in the country or countries in which the parties have hitherto been domiciled (which need not necessarily be the country of habitual residence[108]). At bottom, the intended matrimonial home test insists that it is the law in the State in which the parties are to live together as man and wife that should determine the question of capacity.

While ostensibly there is considerable force in this argument, rather deeper reflection reveals a number of weaknesses in it, some of which might be thought fundamental and thus fatal. In the first place, the intended matrimonial home test is ineluctably chauvinistic. Its central presumption is founded upon an unwarranted pre-eminence that is afforded to the domicile of the husband. If the parties do not intend to establish their home in a new country, the wife's domicile and the law that operates in that country are irrelevant. Secondly, the test can suspend the validity of a marriage between the date of celebration and date when the couple finally settle in their intended country of residence.[109] Such uncertainty about the validity of a marriage at the date of celebration is clearly undesirable when the whole purpose of a private international law rule is to provide a definite solution to a conflict of laws. Thirdly, it is difficult to resist the argument that simple logic requires that pre-nuptial capacity ought not to be assessed on the basis of post-nuptial intentions and events.

Fourthly, the *raison d'être* of the intended matrimonial home test may be called into question where a couple respectively domiciled in Country A and Country B initially establish their home in Country C, but subsequently move to Country D. While it would be highly unrealistic to suggest that the validity of the marriage should be re-evaluated upon their migration to Country D (or elsewhere at some later date), it is also far from clear why the capacity of the parties currently living in Country D should now be adjudged in accordance with the law of Country C where, as events turned out, they may have only lived for a short period of time. In short, the rationale of the intended matrimonial home test is premised upon a misplaced assumption that a married couple's initial intentions *vis-à-vis* country of residence is somehow final and unalterable.

[108] See, eg, *Bowie (or Ramsay) v Liverpool Royal Infirmary* [1930] AC 588 where Mr George Bowie was habitually resident in Liverpool and had no significant connection with his country of domicile, Scotland. Crucially, it was held that in the absence of any evidence to show that he had ever formed the intention to change his domicile, he should be presumed to remain a Scottish domiciliary.

[109] This limbo situation is clearly avoided where there is no inference at that time of celebration that the couple intend to establish their home in a country other than the one in which the husband is domiciled.

Finally, it is often urged that it is far too simplistic to suggest that the capacity of the parties should be judged according to the law of the country in which they establish their home *on the basis* that the laws of that country have the greatest connection with the marriage and the parties to it. In truth, the preconditions of legal capacity are set not merely with *post-marital* concerns in mind. Thus, while it is true that the moral and eugenic concerns that underpin the prohibited degrees of consanguinity reflect such considerations, the same cannot be said of the usual minimum age requirements, which clearly reflect a concern to protect minors and ought therefore to be referred to the law of the parties' domicile at the time of the marriage.[110]

Given such powerful objections, it is clear that the intended matrimonial home test is too anachronistic, too simplistic and too susceptible to impracticability to form a suitable basis for a critical choice of law rule. On the other hand, disavowal of this test should not be viewed, *per se*, as a sufficient basis for the uncritical and wholehearted acceptance of the more orthodox test based on the law of both parties' domicile. Indeed, since domicile in any given country does not *necessarily* require residence there, there need not be any obvious or direct connection between the country of domicile and the marriage in question. As Hartley once aptly put it: 'the English law of domicile is distorted in certain respects and does not always indicate the country to which the parties really "belong"'. Accordingly, he continued, 'the policy justifications for applying the law of the domicile fall away'.[111] It is also the case that, since a domicile of choice is so easy to acquire, the dual domicile test is remarkably easy to evade: an incapacity in Country A can be side-stepped by the simple acquisition of a domicile of choice in Country B prior to the marriage.

These problems amply expose the fact that, in practical terms, the dual domicile test also operates far from perfectly. But, it is difficult to conceive of them as fundamental objections to the test, for they are merely contingent problems stemming from certain inadequacies in the law governing the acquisition and loss of domicile.[112]

2 The relevant authorities

From the point of view of analytical convenience, it is regrettable that the reported cases – admittedly not all of them English – offer some support to both the dual domicile and the intended matrimonial home tests. Matters are further complicated by the fact that there exist cases that are indeterminate on the matter, offering no obvious support to either test. These are

[110] One objection to this approach, however, is that the *lex domicilii* need not have any greater connection with the parties' pre-nuptial residence because the country of habitual residence need not be the country of domicile.

[111] Hartley, *op cit* n 35, at 576.

[112] See further the *Conclusions and critique* at the end of this chapter.

considered later. To begin with, however, we analyse the cases that may be argued to support the orthodox approach, noting in particular the extent to which they do in fact support it.

In *Re Paine*,[113] a woman domiciled in England married a German domiciliary in 1875 who was also her deceased sister's husband. The couple then lived in England until they died in 1919 and 1939, respectively (the husband predeceasing the wife). They left one surviving daughter who, for technical reasons applicable at the time, could only claim a legacy under her mother's will if she could show that she was a legitimate child. Since the daughter's legitimacy turned on the validity of her parents' marriage, and since at that time marriage between a woman and her deceased sister's husband was prohibited under English law, the validity of their marriage came into question. Expressly approving the dual domicile test as it appeared in the then current edition of *Halsbury's Laws of England*, Bennett J held the marriage to be void.[114] The fact that the mother lacked capacity according to the law of her ante-nuptial domicile was fatal to the validity of the marriage (even though it would have been valid under German law).

A similar decision was reached in the later case of *Pugh v Pugh*[115] where a man of English domicile married a fifteen-year-old girl of Hungarian domicile in Austria. The wife subsequently alleged that the marriage was void on the grounds that the husband did not have capacity to marry anyone under the age of sixteen, regardless of where the marriage took place.[116] Emphasising the law of the husband's domicile,[117] the judge stressed the fact that 'by the law of the husband's domicile it was a marriage into which he could not lawfully enter'.[118] On the other hand, the wife had also argued that English law should govern the essential validity of the marriage on the basis that it was the law of the intended matrimonial home. It is certainly noteworthy that had this approach been taken, not just in the present case but also in *Re Paine*, the same finding of invalidity would have resulted. In both cases, English law represented both the law of the husband's domicile and the law of the country in which the matrimonial home was to be established.

In the light of the preceding observation – especially bearing in mind the alternative pleading of the wife in *Pugh v Pugh* – it might realistically be thought that these two cases provide only very limited support for the contention that there has been discernible judicial acceptance of the dual

[113] [1940] Ch 46.

[114] *Ibid*, at 49–50.

[115] [1951] P 482.

[116] Under the Age of Marriage Act 1929 marriage was prohibited 'between persons either of whom is under the age of sixteen'.

[117] Such emphasis was required since the marriage was valid under Austrian law from the outset, and it had subsequently become valid under Hungarian law when the girl reached the age of seventeen.

[118] [1951] P 482, at 494 *per* Pearce J.

domicile theory.[119] Nonetheless, somewhat clearer support for the test has been enunciated. The decision of the then President of the Family Division in *Padolecchia v Padolecchia*, for instance, provides fairly strong implicit support for the dual domicile approach.[120] In that case, evidence of the law of the intended matrimonial home (Denmark) was conspicuous by its absence, thus suggesting the irrelevance of Danish law. Instead, the President focused on whether a Mexican divorce decree was valid under Italian law (that being the law of the husband's domicile); for if the decree was not recognised in Italy, the husband lacked capacity under the law of his domicile. Had the law of the intended matrimonial home been considered relevant, a proper investigation of the validity of the Mexican divorce under Danish law would have been required.

Even stronger (but still not absolute or convincing) support for the dual domicile test is evident in *Sottomayor v De Barros (No 1)*.[121] There, the Court of Appeal assumed that the cousins who married were domiciled in Portugal and adjudged the marriage to be void given that Portuguese law prohibited marriage between first cousins.[122] Cotton LJ was clearly in support of the dual domicile test when he stated forthrightly that, in determining the essential validity of a marriage, 'personal capacity must depend on the law of the domicile; and if the laws of *any country* prohibit [such marriage] . . . this, in our opinion, imposes on the subjects of that country a personal incapacity'.[123]

In relation to the intended matrimonial home test, unequivocal judicial support is equally difficult to identify. This is partly because the scant support that does exist has tended to be couched in inconclusive or confused terms. It is also partly because, even where statements of support for the intended matrimonial home test have been expressed in sufficiently clear terms, those statements were uttered either *obiter*, or in language designed to confine the

[119] One commentator has even argued that the result has little to do with the application of the dual domicile test but rather that 'the solution has always been the application of the forum law where, as has always been the case, one party is domiciled in England': Hartley, *op cit* n 35, 577.

[120] [1968] P 314, at 336 *per* Sir Jocelyn Simon P.

[121] (1877) 3 PD 1.

[122] Regrettably, the question of whether the husband was *in fact* domiciled in Portugal in this case was never demonstrably resolved.

[123] (1877) 3 PD 1, at 5. When the key question of fact concerning the true domicile of the parties at the time of the marriage was later resolved in *Sottomayor v De Barros (No 2)* (1879) 5 PD 94, it was held by Sir James Hannen P that the marriage was valid on the unprincipled and xenophobic basis that the marriage had been celebrated in England and that one of the parties was of English domicile. His approach was later endorsed by the Court of Appeal in *Ogden v Ogden* [1908] P 46. But for criticism of this exception to the dual domicile test, see Law Commission Working Paper No 89, *op cit* n 14, paras 3.45–3.48 and Law Com No 165, *op cit* n 14, paras 2.7–2.8. For an attempt to defend it on the policy ground of 'validation of marriage', see Hartley, *op cit* n 35, at 572, 578.

judgment to a particular type of impediment.[124] An example of the first type of problem can be seen in *Kenward v Kenward.*[125] There, at one point in his judgment, Denning LJ remarked: 'it may be found that a marriage, although valid by the local law, is voidable by reason of a condition imported by the personal law of one of the parties'.[126] But when later considering a hypothetical foreign polygamous marriage between a man domiciled in England and a woman domiciled in a country permitting polygamy he reasoned, somewhat confusingly, thus:

> [i]f he marries her in her homeland, by the ceremonies of her country, intending to live with her there, well knowing the kind of marriage into which he is entering, the substantial [ie, essential] validity of the marriage, as well as its formal validity, should then depend on her personal law and not on his.[127]

In a case of the second kind, where what was actually at issue was whether the English or French courts had jurisdiction to hear a nullity suit, the then Master of the Rolls considered *obiter* the question of how essential validity was to be determined. He said:

> In my opinion [it is to be determined] by the law of France, either because that is the law of the husband's domicile at the date of the marriage or (preferably, in my view) because at that date it was the law of the matrimonial domicile in reference to which the parties may have been supposed to enter into the bonds of marriage.[128]

In the light of this analysis, it is apparent that the authorities, such as they are, reveal only equivocal support for either of the two main tests. Overwhelmingly, the image that emerges is one of a body of case law that is ambiguous, limited of scope, unprincipled in places and (most confusingly of all) equally capable of supporting either test.[129] A classic illustration (perhaps even the source) of this problem is the House of Lords decision in *Brook v Brook.*[130] There, having noted that 'England was to be [the parties'] matrimonial residence', Lord Campbell LC continued in terms of '[t]he doctrine being established that the incidents of the contract of marriage

[124] See *Radwan v Radwan (No 2)* [1973] Fam 35.

[125] [1951] P 124.

[126] *Ibid*, at 144.

[127] *Ibid*, at 145.

[128] *De Reneville v De Reneville* [1948] P 100, at 114 *per* Lord Greene MR.

[129] For an excellent account of the confusion surrounding and within the leading cases see Fentiman, *op cit* n 105. See also *Sottomayor v De Barros (No 2)* (1879) 5 PD 94 which supports neither theory, and in which Sir James Hannen P applied English law to the question of validity on the basis that it was in England that the marriage was celebrated. See also the supporting *dicta* in *Ogden v Ogden* [1908] P 46, at 74–77 *per* Garell Barnes P; *Chetti v Chetti* [1909] P 67, at 81–88 *per* Garell Barnes P; *Vervaeke v Smith* [1981] Fam 77, at 122 *per* Sir John Arnold P.

[130] (1861) 9 HL Cas 193.

celebrated in a foreign country are to be determined according to the law of the country in which the parties are domiciled and mean to reside'.[131]

Against such an uncertain background, neither the intended matrimonial home test nor the dual domicile test serves particularly well as an explanatory account of the decided cases. Indeed, to the extent that there is any consistency or clarity in the law, it seems more by way of accident than design. There is certainly no obvious adherence to any clear, overarching policy on choice of law in this area.[132] Instead, what is discernible is a patchwork of policy objectives that only becomes truly apparent when the law on essential validity is broken down into a series of different types of impediment to capacity. Hartley, writing in 1972, identified no fewer than seven specific (but sometimes conflicting) policy objectives in this area.[133]

An open indication of the courts' preference for treating different types of incapacity differently is evident in the decision of Cumming Bruce J in *Radwan v Radwan (No 2)* where he said:

> It is an oversimplification of the common law to assume that the same test for the purposes of choice of law applies to every kind of incapacity – non-age, affinity, prohibition of monogamous contract by virtue of an existing spouse, and capacity for polygamy. Different public and social factors are relevant to each of these types of incapacity.[134]

It is a preference that was pre-echoed, albeit in less explicit terms, in *Russ v Russ* where Willmer LJ said: '[the court] retains a residual discretion not to apply the law of the domicile where it is not proper to do so in the circumstances of a particular case.'[135] In the light of such judicial statements, we shall for the present leave to one side the idea that one of the rival tests is superior to the other[136] and instead consider the applicable choice of law rules on an impediment-by-impediment basis.[137]

[131] *Ibid*, at 213.

[132] Cf Fentiman, *op cit* n 105, who argues that the cases can be made to fit an account founded on the proper law of status identified by a 'real and substantial connection' with a particular system of law. Yet, however well the cases *could be* accommodated within Fentiman's explanatory model, the truth remains that the overwhelming majority of the cases were simply not decided on that basis.

[133] Hartley, *op cit* n 35, at 571–573. Jaffey, in an attempt to explain why different choice of law rules in relation to different types of impediment are both inevitable and necessary, argued that certain marital restrictions reflect the domestic policy of a country, while others – such as the rule against bigamy – are designed to protect defined individuals. See North & Fawcett, *op cit* n 41.

[134] [1973] Fam 35, at 51. See also *Vervaeke v Smith* [1983] 1 AC 145, at 165–166 *per* Lord Simon.

[135] [1964] P 52, at 64.

[136] It is, however, a matter that is revisited at the end of this chapter.

[137] Cf North & Fawcett, who prefer adherence to a uniform test, albeit with a limited number of exceptions: see North & Fawcett, *op cit* n 41, p 735.

Before considering each category of incapacity, however, it is useful to note and bear in mind the fact that some policy concerns in this context facilitate the validation of foreign marriages, while others do quite the opposite.[138] Those in the second category are intimately bound up with the courts' residual discretion to refuse recognition to 'offensive' foreign marriages and as such are considered more closely in chapter 4.

The impediments

1 Non-age

In many African and Asian countries, marriage laws permit the marriage of girls below the age of sixteen.[139] Under English domestic law, however, any such marriage is void *ab initio.*[140] This stance is taken partly to avoid the instability of premature marriage, partly to preserve the principle of free and informed consent to marriage and partly to protect young girls from sexual exploitation and the responsibilities of married life. The potential for conflicts of laws in this context is therefore clear. And what makes this issue of particular practical importance is the fact that this country has a strong colonial connection with parts of Africa and Asia that for many years supplied significant numbers of immigrants to this country.

In terms of the position under English private international law, the choice of law rules with respect to non-age marriages must be explained according to three different scenarios. First, where a child marriage abroad involves two foreign domiciliaries, the law of the parties' domicile governs the essential validity of the marriage. Thus, if the law of their domicile prescribes a minimum age below sixteen years, the English courts will treat their marriage as valid. As Lord Parker CJ explained in the leading case of *Alhaji Mohamed v Knott*, where thirteen-year-old-girl married a grown man in Nigeria:

> I cannot myself think that decent-minded English men or women, realising the way of life in which this girl was brought up, and this man for that matter, would inevitably say that this [marriage] is repugnant. It is certainly natural for a girl to marry at that age. They develop sooner, and there is nothing abhorrent in their way of life for a girl of 13 to marry a man of 25.[141]

Secondly, where foreign domiciliaries contract a non-age marriage in England, it has been judicially suggested (albeit implicitly) that their marriage

[138] See, eg, *Cheni v Cheni* [1965] P 85; *Vervaeke v Smith* [1983] 1 AC 145 and the academic discussion in Murphy, *op cit* n 36.

[139] For details see Poulter, *op cit* n 9, pp 16–17.

[140] Marriage Act 1949, s 2 (re-enacting the Age of Marriage Act 1929).

[141] [1969] 1 QB 1, at 15. For criticism of the decision, see R. Deech, 'Immigrants and Family Law' [1973] *New Law Journal* 110.

will be void notwithstanding the fact that it would have been valid by the law of their domicile.[142] This approach *may* be justifiable in cases where the parties' matrimonial home will be established in England, but not otherwise. Why should English law prescribe a minimum age for a person who, prior to, and following, the marriage is to have her home in a country whose laws treat her as sufficiently mature for marriage?

Finally, where a child marriage takes place overseas and involves an English domiciliary, the marriage will be treated as void by the English courts regardless of which of the parties was under sixteen, and regardless of whether the non-age spouse possessed capacity according to the law of his or her domicile at that the time of the marriage.[143]

2 Prohibited degrees

Most if not all countries impose certain prohibitions on marriage between persons who are viewed as too closely related, either through common blood (consanguinity), or through marriage (affinity). Under English domestic law, the prohibited degrees of consanguinity and affinity are exhaustively prescribed by statute.[144] While the prohibited degrees of consanguinity have remained firmly fixed since 1603, the modern prohibited degrees of affinity are considerably more liberal than they were a hundred or so years ago.[145] This liberalisation of the prohibited degrees has brought this country increasingly into line with contemporary European States. The result has been a corresponding diminution in the scope for a conflict of laws in this area. On the other hand, certain important inconsistencies remain – such as English law's anomalous prohibition of marriage between an uncle and niece, or between first cousins – which renders the relevant rules of private international law of continuing importance.

In this context, it is necessary to consider the relevant conflicts rules according to same three categories adopted in the previous section. First, in the case of two foreign domiciliaries who marry abroad, it is generally accepted that the marriage will be regarded as valid in this country so long as the marriage was permissible according to the *lex domicilii*. It is largely irrelevant that the marriage would have fallen within the English prohibited

[142] In *Pugh v Pugh* [1951] P 482, at 491–492, Pearce J said of the statutory prohibition of non-age marriages that he could 'see no reason to put upon the words any other limitation than the obvious one that they are not intended to apply to marriages abroad of persons who are not domiciled here'.

[143] *Pugh v Pugh* [1951] P 482.

[144] Marriage Act 1949, s 1 and Sch 1.

[145] Relaxation of these prohibited degrees was achieved incrementally through the Deceased Wife's Sister's Marriage Act 1907, the Deceased Brother's Widow's Marriage Act 1921, the Marriage (Prohibited Degrees of Relationship) Act 1931, the Marriage (Enabling) Act 1960 and the Marriage (Prohibited Degrees of Relationship) Act 1986. For discussion, see McClean, *op cit* n 34, pp 194–196.

degrees of affinity[146] or consanguinity.[147] Indeed, the only significant outstanding question in this context is whether a marriage that would violate the English incest laws[148] should be regarded as valid. Yet even in incest cases – for example, a marriage between a half-brother and half-sister – there seems no reason to disturb the general approach just described. Rather, if it were thought necessary to do so, such cases could be dealt with on the basis of the court's residual discretion to refuse recognition to such marriages.[149] But whether the courts would regard all of the many different kinds of incestuous marriage with the same degree of (eugenic) repugnance is uncertain.[150]

The second situation concerns foreign domiciliaries who attempt to marry in this country in violation of the English prohibited degrees. Here there is no direct authority. Nonetheless, it seems probable that an English court would apply the English law in preference to the law of the parties' domicile.[151] On the other hand, this kind of blanket approach can be criticised on the basis that it lacks proper subtlety and sensitivity. In the cases concerning prohibited degrees of consanguinity, the law is largely underpinned by eugenic concerns which point towards the parties' post-matrimonial lives. By contrast, the prohibited degrees of affinity are based largely on religious and moral concerns; and these arise prior to the marriage. For this reason, they ought sensibly to be referred to the law(s) of the parties' ante-nuptial domicile(s). In short, the policy reasons for applying English law are much weaker in cases of affinity; and this is especially so if the parties do not intend to establish their matrimonial home in this country.

From an analytical perspective, things are more complicated when only one of the parties attempting to marry in this country possesses a foreign domicile. It is certainly an established rule of law (even if only in cases where the foreign rule of law is more restrictive than its English counterpart) that the *lex fori* applies.[152] Yet the simple application of the *lex fori* is open to the twin criticisms of being both starkly at odds with the general approach in this area as well as being xenophobic in its prioritisation of the English capacity rules. Happily, this heavily criticised rule[153] is still technically

[146] *Re Bozzell's Settlement* [1902] 1 Ch 751 (marriage between a widow and her deceased husband's brother was treated as valid although such marriages were prohibited under English law at the time).

[147] *Cheni v Cheni* [1965] P 85 (marriage between uncle and niece).

[148] Sexual Offences Act 1956, ss 10, 11. Note that the uncle–niece marriage in *Cheni, supra*, was not caught by these provisions.

[149] For analysis of this discretion, see ch 4.

[150] Note that although an uncle–niece marriage is not incestuous under English law, a marriage between half-siblings is thus defined. Yet the number of common genes in both cases is *exactly the same.*

[151] See *Dicey & Morris* (London: Sweet & Maxwell, 2000) p 676.

[152] *Sottomayor v De Barros (No 2)* (1879) 5 PD 94; *Chetti v Chetti* [1909] P 67.

[153] See, eg, Law Com Working Paper No 89, *op cit* n 14, para 3.17

open to review by the Higher courts, and they might well abandon it in view of the strong present-day desire to develop the rules of English private international law in accordance with comity and a greater degree of pluralism.[154]

The third situation concerns one or both parties to an overseas marriage possessing an English domicile at the time of the marriage. In such a case, the marriage will be treated as void if it did not comply with the English prohibited degrees. Accordingly, the House of Lords refused to recognise a Danish marriage contracted by two English domiciliaries in *Brook v Brook*;[155] while in *Mette v Mette*[156] and *Re Paine*,[157] two marriages in Germany – both involving only one English domiciliary – were similarly ruled void. In such cases, it is clear that the English conflicts rule is designed to prevent the circumvention of an English domestic law by the simple expedient of travelling to another jurisdiction in order to marry.[158]

3 Previous marriage

Most societies impose a bar on bigamy so that if one of the parties is already married, he or she is generally unable to enter a second marriage until the first has been properly annulled or dissolved. Exceptionally, some countries also impose a bar on the re-marriage of persons who have obtained a valid divorce.[159] But in both cases – and notwithstanding the widespread prohibition of bigamy – there are potential conflicts of law that can arise. This potential is obvious in the case of two countries only one of which prohibits re-marriage following a divorce; but as between two countries that both prohibit bigamy, the scope for conflict is less apparent. Yet the potential for disagreement about the bigamous nature of the second marriage does exist, since there may be disagreement about the validity of the first marriage[160] or the validity of a decree of nullity or divorce obtained in connection with it.[161]

[154] In *The Abidin Daver* [1984] 1 All ER 470 Lord Diplock noted (at 476) that 'the essential change in attitude of the English courts . . . has been achieved step by step during the last ten years as a result of the successive decisions of this House . . . [and] that judicial chauvinism has been replaced by judicial comity'.

[155] (1861) HL Cas 193.

[156] (1859) 1 Sw & Tr 416.

[157] [1940] Ch 46.

[158] It is for this reason that Fentiman has argued that the cases are best explained in terms of an application of the proper law as deduced from the country with which the marriage has its most real and substantial connection: see Fentiman, *op cit* n 105, at 268–273. But this is difficult to square with the language of some of the decisions. In *Mette v Mette*, for example, Sir Cresswell Cresswell said that '[t]here could be no valid contract unless each was competent to contract with the other': (1859) 1 Sw & Tr 416, at 423.

[159] See Dicey & Morris, *op cit* n 151, paras 17-082–17-085.

[160] See, eg, *Kassim v Kassim* [1962] P 224.

[161] See, eg, *Shaw v Gould* (1868) LR 3 HL 55 and *Padolecchia v Padolecchia* [1968] P 314.

For reasons that will become apparent in due course, bigamy cases need to be discussed separately from those in which the *lex domicilii* of one of the parties imposes a bar on re-marriage after divorce.

In cases of bigamy there are two main questions that must be answered. The first is whether the marriage in question is in fact bigamous. But the prior question is whether the first marriage (or decree of dissolution or nullity) was valid. Both these questions present choice of law problems. In particular we must consider (a) which law should be applied to determine the validity of the marriage where the incapacity alleged is bigamy, and (b) if the relevant law is the foreign law, whether that foreign law should determine merely the question of whether bigamy invalidates a second marriage, or whether it should also determine the bigamous nature of the subsequent marriage. In relation to the first question, it was emphatically held in *Padolecchia v Padolecchia* that capacity to marry in cases of bigamy is governed by the dual domicile test.[162] But in relation to the incidental questions of determining the marital status of the parties at the time of the second marriage and whether bigamy invalidates a second marriage, things are slightly more complicated.

In cases in which a prior marriage is alleged to have been terminated by a foreign decree, two possible scenarios may emerge (always assuming that the relevant foreign law does not permit bigamous marriage). On the one hand, the foreign decree may be recognised in England, but not according to the *lex domicilii* of one of the parties. On the other hand, the converse may apply. In both circumstances the choice of law question is crucial since the bigamous nature of the second marriage will turn upon the validity (or otherwise) of the foreign decree.

In the first scenario, the answer is now regulated by statute. Under section 50 of the Family Law Act 1986, where an English court has granted a divorce, or where a foreign divorce is recognised in England, the fact that the decree in question would not be recognised by the law of one of the parties' domiciles will not affect the capacity of that person to marry.[163] In the opposite scenario, however – that is, where the foreign decree is not recognised in this country, but is recognised by the law of the relevant party's domicile – section 50 of the 1986 Act does not apply. As such, the relevant rule is to be gleaned from the common law; and the best guidance available derives from the Canadian case of *Schwebel v Ungar*.[164] There, a

[162] 'Each party must be capable of marrying by the law of his or her respective ante-nuptial domicile': [1968] P 314, at 336 *per* Sir Jocelyn Simon P. There is House of Lords authority to like effect in *Shaw v Gould* (1868) LR 3 HL 55.

[163] This rule supersedes the somewhat inconsistent case law that preceded it. Compare *Padolecchia v Padolecchia* [1968] P 314 and *R v Brentwoood Superintendent Registrar of Marriages, ex p Arias* [1968] 2 QB 956 with *Perrini v Perrini* [1979] Fam 84 and *Lawrence v Lawrence* [1985] 1 All ER 506.

[164] (1964) 48 DLR (2d) 644.

husband and wife domiciled in Hungary divorced informally by Jewish *ghet* (see chapter 5) in Italy while on their way to Israel where they had decided to emigrate. They then settled in Israel where both parties acquired a domicile of choice. Later, during a temporary visit to Canada, the wife married a man domiciled in the province of Ontario. By Hungarian law, the Jewish *ghet* was ineffective to dissolve the first marriage, but it was effective under the law of Israel. The crucial question for the Canadian Supreme Court, therefore, was whether the first marriage should be regarded as having been dissolved by the *ghet*. It was accepted that the divorce was ineffective under the law of Ontario, but the court nonetheless held the second marriage to be valid on the basis that, applying the dual domicile test, the woman had capacity according to the law of her domicile (Israel) at the time of the re-marriage.

The approach in *Schwebel v Ungar* is supportive of the dual domicile test but it is not uncontroversial. If an English court were to take the same approach in the context of a case turning on a foreign divorce not recognised in this country, it would give rise to the rather odd position whereby, under the English conflicts rules, two purportedly monogamous marriages would be afforded recognition. Such a conclusion would be unsatisfactory in terms of the problems it may cause in the future over matters such as succession or matrimonial relief.[165] It *may* be preferable, on this line of argument, if, like the converse situation dealt with by the 1986 Act, the marital status of the parties were to be resolved on the basis of English law, while their capacity alone (having determined their status) should be referred to the *lex domicilii*. On the other hand, there are at least three objections that can be raised here. First, the reasonable expectations of the parties[166] and the principle of comity[167] would appear to be swept aside if the *Schwebel v Ungar* approach is not adopted. Secondly, insisting that a foreign divorce is invalid in this country gives rise to the age-old, and long since lamented, problem of creating a limping marriage. Finally, it can be viewed as both heavy-handed and xenophobic to impose an Anglo-centric rule of law to *all cases* within this category simply to catch the potentially problematic few cases in which difficult questions of succession or matrimonial relief *may*

[165] It would also fail to recognise the legitimate interest of the State in which the matrimonial home is to be established. Cf P. St J. Smart, 'Interest Analysis, False Conflicts and the Essential Validity of Marriage' (1985) 14 *Anglo-American Law Review* 225.

[166] As Hartley, *op cit* n 35, put it (at 571): '[t]he policy of upholding the reasonable expectations of the parties as to the law governing their affairs is based on elementary justice and fairness.' For judicial support of the principle, see *Re Goodman's Trusts* (1881) 17 Ch D 266, at 297–298 *per* James LJ.

[167] For weighty judicial support of the principle, see *The Abidin Daver* [1984] 1 All ER 470, at 476 *per* Lord Diplock.

arise. In utilitarian terms, adoption of the *Schwebel* approach would seem sensible as a damage limitation strategy.[168]

Thus far we have considered only what the courts should do when faced with a dispute about the status of a foreign divorce or nullity decree. It is just as conceivable, however, that a similar pair of questions could arise in relation to the parties' status where a dispute occurs concerning the validity of a previous marriage. More particularly, this would be the case *either* where a marriage would be treated as invalid under a foreign law but valid under English law,[169] *or* where the converse was true. In the absence of any direct authority on the matter, it is suggested here that the preliminary status issue (which centres on the validity of the initial marriage) ought to be referable to English law. Doing so means that English law would not be caught in the bind in which one party's marital status prior to the second marriage could not be reconciled with the decision as to the validity of the subsequent marriage. In determining status, however, the validity of the first marriage should be judged according to the normal rules.

Turning now to prohibitions on re-marriage, it should be noted that there exist some societies that prohibit the re-marriage of divorced persons. These restrictions take a considerable number of different forms, but tend to be imposed for only three reasons: punishment of the 'guilty party', safeguarding the innocent party's right to appeal against the divorce decree, and preventing paternity disputes in relation to children to which the divorced woman later gives birth.[170] Having exposed these concerns, it can be seen that cases of bigamy are analogous to only some of the reasons for prohibition in this context.

The most common kind of prohibition falls into the second category. Here at least part of the concern is with the avoidance of a bigamous marriage being celebrated. If the innocent party's appeal against the divorce succeeds, and if the decree is rescinded but not until the other party has already re-married, that other person would be party to two valid marriages. As such, English private international law generally recognises the validity of such restrictions on re-marriage regardless of where the parties are domiciled.[171] The exceptional instances in which such restrictions will not receive recognition centre on restrictions that operate in a discriminatory fashion. Thus, in *Scott v Attorney General*[172] a restriction on re-marriage imposed upon a

[168] How many *Schebel*-like 'double monogamy' cases are there really likely to be causing difficulties for the State in which the matrimonial home was established?

[169] Eg, if a marriage was formally invalid according to the local law, it might nonetheless fall within one of the recognised exceptions to the rule on formal validity allowed under English law.

[170] See T.C. Hartley, 'Bigamy in the Conflict of Laws' (1967) 16 *International and Comparative Law Quarterly* 680, 691–699.

[171] See, eg, *Warter v Warter* (1890) 15 PD 152.

[172] (1886) 11 PD 128.

woman who had been divorced because of her adultery was ignored on the basis that the same prohibition did not operate with respect to her former husband.[173] Similarly, in the Australian case of *Lundgren v O'Brien (No 2)*[174] a Belgian ten-month restriction on the re-marriage of *divorced women* to avoid paternity disputes was held to be inapplicable by the Australian court by reason of its discriminatory nature.

4 Same-sex

Under section 11(c) of the Matrimonial Causes Act 1973, a marriage between parties who are not respectively male and female is void. In other words, capacity to marry under English law is limited to marriages with persons of the opposite sex. Since virtually all other countries also prohibit same-sex marriages, the question of whether or not to recognise a same-sex marriage has never come before the English courts. However, in 2001 the Netherlands became the first country in the World to legalise same-sex marriages.[175] Belgium and Canada (with other States no doubt to follow) have now also firmly followed suit.[176] That being the case, it would seem a mere matter of time before the English courts will have to grapple with the thorny question of whether or not to afford recognition to a foreign same-sex marriage that would otherwise satisfy the requirements of formal and essential validity. Ultimately, it may of course be that such a case would have to be resolved on the basis of the court's residual discretion to refuse recognition. But for reasons discussed later in this chapter, the need to invoke the discretionary veto seems unlikely.[177] (This discussion is deferred until later in the chapter for convenience: a set of closely related issues emerges for the time being in

[173] This explanation of the decision stems from *Warter v Warter* (1890) 15 PD 152.

[174] [1921] VLR 361.

[175] Act of 21 December 2000, *Staatsblad* 2001, nr 9.

[176] Various States in the United States have attempted to do likewise, but at the time of writing such endeavours have been presented as politically very sensitive, and technically unresolved. For an account of the Belgian Law, see A. Fiorini, 'New Belgium Law on Same-Sex Marriage and its PIL Implications' (2003) 52 *International and Comparative Law Quarterly* 1039.

[177] A similar conclusion might well be reached with respect to marriages involving transsexuals which, although permitted elsewhere in the world, are still prohibited in this country. That said, it has been convincingly argued that such cases should not be viewed as raising questions about the essential validity of marriage, but rather about the status of the parties: see K. Norrie, 'Reproductive Technology, Transsexualism and Homosexuality: New Problems for International Private Law' (1994) 43 *International and Comparative Law Quarterly* 757. In any event, in the light of the decision of the House of Lords in *Bellinger v Bellinger* [2003] 1 FLR 1043 (where their Lordships issued a declaration under s 4 of the Human Rights Act 1998 that s 11(c) of the Matrimonial Causes Act 1973 is now incompatible with the European Convention on Human Rights) it seems inconceivable that the courts would refuse to recognise a foreign marriage involving a transsexual.

connection with the recognition of foreign same-sex registered partnerships, which are discussed there. There is little point in duplicating the material.)

5 Impotence and wilful refusal to consummate a marriage

Unlike the impediments thus far considered, impotence and wilful refusal to consummate a marriage are factors that render a marriage voidable rather than void under English law. In one obvious sense, therefore, such impediments cannot be described as depriving a marriage of its essential validity in quite the same way as those impediments considered in the preceding paragraphs. Another difference worthy of note is that, while impotence is easy to classify as a capacity matter, wilful refusal to consummate a marriage is not so to easy to accommodate under that heading. Nonetheless, wilful refusal does fit squarely within an account of the broader concept of essential validity and both issues are therefore dealt with here.

Conflicts difficulties arise in this context because, while English law treats non-consummated marriages as voidable, other systems of law may regard non-consummation as either immaterial or, alternatively, a basis for divorce. Unfortunately, the case law in this area is rather confused; but the greatest degree of support exists in favour a choice of law rule based on 'the law of the of the husband's domicile at the time of the marriage or . . . the law of the matrimonial domicile in reference to which the parties may have been supposed to enter into the bonds of marriage'.[178] The justice of this approach has been subjected to rigorous criticism on the grounds that what is at issue is a pre-nuptial matter: a desire to protect a person from contracting a marriage radically different to that which they had anticipated.[179] As such, it is more appropriate that the law of the domicile of both parties should be considered rather than the (post-nuptial) law of the country in which the matrimonial home is to be established. It is also susceptible to a criticism that has been levelled against other aspects of the law relating to essential validity: namely, that it is intrinsically chauvinistic. A much better suggestion is that 'a party is entitled to a nullity decree if he [or she] is so entitled by the law of his [or her] domicile at the time of the marriage'.[180]

6 Consent of the parties

The first point to recall in this context is Cohen LJ's statement in *Apt v Apt* that 'the method of giving consent as distinct from the fact of consent is essentially a matter for the *lex loci celebrationis*'.[181] With this in mind it will

[178] *De Reneville v De Reneville* [1948] P 100, at 114 *per* Lord Greene MR. See also *Casey v Casey* [1949] P 420; *Ponticelli v Ponticelli* [1958] P 204. Cf *Robert v Robert* [1947] P 164 (application of the law of the place of celebration).

[179] C.M.V. Clarkson & J. Hill, *Jaffey on the Conflict of Laws* (London: Butterworths, 2002) p 350.

[180] Jaffey, *op cit* n 105, at 49.

[181] [1948] P 83, at 88.

be apparent that, here, we are concerned only with the fact of consent; that is, with whether the consent that has been provided by one of the parties is imperfect in such a way as to provide a basis on which to invalidate the marriage. Under English law, a marriage is voidable if consent has been vitiated in any one of four ways. First, a marriage is voidable if either party's consent was invalidated by reason of duress, mistake, unsoundness of mind or otherwise.[182] Secondly, an annulment may also be sought where either party, though capable of giving a valid consent, was suffering from mental health within the meaning of the Mental Health Act 1983 at the time of the marriage.[183] Thirdly, a petitioner may also seek a decree of nullity where he can show that the respondent was infected with venereal disease in a communicable form at the time of the marriage, and that he was ignorant of that fact.[184] Finally, a marriage may be annulled where the respondent, unbeknown to the petitioner, was pregnant by a third party at the time of the marriage.[185] (It is well established in respect of the first of these grounds that mistake refers only to the identity (not the attributes) of the respondent,[186] and that the third and fourth grounds provide very limited statutory exceptions to this rule.)

The potential for conflicts of law in this context arises from the fact that not all other legal systems attribute the same significance to these factors as English law. For example, the sacrosanct nature of consensual marriage under the law of this country is wholly alien to those systems that permit, even encourage, forced marriages.[187] The question then, is the familiar one concerning choice of law. The answer, however, is far from clear. For while the judge in *Way v Way* said that 'questions of consent are to be dealt with by reference to the personal law of the parties rather than by reference to the law of the place where the contract was made',[188] other cases suggest alternative approaches.[189] For instance, the court in *Parojcic v Parojcic*[190] applied the law of the place of celebration, while in *Szechter v Szechter*,[191]

[182] Matrimonial Causes Act 1973, s 12(c).

[183] *Ibid*, s 12(d).

[184] *Ibid*, ss 12(e), 13(3). Whether HIV infection counts for these purposes is undecided; but for extensive discussion, see J. Murphy, 'Aids, Human Rights and Family Law' in M. Brazier *et al* (eds), *AIDS, Europe and Human Rights* (Oxford: Oxford University Press, 2005, forthcoming).

[185] *Ibid*, ss 12(f), 13(3).

[186] See, eg, *Militante v Ogunwomoju* [1993] 2 FCR 335.

[187] For examples, see Poulter, *op cit* n 9, ch 2.

[188] [1950] P 71.

[189] But even in *Way v Way* this approach would have been possible given the fact that the wife's domicile (Russia) coincided with the place of celebration. The same is true of the decision in *Szechter v Szechter* [1971] P 286 where the law of both parties' domicile (Poland) again coincided with the place of celebration.

[190] [1958] 1 WLR 1280.

[191] [1971] P 286, at 294–295 *per* Sir Jocelyn Simon P.

the then President suggested *obiter* that either party may seek an annulment if his or her consent was invalid either by the law of his or her own domicile, or by that of the respondent.[192] On principle, however, it can be argued that a straightforward application of the dual domicile test should be adopted in this context. For, as Jaffey put it:

> [a] party should not be held unwillingly bound to a marriage which, according to the notions of his own community, is a defective marriage . . . In other words, a party's expectations as to what amounts to a complete as opposed to a defective, marriage can be presumed to be those of the community to which he belongs at the time of the marriage.[193]

Polygamous marriages

The recognition of polygamous marriages involves a number of particular problems which require such unions to be afforded separate treatment even though their recognition often turns on questions of capacity. Apart from anything else, such marriages are distinctive in that, when they are recognised by the English courts, they receive recognition only for specific purposes. This tradition of limited recognition can be traced to the nineteenth-century case of *Hyde v Hyde*[194] where an Englishman married an American woman in Utah according to Mormon rites.[195] After a convoluted series of events, the husband returned to England and sought to divorce his wife. Lord Penzance refused to entertain the divorce petition on the ground that Mormon marriages were polygamous in nature and therefore did not warrant the recognition of the English divorce courts. Yet he was markedly reserved in giving judgment. He said:

> This court does not profess to decide upon the rights of succession or legitimacy which it might be proper to accord to the issue of polygamous unions . . . All that is intended to be here decided is that as between each other they are not entitled to the remedies, the adjudication, or the relief of the matrimonial law of England.[196]

[192] Furthermore, although the case was avowedly decided by following *Way v Way*, it has been questioned whether it was in truth Polish law that was applied: would a Polish court have held that the threat of imprisonment by the Polish authorities constituted duress as the English court did? See further Hartley, *op cit* n 35, at 580.

[193] Jaffey, *op cit* n 105, at 48.

[194] (1866) LR 1 P & M 130.

[195] Technically, there is no Mormon church though this seems to be the ecumenically accepted shorthand. To give it its full title, it is the Church of Jesus Christ of the Latter Day Saints.

[196] *Ibid*, at 138. Cf *A-M v A-M (Divorce: Jurisdiction: Validity of Marriage)* [2001] 2 FLR 6, and for further analysis, see Poulter, *op cit* n 3.

Apart from illustrating the fact that a distinctive approach is taken towards the recognition of polygamous marriages, the case also reveals the general hostility that was historically shown towards marriages that were both actually and potentially polygamous.[197] Over time, this hostility has gradually declined[198] so that nowadays special treatment is effectively confined to marriages that are actually polygamous.

Determining the nature of the marriage

A preliminary problem that arises in this context is when a marriage will be characterised as polygamous for the purposes of English private international law. It has already been noted that potentially polygamous marriages qualify as such.[199] But other cases – including one in which the local customary law permitted a man to take a single wife *plus* a plurality of concubines[200] – have also presented difficulties of classification in this context.[201] The key question is whether the nature of the marriage is to be decided by reference to the law of the parties' domicile, the law operative at the place of celebration, or the law of the forum in which the particular matrimonial dispute has fallen for consideration. While there is but scant and equivocal support for the third possibility,[202] the cases are fairly evenly divided in relation to the other two. In *Hussain v Hussain*, for example, there was a clear intimation that the matter is to be resolved by reference to the law of the parties' domicile: 'a marriage can only be potentially polygamous if at least one of the spouses *has the capacity* to marry a second spouse'.[203] By contrast, support for the law of the place of celebration was clearly evident in *Qureshi v*

[197] For further examples, see *Sowa v Sowa* [1961] P 70 and *Cheni v Cheni* [1965] P 85.

[198] See Poulter, *op cit* n 9.

[199] But the extent to which the courts are at liberty to deal with them in the same way is now limited by virtue of the Private International Law (Miscellaneous Provisions) Act 1995, ss 5–8. Under that Act, any potentially polygamous marriage involving one or more English domiciliaries is to be treated as a monogamous marriage.

[200] In *Lee v Lau* [1967] P 14 it was noted that there was only one marriage ceremony as such, yet it was remarked (at 20) that, 'that ceremony cannot be said to bring about a union to the exclusion of all others since the husband can take fresh partners to whose status some legal recognition is given'.

[201] See, eg, *Sowa v Sowa* [1961] P 70; *Mehta v Mehta* [1945] 2 All ER 690.

[202] In *Lee v Lau* [1967] P 14, Cairns J said confusingly (at 20) that 'once the nature and incidents of the union have been ascertained according to the local law, the question of whether the union is a monogamous marriage is for this court a question of English law'.

[203] [1983] Fam 26, at 32 *per* Ormrod LJ (emphasis added). See also *Ali v Ali* [1968] P 564, at 576–577 *per* Cumming-Bruce J and *Russ v Russ* [1964] P 315, at 323 *per* Willmer LJ.

Qureshi[204] where a woman of Indian domicile and a man with a Pakistani domicile married in England. It was held that, 'having taken place in England, where monogamy is the rule, [the marriage] must be regarded as monogamous for the purpose of invoking the jurisdiction of the court'.[205]

The majority of writers seem to favour the place of celebration test over the test based on the law of the parties' domicile; but there are arguments both ways. In support of the latter it has be urged that it is a 'fundamental principle that matters of status, especially the status of husband and wife, are regulated by the law of the domicile'.[206] While this may be true, this approach leads to profound problems in cases such as *Qureshi* where two foreign domiciliaries marry in England, the law of which country prohibits polygamous marriage. On balance, it seems that a test based on the place of celebration is preferable. The normal reason for having recourse to the law of the domicile(s) is to uphold the reasonable expectations of the parties.[207] But if, for instance, two Muslims from Pakistan were to marry in England, one could hardly describe as reasonable their expectation that the marriage would be treated as potentially polygamous. The parties' expectations as to the nature and incidents of the marriage are likely to be conditioned more by reference to where they are when they marry, than by reference to where they are domiciled at that time. For example, it would be inconceivable that a man who marries in this country could reasonably suppose himself to be outside the English marital rape prohibition simply because he has a foreign domicile.

Leaving to one side the question of which law governs the nature of the marriage, a second question that has posed problems in terms of classifying foreign marriages as either monogamous or polygamous centres on the time at which the status of the marriage falls to be determined. This problem stems from the fact that, in a country that has both polygamous and monogamous marriages, a crucial change of circumstances may sometimes convert a marriage that was polygamous at its inception into a monogamous union. In such circumstances, the characterisation of the marriage may differ depending on whether it is judged at the date of celebration, or at the commencement of the legal proceedings in which its character falls to be determined. The

[204] [1972] Fam 173. See also *Re Bethel* (1888) 38 Ch D 220 and *Chetti v Chetti* [1909] P 67.

[205] *Ibid*, at 182. Further (if not entirely unambiguous) support for this test is to be gleaned from *Iman Din v National Assistance Board* [1967] 2 QB 213, at 218–219 *per* Salmon LJ.

[206] North & Fawcett, *op cit* n 41, p 745.

[207] See, eg, the comments of James LJ in *Re Goodman's Trusts* (1881) 17 Ch D 266, at 297–298. A further reason is that two foreign domiciliaries marrying in England could otherwise claim to have contracted a valid polygamous marriage in an English register office based on the fact that law of their domicile permits polygamy.

modern view in relation to marriages that are initially polygamous is that certain limited later events may convert them into monogamous unions;[208] and that the critical time for determining the nature of the marriage is the time at which the proceedings in which its nature falls to be determined are commenced.[209] In one case, for example, it was held that the marriage had become monogamous by virtue of the birth of a child where the parties' religion forbade the husband the right to take any further wives if a child was born within ten years of the marriage.[210]

A change in character of a marriage is most likely to occur in relation to marriages that were only potentially polygamous at their inception. An actually polygamous marriage in which a man *presently* has a plurality of wives can never become monogamous. But if one wife dies or obtains a divorce, there seems no reason in principle why the nature of the man's *one* remaining marriage may not become *de jure* monogamous by virtue of a later valid monogamous ceremony, or a change of religion, law or domicile. Such an issue might be crucial, for the English courts are still reluctant to grant total recognition to an actually polygamous marriage.[211]

A second practical problem in this context is whether a marriage that was monogamous at its inception may subsequently become polygamous. The question has never arisen directly under English law. But the Privy Council has suggested in connection with another jurisdiction that the courts should, *so far as the marriage in question is concerned*, ignore any subsequent events that purportedly convert a monogamous marriage into a polygamous one.[212] As such, if a male domiciliary of Pakistan were to marry an English domiciliary in England, their marriage would be monogamous since English law permits only monogamy. If, however, the man were later to fly back to Pakistan and take a second wife domiciled there, it is submitted that the first marriage would remain monogamous for the purposes of matrimonial causes heard by the English courts. But if the validity of the second marriage were

[208] Early cases such as *Hyde v Hyde* (1866) LR 1 P & D 130 and *Mehta v Mehta* [1945] 2 All ER 690 rejected the possibility of any such change.

[209] *Parkasho v Singh* [1968] P 233, at 254–255 *per* Sir Jocelyn Simon P.

[210] *Cheni v Cheni* [1965] P 85. Other occurrences with like effect include the following: subsequent legislation in the country of celebration that renders the marriage monogamous (*Parkasho v Singh* [1968] P 233); a change of domicile to a country that prohibits polygamy (*Ali v Ali* [1968] P 564); going through a subsequent, valid monogamous ceremony (*Ohochucku v Ohochucku* [1960] 1 All ER 253).

[211] At the time the cases referred to in the preceding paragraph were decided, the English courts treated potentially polygamous marriages with similar hostility; but see now s 47 of the Matrimonial Causes Act 1973 (as amended by the Private International Law (Miscellaneous Provisions) Act 1995), rendering the classification 'potentially polygamous' a largely academic one.

[212] *A-G of Ceylon v Reid* [1965] AC 720. The Privy Council confined its decision to the law of Ceylon and expressly declined (at 734) to conjecture as to the legal position 'in a purely Christian country'.

to be tested – and if it satisfied the usual requirements in relation to form and essence – the English courts would face a real quandary. If recognition were afforded, the court would be admitting, somewhat nonsensically, that the man was simultaneously a party to a monogamous and a polygamous marriage. Equally, in recognising the man's legal obligations towards his second wife, the courts would effectively be diluting his responsibilities towards the first.[213] The combination of these two factors might therefore be argued to form sufficient grounds for invoking the court's residual discretion to refuse recognition of the second marriage.[214]

Relevance of the parties' domicile

Although the nature and incidents of a particular form of marriage ceremony are to be determined by reference to the law of the country in which it was celebrated, the law operative in the country or countries of the parties' ante-nuptial domicile(s) remains an important factor since it determines the capacity of those parties to contract a polygamous union. Because English domiciliaries are prohibited by statute from entering *actually* polygamous marriages,[215] we must consider the role of the parties' personal law(s) under two separate heads.

1 Persons domiciled in England

Two unsatisfactory decisions relating respectively to the choice of law rules in relation to polygamous marriages[216] and the interpretation of the original section 11(d) of the Matrimonial Causes Act 1973[217] made legislative reform

[213] If the second wife, for instance, petitioned for divorce on the basis of the husband's adultery, how much would his duty to support his second wife affect the financial payments he would be ordered to make in respect of the first?

[214] This residual discretion is discussed in ch 4.

[215] Matrimonial Causes Act 1973, s 11(b).

[216] *Radwan v Radwan (No 2)* [1973] Fam 35. This case seemed to suggest that a woman domiciled in England could contract an *actually* polygamous marriage so long as the intended matrimonial home would be in a country accepting polygamy (Egypt). For criticism, see I.G.F. Karsten, 'Capacity to Contract a Polygamous Marriage' (1973) 36 *Modern Law Review* 291, J.A. Wade, 'Capacity to Marry: Choice of Law Rules and Polygamous Marriages' (1973) 22 *International and Comparative Law Quarterly* 571 and D. Pearl, 'Capacity for Polygamy' [1973] *Cambridge Law Journal* 43.

[217] *Hussain v Hussain* [1983] Fam 26. According to this decision, a man with an English domicile could validly marry a woman domiciled in Pakistan, but not *vice versa*. It therefore benefited men, but not women. For elaborate criticism, see D. Pearl, 'Polygamy for English Domiciliaries' [1983] *Cambridge Law Journal* 26, A. Briggs, 'Polygamous Marriages and English Domiciliaries' (1983) 32 *International and Comparative Law Quarterly* 737 and R. Schuz, 'When is a Polygamous Marriage Not a Polygamous Marriage?' (1983) 43 *Modern Law Review* 653.

in this area imperative. That reform appeared in the shape of Part II of the Private International Law (Miscellaneous Provisions) Act 1995, which amended section 11(d) of the 1973 Act so that its operation was specifically confined to actually polygamous marriages.[218] In addition, section 5(1) of the 1995 now provides that:

> A marriage entered into outside England and Wales between parties neither of whom is already married is not void under the law of England and Wales on the ground that it is entered into under a law which permits polygamy and that either party is domiciled in England and Wales.

The main point to note here is that English law now permits all English domiciliaries to enter marriages abroad that are characterised by the local law as polygamous in form, but only so long as the marriage is in fact monogamous. Put otherwise, if neither party to the marriage already has a spouse at the date of its inception, the marriage will be treated as monogamous even though it would otherwise be styled *potentially polygamous*. A second observation that must be made here is that the question of capacity to contract a marriage in polygamous form is merely *one* important issue. The broader question concerning the validity of the marriage in more general terms remains also relevant, and nothing in the 1995 Act affects the common law conflicts rules that must be applied to in order determine this matter.[219]

2 Persons domiciled abroad

Where neither party to the marriage is an English domiciliary, his or her capacity to enter a polygamous marriage is determined by reference to the *lex domicilii*. Where, then, both parties are domiciliaries of country X (which permits polygamy), their marriage may be treated as valid for the purposes recognised by English conflicts rules. But where only one of the parties is domiciled in country X, and the other party is domiciled in country Y (which does not permit polygamy), the validity of the marriage in country X is to be determined by reference to the private international law rules operative in country Y. In other words, the English court when asked to consider the validity of the marriage will have to enquire whether country Y permits its own domiciliaries to contract foreign marriages that are actually polygamous, potentially polygamous, or neither.

Extent of recognition of polygamous marriages

English law, in a notable *volte face*, now predominantly recognises foreign polygamous marriages so long as they were validly created both in terms of

[218] By virtue of the Private International Law (Miscellaneous Provisions) Act 1995, Sched, para 2(2).
[219] *Ibid*, s 5(2).

the formal requirements of the local law and in terms of the capacity of the parties.[220] Indeed, as one judge put it, 'a polygamous marriage will [now] be recognised in England as a valid marriage unless there is some strong policy reason to the contrary'.[221] As such, parties to a valid polygamous marriage can nowadays expect it to attract recognition for nearly all purposes.[222] So, for instance, despite the decision in *Hyde v Hyde*, it is now clear that the matrimonial relief which was denied the petitioner in that case would now be available.[223] So, too, would the other matrimonial remedies that may be dispensed under section 47 of the Matrimonial Causes Act 1973.[224] Similarly, a respondent who has attempted to take a second spouse in this country will find that the first marriage is recognised for the purposes of entitling either party to the subsequent 'marriage' to a nullity decree based on the bigamous nature of that union.[225]

Turning to succession rights, it seems broadly immaterial that the deceased was party to a polygamous marriage. Certainly, in the case of children born within both actually and potentially polygamous marriages, there is a right to succeed to a deceased parent's property.[226] Furthermore, the children of potentially polygamous marriages may also succeed to titles of honour (although the matter is unclear in relation to children within actually

[220] In *Re Bethell* (1888) 38 Ch D 220 the husband's incapacity to contract a polygamous marriage according to his personal law was fatal to the claim in that case.

[221] *Alhaji Mohamed v Knott* [1969] 1 QB 1, at 13–14 *per* Lord Parker CJ. But for the view that there is still some way to go before polygamous marriages get treated like any other foreign marriage, see P.A. Shah, 'Attitudes to Polygamy in English Law' (2003) 52 *International and Comparative Law Quarterly* 369, 370.

[222] The narrow rule in *Hyde v Hyde* was abolished by statute: Matrimonial Proceedings (Polygamous Marriages) Act 1972, s 1 (since repealed, then re-enacted with only minor amendments as s 47 of the Matrimonial Causes Act 1973). For comment on the repeal, see I. Saunders & J. Walter, 'The Matrimonial Proceedings (Polygamous Marriages) Act 1972' (1972) 21 *International and Comparative Law Quarterly* 781.

[223] See *A-M v A-M (Divorce: Jurisdiction: Validity of Marriage)* [2001] 2 FLR 6.

[224] Technically *Hyde v Hyde* concerned only the matrimonial relief that could be obtained from the High Court. But a similar approach was later taken with respect to the dispensation of the *magistrates'* matrimonial jurisdiction in *Sowa v Sowa* [1965] P 70.

[225] *Srinivasan v Srinivasan* [1946] P 67; *Baindail v Baindail* [1946] P 122. Interestingly, the party at the heart of a polygamous marriage is not treated as being married for the purposes of grounding a criminal charge of bigamy: *R v Sagoo* [1975] QB 885.

[226] See, eg, *Bamgbose v Daniel* [1955] AC 107 (children from *nine* marriages succeeded to the property of their father who died intestate). The court held that the word 'children' in the English Statute of Distribution 1670 (which applied in Nigeria at that time) was broad enough to cover children of polygamous marriages. The equivalent interpretation would no doubt be extended to the word 'issue' used in the Administration of Estates Act 1925.

polygamous marriages).[227] On the matter of a widow's succession rights, the law lacks absolute authority. Nonetheless, it was observed in *Re Sehota*[228] that the question of a widow's succession rights was never intended to fall within the rule in *Hyde v Hyde*, and accordingly, in the absence of any obvious policy reason for denying such a right, it would seem that the deceased's widow ought to be able to succeed to his property on intestacy,[229] just as she may make a claim for financial provision under the Inheritance (Provision for Family and Dependants) Act 1975.[230]

During the parties' lifetime, it is noteworthy that statute provides a range of remedies for domestic violence – including orders regulating the occupation of the matrimonial home[231] – and that these are available regardless of whether the marriage is polygamous. Equally, the summary procedure available for resolving property disputes between spouses contained in the amended Married Women's Property Act 1882[232] may also be invoked by a party to a polygamous union. Statute further treats potentially polygamous marriages as equivalent to monogamous marriages for *some*, but not all, social security benefit purposes.[233] There is also a miscellany of cases in which polygamous unions have been recognised for various other, *ad hoc* purposes.[234]

It is thus clear that the significance of being a spouse within a potentially polygamous marriage has all but disappeared. It is equally clear that even actually polygamous marriages will now be recognised for virtually all purposes[235] so long as there is no strong policy reason for refusing recognition in

[227] *The Sinha Peerage Claim* [1946] 1 All ER 348. There is some doubt as to the ability of children of actually polygamous marriages to succeed to titles of honour. The problem is that the deceased's first-born son may have been born to his second or subsequent wife, while a later son was born to his first wife. Lord Maugham explicitly declined to express a view on the matter in this case: see *ibid*, at 349.

[228] [1978] 3 All ER 385.

[229] Administration of Estates Act 1925, Part IV.

[230] In *Re Sehota* [1978] 3 All ER 385 the court held that the word 'wife' in the Inheritance (Provision for Family and Dependants) Act 1975 was broad enough to cover the second wife of the deceased. The equivalent interpretation would no doubt be extended to the word 'spouse' which is used in the Administration of Estates Act 1925. See also the parallel approach adopted in *Coleman v Shang* [1961] AC 481 in connection with a widow's power to grant letters of administration to the deceased's estate.

[231] Family Law Act 1996, s 63.

[232] Section 17.

[233] See, eg, Social Security and Family Allowances (Polygamous Marriages) Regulations 1975 (SI 1975, No 561) rr 1(2), 2(2); Child Benefit (General) Regulations 1976 (SI 1976, No 965) r 12.

[234] For details see McClean, *op cit* n 34, pp 221–222.

[235] For immigration purposes, however, a polygamous wife is not recognised so as to entitle her to migrate to this country if there is currently, or has already been, another wife in the United Kingdom: Immigration Act 1988, s 2(2). Similarly, it is unclear how an English Court would approach an adoption application made by a polygamist and *one* of his plurality of wives, given that s 50 of the Adoption and Children Act 2002 speaks of adoption by a 'couple'.

accordance with the court's residual discretion.[236] This represents a welcome step in the direction of cultural pluralism on the part of the English courts and legislature.

Same-sex marriages and registered partnerships[237]

In addition to the Netherlands, which was the first country in the world to permit same-sex marriage,[238] several other States have now also formally permitted marriages between persons of the same sex.[239] Other European countries will almost certainly follow suit in making marriage available to same-sex couples. It would thus seem, bearing in mind the free mobility of persons within the European Union and the long-standing connections between this country and Canada, that it will be a mere matter of time before the English courts will be required to apply the rules of private international law to the question of whether such unions should be recognised as valid.[240] A related question, no less likely to arise, and no less important, is whether the English courts would be prepared to recognise the status created by a foreign, registered partnership (including, for the time being, one between two adults of the same sex). The facility to contract such partnerships of this kind has certainly proliferated since Denmark paved the way in 1989.[241]

Same-sex marriages

Just as with polygamous marriages, there is a specific domestic statutory bar to marriages between persons of the same sex. Section 11(c) of the Matrimonial Causes Act 1973 prohibits the marriage of persons who are not respectively

[236] On the courts' discretion to refuse recognition of foreign marriages, see ch 4.

[237] For fuller discussion see J. Murphy, 'The Recognition of Same-Sex Families in Britain: The Role of Private International Law' (2002) *International Journal of Law, Policy and the Family* 181 and K. Norrie, 'Would Scots Law Recognise a Dutch Same-Sex Marriage?' (2003) 7 *Edinburgh Law Review* 147.

[238] See K. Waaldijk, 'Small Change: How the Road to Same-Sex Marriage got Paved in the Netherlands' in R Wintemute & M. Andenæs (eds), *Legal Recognition of Same-Sex Partnerships* (Oxford: Hart Publishing, 2001).

[239] For the Canadian position, see N. Bala, 'Controversy over Couples in Canada: The Evolution of Marriage and other Adult Interdependent Relationships' (2004) 29 *Queen's Law Journal* 41. For the Belgian initiative, see Fiorini, *op cit* n 176.

[240] Importantly, for policy and other reasons, domestic legislation permitting same-sex marriage in England looks distinctly unlikely at present: see Murphy, *op cit* n 237, at 182–185.

[241] Act No 372 of 7 June 1989. Since then, and as of 2004, Australia, Belgium, Canada, Denmark, Finland, France, Germany, Hungary, Iceland, Luxembourg, The Netherlands, Norway, Sweden and the State of Vermont were among those permitting the registration of civil partnerships.

male and female. The immediate consequence of this is that persons domiciled in England have no capacity to contract a valid same-sex marriage.[242] In private international law terms, such a marriage would be invalid on account of its essential invalidity.[243] It is also likely that any purported same-sex marriage in this country would also be regarded as invalid, even if the parties were domiciled in a country that permits such unions.[244] If, by contrast, and for the sake of argument a Dutch couple contracted a same-sex marriage in the Netherlands, difficult questions could conceivably arise in relation to its essential validity if the parties subsequently moved to this country. For while on one view there should be no problem with the essential validity of the marriage because the parties' personal law was suitably permissive,[245] things may in reality become a little more complicated than this. Certainly, there would be a strong case for revisiting the dual domicile *versus* intended matrimonial home debate in this context.[246] For while the dual domicile test *generally* enjoys greater judicial favour than its rival, it is conceivable that a court might revert to the intended matrimonial home test in such a case for two reasons. First, impediments to marriage are often put in place to protect the parties concerned. This is obviously the basis for stipulating that there be a minimum age and for insisting upon a genuine consent to marriage. In relation to same-sex marriages, however, the concern is not to protect the parties, but to protect the institution of heterosexual marriage in the country in which the couple intend to establish their home.[247] For this reason, it could be argued that the intended matrimonial home test would be appropriate:

[242] For the argument that this provision may be inconsistent with England's Human Rights Commitments under the Human Rights Act 1998, see J. Murphy, 'Some Wrongs and (Human) Rights in the English Same-Sex Marriage Debate' [2004] *Brigham Young University Journal of Public Law* 543.

[243] See *Berthiaume v Dastous* [1930] AC 79, *Ogden v Ogden* [1908] P 46 and *Simonin v Mallac* (1860) 2 Sw & Tr 67.

[244] See *Dicey & Morris* (London: Sweet & Maxwell, 2000) p 684.

[245] Essential validity requires the parties to have both the capacity to marry in general and to marry one another. For the legal position in cases where one of the parties *may* be British, see W.A. Adams, 'Same-Sex Relationships and Anglo-Canadian Choice of Law: An Argument for Universal Validity' (1996) 34 *Canadian Yearbook of International Law* 103.

[246] Kenneth Norrie, *op cit* n 237, at 159, has suggested that a marriage of this kind should be seen as valid on the basis that 'Dutch marriage law requires only one of the parties to be Dutch and would hold valid a marriage between a person domiciled or habitually resident in, or a national of, the Netherlands at the time of the marriage and a person domiciled in [this country]'. But this would seem to address only the question of the formal validity of the marriage. It surely cannot be that Dutch legislation has the capacity to affect the matrimonial capacities of persons domiciled in this country!

[247] For staunch criticism of the notion that permitting same-sex marriage would somehow undermine heterosexual marriage, see Murphy, *op cit* n 237; *id*, *op cit* n 242; Norrie, *op cit* n 237.

it avowedly refers the choice of law to the country with the greatest interest in the marriage. Secondly, if a court were minded to refuse recognition, it may well find the intended matrimonial home test a convenient and effective means by which this could be achieved, and one which would avoid the need to invoke its discretionary veto under the banner of public policy.

Notwithstanding the uncertainty that inevitably surrounds this yet to be litigated question, it is nonetheless submitted that strong reasons exist for granting recognition to such marriages.[248] Not least among these are the many judicial utterances about giving effect to the parties' reasonable expectations, and showing broadmindedness and tolerance while upholding the principle of international comity.[249] In addition, however, human rights arguments based on respect for private and family life (developed fully below in connection with the recognition of registered partnerships), might be invoked to persuade a court in favour of recognition. It is certainly noteworthy that it was a human rights argument that persuaded the Canadian courts to open up marriage to same-sex couples in 2003.[250]

Registered civil partnerships[251]

In relation to the recognition of a foreign registered civil partnership, two broad problems would face an English court: first, whether the case should be dealt with as raising a *contract* issue or a *status* issue; and, secondly, what to do in view of the fact that there are many different models of such registered partnerships.

1 Contract versus status

If a court were to treat a registered civil partnership as a foreign contract, then the contractual choice of law rules – quite irrelevant in the context of the recognition of foreign marriages[252] – would apply. Accordingly, the first

[248] See Murphy *op cit* n 237, at 185–189. See also the interesting argument advanced by Norrie, *op cit* n 237, that an approach akin to that adopted with respect to polygamous marriages ought to be adopted whereby recognition is afforded for specific purposes on the basis that the marital status *per se* is not so important, but rather the legal consequences that flow from it.

[249] See ch 4.

[250] See *EGALE Canada Inc v Canada (Attorney General)* [2003] BCJ 994; *Halpern v Attorney General of Canada* [2003] OJ 2268.

[251] The analysis that follows will clearly be of less significance in relation to same-sex registered partnerships once the Civil Partnership Act 2004 comes into force. That is due to happen in December 2005.

[252] Art 1(2) of the Rome Convention on the Law Applicable to Contractual Obligations expressly excludes its operation in respect of questions concerning 'status' and 'rights and duties arising out of a family relationship'. The common law contract rules that operate by default have never covered foreign marriages, for as we have seen, a discrete set of rules operate in that context.

matter for any English court called upon to recognise such a partnership would be whether it was more appropriate for the contract or status choice of law rules to apply. There are arguments both ways, and in the absence of any precedents or other judicial guidance, the best that can be offered here is reasoned speculation.

On balance, and notwithstanding the increased emphasis on reciprocal rights and duties in family relationships in the *domestic* context,[253] it is submitted that the application of the contract rules would be misplaced. This is because, even though registered partnerships are dependent upon the mutual agreement of the parties, there remain a number of weighty reasons why they should not be thought of, or treated as, contracts for recognition purposes. To begin with, marriages (like registered partnerships) typically require the agreement of the parties; yet their recognition is dealt with as a status, not a contract, issue. Given, then, that the clear intention behind most of the registered partnership legislation in Europe is that they should be viewed more like marriage rather than cohabitation contracts,[254] there would appear a strong *prima facie* case for treating such partnerships as akin to marriages.[255]

[253] For details, see G. Douglas, *An Introduction to Family Law* (Oxford: Oxford University Press, 2001) pp 12–13.

[254] The model least like marriage is the French PaCS model which, among other things, does not insist on cohabitation, does not contain provision as to succession and does not automatically confer the tax concessions offered to spouses: see D. Bradley, 'Regulation of Unmarried Cohabitation in West European Jurisdictions – Determinants of Legal Policy' (2001) 15 *International Journal of Law, Policy and the Family* 22, 33–37. On the other hand, even registration of a PaCS has profound status repercussions in public law. For example, a PaCS partner may succeed to a tenancy (*CC*, Art 14), rely upon the health insurance and social security contributions made by the other (*CC*, Art 7) and enjoy the same tax status as a married person (*CC*, Art 4). It is for such reasons that PaCS has variously been described as 'a replica of marriage' (E. Steiner, 'The Spirit of the New French Registered Partnership Law – Promoting Autonomy and Pluralism or Weakening Marriage' [2000] *Child and Family Law Quarterly* 1, 7) and 'a variation of traditional marriage by a different name' (R. Probert, 'From Lack of Status to Contract: Assessing the French *Pacte Civil de Solidarité*' [2001] *Journal of Social Welfare and Family Law* 257, 258).

[255] In the Nordic countries (including Iceland), the relevant legislation requires the parties to fulfil the same basic conditions (regarding age, monogamy, etc) as heterosexual married couples. It also States that the parties be treated as married couples to whom, in the absence of express provision, the rights and obligations of married persons contained in other legislation shall be extended: see I. Lund-Andersen, 'Cohabitation and Registered Partnership in Scandinavia: The Legal Position of Homosexuals' in J. Eekelaar & T. Nhalpo (eds), *The Changing Family: Family Forms and Family Law* (Oxford: Hart Publishing, 1998). The Dutch partnership model is drafted in very similar terms: see W.M. Schrama, 'Registered Partnership in the Netherlands' (1999) 13 *International Journal of Law, Policy and the Family* 315, 318–321.

A second reason for rejecting the contract choice of law rules is that registered partnership legislation tends substantively to be more concerned with the parties' status than with their reciprocal obligations. This is certainly true, for example, of the Scandinavian and Dutch legislation.[256] So, for example, of the fifteen legal effects noted by Wendy Schrama in the context of the Dutch model, only three concern mutual obligations while the remaining twelve concern status.[257] Thirdly, unlike commercial or other contracts, where the principle of freedom of contract rides high, the agreements embodied in registered civil partnerships derive their legal significance only from the act of being formally and institutionally sanctioned in much the same way that consent orders do.[258] Even in the most contract-like version of a registered partnership – that is, the French PaCS model[259] – any change in the terms of the agreement must be communicated to, and recorded by, the appropriate official.[260] Fourthly, registered same-sex partnerships can normally be terminated only by way of formal, institutional dissolution. This, again, stands in stark contrast to the normal rules of contract according to which, for instance, we might expect something so fundamental as infidelity to be treated as a repudiatory breach of contract rather than merely as a basis upon which the 'innocent' party may apply to have the partnership formally dissolved.[261] Taken together, these factors suggest strongly that the status approach is preferable to any contract analogy.

2 Registered partnership: an unfamiliar juridical entity

In terms of recognition, the fact that registered partnerships do not currently exist as a juridical entity in this country is the source of the second potential difficulty for the English courts. Since such partnerships are unavailable, and because it is uncertain if and when Parliament will legislate to create a facility for heterosexuals to register a partnership, the question of how a migrant couple's registered partnership should be regarded for recognition purposes necessarily remains open. The courts' problem inheres principally

[256] Typically, the provisions confer special tax status, succession rights, rights to use each other's names, rights under domestic violence legislation and the like.

[257] See Schrama, *op cit* n 255, at 319–20. Similarly, the registered partnership laws of Nova Scotia, Manitoba and Quebec confer upon the partners the status of spouse for the purposes of Provincial statutes concerning matrimonial property, succession and support obligations: see Bala, *op cit* n 239.

[258] *de Lasala v de Lasala* [1980] AC 546; *Thwaite v Thwaite* (1981) 2 FLR 280; *Masefield v Alexander* [1995] 1 FLR 100.

[259] See Probert, *op cit* n 254 and C. Richards, 'The Legal Recognition of Same-Sex Couples – The French Perspective' (2002) 51 *International and Comparative Law Quarterly* 305.

[260] *CC*, Arts 515–517.

[261] That fidelity is central in such partnerships is evident in the Danish model whereby it is a criminal offence to marry or register another partnership during the subsistence of the first partnership.

in the fact that there are so many different kinds of such partnerships, each having different legal effects, depending on the country of registration. This contrasts sharply with marriage, for which there is a fixed range of statutory consequences. Furthermore, the expectations of the parties as to legal consequences of their registered partnerships will vary from one couple to the next, depending on country of origin and whether they are of the same sex. How, then, should the English courts approach the question of recognition?

It is suggested here, in accordance with the central principle that our system of private international law should seek to fulfil the reasonable expectations of the parties, that such partnerships ought to be dealt with in a manner akin to that applied to polygamous marriages. In other words, such partnerships should be recognised for specific purposes decided on a case-by-case basis. But first we need to consider why the courts should even recognise these unions at all. After all – and this is the main point – there is no current equivalent juridical entity in English law.

The most important criterion here is likely to be Article 8(1) of the European Convention on Human Rights[262] given that the English courts must now adjudicate mindful of, and consistently with, this and the other rights embodied in the Convention.[263] Article 8(1) provides that '[e]veryone has the right to respect for his private and family life, his home and his correspondence'. Thus, if a civil partnership could be equated with either 'family life' or 'private life' for these purposes, it would be very difficult for an English judge to refuse recognition yet at the same time claim to be respecting the parties' family and/or private lives.

Before the Civil Partnership Act 2004 becomes operative, one potential obstacle to treating same-sex partnerships as 'familial' for these purposes is the fact that a significant body of European Human Rights jurisprudence has rejected the notion that same-sex relationships should qualify as 'family life'.[264] On the other hand, the English courts are not strictly bound by the decisions of the Strasbourg court. Instead, and for two reasons, they should be viewed only in terms of setting a *minimum* standard in the protection of Convention rights.

The first of these reasons is the fact that the Human Rights Act 1998 was deliberately drafted so as not to bind the English courts to Strasbourg decisions:[265] it is couched in terms that permit the domestic courts to be more

[262] The claim that, *in practice* the most important criterion will be Art 8(1) is made on the assumption that the usual (marriage) requirements as to formal and essential validity are satisfied.

[263] Human Rights Act 1998, ss 2, 6.

[264] See, eg, *Kerkhoven v The Netherlands* (Application No 15666/89) (unreported) 19 May 1992; *X, Y and Z v United Kingdom*; *Salgueiro da Silva Mouta v Portugal* [2001] 1 FCR 653.

[265] Under s 2 of the 1998 Act the English courts are required *only to* take into account the decisions and opinions of the of the European Court of Human Rights and the Commission.

progressive, but no more restrictive, than the European court in interpreting the Convention.[266] Secondly, if a domestic tribunal were to attempt to interpret the Convention more narrowly than the Strasbourg court, the offended individual would simply take his or her case to the latter in order to obtain a predictable, contrary outcome. There would be little point, then, in a domestic tribunal attempting to insist on a narrower interpretation of the Convention than that of the Strasbourg court.

Technically, therefore, the English courts are free to interpret the phrase 'family life' as including same-sex partners, even though in *Ghaidan v Godin-Mendoza*[267] the House of Lords stopped short of doings so.[268] It is also worth noting that the European court is itself not bound by its own earlier decisions, and that the Convention is a 'living instrument' that must be interpreted in the light of prevailing conditions.[269] For as those conditions change, so too will the European court's own interpretation of the Convention (and particularly, the phrase 'family life'). As the court explained *Marckx v Belgium*:[270]

> It is true that, at the time when the Convention was drafted, it was regarded as permissible and normal in many European countries to draw a distinction between the 'illegitimate' and the 'legitimate' family. However, the Court

[266] While the Human Rights Bill was before Parliament it was actually mooted whether Strasbourg decisions should bind the English courts; the Lord Chancellor said: '[w]e must remember that the interpretation of the Convention rights develops over years . . . We feel that to accept this amendment [in favour of making Strasbourg case law binding] removes from the judges the flexibility and discretion they require in developing human rights law': *Hansard* HL, 19 January 1998, col 1270. The clear tenor of this statement is that the English courts *may* depart from Strasbourg case law, *but only* in instances where such a departure would *expand* the scope of any given Convention right.

[267] [2004] UKHL 30.

[268] The case turned upon a matter of sexual orientation discrimination in relation to statutory succession rights. Baroness Hale emphasised (*passim*) the question of whether there was any justification for treating homosexual 'marriage-like' relationships in a different manner to heterosexual 'marriage-like' relationships. In similar vein, Lord Nicholls (*ibid*, at [16]) stressed the fact that 'there is no reason for believing [that certain] . . . factual differences between heterosexual and homosexual couples have any bearing on why succession rights have been conferred on heterosexual couples but not homosexual couples'. He also conclusively said (at [15]) that '[s]ame sex partnerships cannot be equated with family'; and Lords Steyn, Millett (but only on this matter) and Rodger all agreed with him: *ibid*, at [37], [55] and [103], respectively.

[269] In this context it is noteworthy that the Canadian Supreme Court has already taken the step of extending the definition of 'family' to include same-sex relationships in *M v H* [1999] 2 SCR 3. For discussion see, A. Harvison Young, 'The Changing Family, Rights Discourse and the Supreme Court of Canada' (2001) 80 *Canadian Bar Review* 749, esp 787–791; and for some of the background N. Bala, 'The Evolving Canadian Definition of the Family: Toward a Pluralistic and Functional Approach' (1994) 8 *International Journal of Law and the Family* 293.

[270] (1979) 2 EHRR 330.

recalls that this Convention must be interpreted in the light of present-day conditions.[271]

Furthermore, in *Kjeldsen v Denmark*[272] it was said that the Convention is an 'instrument designed to maintain and promote the ideas and values of a democratic society';[273] while in *Handyside v UK*[274] it was explained that the important features of a democratic society were 'pluralism, tolerance and broadmindedness'.[275] Accordingly, and in line with the example set by the Canadian Supreme Court,[276] it is suggested that the ever-expanding legal recognition of same-sex relationships will soon, in any event, be reflected not just in the 2004 Act, but in the evolutionary jurisprudence of the Human Rights Court.[277] Indeed, it is arguable that the initial basis for the Strasbourg court's decision to exclude same-sex relationships from the definition of family life has already begun to disintegrate. Gillian Douglas has suggested that its refusal in the past to treat same-sex relationships as family life 'may, to some extent, stem from its focus [hitherto] on the parent/child relationship rather than adult partnerships'.[278] But now that some European States permit step-parent adoption within a registered partnership,[279] and now that the Netherlands and Belgium allow actual marriage between persons of the same sex, it has become more or less impossible for the Strasbourg court to continue to exclude cohabiting same-sex partners from its definition of 'family life'. Against this background, and bearing in mind the English courts' abiding duty to uphold international comity and to give effect to the reasonable expectations of the parties, it would seem that a strong case for recognition of a same-sex (and, by necessary extension heterosexual) partnership on the first limb of Article 8(1) exists.

[271] *Ibid*, at para 30.
[272] (1976) 1 EHRR 711.
[273] *Ibid*, at 731.
[274] (1976) 1 EHRR 737.
[275] *Ibid*, at 754.
[276] See *M v H* [1999] 2 SCR 3.
[277] The case of *D v Council* (Case C-122/99 P, 31 May 2001) – holding that it did not amount to a breach of Article 8 to refuse an employee of the Council a household allowance on the basis that a registered partnership did not qualify for such purposes – should not be taken to have any bearing on this prediction. First, the case was a decision of the ECJ not the ECHR. Secondly, it concerned a very narrow question of whether the applicant was 'a married person' for the purposes of Art 1(2) of Annex VII to the Staff Regulations of Officials of the European Communities. And thirdly the decision seems wrong insofar as the court found that the refusal of the allowance 'was not . . . capable of constituting interference in private and family life', whereas for Art 8 purposes the proper question should have been whether the refusal was a failure to 'respect' private or family life.
[278] Douglas, *op cit* n 253, at p 46. Douglas' contention certainly explains the court's recognition in *Salgueiro da Silva Mouta v Portugal* [2001] 1 FCR 653 that homosexual parents enjoy family life with their children, but not with one another.
[279] See, eg, Denmark's Law No 360 of 2 June 1999, s 2.

Even if it does not, a separate argument in support of the recognition of registered civil partnerships can be grounded on the second limb of Article 8(1): namely, the right to respect for one's private life. There are certainly Strasbourg decisions that reveal a willingness to recognise same-sex relationships for these purposes.[280] Furthermore, the obligation to respect private life has been held to entail both a positive and negative aspect comprising not just a duty to refrain from interfering in private relationships, but also an obligation to ensure that they are properly respected.[281] Taken together, these factors suggest that it would be difficult for an English court to refuse to recognise a properly contracted registered partnership yet at the same time claim to be fulfilling its Human Rights Act duty to afford positive respect to the private lives of the parties to it.

How, then, given the juridical unfamiliarity of registered partnerships in this country, should an English court proceed? A strategically guarded approach might be called for according to which recognition is afforded *only* for the purpose for which it is actually being sought on a case-by-case basis. So, for example, Canadian same-sex partners migrating to this country because one of them has been offered a job here may seek to claim immigration rights for the other partner on the basis of family membership. The court, may then decide whether recognition should exist for this purpose. Alternatively, following the breakdown of a Swedish partnership between a heterosexual couple who moved here and have a child together, the male partner may seek to argue that the other, who now lives alone, would commit an abduction within the Hague Convention if she tried secretly to remove the child to Sweden.[282] While recognition for both these purposes may well be forthcoming,[283] the courts may still be guarded in allowing registered opposite-sex partners to claim the benefit of statutory *spousal* support obligations, even if the claimant could point to such a right in his or her country of origin.[284] This may be viewed as a wholly inappropriate since, as Kenneth Norrie has pointed out, '[t]hese rules are designed, if somewhat clumsily, to harmonise the wealth of both parties in [opposite-sex] relation-

[280] See, eg, *ADT v UK* [2000] 2 FLR 697 and *Smith and Grady v UK* (1999) 29 EHRR 493.

[281] *Kroon v Netherlands* (1994) 19 EHRR 263. See also N. Bamforth, 'The Application of the Human Rights Act 1998 to Public Authorities and Private Bodies' [1999] *Cambridge Law Journal* 159.

[282] For the definition of wrongful removal contrary to custody rights under this Convention, see Ch 8.

[283] For doubt as to whether recognition would be afforded for the purpose of creating immigration rights, see Clarkson & Hill, *op cit* n 179, p 354.

[284] The reason for such possible reluctance would no doubt derive from the fact that the Civil Partnership Act 2004 will exclude opposite-sex couples from the benefits of registration.

ships which, by and large, are between individuals who in terms of wealth creation, tend to be unequal'.[285] It would seen foolish to ignore this fact.

Three main reasons might be advanced to support the approach suggested here. First, it would allow the courts to eliminate the possibility of an otherwise inevitable, and problematic constitutional law issue. Registered partnerships exist according to a number of different models that vary from country to country; yet none of these models is available under domestic law.[286] If recognition were granted for 'all purposes', would this mean that an immigrant heterosexual couple from, say, the Netherlands would have their partnership recognised for all the purposes granted by Dutch law? If so, this could scarcely be justified in constitutional law terms. For the Dutch legislature is plainly incompetent to confer rights on couples who migrate from the Netherlands to this country when this country's legislature does not afford such rights to its own citizens.[287]

Secondly, the case-by-case approach allows the courts to afford the *same* limited recognition to all immigrant couples, regardless of country of origin. This averts any need to consider whether some forms of registered partnership are more acceptable than others (and thus avoids any accusations of discrimination based on differential treatment). Thirdly, confining recognition to certain limited purposes in preference to tackling the broader question of the legal status of registered partnerships more generally, carries with it all the advantages of what Cass Sunstein has termed 'judicial minimalism'. In essence, Sunstein suggests that there are two main bonuses associated with minimalist decision-making. In the first place, such an approach 'is likely to reduce the burden of judicial decision', while secondly – and at the same time – it renders 'judicial errors less frequent and (above all) less damaging'.[288]

In the background, however, and regardless of the purpose for which recognition is sought, the courts should bear in mind the cardinal principle uttered in a case concerning the recognition of a polygamous marriage that

[285] K. Norrie, 'Marriage is for Homosexuals – May the Rest of us be Saved From it' [2000] *Child and Family Law Quarterly* 363, 366. As he rightly continues, these rules 'are uniquely appropriate for [only] opposite-sex couples . . . [For] [r]esearch has long shown that same-sex couples: (1) tend to be economically closer to each other, in terms of both wealth and earning power than opposite-sex couples; and (2) tend to avoid the economic inter-dependency on each other that so often characterises opposite-sex couples': *loc cit*.

[286] When the Civil Partnership Act 2004 becomes operative, no doubt foreign same-sex partnerships will be treated in the same way as those under the 2004 Act.

[287] In *Baindail v Baindail* [1946] P 122, Lord Greene MR was aware of the corresponding problem associated in recognising a polygamous marriage for all purposes. After cautioning (at 130) 'I must not be taken as suggesting that for every purpose . . . [a] marriage such as this would be regarded as a valid marriage' he stressed the fact 'nothing that I have said . . . [has] the slightest bearing on the law of bigamy'.

[288] See C.R. Sunstein, *One Case at a Time: Judicial Minimalism on The Supreme Court* (Cambridge, MA: Harvard University Press, 1999) p 4.

'on a question which is not covered by authority, considerations [about the adverse effects of non-recognition] must carry very great weight'.[289] In other words, the English courts should be extremely cautious about refusing recognition.

Conclusions and critique

This chapter has been a long and involved one setting out a good deal of the detailed rules of private international law governing the recognition of foreign marriages. In so doing, and in traversing much of the same detailed ground that one would find in a good private international text, it might be wondered what particular value there is to affording such in-depth discussion to those rules here. After all, this is designed to be a book primarily about family law, not the conflicts of law. The answer inheres in the paragraphs that follow. For while they are intended to form a general critique of this area of the law, they nonetheless refer frequently to some of these rather esoteric rules. And although the particular rules may seem somewhat abstruse, the points of critique drawn from them form a pattern that raises issues of general principle. The points are gathered under three headings.

Pockets of xenophobia

Perhaps the most important observation to offer is that within this immensely complex body of rules, there remains a sizeable number – of both judicial and legislative provenance – that cut very much against the grain of modern family law which has become much more pluralistic and sensitive towards the treatment of cultural and ethnicity issues,[290] as well as those

[289] *Baindail v Baindail* [1946] P 122, at 130.

[290] Given the modern tendency within family law to minimise the regulation of adult relationships (see text associated with n 303, below), most statutory examples exist within the law relating to children. See, eg, the Children Act 1989, s 22(5)(c) (a local authority looking after a child 'shall give due consideration to the child's religious persuasion, racial origin and cultural and linguistic background') and Sched 2, para 11 (a local authority making available support services shall 'consider racial groups to which children belong'). Official Guidance on this Act further states that 'children should have the right to be cared for as part of a community which values the religious, cultural and linguistic identity of the child': Department of Health, *The Children Act 1989 Guidance and Regulations Volume 2: Family Support, Day Care and Educational Provision for Young Children* (London: HMSO, 1991) para 6.28. A further statutory example of such provision can be found in the Adoption and Children Act 2002, s 1(5). For welcome judicial recognition that culture differences are not merely synonymous with colour differences, note Bush J's observation that 'emphasis on colour rather than cultural upbringing can be mischievous and highly dangerous when you are dealing in practical terms with the welfare of children':

involving matters of gender.[291] Three pertinent examples will be supplied here, although several more exist.[292]

First, although as we have seen, the question of whether to categorise consent to marriage as a matter of formal or essential validity is a difficult one, there can be no convincing argument to support the retention of certain xenophobic rules that ride roughshod over aspects of a party's personal law nor of those rules which, if the best explanation of their curious nature is to be believed,[293] afford special treatment to the consent of English male domiciliaries.[294]

Secondly, and in similar vein, is the dubious rule in *Sottomayor v De Barros (No 2)*.[295] According to this rule, any marriage celebrated *in England* in which one of the parties has an English domicile at the time of the marriage is to be governed exclusively by reference to *English law*.[296] Any lack of capacity on the part of the *foreign domiciliary* according to *the law of his or her domicile* is entirely disregarded. The rule constitutes a patently Anglocentric exception to the dual domicile test: there is no equivalent in cases where the marriage was celebrated elsewhere than in England.[297] And while it has been argued that the rule can be defended (if not justified) on the grounds that the conflicts of laws often exhibits forum preferences of this kind,[298] this is essentially a technocratic answer to a question brimming with policy concerns.[299] As we noted earlier, when discussing *Schwebel v Ungar*,

---

Re N (A Minor) (Adoption) [1990] 1 FLR 58, at 63. At international level, too, recognising the modern-day multi-cultural make-up of many States, the United Nations Convention on the Rights of the Child requires due regard to be paid to a child's ethnic, religious, cultural and linguistic background: see Arts 2, 8, 20, 30. See also, more generally ch 9 and J. Murphy (ed), *Ethnic Minorities, Their Families and the Law* (Oxford: Hart Publishing, 2000).

[291] Cf *Ogden v Ogden* [1908] P 46 (criticised heavily by the see Law Commission: see Working Paper No 89, *op cit* n 14, paras 3.45–3.48 and Law Com No 165, *op cit* n 14, paras 2.7–2.8) and *Lodge v Lodge* (1963) 107 *Sol Jo* 437.

[292] See, as an example of a legislative provision falling into this category, s 50 of the Family Law Act 1986.

[293] McClean, *op cit* n 34, p 209.

[294] *Sottomayor v De Barros (No 2)* (1879) 5 PD 94.

[295] (1879) 5 PD 94.

[296] Section 50 of the Family Law Act 1986, as we observed earlier, is similarly questionable.

[297] See, eg, *In the Will of Swan* (1871) 2 VR (IE & M) 47; *Breen v Breen* [1964] P 144; *Schwebel v Ungar* (1964) 48 DLR (2d) 644; *Reed v Reed* (1969) 6 DLR (2d) 617.

[298] See C. Clarkson, 'Marriage in England: Favouring the *Lex Fori*' [1990] *Legal Studies* 80.

[299] Thus it is no real answer to say that English law, being the *lex loci*, has a sufficient interest in the essentials of a marriage to impose an extra hurdle to marriage. It seems preferable to say that where the parties are aware that English law would not countenance the kind of marriage in question, by reason of whatever impediment under the local law, they would not have a reasonable expectation that

difficult questions concerning the reasonable expectation of the parties, the interests of the State in which the matrimonial home is to be established, limping marriages and the principle of comity arise. These, it is submitted, ought to be in the forefront of the minds of those called upon to adjudicate such questions rather than tendencies within the broad corpus of private international law more generally.

The final example of a xenophobic trait within this area of the law can be observed in the decision in *Pugh v Pugh* in relation to non-age marriages. Whereas the decision in *Sottomayor v De Barros (No 2)* permits the English courts to ignore a foreign incapacity, *Pugh*, it will be recalled, entitles them to impose upon the foreign party an English incapacity. It remains a singularly difficult decision to justify or accept in so far as it confounds the ascendant dual domicile test by virtue of its culturally imperialistic essence.[300] As will be recalled, the Age of Marriage Act 1929 was given extra territorial effect in that case in order to render a Hungarian girl of fifteen incapable of marrying an English man in Austria. Although both had capacity according to their personal laws, and although the marriage satisfied the Austrian formalities, the marriage was declared void. Sebastian Poulter, noting that 'the Act was held applicable to . . . [a] foreign domiciliary who was below the minimum age, even though her *lex domicilii* treated the marriage as valid' has nonetheless contended that the decision can 'still be justified as a valuable protection for English domiciliaries against the risks of an unstable marriage'.[301] But this is difficult to accept, for two reasons. First, it merely props up the notion that there is something special, something more deserving of the courts' protection about *English* domiciliaries.[302] Secondly, and more importantly although it is a point entirely overlooked in all the leading texts on private international law, it is a stance that is entirely at odds with the dwindling State interest in matrimonial matters. The point has been put succinctly, thus:

> The traditional understanding is that the state has a vital interest in the legal relationship between couples . . . But this doctrine has become increasingly

---

the marriage would be held valid and the court would therefore be free to strike it down on the basis of its residual discretion. The other solution is to extend the notion that the *lex loci* is relevant to all cases. But this means abolishing, not attempting to justify, the rule in *Sottomayor v De Barros (No 2)*: see Law Com No 165, *op cit* n 14, paras 2.13–2.14

[300] Note also the argument that it failed to serve either the interests of English or Hungarian law to invalidate the marriage: see Smart, *op cit* n 166, at 233–234.

[301] Poulter, *op cit* n 9, p 19. For similar arguments, see Jaffey, *op cit* n 105, at 45 and Hartley, *op cit* n 35, at 577. But since when did English domestic law ever try to protect *adult* parties from other kinds of statistically unstable marriage?

[302] Cf the child marriage involving two Nigerians in *Alhaji Mohamed v Knott* [1969] 1 QB 1 that was recognised as valid.

difficult to reconcile with the changing nature of marriage (which, as has been said is now seen primarily a concern of the individuals involved, governed by their individual sense of ethics or utility).[303]

In truth, the only instance in which the courts could legitimately seek to save an English domiciliary from himself in this way is if the English domiciliary were a child. In such a circumstance, were it necessary so to do (which it is not[304]), the court would presumably wield its discretionary veto to deny recognition to a marriage that otherwise satisfied the requirements of formal and essential validity. This it could conceivably do either on the basis of its inherent protective jurisdiction with respect to minors,[305] or in line with the child's Convention Rights to protection from any form of exploitation.[306] It is suggested here that this would be a far better way of resolving the issue than creating an essentially xenophobic exception to the general rule concerning essential validity.[307]

Before turning to the second general insight provided by this chapter, it is important to provide a proper context in which to view the above criticisms. It is true that a number of these exceptions to the general rules on the recognition of foreign marriages bear culturally imperialistic elements, but it must also be remembered that they are just that: exceptions. It must equally be recalled that judicial attitudes have softened over the last half-century or so, and that they increasingly reflect the liberal, tolerant, pluralist society that has emerged in this country.[308] Furthermore, the exceptions adverted to are of limited scope and are probably also of limited practical significance. Notwithstanding any of this, however, they are far from insignificant. Apart

[303] Cretney *et al*, *op cit* n 9, p 4. For a corresponding judicial view, see *Bellinger v Bellinger* [2001] 2 FLR 1048, at 1082 *per* Thorpe LJ: 'Marriage has become a state into which, and from which, people choose to enter and exit. Thus I would now redefine marriage as a contract for which the parties elect.' See also M. Glendon, *State, Law and Family* (New York: North-Holland, 1977) p 323.

[304] The child would lack capacity according to his or her personal law, the law of England and Wales.

[305] See J. Seymour, '*Parens Patriae* and Wardship Powers: their Nature and Origins' (1994) 14 *Oxford Journal of Legal Studies* 159.

[306] United Nations Convention on the Rights of the Child, Arts 32, 34, 36.

[307] For those in whose view the interest of the *lex loci* outweighs the concerns centring on comity as well as, sometimes, limping marriages, the suggestion of the Law Commission that the *lex loci* should always be a relevant factor – not merely in cases in which the marriage was celebrated in England – will no doubt be of greater appeal: see Law Com No 165, *op cit* n 14, paras 2.13–2.14.

[308] Compare, eg, the Victorian/Christian values evident in *Hyde v Hyde* with those at play in *Alahaji Mohamed v Knott* [1969] 1 QB 1, *Cheni v Cheni* [1965] P 85, *Bellinger v Bellinger* [2003] 1 FLR 1043 and *Ghaidan v Godin-Mendoza* [2004] UKHL 30. Recall also the gradual liberalisation of judicial attitudes towards polygamy discussed at length in Poulter, *op cit* n 3 (as well as the corresponding steps taken by Parliament in the Private International Law (Miscellaneous Provisions) Act 1995).

from revealing how family law issues within the rules of private international law seem to have been overlooked (or at least downgraded[309]) to some extent, they also sit uncomfortably beside both the current concern to minimise the State interest in matrimonial matters and (in being highly technocratic) the prevalence of discretionary decision-making within modern domestic family law.[310] Finally, they hint at our next major insight: that a strong case for codification of this branch of the law may be made.

A case for codification?

There are at least three plausible strands to the claim that the law in relation to the recognition of foreign marriages ought to codified. These are based, in turn, on the need for clarification of the law, the need for greater simplicity and the need for a certain measure of modernisation.

As regards clarification, there is first and foremost a pressing need to resolve finally the question of whether essential validity is, or ought to be, determined by reference to the law of the parties' domicile or the law of their intended matrimonial home. As we noted at the time, the case law exhibits some support for both tests. What we also noted briefly[311] was that there are other competing accounts of the basis for the choice of law rule in relation to essential validity. Amidst such confusion – neither the courts nor academic commentators seem able to resolve it – the case for clarification by way of codification would seem overwhelming. Similar confusion, as we also saw, exists in the case law concerning the formal validity of marriages celebrated in consulates and embassies.[312] It is equally in need of legislative attention given that the confusion centres on the fact that marriages celebrated in embassies situated in this country are apparently treated differently to those taking place in embassies located in any other country. Finally, the debate about whether the *renvoi* doctrine applies in the context of formal validity ought finally to be settled.[313]

[309] Recall the Law Commission's unconvincing reason for inaction – that it would be best to leave things as they are until the courts have had the chance to eradicate some of the controversy and inconsistency in the current law: see Law Com No 165, *op cit* n 14. Cf North & Fawcett's pertinent comment that '[t]he experience of the last hundred years is unlikely to convince those varied officials who have to advise on and apply marriage choice of law rules that the much needed clarification will in fact be forthcoming through judicial decisions': North & Fawcett, *op cit* n 41, p 742.

[310] J. Dewar, 'Reducing Discretion in Family Law' (1997) 11 *Australian Journal of Family Law* 309.

[311] *Supra*, n 105.

[312] Compare *Radwan v Radwan (No 2)* [1973] Fam 35 with *Bailet v Bailet* (1901) 17 TLR 317.

[313] There are finely balanced arguments both ways in this context (see Law Com Working Paper 89, *op cit* n 14, para 2), but clarification one way or the other would seem preferable to lingering uncertainty.

Turning to the need for simplification of the law, it is notable that the leading English conflicts textbooks typically deal with the topic of recognition of foreign marriages in long, sometimes very long, chapters.[314] This is some testimony to the complexity of the law founded, as it is, on a preponderance of intricate and uncertain common law rules laced intermittently with a miscellany of no less complicated statutory rules. By contrast, the statutory rules that operate in Australia have been described in detail by one leading commentator in a comparatively short article.[315]

Of course, ease of exposition for textbook writers is hardly a reason in itself for simplifying the law; especially when one recalls the usual trade-off between simple rules and the capacity for justice in hard cases.[316] Nonetheless, several substantive elements of the law call out for principled and pragmatic rationalisation. First, there seems little point in retaining much of the specious legislation and some of the common law exceptions to the general rule concerning formal validity. Many of these rules, as we noted at the time, are remarkably dated and of little to no practical contemporary significance. Secondly, it is often non-lawyers that are called upon to give everyday application to the rules concerning the recognition of foreign marriages. If these rules are to be properly applied, they must be properly understood. The pragmatic argument for simplification is thus manifest in this context, and it featured prominently in the Irish Law Reform Commission's proposal that the equivalent uncertainty and complexity in the Irish rules should be removed.[317] Finally, the case for simplification appears grounded when we bear in mind the fact that the complexity and uncertainty in the law has been around a long time and shows no sign of being resolved by the courts. It has thus been pithily observed in relation to the joint decision of Law Commissions of England and Scotland to do nothing for the present that:

[314] *Dicey & Morris*, *op cit* n 151, is sixty-four pages long; North & Fawcett, *op cit* n 41, is fifty-eight pages long; Clarkson & Hill, *op cit* n 180, is seventy pages long, McClean, *op cit* n 34, is forty-two pages long.

[315] M. Neave, 'The New Rules on Recognition of Foreign Marriages – Insomnia for Lawyers' [1990] *Australian Journal of Family Law* 190–221. See also P.E. Nygh, *Conflict of Laws in Australia* (Sydney: Butterworths, 1995) ch 24; E.I. Sykes & M.C. Pryles, *Australian Private International Law* (Sydney: Law Book Co, 1991) ch 11.

[316] But note, also, North & Fawcett's comment that '[t]he solution of complex problems does not necessarily lead to complex legislation [especially given that] [a]spects of the current law are undoubtedly undesirable': North & Fawcett, *op cit* n 41, p 742.

[317] Law Reform Commission Report No 19, *Private International Law: Aspects of Capacity to Marry and Choice of Law in Proceedings for Nullity of Marriage* (Dublin: Law Reform Commission, 1985). An English academic, noting the fact that 'the law is unacceptably uncertain and incoherent' recommended simplification not merely in the interests of the spouses affected but also in the interests of those 'officials in the great variety of government departments with whom they have to deal': Poulter, *op cit* n 9, p 61.

> [i]t is perverse then to rely, as in effect the Commissions did, on that uncertainty as a reason for doing nothing, in the hope that the courts will in due course provide the appropriate new, clear rules. The experience of the last hundred years is unlikely to convince those varied officials who have to advise on and apply marriage choice of law rules that the much needed clarification will in fact be forthcoming through judicial decisions.[318]

As regards the need for modernisation of the law, all the objections we have just considered that relate to the current set of rules' occasional tendency to display traits of cultural imperialism and a lack of adherence to the comity principle would of course need to be tackled. In addition, however, any codification of the law should also seek to deal with the twin contemporary problems posed by foreign same-sex marriages and registered partnerships.[319] Lengthy arguments were advanced earlier to the effect that, so far as possible, parties to such unions should have their status recognised by the English courts, and we need not revisit them here. It is, however, perhaps worth reiterating that a same-sex marriage between foreign domiciliaries who intend to establish their home in this country would throw the question about whether capacity ought to be judged according to the dual domicile or intended matrimonial home test into the sharpest possible relief. What would not appear appropriate, however, is the suggestion that a modified version of the intended matrimonial home test should be adopted for such unions. Yet this has been argued on the spurious basis that since '[p]rohibitions against homosexual marriages are designed to buttress the institution of heterosexual marriage . . . [rather than] protect the parties to the marriage' it follows that 'it is the country where the marriage or partnership is to based that has the most interest in the validity of such a marriage or relationship'.[320] The argument is bogus because permitting same-sex couples the right to marry in no way undermines the traditional institution of heterosexual marriage. As Norrie has remarked:

> [c]hanging the terms of entry into the state-sanctioned relationship we call marriage is not in itself an attack on marriage as previously understood, otherwise parliament has frequently attacked marriage, such as . . . every time it loosened the forbidden degrees. Did the Supreme Court of the United States of America attack marriage when it struck down various States' rules prohibiting inter-racial marriage in *Loving v Virginia* 388 US 1 (1967)? 'Traditional' marriage is, in reality, an ever-changing, ever-evolving beast.[321]

[318] North & Fawcett, *op cit* n 41, p 742.

[319] Especially those between partners of the opposite sex.

[320] See Clarkson & Hill, *op cit* n 179, p 354.

[321] Norrie, *op cit* n 237, at 156. For further counter-argument to the allegation that allowing same-sex couples the right to marry undermines traditional, heterosexual marriage, see Murphy, *op cit* n 237, at 186–187.

On the other hand, there is no reason in principle why special provisions could not be adopted to meet the problems posed by the three kinds of union in respect of which there is currently no juridical equivalent in this country: same-sex marriages, actually polygamous marriages and registered civil partnerships. Any such special provisions could specify authoritatively the purposes for which each kind of union may be afforded recognition in this country and the circumstances in which this may be done (always assuming that the arguments advanced earlier about what *ought to be done* in the light of this country's human rights commitments are accepted by the legislature).

A final point worth making in this context is that it is one thing to decide on the appropriate content of legislation; it is quite another to settle upon the appropriate form of that legislation. In fact, there is an important question to be addressed here about whether any codifying legislation should seek to put in place a model of regulation that is essentially rigidly rule-based, or whether it ought to have inbuilt flexibility that affords the courts structured discretions on how to tackle recognition cases. Both models exist within modern English family law. But while legislative discretions can give rise to injustices attributable to their vastly differential deployment in the hands of different judges, properly structured discretions seem overwhelmingly to be preferable to a regime that is too tightly rule-bound. The history of the child support legislation amply demonstrates how a reduction in discretion in family law legislation – something that is now rather common[322] – can fail to fulfil the objective it was designed to achieve.[323]

In its first incarnation, and largely as a response to the very different amounts that the courts were ordering non-residential divorcing parents to pay by way of child maintenance,[324] the Child Support Act 1991 established a rule-bound agency to apply a strict formula in computing amounts of child support. It soon became apparent, however, that injustices were being done in that, for example, some absent parents were left unable to afford to see their children because of the costs of travel involved.[325] To meet such cases, the 1995 Act of the same name introduced an element of discretion to allow exceptional cases to be dealt with according to a system of 'variations'

[322] See Dewar, *op cit* n 310. Note that the concern that underlies this objective is not always better justice. As Dewar observes *loc cit*, at 310, this reduction in discretion is sometimes simply driven by 'the concern of government to reduce the costs associated with family breakdown'.

[323] Noting the inability of rigid, rule-based legislation to cope with the kinds of rights-based claims that have come to the fore in family law litigation, see J. Dewar, 'The Normal Chaos of Family Law' (1998) 61 *Modern Law Review* 647.

[324] In one case documented in *Children Come First: The Government's Proposals on the Maintenance of Children*, Cm 1264 (1990), there is an account of two fathers both with a net income of £150 per week; yet whereas one was paying £5 per week, the other was paying £50.

[325] See, eg, R. Collier, 'The Campaign Against the CSA' [1994] *Family Law* 384.

from the normal computation.[326] These variations were not made available according to any kind of free-and-easy discretion on the part of the Agency, however. Instead, they were permitted only upon meeting the desiderata set out in the form of one or more specified factors.[327]

It is this kind of factor-based discretion that appears to work best in achieving the greatest degree of justice within a body of law that applies to families varying greatly in their constitution and needs. Cass Sunstein has suggested that where rules are to be operated by able officials, there is more scope for flexibility than where legislation simply seeks to regulate the conduct of individual members of the public. 'Legislatures', he asserts, 'should lay down rigid rules for the public – "conduct rules" . . . [But] [o]fficials might follow more flexible "decision rules"'.[328] Subsequently, he has argued more broadly that factor-based rather than rigid rule-based decision-making is essential in societies that are characterised by diversity and lack of consensus.[329]

The problems with the rules governing domicile

The final insight to be gleaned from this chapter relates to the current law on domicile. As we noted earlier, the balance of the argument concerning the appropriate test for the choice of law in matters of essential validity lay in favour of the dual domicile test rather than the rival intended matrimonial home test. Nonetheless, in the course of that discussion, we also noted that the dual domicile test is far from perfect and that chief among its inadequacies was the fact that it is parasitic upon a deficient set of rules governing domicile. We must now elaborate upon the two main shortcomings in this set of rules on domicile, for these were not explained earlier.

First of all, we may usefully recall Hartley's objection that, 'the English law of domicile is distorted in certain respects and does not always indicate the country to which the parties really "belong"'.[330] This observation – grounded as it is in a wealth of authority[331] – obviously has profound potential consequences for a choice of law rule based upon the parties' ante-nuptial domicile. We noted in passing the case of *Bowie*[332] in which a man was held

[326] 'Departures', as they were originally known, were re-named 'variations' by the Child Support, Pensions and Social Security Act 2000.

[327] See the Child Support Act 1991, s 28E(2); Sched 4B, para 3.

[328] C. Sunstein, 'Problems with Rules' (1995) 83 *California Law Review* 953. See also C. Schneider, 'Discretion and Rules: A Lawyer's View' in K. Hawkins (ed), *The Uses of Discretion* (Oxford: Oxford University Press, 1995).

[329] C. Sunstein, *Legal Reasoning and Political Conflict* (New York: Oxford University Press, 1996) ch 6.

[330] Hartley, *op cit* n 35, at 576.

[331] See North & Fawcett, *op cit* n 41, pp 140–143.

[332] *Bowie (or Ramsay) v Liverpool Royal Infirmary* [1930] AC 588.

to have retained his Scottish domicile although he had a long since ceased to have any real connection with that country. An even more striking example, however, is evident in the case of *IRC v Bullock*.[333] For there, a man who had lived in England for over forty years and held only a contingent intention to return to Nova Scotia, was nonetheless held to have retained his domicile there.[334] One pressing sort of problem to which this aspect of the domicile rules may give rise has been neatly identified by Sebastian Poulter:

> One can well envisage two Pakistani neighbours or even brothers with only marginally differing intentions as to the permanence of their future here who find as a result that they have entirely different capacities *vis-à-vis* the contracting of a polygamous marriage. If the validity of a marriage is to turn on such an elusive concept as intention in this type of situation, it can surely be argued that the law is unacceptably uncertain and incoherent.[335]

Conversely, a domicile of choice can be extremely easy to obtain where the settled intention to move permanently to a new country is unequivocal. Thus, in *Hodgson v Beauchesne*[336] it was recognised that a man who emigrates can obtain a new domicile in the country to which he moves upon his very arrival there. Winding up all his affairs in his country of origin signalled an unequivocal intention to become permanently resident elsewhere, and the bi-partite test for the acquisition of a domicile of choice – intention *plus* residence – was satisfied the moment his residence in Australia began. The problem here is that the law does not question the reason for the intention; it is merely concerned that there should be such intention. Thus, one might legitimately obtain a new domicile simply to overcome an incapacity imposed by one's original personal law. One might, in other words, take advantage of the rule in order to subvert the very idea propping up the dual domicile test in the first place: namely, that matters of marital capacity should be referred to the law of the party's ante-nuptial domicile.

The second objection to the current law on domicile centres on the rules governing the revival of a domicile of origin. Under English law, domicile of origin is a most tenacious creature. Thus, although a domicile of choice elsewhere is comparatively easy to obtain, any indecision about where to

[333] [1976] 3 All ER 353. See also *Jopp v Wood* (1865) 4 De GJ & Sm 616 (twenty-five years spent in India were not enough because of a lingering – albeit remote – ambition to one day return to Scotland) and *A-G v Yule* (1931) 145 LT 9.

[334] The man intended to return to Nova Scotia if his wife should predecease him and this was sufficient to invoke the presumption against the formation of the necessary fixed intention to remain permanently in England. On the certainty with which the requisite intention must be formed, see *Winans v A-G* [1904] AC 287 and *Bowie (or Ramsay) v Liverpool Royal Infirmary* [1930] AC 588.

[335] Poulter, *op cit* n 9, p 61.

[336] (1858) 12 Moo PCC 285.

live next will cause the domicile of origin to revive.[337] Imagine that a man, A, leaves this country in order to escape one or other of the English marriage impediments that would otherwise deny him the capacity to marry woman B. Suppose also that A then acquires a domicile of choice in country Y (which would permit such a marriage) with every intention of marrying B, and settling down there. Imagine finally that before A and B marry, they leave Y and move to Z (which would also permit their marriage), but with no fixed intention of staying in Z. Should A and B ever return to this country, their marriage would be deemed invalid because A's domicile of origin will have revived when he left Y without the settled intention to acquire a new domicile of choice in Z. The offence in this case, of course, is that, without returning to England before marrying B, and quite contrary to A's reasonable expectations, England would extraterritorially re-impose a domicile of origin.[338]

Even if *all* the points of criticism made here were to be taken on board by the legislature, it is doubtful whether the law would operate perfectly. Legislation seldom acts as a panacea. Accordingly, whether there is legislative reform or not, it would be sensible if the courts were to retain their current residual discretion to veto foreign marriages that offend against English public policy. As we shall see in several subsequent chapters, legislation and international Conventions often provide for public policy vetoes of this kind. As things stand, however, it is the common law that provides this facility in the context of foreign marriages. We consider it in detail in chapter 4.

[337] *Udny v Udny* (1869) LR 1 Sc & Div 441. The doctrine of revival has been rejected in Australia (Domicile Acts 1982, s 7) and New Zealand (Domicile Act 1976, s 11). Furthermore, it was never accepted in the United States: *Re Jones' Estate* (1921) 192 Iowa 78.

[338] To no ultimate avail, the Law Commission suggested the abolition of this rule for just this reason in 1985: see Law Com No 168, *Private International Law: The Law of Domicile* (London: HMSO, 1987) para 5.

4

The discretionary refusal to recognise foreign marriages

Even if a foreign marriage satisfies the twin tests for formal and essential validity, the English court retains a residual discretion to refuse to recognise the union. It has generally been understood that this discretionary veto is to be wielded in accordance with the dictates of 'public policy'. As long ago as 1945, Lord Greene MR stated that such matters were to be resolved 'with due regard to common sense and *some attention to reasonable policy*'.[1] Almost forty years later, and speaking in the House of Lords, Lord Simon was of similar mind. Yet he was considerably more emphatic: he said, [t]here is abundant authority that an English court will decline to recognise or apply what would otherwise be the appropriate foreign rule of law when to do so would be against English public policy.[2]

Notwithstanding his Lordship's allusion to a wealth of authority supporting the existence of this discretionary veto, it is noteworthy that it has attracted only very limited academic discussion.[3] This chapter therefore begins by unearthing the kinds of particular concern that are thought to ground the use of this veto – and it will be noted that these vary from one type of

[1] [1946] P 122, at 129 (emphasis added). Approved and re-stated in *Alhaji Mohamed v Knott* [1969] 1 QB 1, at 13 *per* Lord Parker CJ.

[2] *Vervaeke v Smith* [1983] 1 AC 145, at 164. For other occasions on which members of the judiciary have acknowledged the role of 'public policy' in this context, see *Russ v Russ* [1964] P 315, at 327–328 *per* Willmer LJ and *Cheni v Cheni* [1965] P 65, at 97 *per* Simon P.

[3] It seems to have been accepted but not rigorously examined by a number of writers. See, eg, A.J.E. Jaffey, 'The Essential Validity of Marriage in the English Conflict of Laws' (1978) 41 *Modern Law Review* 38, 50; S. Poulter, *English Law and Ethnic Minority Customs* (London: Butterworths, 1986) pp 13–14; C.M.V. Clarkson & J. Hill, *Jaffey on the Conflict of Laws* (London: Butterworths, 2002) pp 362–364; J. O'Brien, *Smith's Conflict of Laws* (London: Cavendish, 1999) p 462; *Dicey & Morris* (London: Sweet & Maxwell, 2000) p 688.

foreign marriage to another. The next part of this chapter will take a critical view of the leading authorities, suggesting that it is inadequate for the courts and for academic commentators to state laxly that this discretion is grounded in concerns of 'public policy' as if these concerns were somehow obvious.[4] It will be suggested that incompletely articulated reasons for their decisions lay the courts open to accusations of both cultural imperialism and irrational adjudication.

Particular domestic policy concerns

In chapter 3, we saw that English law contains a number of impediments to marriage. While these impediments circumscribe the marital capacities of English domiciliaries, they do not affect the capacity of foreign domiciliaries who marry abroad.[5] Accordingly, unless the relevant foreign legal system imposes the same impediments to marriage, it is in theory possible for a foreign domiciliary to contract a marriage that would be prohibited under English law and then, later, move to this country where the union would be recognised. However, the matter is more complex than this; for underlying each of the domestic impediments is a particular policy concern, or set of such concerns. It is these *particular* policies – which differ from case to case – that lie at the heart of the courts' discretionary power to veto specific kinds of 'offensive' foreign marriage. As Cumming-Bruce J explained in *Radwan v Radwan (No 2)*:[6]

> [I]t is an over-simplification of the common law to assume that the same test . . . applies to every kind of incapacity – non-age, affinity, prohibition of monogamous contract by virtue of an existing spouse, and capacity for polygamy. Different public and social factors are relevant to each of these.

We therefore turn next to consider the actual policy factors that underpin each of the relevant incapacities – that is, most of the incapacities set out in s 11 of the Matrimonial Causes Act 1973[7] – for these render a marriage void

[4] See, eg, Poulter, *op cit* n 3, ch 3 and Jaffey, *op cit* n 3, at 49–50.

[5] In chapter 3 we noted that, anomalously, foreign domiciliaries who marry in this country might still need to satisfy the capacity requirements imposed by English law. For a more detailed account of this phenomenon, see C. Clarkson, 'Marriage in England: Favouring the *Lex Fori*' [1990] *Legal Studies* 80.

[6] [1972] 3 All ER 1026, at 1037.

[7] We need not consider same-sex marriages prohibited under s 11(d), for these were dealt with exhaustively in ch 3 and overwhelmingly thought to be suitable for recognition. Nor need we consider non-compliance with certain formalities set out in s 11(a)(iii) of the 1973 Act, for these requirements have no application in respect of marriages contracted abroad.

ab initio[8]. We also consider briefly, because of the particular problems they may pose in this context, the policy factors associated with proxy marriages.[9]

Prohibited degrees

The impediments to marriage constituted by the prohibited degrees of consanguinity and affinity vary considerably from one country to the next. They are, therefore, particularly apt to cause a conflict of laws that cannot be resolved simply by recourse to the requirements of formal and essential validity. Indeed, the crux of the conflict is based on different notions of what amounts to essential validity. In short, foreign marriages that do not meet the standards of the English prohibited degrees, are prime candidates for the invocation of the discretionary veto.

Historically, Canon law justified the prohibited degrees by reference to Biblical authority.[10] But the modern reasons behind these impediments are located in three (not uncontroversial) kinds of concern:[11] namely, eugenic, social and moral considerations. As regards the eugenic concerns, these are reflected in the prohibited degrees of consanguinity, and they serve to avoid the dangers associated with inbreeding. Yet while it is true that there *can* be certain scientific risks for the children born within such marriages,[12] it is also true that genetic screening and counselling is nowadays so easily available that any such risks can be minimised if not eliminated.

[8] The other grounds upon which a nullity petition may be based are contained in s 12 of the Matrimonial Causes Act 1973 and render a domestic marriage valid yet voidable. Given the *prima facie* validity of such marriages, it is beyond serious suggestion that they would ground the non-recognition of a foreign marriage.

[9] That is, a marriage at which one or both parties was not present. See, eg, *McCabe v McCabe* [1994] 1 FLR 410 (discussed at p 44, above).

[10] *Leviticus*, 18. Christian doctrine also treated a man and his wife as 'one flesh' thus grounding the prohibitions based on relationships of affinity: a marriage between a man and his sister-in-law, for example, would be viewed as a marriage between brother and sister. Biblical reasons cannot now be justified in such a multi-racial, pluralist society: see D. Bradley, 'Comparative Law, Family Law and Common Law' (2003) 23 *Oxford Journal of Legal Studies* 127, at 129–132.

[11] By a combination of two Articles of the European Convention on Human Rights – Art 12 (the right to marry and found a family) and Art 14 (the right to enjoy the other Convention rights free from discrimination based on, among other things, religion) – it can at least be argued that certain of the English prohibited degrees are incompatible with the Convention. For instance, the prohibition on marrying one's uncle or aunt (Marriage Acts 1949, Sched 1, Part I) is not present in Jewish Law, which permits such unions (*Deuteronomy* 25: 5–6).

[12] See the Report of the Kilbrandon Committee, *The Marriage Laws of Scotland* Cmnd 4011 (1969); V. Bailey & S. McCabe, 'Reforming the Law of Incest' [1979] *Criminal Law Review* 749, 757–758.

By contrast, the moral concern that is sometimes advanced to justify the prohibited degrees both of consanguinity[13] and affinity is rooted in the notion that it is contrary to the natural order of things for such marriages (and sexual intercourse within them) to take place. This objection is so widespread that most societies proscribe marriages between blood relatives while some also prohibit marriages between persons *closely related* through marriage. The potential for a conflict of laws arises out of the fact that not all States agree on how close a blood or marital relationship must be before one considers it immoral for the persons concerned to marry one another. Thus, while English law prohibits marriages between relatives of the half-blood,[14] other systems can be more permissive.[15] Equally, although there has been a marked reduction in the range of the prohibited degrees of affinity over the last century or so,[16] it is still the case that this country continues to apply a sizeable number, while Australia, for example, has abandoned such prohibitions altogether.[17]

Finally, as regards the social reasons for imposing prohibited degrees of affinity – and it is only here that they apply – there appear to be two main concerns. The first is that, if men were generally permitted to marry their step-daughters, this might facilitate (or at least not strongly enough discourage) adult abuse of relatively young girls. In addition, it might also be thought objectionable if step-parents were permitted to marry their step-children, especially where there is a history of the latter having been treated as children of the family. Such quasi-incestuous marriages are perceived as having the capacity to destabilise 'normal' family life.

Given that most of the English prohibited degrees are to some extent controversial, and given also that other societies seem able to function satisfactorily even though they do not impose the same impediments, it might be thought that the English courts would be entitled to recognise a *foreign* marriage of this kind even though it fell within the English prohibited degrees.

[13] To an extent, these are reflected in the prohibitions on sexual intercourse between certain family members contained in the Sexual Offences Act 1956, ss 10, 11. But notably, the 1956 Act proscribes intercourse between fewer relationships than are prohibited from marrying under the Marriage Act 1949.

[14] The terms 'brother' and 'sister' are defined in s 78 of the Marriage Act 1949 to include brothers and sisters of the half-blood.

[15] Eg, Swedish law permits marriages between brothers and sisters of the half-blood in certain circumstances with the Dispensation the Monarch in Council: see I.F.G. Baxter, 'Recent Developments in Scandinavian Family Law' (1976) 26 *International and Comparative Law Quarterly* 150.

[16] See, eg, the Marriage (Enabling) Act 1960 and the Marriage (Prohibited Degrees of Relationship) Act 1986. For further examples, and for details of the remaining prohibitions, see S.M. Cretney, J.M. Masson & R. Bailey-Harris, *Principles of Family Law* (London: Sweet & Maxwell, 2002) pp 43–44.

[17] See H.A. Finlay, 'Farewell to Affinity and the Calculus of Kinship' [1976] *University of Tasmania Law Review* 16.

There is certainly some support for this idea in the case law, for in *Cheni v Cheni* the English court recognised a marriage contracted in Egypt between an uncle and niece who were both of Egyptian domicile. In the course of reaching his decision, Simon P noted that, 'it would be altogether too queasy a judicial conscience which would recoil from a marriage acceptable to many peoples of deep religious convictions, lofty ethical standards and high civilisation'.[18]

On the other hand, we must be cautious not to read too much into this *dictum*. In the course of his speech, the then President acknowledged that he was influenced in reaching his decision by the fact that the uncle–niece relationship does not fall within the criminal law of incest.[19] Arguably, then, he may have been minded to veto a marriage had it fallen on the wrong side of the incest definition.[20] An example would be that of a marriage between a half-brother and half-sister.[21] It is difficult to speculate what a modern-day court would do, although for consistency's sake, it would make sense to veto marital relationships – presumably sexual in nature – where they would transgress the criminal law.

Bigamy and polygamy

In respect of the policy concerns that underpin the domestic law's prohibition of bigamous and polygamous marriages,[22] it might again be noted that, historically, opposition to such unions stemmed from Christian doctrine. Of course, such an objection could not be invoked in today's more secular and pluralist society (even if it were uncontroversial, which it is not[23]). Instead,

[18] [1965] P 65. Note in similar vein the decision in *Husey-Hunt v Bozzelli* [1902] 1 Ch 751 in which a marriage contracted in Italy was recognised even though it fell within what were at the time in England the prohibited degrees of affinity.

[19] *Ibid*, at 97.

[20] For details, see the Sexual Offences Act 1956, ss 10(2) and 11(2).

[21] In the case of a half-brother–half-sister marriage, eugenic concerns would be difficult to invoke since the number of shared genes would be exactly the same as in the case of an uncle–niece marriage. Any such disapproval would have to be on the moral grounds reflected in the criminal law. But why are such marriages so immoral when those between adoptive siblings are permitted? By contrast, the courts might also refuse to recognise a step-parent–step-child marriage even though this relationship would fall outside the present law on incest (see Sexual Offences Act 1956, ss 10, 11). In this case, any such denial would have to be based on the risks of sexual exploitation mentioned above.

[22] Matrimonial Causes Act 1973, s 11(b), (d).

[23] Famously, the Mormons used to permit polygamy believing there to be no prohibition on polygamy to be found in the New Testament. This doubt has since been reiterated by a number of more recent theologians. See, eg, J. Cairncross, *After Polygamy Was Made a Sin: The Social History of Christian Polygamy* (London: Routledge, 1974); E. Hillman, *Polygamy Reconsidered: African Plural Marriage and the Christian Churches* (New York: Orbis, 1975); A. Hastings, *Christian Marriage in Africa* (London: SPCK, 1973).

several other considerations are now used to justify the prohibition on having a plurality of spouses.

For a start, there are social concerns about individuals having one more than one husband or wife. Beyond the familiar objections associated with the presumptive immigration rights of foreign spouses,[24] these are commonly expressed in terms of the tendency of polygamous marriages to be both exploitative and abusive of women. Yet there is an absence of empirical data to vindicate these claims.[25] More plausibly (but no more compellingly) there are also economic considerations that are sometimes thought to militate against recognising polygamous marriages. These, as Nicholas Bala has pointed out, centre on the 'concerns about costs to employers and others if, for example, a man can claim that he has two or more wives, each of whom is entitled to 'spousal' benefits'.[26] While there is an element of truth in this argument, it is also true that polygamy would not be commonplace in this country even if it were to be permitted. That being the case, the costs involved would be marginal. Furthermore, any such additional costs to employers would more than likely be passed on to ultimate consumers of their goods and services. But in any event, there is a point of principle here: whether an employer's financial welfare should be seen as more worthy of the law's support than an individual's marriage rights.

Finally, there is the argument that polygamy should not be permitted for the simple reason that it runs counter to the tradition and culture, not just in England but across Europe, of tolerating only monogamous marriages.[27] Of course, the immediate response here is that the tradition in question hails from an age in which the multi-cultural European societies of today could scarcely have been envisaged, making this an outmoded yardstick by which to gauge the acceptability of polygamy. Furthermore, any opposition to what are generally Asian and African customs on the basis of an overtly Euro-centric perspective is ineluctably xenophobic, and thus untenable.[28]

[24] See P.A. Shah, 'Attitudes to Polygamy in English Law' (2003) 52 *International and Comparative Law Quarterly* 369, 388–396.

[25] See, eg, the various anecdotal newspaper accounts cited in N. Bala, 'Controversy over Couples in Canada: The Evolution of Marriage and other Adult Interdependent Relationships' (2004) 29 *Queen's Law Journal* 41, 70. See also Poulter's observation that '[there] is a belief (almost certainly erroneous) that it is an inevitable consequence of polygamy that wives will be lowly rated and ill-treated': Poulter, *op cit* n 3, p 46.

[26] Bala, *op cit* n 25, at 72.

[27] Monogamy apparently pre-dates Christianity in Europe: see O.M. Stone, '*Sowa v. Sowa:* Maintenance of Family Dependants' (1961) 24 *Modern Law Review* 501.

[28] On the other hand, the kinds of reasons used to justify polygamy in parts of the developing world – such as the security guarantees that it can provide for women who would otherwise have no husband – cannot legitimately be raised in this country. That being the case, it follows that beyond accommodating the desires of a very small minority of citizens, there are no especially strong reasons for legalising polygamy at a domestic level.

As we have seen, none of the stated objections to non-monogamous marriages are especially strong. As such, when it comes to the domestic courts being asked to recognise foreign polygamous marriages, it is unsurprising to find that there has been a progressive willingness to recognise such unions where they satisfy the twin tests of formal and essential validity.[29] Indeed, as we saw in chapter 3, the significance attached to potentially polygamous marriages has all but been confined to the history books, while actually polygamous marriages now receive the recognition of the courts for practically all purposes. In short the social and economic reasons that *perhaps* justify the continuance of a domestic prohibition against such unions can hardly be thought of as sufficiently cogent or weighty to justify the courts in refusing recognition on the grounds of public policy as happened in *Hyde v Hyde* over a century ago. There, it will be recalled, Lord Penzance declared (with an unintended ironic sting in the tail):

> It may well be doubted whether it would become the tribunals of this country to enforce the duties (even if we knew them) which belong to a system so utterly at variance with the Christian conception of marriage, and so revolting to the ideas we entertain of the social position to be accorded to the weaker sex.[30]

Child marriages

Foreign marriages involving children – particularly young girls – are common in a number of African, Asian and Latin American Societies. By contrast, English domestic law imposes an absolute minimum age for marriage of sixteen years.[31] In relation to foreign domiciliaries who are permitted to contract such marriages abroad, however, it is not entirely clear when the English courts will afford such unions recognition. Such guidance as exists goes no further than to indicate that non-age *may occasionally* be a suitable basis on which the courts may exercise their discretionary veto.[32] What, then, are the underlying considerations that affect this discretion?

To begin with, there is a concern to protect vulnerable minors from the instability of premature marriages. As Ruth Deech has argued in connection with leading case of *Alhaji Mohamed v Knott*[33] (which involved the recognition of a marriage involving a thirteen-year-old girl):

[29] See S. Poulter, '*Hyde v Hyde* – A Reappraisal' (1976) 25 *International and Comparative Law Quarterly* 475.

[30] (1866) LR 1 P & D 130.

[31] The Marriage Act 1949, s 2 provides that '[a] marriage solemnised between persons either of whom is under the age of sixteen shall be void'.

[32] *Alhaji Mohamed v Knott* [1969] 1 QB 1. Although the marriage was recognised in this case, it is clear from Parker CJ's judgment that the court reserved the right in other cases to refuse recognition.

[33] [1969] 1 QB 1.

> If the statistics on teenage brides are anything to go by, the marriage seemed destined to break down and one can easily imagine the wife as a future deserted, uneducated mother incapable of earning a living or bringing up her children.[34]

Alarming though this image may be, it is by no means clear that it is a realistic one. Stripping away the rhetoric, we might reasonably question whether the statistics upon which Deech relies have any meaningful bearing on the situation. This is because the statistical evidence about teenage brides *in this country* is an unsuitable basis on which to draw conclusions about the stability of child marriages contracted in Nigeria where vastly different traditions and culture no doubt have a significant bearing. In short, what Deech would require in order properly to substantiate her claim would be statistics pertaining the marital failure rate of teenage brides from Nigeria. Recognising the importance of the cultural context, Parker CJ noted that, '[i]t is certainly natural for a girl to marry at that age [in Nigeria]. They develop sooner and there is certainly nothing abhorrent in their way of life for a girl of 13 to marry a man of 25'.[35]

A second concern in this context centres on the question of whether children are able to give a genuine, free and informed consent to marriage. In western societies, the institution of marriage centres on notions of love, compatibility and individual choice. Accordingly, the multilateral Convention on Consent to Marriage 1964 (overwhelmingly ratified by Western states) provides that:

> No marriage shall be legally entered into without the full and free consent of both parties, such consent to be expressed by them in person after due publicity and in the presence of the authority competent to solemnise the marriage and of witnesses.[36]

Underpinning this provision is a clear, deep-seated respect both for human individuality and the highly cherished value of autonomous choice. By contrast, according to some African and Asian traditions and religions, arranged marriages for children are regarded as perfectly acceptable. This is often because they are sanctioned and affirmed by patriarchal doctrines.[37] Given the profundity of these cultural justifications, it would be a brave English court that ignored them.[38]

[34] R. Deech, 'Immigrants and Family Law' (1973) *New Law Journal* 110, 111.

[35] [1969] 1 QB 1, at 15.

[36] Art 1(1). Recall also the presumption of adulthood built into Art 12 of the European Convention on Human Rights and Fundamental Freedoms which confers an equal right to 'marry and found a family' upon all '*men and women of marriageable age*' (emphasis added).

[37] See, eg, S. Shan, *In My Own Name* (London: The Women's Press Ltd, 1985) p 24; C. Ballard, 'Arranged Marriages in the British Context' [1978] *New Community* 181.

[38] See further, J. Murphy, 'Rationality and Cultural Pluralism in the Non-Recognition of Foreign Marriages' (2000) 49 *International and Comparative Law Quarterly* 643.

A third objection to child marriage focuses on the psychological and moral dangers for developmentally young children[39] that are associated with their engaging in sexual relationships at too early an age.[40] These dangers are recognised by the criminal law, for section 6(1) of the Sexual Offences Act 1956 makes it an offence 'for a man to have unlawful sexual intercourse with a girl . . . under the age of sixteen'. But notwithstanding this provision Parker CJ's judgment in *Knott's* case recognised the importance of the cultural context:

> Granted that this man may be said to be a bad lot, that he has done things in the past which perhaps nobody would approve of, it does not follow from that that this girl, happily married to this man, is under any moral danger by associating and living with him . . . [I]t could only be said that she was in moral danger if one was considering somebody brought up and living in our way of life, and to hold that she is in moral danger in the circumstances of this case can only be arrived at, as it seems to me, by ignoring the way of life in which she was brought up.[41]

While the recognition of the cultural context is important, it must not, as we shall see later, become the sole determinant of such cases.[42] Thus, while it is true that his Lordship did not ignore the Sexual Offences Act in reaching his decision, it is also true that his explanation of why it did not apply is a long way short of convincing. To his mind, the Act did not apply since the offence in section 6(1) hinged upon 'unlawful sexual intercourse', which could not have been an apt description of the sexual intercourse between a man and his wife. But his reasoning seems inadequate in two key respects. First, he should have recognised the circularity of the wording of the subsection

[39] There is no point in fixing an age for child marriages where the avowed reason for so doing is to protect the vulnerabilities of the child that stem from her immaturity. The better approach is to set a limit based upon the child's stage of development. It is implicit from his judgment in *Alhaji Mohamed v Knott* [1969] 1 QB 1 that Parker CJ (at 15–16) was sympathetic to this approach. Cf I.G.F. Karsten, 'Child Marriages' (1969) 32 *Modern Law Review* 212, esp at 215–216 (where a minimum age approach is preferred).

[40] It is just such dangers that prompted Mrs Victoria Gillick into litigation in the landmark case of *Gillick v West Norfolk and Wisbech AHA* [1986] AC 112.

[41] [1969] 1 QB 1, at 16.

[42] The problem with this excerpt from his Lordship's speech is that it is couched in terms of cultural relativism – an ostensibly appealing, but ultimately flawed approach. Whether an English judge with no expertise in the cultural values in question is able properly to evaluate their significance is highly questionable. Furthermore, as will be explained more fully below, to attribute worth *no matter what* to foreign cultural practices is to run the risk of abandoning one's own moral commitments. On cultural relativism more generally, see M. Herskovits, *Cultural Relativism: Perspectives on Cultural Pluralism* (New York: Random House, 1972); E. Hatch, *Culture and Morality: The Relativity of Values in Anthropology* (New York: Columbia University Press, 1983).

according to which the sexual intercourse in question is an offence only if it is 'unlawful'. If it were unlawful to start with, there would be no need of the subsection. Secondly, his own reasoning was circular in that he effectively suggested that there was no offence under the Act because there was a valid marriage, and that there was a valid marriage because there was no offence (providing a basis on which to deny recognition).

A final objection to non-age marriages centres on the fact that, nearly always, it is a child bride that is involved.[43] As such, a legitimate concern arises as to the exploitation or oppression of women. Indeed, with this very danger in mind, the UN Convention on the Elimination of All Forms of Discrimination against Women 1979 provides that, '[t]he betrothal and marriage of a child shall have no legal effect'.[44] And although the Convention has not been ratified by this country, the sentiment that it embodies is one with which the English courts would no doubt be in agreement. It is therefore submitted that it would be quite proper for them to take account of the fact that any given foreign marriage was contracted in a country where the number of child brides was not even remotely matched by the number of child grooms.

In sum, none of the above considerations comprise absolute objections to child marriage: such marriages may be short-lived (but we have insufficient evidence to be certain); such marriages may involve risks to children, especially girls (but they may also involve benefits in the form of spousal maintenance and inheritance); such marriages may seem immoral (but the time at which this is judged – for example ten years after celebration – will be a material consideration). Nonetheless, they from time to time form suitable bases on which the courts may wield their residual discretion to refuse recognition to such marriages. Everything depends on the particular circumstances of the case. Thus, notwithstanding the decision in *Knott's* case, it is hard to imagine that an English court would recognise a marriage involving a pre-pubescent girl who, on any view, was unable to give a valid consent.[45]

Proxy marriages

Proxy marriages raise two particular types on concern. First, there is the idea that they lack proper formality and solemnity given that, by definition,

[43] This is true of South American, African and Asian societies where child marriages are prevalent: see Poulter, *op cit* n 3, pp 16–17.

[44] Art 16(2). Regrettably, the Convention does not specify any definition of child, nor does it recommend a particular minimum age for marriage. Partly for this reason, it has not been ratified by the United Kingdom.

[45] For the view that '[p]hysical and psychological considerations dictate that [the line] should not be much below the age of puberty', see Karsten, *op cit* n 39, at 215–216.

one or both parties was absent from the actual wedding ceremony, and may even have been residing in another country at the time.[46] Secondly, such unions could in theory be used as a surreptitious means by which an English domiciliary could create immigration rights in favour of someone domiciled outside this country. The leading case is *Apt v Apt*[47] in which a woman who was resident and domiciled in England married by proxy a man resident and domiciled in Argentina. At first instance, Lord Merriman P specifically adverted to the danger that such 'prostitute marriages' might be employed as a means of circumventing immigration rules.[48]

The first objection constitutes a very weak basis on which to attempt to ground the use of the courts' discretionary veto. It relates entirely to a matter of form and, as we saw in chapter 3, there is a very strong body of case law supporting the eminently sensible rule that matters of form are to be determined by the law of the place of celebration. Indeed, in *Apt v Apt*, the President conceded as much. Feeling that it would be inappropriate for a member of the judiciary to disturb such an entrenched rule, he deflected the matter in the direction of the legislature, noting that, '[t]here is nothing whatever to prevent Parliament from enacting in relation to domiciled British subjects generally that proxy marriages shall not be recognised in this country wherever celebrated'.[49] The second objection is rather stronger, however, for a marriage celebrated purely to circumvent immigration restrictions might very well be questioned as a legitimate form of marriage. We explore this matter in greater depth below.

Critique of the discretionary veto as commonly presented

Thus far we have identified a number of particular policy considerations that arise in connection with each of the kinds of marriage discussed in the preceding section. Having unearthed these specific concerns, it becomes clear that it is wholly unsatisfactory merely to say of the courts' public policy based veto that, '[t]he premise [for its invocation] should be that . . . there is a *good reason* for its application'.[50] This statement merely recasts one

[46] Under the Marriage Act 1949, s 44(3), it is implicitly required that the parties be present, for this subsection requires that they make certain declarations at the ceremony. Cf *McCabe v McCabe* [1994] 1 FLR 410 where a man domiciled in Eire married a woman domiciled in Ghana although, at the time of the marriage, both parties (who were resident in London) never in fact left London. The case is discussed at length in J. Murphy, 'The Recognition of Overseas Marriages and Divorces: Some Opportunities Missed?' (1995) 46 *Northern Ireland Legal Quarterly* 35.

[47] [1948] P 83.

[48] [1947] P 127, at 141.

[49] *Ibid*, at 139.

[50] Jaffey, *op cit* n 3, at 38 (emphasis added).

nebulous term, 'public policy', as another, 'a good reason'. And Lord Simon's famous enjoinder to use 'common sense, good manners and a reasonable degree of tolerance' in the use of this discretion is scarcely any clearer.[51] Indeed, it is susceptible to the familiar criticism that the use of such opaque terms as 'common sense', 'good manners' and 'a reasonable degree of tolerance' deny the law the clarity, consistency and objectivity that is often thought necessary to constrain and legitimate the adjudicative function.[52] But even beyond the problem of the way in which such obscure terms are perceived by objective onlookers, two further objections of a fundamental nature can be raised against the invocation of 'public policy', without further explanation, as the basis for a decision to refuse recognition to an 'offensive' foreign marriage. First, blanket use of the term 'public policy' can easily be seen in terms of judicial cultural imperialism rather than adherence to some form of universal norm or social value.[53] Secondly, use of such an unclear phrase also tends to conceal the real issues at stake – not just from the litigants, but also from adjudicators. It can thus contribute to the danger of irrational decision-making. Each of these objections requires some elaboration.

Public policy as cultural imperialism

The notion that 'public policy' can adequately resolve questions concerning the validity of foreign marriages arguably carries with it the implicit suggestion that there is some obvious and universal (yet unstated) conception of what 'public policy' entails, and that it represents some sort of accepted, dominant ideology. The danger here, of course, is that this putative universal ideology may in fact be an illusion. As Gutmann has cautioned in relation to denying minority groups the right to contract polygamous marriages, '[e]ven when the dominant understanding is widely shared, it may still [only] be the standard of the most powerful ("dominant") groups in society'. And furthermore, as she continues, 'the understandings of a dominant group or groups not only prevail but also are widely considered to be just because those understandings [misleadingly] appear to be *the* social understandings of that culture'.[54] Yet in modern, pluralist Britain – especially when confronted with a question that tests the very nature and extent of that pluralism – the assumption that there exists any such unitary notion of what constitutes

[51] *Cheni v Cheni* [1965] P 65, at 99.

[52] See L. Fuller, 'The Forms and Limits of Adjudication' (1978) 92 *Harvard Law Review* 353, 369.

[53] The recognition of foreign marriages is an arena particularly susceptible to accusations of cultural imperialism because of the diverse religious and cultural traditions discernible in modern society: see A. Gutmann, 'The Challenge of Multiculturalism in Political Ethics' [1993] *Philosophy and Public Affairs* 171.

[54] Gutmann, *op cit* n 53, at 176.

sound public policy is without foundation. Only to some of the indigenous population would, say, the proxy marriages we have just considered seem unconscionable.[55] To a significant minority, such marriages would be perfectly acceptable (as would, for example, polygamous or arranged marriages). At the very least, there would certainly be no universal sense of impropriety or repugnance. Indeed, as Lord Merriman P recognised at first instance in *Apt v Apt*,[56] there is no single problem of general unconscionability associated with proxy marriages. Rather, as we identified earlier, there are at least two possible problems: one concerning the circumvention of immigration rules, and the other concerning the lack of proper form or solemnity. Recognising this, Lord Merriman explained that:

> the problem should be sub-divided into categories and the test of public policy be applied, if at all, to each category separately . . . I do not think it is necessary to pursue this topic further than to say that I am not satisfied that a single test of public policy can be applied to all proxy marriages indiscriminately.[57]

To this suggestion one might, of course, respond that the judges have recourse to obscurities such as 'public policy' *precisely because* there would otherwise be profound disagreement over the appropriate basis for the denial of recognition. For example, Judge X may consider immigration concerns to be the crux of the case. She may also see such concerns to be a matter of public policy and, hence, be happy that 'public policy' should be stated as the basis for her decision to refuse recognition to the marriage. By contrast, Judge Y may feel the same way about the strong suspicion in the case that family pressure lies behind the consent of the party resident and domiciled in England. Accordingly, the two judges can agree to refuse recognition on the basis of 'public policy' although the policy concerns of each would be different from those of the other. Sunstein has captured the point thus:

> [L]egal systems tend to adopt a special strategy for producing stability and agreement in the midst of social disagreement and pluralism: arbiters of legal controversies try to produce *incompletely theorized agreements* . . . [for] [t]hey are an important source of social stability and an important way for people to demonstrate mutual respect, in law especially but also in liberal democracy as a whole.[58]

[55] At one point in his famous judgment in *Cheni v Cheni*, Simon P recast 'public policy' in terms of unconscionability. He said: '[t]he courts of this country will exceptionally refuse to recognise [a marriage] . . . on the ground that to give it recognition and effect would be unconscionable in the circumstances': [1965] P 85, at 98. See also Lord Parker CJ's equally crepuscular re-formulation in terms of 'repugnance' occasioned to 'decent-minded men or women' in *Alhaji Mohamed v Knott* [1969] 1 QB 1, at 15.

[56] [1947] P 127.

[57] *Ibid*, at 141.

[58] C. Sunstein, *Legal Reasoning and Political Conflict* (New York: Oxford University Press, 1996) pp 4–5 (emphasis added).

In advocating recourse to such incomplete theorisation, Sunstein suggests that decision-makers (including judges in multi-member courts) should produce decisions based on their agreement over certain broad issues; for here consensus can be reached without the need to supply a grand and fully articulated account of any background theory. As he contends, 'incompletely theorized agreements are well-suited to a world – and especially a legal world – containing social dissensus on large-scale issues'.[59] The decision – or agreement, to use Sunstein's word – 'is incompletely theorized in the sense that it is *incompletely specified*'.[60] The perceived virtue of such incompletely theorised decision making, especially in pluralistic societies,[61] is that 'judges on multimember bodies . . . [can] find commonality and thus a common way of life without producing unnecessary antagonism' because 'low-level principles[62] make it unnecessary to reach areas in which disagreement is fundamental'.[63] He argues further that this also allows mutual respect among differently minded society members to flourish, and that 'judges, perhaps even more than ordinary people, should not challenge a litigant's or even another person's, *most defining* commitments'.[64]

Yet silence on what for the litigant is a crucial and deeply held cultural or religious conviction can, on reflection, be perceived as insult rather than respect. To ignore, for example, the litigants' deeply held belief on a specific matter in favour of some 'low-level principle' about which each of the (English) judges on the multi-member tribunal can agree may be perceived by the litigants as disrespect for their core religious or cultural value. Take as an example a society in which child marriage is permitted and imagine that the Court of Appeal is called upon to decide the validity of a non-age marriage celebrated there. Suppose further that each member of the Court holds a different view about the morality and propriety of such marriages – one judge may be concerned about the exploitation of girls, another about the instability of such marriages, a third about the fact that it seemed to be a forced marriage. In such circumstances the various members could agree not to recognise the marriage on the simple ground that it was contrary to public policy. Yet, in avoiding any consideration of the cultural or religious

[59] *Loc cit*, p 39.

[60] *Loc cit*, p 35.

[61] *Loc cit*, p 47.

[62] Sunstein states that commonality is reached at low levels of abstraction but it is more plausible that agreement is easier to reach at higher levels of abstraction: see N. Duxbury, 'Ambition and Adjudication' (1997) 47 *University of Toronto Law Review* 161, 166–167.

[63] C. Sunstein, *op cit* n 58, p 39.

[64] *Loc cit*, p 40 (emphasis added). The importance of highly valued commitments to rational decision-making are discussed in the next section.

reasons for the marriage,[65] the three judges may nonetheless expose themselves to the criticism that they treated such features of the case as 'not even worthy of a mention or discussion'. In short, their deliberate silence on the putative cultural values associated with child marriages may appear as though those values were treated, in legal terms, as 'non-issues'.[66] And it is when deeply held convictions associated with particular foreign religions or cultures are treated as non-issues that a court lays itself open to the accusation of being culturally imperialistic. The decision is reached only by reference to a value or norm prevalent among the endogenous cultural majority.

But there is a need for clarification here. The problem does *not* lie with the prioritisation of domestic cultural value X over foreign cultural value Y, because Y has never been acknowledged to be a relevant value in the first place. It is, therefore, the very failure to take account of value Y, or at least acknowledge that it is value at all, that is the source of the *perceived* offence. The emphasis in the last sentence is necessary since it is not suggested here that there will inevitably be any cultural imperialism on the part of the court. Nor is it implied that, whatever else is at stake, foreign cultural values should always play a part in judicial decisions. It is simply suggested that crepuscular references to 'public policy', or references to certain (but not all) of the cultural values at stake in hard cases, can legitimately be viewed as derogatory. At bottom, the contention here is that, regardless of whether there is consensus over any particular (foreign) cultural value, there is no need to dismiss that value cursorily. Often, such values may harmlessly be acknowledged without necessarily assuming any particular significance in the judge's final decision. But a note of caution should be entered here; for the previous proposition must be distinguished from the assertion that, in all hard cases, the worth of (supposedly) dominant cultural value X should be compared with, and weighed against, minority cultural value Y. Such comparisons may often prove to be impossible. All that is suggested here – no more and no less – is that, as a minimum, explicit acknowledgement of (minority) cultural value Y ought to be provided if the decision is to *appear* both rational and non-ethnocentric.

Of course, this in turn begs the question: 'why is *mere acknowledgement* of a minority cultural value any less derogatory than no acknowledgement at all?' After all, in both instances the minority cultural value plays no part in the final decision. This issue is addressed next.

[65] Arranged marriages, for example, are sometimes explained (if not justified) in terms of the endeavour to preserve a particular ethnic identity: see P. Constantinides, 'The Greek Cypriots: Factors in the Maintenance of Ethnic Identity' in J.L. Watson (ed), *Between Two Cultures: Migrants and Minorities in Britain* (Oxford: Basil Blackwell, 1978).

[66] Sunstein views such silence in 'constructive terms'. His argument is that it can 'help minimize conflict, allow the present to learn from the future, and save a great deal of time and expense': *op cit* n 58, p 39.

Public policy and irrational decision-making

Apart from its capacity to engender suspicions about cultural imperialism, the failure to acknowledge certain foreign religious beliefs or cultural traditions may lead to inadequate decision-making in at least three ways. First, where value Y can and ought to be weighed against value X – even if, ultimately, value X holds sway – any decision based only on consideration of value X might legitimately be condemned as irrational. The irrationality of a decision taken without due weight being afforded to a relevant and material factor is the very stuff of a significant body of administrative law.[67] Secondly, and again where competing values X and Y should be weighed against one another, any decision taken without such a comparison being made will necessarily fail to reveal the extent of the decision-maker's commitment to the dominant value – value X for the sake of argument.[68] Such a failure means, in turn, that future hard cases are rendered unnecessarily difficult to resolve because the reasons for, and the level of commitment to, value X was never made clear in the initial case.[69] Thirdly, in cases where values X and Y are incommensurable, it may be only by acknowledging that Y *is* a background factor, that a decision-maker may become aware of the depth of his or her commitment to value X and, hence, the problem of incommensurability. The value in identifying the depth of one's commitment to value X – especially where this commitment is absolute – is that it again helps remove the prospect of unnecessary litigation in the future.

The preceding paragraphs have been largely based on theoretical argument.[70] But this book seeks to address practical family law problems with an international element from the perspective, at least primarily, of a family lawyer. It is not a central concern that we consider the intricacies of the rules of private international law; nor is it chiefly the present aim to add a further dimension to the modern jurisprudential commensurability debate. What must now, therefore, be undertaken, is an application of the above arguments to the particular problem of elucidating some clearer touchstones of adjudication than currently exist for those courts considering the use of

[67] See G.D.S. Taylor, 'Judicial Review: Improper Purposes and Irrelevant Considerations' [1976] *Cambridge Law Journal* 272.

[68] Deciding on the basis 'X is preferable to Y' compels the decision-maker to question the depth of his or her commitment to *both values*. In cases where value X is the only one acknowledged to be at play, no such evaluation is necessary.

[69] The fact that balancing exercises of this kind are considered to be a vital part of the adjudicative process should not be seen as an attachment to Dworkinian principle-based decision-making. I am as happy for the decision-maker to take account of policy considerations as principles, not least because, ultimately, the distinction between the two is unsustainable (see, eg, S. Fish, *Doing What Comes Naturally: Change, Rhetoric and the Practice of Theory in Literary and Legal Studies* (Oxford: Clarendon Press, 1989) pp 369–370).

[70] This argument has been drawn from Murphy, *op cit* n 38.

their residual discretion to refuse recognition to certain forms of foreign marriage.

It is often assumed (or, at least, seldom questioned) that the key to this particular area of the law is 'a proper balance' of 'practicality, commonsense, individual liberty, religious tolerance and the promotion of racial harmony'.[71] Unsurprisingly, this list of considerations commands wide appeal. It appears to be an enumeration of precisely the kinds of 'reasons' that most liberally minded lawyers would like to think were relevant, ultimately, in deciding whether or not to veto a foreign marriage. Put otherwise, these considerations are often thought to be the proper factors to form the basis for a legal decision. Yet what seems to go unquestioned is whether, on occasion, certain of these factors are irrelevant in strict legal terms; whether, in other words, they may sometimes be *non-reasons* in the sense described above. If any given factor is, strictly, a non-reason, it follows that it should not persuade the judge one way or the other in reaching his or her decision. That decision must, of necessity, be an irrational one. Again, this is this stuff of much administrative law.[72]

The example of arranged marriages may be used to illustrate the point. On the one hand – assuming the marriage to be otherwise valid – the court may be minded to invoke 'religious tolerance' from the above list of considerations and afford recognition on the basis that both spouses were committed to the religion in question and accepted such unions. Alternatively, the court may equally be 'offended' if it found the marriage to be non-consensual in nature. It might be tempting to think that the judge could balance the potential offence to the court (non-consensual marriage) against the religious tolerance ideal. But that would be attempting the impossible. For how does one genuinely compare the religious and cultural values of society X with the quite different value system that dominates in western society Y?[73] No judge brought up within one value-system is truly in a position to evaluate meaningfully the significance or centrality of doctrines and customs upon which a quite alien value-system is anchored. It is therefore irrational to decide cases on the ground that the religious tolerance ideal trumps incommensurable, countervailing considerations about freedom of choice in marriage. Instead, what the judge ought to do is to examine whether there is an absolute commitment to the values associated with personal freedom and

[71] See, eg, S. Poulter, *op cit* n 3, p v.

[72] For reported examples see *R v Birmingham Licensing Planning Committee, ex p. Kennedy* [1972] 2 QB 140; *Pilling v Abergele UDC* [1950] 1 KB 636.

[73] As Catherine Ballard, *op cit* n 37, comments (at 181): '[t]here is an obvious contradiction between the South Asia view of marriage as a *contract between two families* which should be arranged by parents on their children's behalf, and the contemporary Western ideal that an intimate personal relationship should exist between a couple before *they* make a decision to marry' (emphasis added).

then, if there is, exclude any evaluation (but not acknowledgement) of the foreign cultural tradition.[74]

Put bluntly, in the context of the discretionary non-recognition of foreign marriages, many of the considerations that *might* be taken into account are, in truth, incommensurable with one another. The various cultural values that are at stake and that are in binary opposition to one another have intrinsic rather than instrumental worth and are impossible to compare.[75] As such, any decisions reached on the basis of *supposed* comparisons must be irrational; they must be claims to have achieved the impossible. Instead, what is required is that such decisions must do at least the following four things.

First, and as a minimum, there must always be explicit *acknowledgement* of the diverse competing cultural values that arise in any particular case. In the second section of this chapter, we identified the specific policy concerns that underpin the domestic prohibitions on certain types of marriage that may be contracted abroad and thus pose potential conflicts problems. It is impossible even to begin to list the various justifications for certain marriage practices abroad, for these can differ drastically from one country to the next. On the other hand, they ought to be discovered as far as is reasonably practicable in each case that comes before the courts. This is because, powerful as his arguments are in general terms, there is no place for Sunstein's 'constructive use of silence' in this context.

Secondly, the courts must also take note of the fact that, having identified the particular policy and cultural values in issue, there is likely to be a problem of incommensurability. This will necessitate hard decision-making. Thus, thirdly, where such incommensurabilities arise, they must decide those cases in terms of commitments (in the absolute sense) and non-comparative

[74] It is not suggested here that all arranged marriages should be denied recognition. We have already noted that the absence of proper consent merely renders a domestically contracted marriage voidable under s 12 of the Matrimonial Causes Act 1973. As such, Parliament has deliberately chosen not to lay down an absolute commitment to the free consent principle. As such, it is difficult to imagine that the courts, at least in the case of an arranged (as opposed to a forced marriage), would deny that marriage recognition. In any event, not all arranged marriages are *ipso facto* non-consensual. Often, *both* spouses will accept the practice (albeit with some trepidation) because of their own commitment to the religious or cultural premise for such marriages.

[75] Values of instrumental worth can normally be measured in financial terms; values of intrinsic worth cannot. Neil Duxbury has captured the point well. 'Whereas fungible property has a purely economic or instrumental value, personal property is property that the owner is bound up with to such a degree that its loss would cause him or her pain that could not be relieved simply by replacing the object with other goods of equal market value. Thus, a credit card is likely to be fungible, whereas many items of jewellery [such as a wedding ring] will (for their owners) have more personal significance': see N. Duxbury, 'Trading in Controversy' (1997) 45 *Buffalo Law Review* 615, 616.

exclusions of non-reasons. It is only by the explicit exclusion of legal irrelevancies that their decision-making will remain rational.

Finally, all of this must be set within the framework of an abiding dedication to the principle of cultural pluralism. To reiterate a point made earlier, this does not mean that we should invoke ideas such as 'tolerance' and 'broadmindedness' as the English courts have done in the past. Such an approach is flawed in that it necessarily entails the uncritical ascription of weight to (sometimes incommensurable) foreign cultural and religious values. Rather, as Michael Freeman has explained:

> For the cultural pluralist, there are values [commitments, in present terms] independent of the context of the culture in question to which we can appeal in settling conflicts . . . There are, in other words, certain minimum requirements of human welfare. They must be met whatever the conception of what constitutes the good life, and regardless of what other values are upheld in any particular culture.[76]

It will be noted that there is nothing inconsistent between a pluralist approach and what has been suggested at length in the preceding two sections. Indeed, the adoption of the approach suggested there ought to guarantee suitably pluralistic decision-making.[77] For this reason, it has not been necessary to attempt to lay down a definitive guide to the preconditions of pluralism in respect of each kind of potentially problematic foreign marriage.[78]

Conclusion and critique

This chapter began by identifying what appear to be two fundamental flaws in the case-law governing the discretionary refusal of recognition of foreign marriages: the occasional willingness to decide cases in accordance with unarticulated concerns of 'public policy', and the (sometimes accompanying) tendency to fail to acknowledge certain cultural values that (at least by the litigants concerned) are perceived to be at stake. It then proceeded to unearth more precisely just what it is about certain forms of 'problematic'

[76] M. Freeman, 'Images of Child Welfare in Abduction Appeals' in J. Murphy (ed), *Ethnic Minorities, Their Families and the Law* (Oxford: Hart Publishing, 1999) p 13.

[77] Borrowing from, and extending the analysis of, Joseph Raz, the fact that the judges are able to acknowledge and choose between different cultural norms 'inevitably upholds a pluralistic view' for '[i]t admits the value of a large number of greatly differing pursuits among which . . . [the judges] are free to choose': see J. Raz, *The Morality of Freedom* (Oxford: Oxford University Press, 1986) p 399.

[78] On the virtues of pluralism (and its distinctiveness from relativism) see Gutmann, *op cit* n 53. And for one family lawyer's application of it, see M. Freeman, 'Cultural Pluralism and the Rights of the Child' in J. Eekelaar & T. Nhalpo (eds), *The Changing Family: Family Forms and Family Law* (Oxford: Hart Publishing, 1998).

foreign marriage that actually vexes the English courts from time to time. In so doing, these more precise concerns were subjected to critical analysis to test their weight and cogency. This was done because there is little point in getting to the bottom of what is really the reason for a court's decision to deny recognition to a particular foreign marriage if there is not also to be some scrutiny of the soundness (or otherwise) of that reason.

Having identified from a domestic perspective what is in issue in relation to the recognition of certain kinds of foreign marriage, this chapter has attempted to argue that adjudication ought to take place according to a taxonomy of 'commitments', 'reasons' (where comparison between competing values is possible) and 'non-reasons' (where there is a prior commitment to some inalienable domestic value). Only within such a framework, and *only* where domestic 'commitments' (probably few in number) arise can foreign cultural or religious values be excluded, on the basis of incommensurability, from the final decision. Assuming this pluralistic approach were to be adopted, with the reasons for vetoing foreign marriages being fully articulated, cases could be decided in the future with the flexibility and sensitivity normally associated with the family courts.

5

The acquisition and recognition of foreign divorces, annulments and separations

Just as in chapter 3 dealing with the recognition of foreign marriages, there is a need at the outset of this chapter to identify the three senses in which the term 'foreign divorce'[1] might be used. In the first place, it might be used to describe a putative divorce in England involving two foreign spouses seeking to dissolve their marriage according to some form of religious, customary or other informal method that is alien to the laws of this country.[2] As we shall see, with one possible exception relating to what are generally known as 'transnational' divorces, such divorces are unproblematic and are not regarded as effective in this country.[3] Secondly, divorces might be referred to as 'foreign' for the simple reason that they were obtained abroad. These are considerably more problematic. Finally, a divorce involving one English and one foreign domiciliary may also be described as 'foreign' to the extent

[1] For convenience, the term 'divorce' will be used in this chapter to refer to divorces, annulments and legal/judicial separations save where context demands that specific reference to annulment or separation is required. References to 'dissolutions' should be interpreted similarly.

[2] For a good introduction to various forms of religious and customary divorce, see S. Poulter, *English Law and Ethnic Minority Customs* (London: Butterworths, 1986) ch 5.

[3] Under the Family Law Act 1986, s 44(1) no divorce obtained in any part of the British Isles is regarded as effective unless it is granted by a court of civil jurisdiction; and it is pointless arguing that a foreign-style divorce constitutes an overseas divorce where it is effected in this country: see *Sulaiman v Juffali* [2002] 1 FLR 479. Furthermore, once the English court is seised of jurisdiction, it will apply only English law to the question of whether a divorce (or separation) should in fact be granted: *Zanelli v Zanelli* (1948) 64 TLR 556; *Quoraishi v Quoraishi* [1985] FLR 780. By contrast, in nullity cases involving foreign domiciliaries, the English court may well have to unravel choice of law questions associated with either the formal or essential validity of the marriage, which issues can easily turn on aspects of foreign law: see P.M. North & J.J. Fawcett, *Cheshire and North's Private International Law* (London: Butterworths, 1999) pp 776–788.

that we may have to consider the possibility of an overseas (not just an English) forum in which the divorce proceedings *ought* to be heard.

Between them, these three categories of 'foreign divorce' require us to consider two sets of rules. The first set centres on the question of jurisdiction: whether and when a marriage involving at least one foreign domiciliary may validly be dissolved in this country. The second set of rules concerns the more obvious matter of when the English courts will recognise a divorce that has been obtained overseas.

The rules relating to the acquisition and exercise of jurisdiction are rather complex. Simply being in England when one decides to get divorced is, by itself, an insufficient jurisdictional basis for the English courts to be able to grant a divorce. Instead, as we shall see, at least one of the spouses must have one of a range of stipulated connections to this country before a court of civil jurisdiction may entertain a divorce petition.[4] In relation to the second set of rules that are discussed in this chapter – that is, those concerning the recognition of divorces obtained abroad – we must examine the relevant statutory provisions contained in the Family Law Act 1986.

The complexities of this topic must be unfolded one layer at a time, and should not be underestimated. But before to turning to the substantive law, it is perhaps useful to sketch something of the practical significance that may very well attach to the twin questions of jurisdiction and the recognition of foreign divorces. First, the right to re-marry will normally depend upon the first marriage having been properly dissolved. Secondly, and in similar vein, an applicant's entitlement to certain social security benefits will depend upon his or her single status. Thirdly, and as we shall see later in greater detail, English court orders concerning post-divorce financial provision and property adjustment also require there to have been a valid divorce.[5] In short, crucial questions concerning status and finance often turn upon the validity of a foreign divorce.

Jurisdiction of the English Courts

Bases of jurisdiction

Under section 5(2) of the Domicile and Matrimonial Proceedings Act 1973, an English court shall have jurisdiction to entertain divorce and judicial

[4] Domicile and Matrimonial Proceedings Act 1973, s 5 as amended by the European Communities (Matrimonial Jurisdiction and Judgments) Regulations 2001 (SI 2001, No 310).

[5] Matrimonial Causes Act 1973, ss 23, 24 (in relation to divorces obtained in this country); Matrimonial and Family Proceedings Act 1984, s 12 (in relation to divorces obtained abroad).

separation proceedings in two alternative situations. The first of these is where it has jurisdiction under an EC Regulation that might conveniently be called Brussels IIA[6] (in which case it must exercise its jurisdiction in accordance with that Regulation). The second possibility is where no other court of a Member State has jurisdiction *and* the applicant is domiciled in England on the date when the proceedings are begun (in which case jurisdiction exists under the 'traditional rules').[7] The fact that the statute is framed in this way means that, in practical terms, the traditional rules are now very much the residual rules. Any question concerning an English court's jurisdiction in this area must begin with consideration of the jurisdiction provisions of Brussels IIA. If jurisdiction is conferred according to Articles 3, 4 or 5 of the Regulation, that will be the end of the matter subject to the applicability of various staying provisions. If jurisdiction is not thus conferred, Article 6 becomes relevant. For it is there provided that jurisdiction under Brussels IIA is exclusive where the respondent is either 'habitually resident in the territory of a Member State'[8] or a national of a Member State other than the United Kingdom or Ireland or a domiciliary of the United Kingdom or Ireland. In short, the thrust of Article 6 is that, in respect of respondents with strong links to Member States, jurisdiction exists either under the Regulation or not at all.

To some extent, Article 7 elaborates upon the residual nature of the traditional rules by providing that those rules may be applied only where no court of a Member State has jurisdiction under the Regulation and the respondent spouse does not fall within Article 6. What may be distilled from all of this is the very significant primacy of the Brussels IIA regime and the fact that the traditional rules will now apply only where an English domiciliary seeks to divorce a non-English and non-Irish domiciliary who is neither habitually resident in an EU country nor a national of any such country.

[6] Council Regulation (EC) No 2201/2003 (repealing but, so far as divorce is concerned, almost precisely re-enacting parts of Council Regulation (EC) No 1347/2000 – sometimes called 'Brussels II' – to which some of the referenced literature in this chapter relates). This Regulation applies to all Member States in the European Union with the exception of Denmark.

[7] Strictly, the Act states that the residual jurisdiction is granted 'if either of the parties to the marriage is domiciled in England and Wales on the date when the proceedings are begun'. But since Art 6 of the Regulation makes its own jurisdiction rules applicable to any respondent domiciled in the United Kingdom, s 5(2) must be read more narrowly than its actual wording suggests.

[8] For the purposes of the Regulation, the term 'habitual residence' will have to be given its European (not domestic) meaning as determined by the European Court of Justice: see A. Borrás, *Explanatory Report on the Convention, Drawn up on the Basis of Article K.3 of the Treaty on European Union, on Jurisdiction and the Recognition and Enforcement of Judgments in Matrimonial Matters* OJ 1998 C221/27, para 32; see also *Swaddling v Adjudication Officer* [1999] 2 FLR 184.

So far as the Regulation's jurisdiction rules are concerned, it is Article 3 that sets out the main criteria according to which it may be exercised.[9] The majority of the detailed criteria are contained in Article 3(1)(a) of Brussels IIA, which provides that:

> In matters relating to divorce, legal separation or marriage annulment, jurisdiction shall lie with the courts of the Member State in whose territory
>
> [i] the spouses are habitually resident, or
> [ii] the spouses were last habitually resident, in so far as one of them still resides there, or
> [iii] the respondent is habitually resident, or
> [iv] in the event of a joint application, either of the spouses is habitually resident, or
> [v] the applicant is habitually resident if he or she resided there for at least a year immediately before the application was made, or
> [vi] the applicant is habitually resident if he or she resided there for at least six months immediately before the application was made and is either a national of the Member State in question or, in the case of the United Kingdom and Ireland, has his 'domicile' there.

There is also a supplemental ground for jurisdiction contained in Article 3(1)(b): namely, that *both spouses* are nationals of the State concerned, or, in the case of the United Kingdom and Ireland, are domiciled there.[10] Although these criteria may seem complex, their main thrust may be captured fairly succinctly.[11] For the most part, jurisdiction turns on one or both of the spouses actually being, or having recently been, habitually resident in the Member State in which the court seised of jurisdiction is situated. Where only the applicant is habitually resident in the Member State concerned, he or she must also satisfy certain minimum residence requirements (which vary from twelve to six months depending on whether the applicant is also a national[12] of that State). Beyond habitual residence, the only alternative basis according to which jurisdiction is ascribed is that *both* spouses are nationals – or domiciliaries, in the case of the United Kingdom and Ireland – of the State concerned. In short, whether based on a test of habitual residence, nationality or domicile, Brussels IIA confers jurisdiction on the

[9] Subsidiary rules relating to jurisdiction over counterclaims and the conversion of a judicial separation into a divorce are contained in Arts 5 and 6 of the Regulation.

[10] Under Brussels IIA, Art 3(2) the term 'domicile' is given 'the same meaning as it has under the legal systems of the United Kingdom and Ireland'.

[11] Perhaps a little too briefly, Truex has said that 'the test is based on habitual residence or nationality . . . [while] [i]n the UK and the Republic of Ireland domicile replaces nationality as a criterion': D. Truex, 'Brussels II – Beware!' [2001] *Family Law* 233, at 233.

[12] In the case of the United Kingdom and Ireland, the nationality rule is replaced by one pertaining to domicile.

basis of a genuine link between the party or parties concerned and the Member State exercising jurisdiction.

Stays of proceedings

While it is undoubtedly correct that the test for jurisdiction should be based on a real link with the country in which a court is seeking to exercise jurisdiction, the complexity of the rules means that a suitable link may exist with more than one country at a time. If, for example, a German national leaves his English wife, returns to Germany with a new girlfriend and then petitions the German court for a divorce some six months later, the German court would be seised of jurisdiction according to criterion [vi] above. But the English court, too, would have jurisdiction under criterion [iii], if the English wife were to seek a divorce in this country. In such circumstances, one or other of the courts would need to stay its proceedings, and Brussels IIA imposes certain mandatory rules in this connection.

The first provision of relevance in this context is Article 18(1) which provides, in accordance with natural justice principles, that where a respondent who is habitually resident in a different Member State does not enter an appearance, the proceedings must be stayed unless it is shown that the respondent has been able to take receipt of the document instituting proceedings in time to arrange his or her defence *or* that all necessary steps to this end have been taken. The second relevant staying provision is Article 19(1). This requires that, if proceedings involving the same cause of action and the same parties is brought before the courts of different Member States, the court second seised of jurisdiction *must* stay its proceedings. This begs the question of when a court actually becomes seised of jurisdiction. To this end it is provided that a court is so seised when the document instituting proceedings is either lodged with the court or received by the authority responsible for service in cases where service must occur beforehand.[13] In cases of disputed jurisdiction – that is, where it is unclear which court was first seised of jurisdiction – it is the court which first claims jurisdiction that shall be regarded as the court first seised. Thus, in one case where there was a dispute as to whether the German court was the court first seised, it was held (according to the equivalent provision of the former Regulation) that the English court must respect the fact that the German court was the first one to hold itself out as being seised. It had to stay its own proceedings. As Thorpe LJ said:

> [W]e must espouse the Regulation and apply it wholeheartedly. We must not take or be seen to take opportunities for usurping the function of the judge in the other member state. Once another jurisdiction is demonstrated to be

[13] Brussels IIA, Art 16(1)(a), (b).

apparently first seised, this jurisdiction must defer by holding itself in waiting in case that apparent priority should be disproved or declined.[14]

The final point worthy of note is that Article 19(1) also extends to dependent actions.[15] So much is clear from the title of the Article: '*Lis pendens* and dependent actions'. What this means is that the court second seised of jurisdiction must stay its proceedings in cases where two *different* matrimonial causes have been commenced in different Member States *so long as* they involve the same two parties. Thus, English nullity proceedings would have to be stayed if Dutch divorce proceedings had already begun.

The exclusive nature of the staying provisions in Articles 18 and 19 has been the subject of debate and criticism. One particular cause of vexation has been the fact that Article 19 makes no provision for voluntary stays on the basis that one forum is clearly more suitable than the other (because of a strong connection between both parties and that Member State). It has been suggested that the mandatory nature of the staying provisions can generate a race to the most advantageous forum.[16] In our earlier example, then, the English domiciled wife could not institute proceedings in this country if her German husband had already begun proceedings in Germany (which may be more advantageous for him). This would be the case despite the fact that the parties may have lived for many years in England having established their matrimonial home here.[17] A further criticism of the inflexible rules contained in Article 19 is that efforts at conciliation and mediation are likely to suffer where there is a powerful in-built incentive to get proceedings on foot as quickly as possible in order to secure one's forum of choice.[18]

By contrast with the inflexible staying rules under Brussels IIA, the traditional rules provide almost exclusively for discretionary stays of proceedings.[19] And while it is not wholly clear from the wording of the Act, it seems probable that the traditional rules on discretionary stays will operate

[14] *Wermuth v Wermuth* [2002] EWCA Civ 50, at [34] (emphasis added).

[15] A dependent action in this context is a different matrimonial cause.

[16] See N. Mostyn, 'Brussels II – The Impact on Forum Disputes' [2001] *Family Law* 359, 363–365 and P. McEleavy, 'The Brussels II Regulation: How the European Community has Moved into Family Law' (2002) 51 *International and Comparative Law Quarterly* 883, 887. See also I. Karsten, 'Brussels II – An English Perspective' [1998] *International Family Law* 75.

[17] For a counter-argument identifying the benefit associated with avoiding the application of the discretionary doctrine of *forum non conveniens*, see C.M.V. Clarkson & J. Hill, *Jaffey on the Conflict of Laws* (London: Butterworths, 2002) p 388.

[18] See Karsten, *op cit* n 16.

[19] There is one circumstance in which a stay of proceedings is obligatory under the traditional rules. But it relates only to divorce or nullity proceedings that are already on foot in another jurisdiction in the British Isles and is hedged by detailed requirements as to residence in that other jurisdiction: Domicile and Matrimonial Proceedings Act 1973, s 5(6).

in respect of any case not caught by Articles 18 and 19 of the Regulation.[20] Under the statute, this discretion is to be deployed according to the balance of fairness and convenience.[21] This is an uncertain phrase, but it is at least clear that the case law associated with the *forum non conveniens* principle is relevant to its interpretation.[22] As such, illustrative considerations would include the ancillary powers of the respective courts,[23] the location of the matrimonial home and other matrimonial assets,[24] the country in which the marriage took place[25] and the question of whether an English divorce would be recognised in the country in which the alternative court is located.[26]

Further jurisdictional significance of Brussels IIA

It is worth noting finally that the jurisdictional significance of the rules contained in Brussels IIA goes beyond the mere delimitation of the residual sphere in which the traditional rules will apply and its mandatory requirements concerning stays of proceedings. In making the acquisition of jurisdiction hinge mainly upon habitual residence *simpliciter*, the Regulation is a good deal more generous than the traditional rules, which, by contrast, insisted either on domicile or on habitual residence *for a minimum period of one year* prior to the commencement of the proceedings. On the other hand, the Regulation is also in one sense less generous than the traditional rules it replaced. It does not allow the English courts to entertain a petition from a foreign domiciliary to divorce an English domiciliary where the couple has established an habitual residence outside the European Union.[27] And while

[20] The Domicile and Matrimonial Proceedings Act 1973, Sched 1, para 9(1) simply states that the traditional staying rules apply to matrimonial proceedings 'other than proceedings governed by the Council Regulation'. This could mean, literally, that where jurisdiction is governed by the Regulation, the traditional staying rules are inapplicable. However, a preferable, purposive interpretation would confine the reference to the Council Regulation to the staying rules located therein. This would mean that the traditional rules would apply to any case in which proceedings were already on foot elsewhere than in a Member State.

[21] Domicile and Matrimonial Proceedings Act 1973, Sched 1, para 9(1).

[22] *De Dampierre v De Dampierre* [1988] AC 92; *S v S* [1997] 1 WLR 1200; *B v B (Divorce: Stay of Foreign Proceedings)* [2003] 1 FLR 1. For details of how the *forum non conveniens* principle operates, see *Spiliada Maritime Corp v Cansulex Ltd* [1987] AC 460.

[23] *R v R (Divorce: Stay of Proceedings)* [1994] 2 FLR 1036; *S v S* [1997] 2 FLR 100.

[24] *C v C* [2001] 1 FLR 624.

[25] *Krenge v Krenge* [1999] 1 FLR 969.

[26] *C v C* [2001] 1 FLR 624.

[27] They will not be caught by the main jurisdiction rules of the Regulation for want of habitual residence in a Member State. They will not be caught by the secondary rule because only one spouse is a national/domiciliary of the State in which the divorce is sought. They will not be caught by the traditional rules because the respondent is an English domiciliary thus invoking Art 6 (making Brussels IIA jurisdiction the exclusive jurisdiction in such a case).

it might be contended that the new country of habitual residence ought to be the appropriate forum in which the parties should seek a divorce, this presupposes that the spouses would meet the jurisdictional and substantive criteria for obtaining a divorce in any such country.

Recognition of foreign decrees

The avoidance of 'limping marriages' – whereby a marriage continues to subsist by the law of this country, but has been validly dissolved according to the law of another country – provides a good policy reason for English law to be reasonably generous in terms of its recognition of foreign divorces. On the other hand, however, it must also guard against the fact that unscrupulous individuals might seek to divest themselves of unwanted spouses by obtaining unilateral divorces in countries with which they have no real connection, but which permit foreigners to obtain divorces there on comparatively flimsy grounds.[28] Equally, an element of caution must be shown in relation to the recognition of foreign divorces that are obtained with little to no formality and which may run counter to certain fundamental principles of human rights. Balancing these countervailing considerations against one another, the statutory rules governing the recognition of foreign decrees – whether of divorce, annulment or legal separation[29]– seek to strike an appropriate balance between free-and-easy recognition, and being overly restrictive.

Just as there were in relation to jurisdiction, so are there here two set of rules governing the recognition of foreign decrees. They are, first, those contained in Brussels IIA (governing decrees obtained in a Member State) and, secondly, those located in Part II of the Family Law Act 1986 (relating to decrees obtained from non-Member States). The two sets of rules operate independently of one another, and each is therefore considered separately.

Brussels IIA

Brussels IIA contains detailed provisions as to the recognition of any judgment obtained from a 'court or tribunal' in relation to 'civil matters'.[30] And the term 'court' is defined broadly enough to encompass civil proceedings

[28] See, eg, the 'mail order' divorce available from Guam that featured in *Kellman v Kellman* [2000] 1 FLR 785.

[29] For the purposes of the recognition of foreign decrees, ss 46–52 of the Family Law Act 1986 use the term 'legal separation'. In relation to British decrees, s 44 of that Act refers to 'judicial separation'. It would appear to be a semantic (not substantive) difference. But since Brussels IIA also employs the term 'legal separation', that term shall be preferred here.

[30] Brussels IIA, Art 1(1).

dealt with by a non-judicial, administrative authority.[31] This then means that both judicial and administrative divorces are within the remit of the Regulation.[32] But what it does not apply to is any divorce that is obtained purely by recourse to customary or religious proceedings.[33]

As to its recognition provisions, Article 21 lays down the basic principle that there should be presumptive recognition of any decree of divorce, nullity or legal separation.[34] And recognition of the decree carries with it an automatic right to the recognition of a party's change of status. Thus, in the words of the Regulation, 'no special procedure shall be required for up-dating the civil-status records'.[35] The only two conditions attached to the automatic recognition principle are first, that the decree must be a final one (so any judgment equivalent to the English *decree nisi* does not suffice) and, secondly, that none of the grounds for refusal of recognition set out in Article 22 is satisfied.

Under Article 22, there are four grounds on which a foreign decree *will* be denied recognition[36] in another Member State. To begin with, recognition will be refused where to do otherwise would be 'manifestly contrary to public policy'.[37] Although ostensibly broad in compass, this ground is actually very limited in scope. For example, a recognising State cannot refuse recognition on grounds associated with what it considers to be the spurious jurisdiction of the granting court.[38] Nor may a recognising State object to recognition on the basis that the judgment of the granting court seemed substantively wrong,[39] or that it was premised on a ground for divorce that would not entitle the applicant to a divorce in the recognising State.[40] Furthermore, given the background policy objective of seeking to avoid limping

[31] Art 2(1) of the Regulation provides that, 'the term courts shall cover all the authorities in the Member States with jurisdiction in the matters falling within the scope of this Regulation'.

[32] Denmark permits administrative divorces, but has excepted herself from the Regulation. It is possible – but not known at the time of writing – whether others of the new EU States allow for administrative divorces.

[33] For examples of both customary and religious divorces, see Poulter, *op cit* n 2, pp 98–100.

[34] While this provision extends to all matrimonial judgments made under a Member State's residual rules (Arts 2(4), 21(1)), there is no requirement to recognise decisions in which a divorce is refused. No issue estoppel therefore arises to prevent the applicant seeking a divorce in an alternative Member State with jurisdiction. See further, W. Kennett, 'Current Developments: The Brussels II Convention' (1999) 48 *International and Comparative Law Quarterly* 465.

[35] Brussels IIA, Art 21(2).

[36] The Regulation provides for *mandatory* refusals of recognition.

[37] Brussels IIA, Art 22(a).

[38] The jurisdiction of the granting court is specifically exempt from review: *ibid*, Art 24.

[39] *Ibid*, Art 26.

[40] *Ibid*, Art 25.

marriages, there remain only a few circumstances in which one might envisage the invocation of this ground. It has been suggested that conceivable examples include cases in which the applicant obtained a decree by substantial fraud, or in which the decree was granted in circumstances appearing to be inconsistent with the respondent's rights under the European Convention on Human Rights.[41] However, there is case law decided in relation to the equivalent test in section 51 of the Family Law Act 1986 that suggests that fraud will not, *per se*, suffice to invoke this ground.[42] And a subsequent decision (also relating to the equivalent test in section 51) has indicated that, since the offence to public policy must be manifest, the test constitutes a 'very high hurdle to clear'.[43] As such, public policy might be invoked to refuse recognition of a foreign divorce in only the most exceptional cases.[44]

Secondly, a divorce will presumptively be refused recognition if it was granted contrary to the natural justice requirement of a fair hearing. Article 22(b) of Brussels IIA provides that a divorce shall presumptively be refused recognition where it is granted in default of appearance by the respondent, and in circumstances where the respondent was not notified in sufficient time and in such manner as to enable a defence to be satisfactorily arranged.[45] To this presumption, Article 22(b) contains one caveat. It is this: if the respondent, despite his or her inability to arrange a proper defence, has 'accepted the judgment unequivocally', the decree must nonetheless be recognised. The Regulation does not elaborate on what amounts to unequivocal acceptance, but the example given in the official explanatory report[46] is that of a respondent who has re-married.

The third basis for a refusal of recognition is triggered where a judgment obtained abroad is irreconcilable with a judgment obtained in the recognising State.[47] There is no requirement that the irreconcilable judgments must relate to the same cause of action. But where the two judgments are irreconcilable, denial of recognition is mandatory. So, for example, this provision would have to be applied by the English courts where a legal separation obtained in Germany was impossible to reconcile with a divorce granted in

[41] See, Clarkson & Hill, *op cit* n 17, p 400.

[42] *Eroglu v Eroglu* [1994] 2 FLR 287. Although this case held that fraud was insufficient to meet the test of 'manifestly contrary to public policy' in s 51(3) of the Family Law Act 1986, it is not a direct authority on the precise same test under Brussels IIA. That said, it seems inconceivable that the courts would interpret the exact same words in the Regulation differently.

[43] *Kellman v Kellman* [2000] 1 FLR 785, at 798 *per* Judge Paul Coleridge QC. The divorce in that case was described as a 'mail order divorce' obtained from Guam with which State neither party had the remotest connection.

[44] In *Eroglu v Eroglu* [1994] 2 FLR 287, at 289 Thorpe J advocated that public policy should be invoked 'sparingly' under the 1986 Act.

[45] Brussels IIA, Art 22(b).

[46] Borrás, *op cit* n 8, para 70.

[47] Brussels IIA, Art 22(c).

this country. In such a case, the intermediate nature of the German judgment precludes it being reconciled with the finality of the English decree. If, however, the respective judgments were obtained conversely – that is, if there was an English separation and a German divorce – the English courts could recognise the German judgment with no difficulty, since the German divorce could easily be reconciled with the English separation.

The fourth ground for refusal is, in a way, an extension of the third to the scenario in which there are *three* States involved: the recognising State, plus two further States from which the irreconcilable judgments emanate. Under Article 22(d) of Brussels IIA, there shall be no recognition of a decree obtained in a Member State if that decree is irreconcilable with an earlier judgment obtained in either another Member State or a non-Member State, so long as that earlier judgment meets the conditions necessary for its recognition in the recognising State. Unlike the preceding ground in which the timing of the irreconcilable judgments is irrelevant, under this ground timing is of the essence. This is because its invocation depends on the second judgment (for which recognition is sought) being irreconcilable with the first. So, for example, if a valid separation were to be obtained in Canada prior to a divorce in Belgium, there would be no difficulty for the English courts in recognising the Belgian divorce and therefore no prospect of invoking this ground. If, however, a valid Canadian divorce were to be followed by a Belgian separation for which latter recognition were sought in this country, the English courts would be required under this ground to deny recognition to the Belgian judgment.

The traditional rules

At common law, the test applied to determine whether the English courts would recognise a foreign divorce was one of 'real and substantial connection' between *either* of the parties to the marriage and the country from which the divorce was obtained. This largely unworkable test gave way to somewhat clearer legislative rules in the shape of the Recognition of Divorces and Legal Separations Act 1971. This in turn has now been replaced by Part II of the Family Law Act 1986 which, unlike the 1971 Act, makes its recognition provisions applicable to nullity decrees as well as divorces and legal separations.[48] Under the 1986 Act, the recognition of foreign decrees outside the Brussels IIA regime[49] falls into two broad categories: those

[48] The Act also applies retrospectively (save in the case of two insignificant exceptions that need not be considered here).

[49] The Family Law Act 1986, s 45(1) (as amended by the European Communities (Matrimonial Jurisdiction and Judgements) Regulations 2001 (SI 2001, No 310) r 10) makes it clear that the statutory rules operate only where Brussels IIA is inapplicable.

decrees obtained in other parts of the British Isles and those obtained 'overseas'.[50] Within the latter category, there are two further subcategories, namely, those obtained by means of proceedings, and those obtained otherwise than by means of proceedings. For convenience, we shall adopt a tripartite classification. We will then consider the issues associated with transnational divorces, refusals of recognition and retrospective foreign annulments.

1 British Isles decrees

Under section 44(2) of the Family Law Act 1986, specific provision is made with respect to decrees granted by courts of civil jurisdiction in any part of the British Isles.[51] As one would expect, the Act requires all such decrees to be recognised throughout the United Kingdom *unless* one of two general grounds for non-recognition in section 51 of the Act is satisfied. And even where one of these grounds (considered below) is satisfied, there is no obligation on the part of the English court to refuse recognition: it has a discretion.[52] In practice, divorces obtained in other parts of the British Isles tend not to be problematic nowadays.[53] This is in sharp contrast to the many difficulties that surround overseas divorces.

2 Overseas decrees obtained by means of proceedings

Under section 46(1) of the Family Law Act 1986, an overseas decree – whether of divorce, annulment or legal separation – shall[54] be recognised as valid if it was effective under the law of the country in which it was obtained *and*, at the date of the commencement of the proceedings,[55] either spouse was habitually resident or domiciled in, or a national of, that country. Although this ground for the recognition of overseas 'proceedings' divorces

[50] By virtue of s 45 of the 1986 Act, an 'overseas divorce' is one 'obtained in a country outside the British Islands'.

[51] The British Isles consists of the United Kingdom *plus* the Channel Islands and the Isle of Man.

[52] Under s 51(1) of the 1986 Act, an English court *may* refuse to recognise a divorce or separation when, according to English law, there was no subsisting marriage between the parties. Under s 51(2), the court is granted a discretion to refuse a decree of divorce on the basis that it is irreconcilable with some effective, prior judgment concerning the validity of the marriage.

[53] Historically, the question of whether the English courts would recognise a foreign marriage was one that first arose in connection with a Scottish divorce: see *R v Lolley* (1812) Russ & Ry 237.

[54] Recognition is mandatory, so long as none of the grounds for refusing recognition under s 51 of the 1986 Act are met.

[55] Family Law Act 1986, s 46(3). Where there are cross-proceedings in a second country, habitual residence or domicile in, or nationality of, the second country on the date the cross-proceedings began will suffice equally well: *ibid*, s 47(1)(a). A further substitution of the critical time is provided for by s 46(4) in cases in which a nullity decree is sought after the death of one of the spouses.

can be stated with ease, it can be understood properly only after the elucidation of some deceptively simple terms.

(a) Effective The meaning of an 'effective' divorce for the purposes of section 46 is far from obvious. In *Kellman* v *Kellman*[56] it was held that an effective divorce need not be a valid divorce. This somewhat perplexing finding can best be explained by reference to the facts. The husband and wife were both US citizens who married in the United States in 1980. Two years after the marriage they moved to England and settled there for five years before their relationship broke down. Although neither party had any connection with Guam, an unincorporated territory of the United States, they obtained what the judge called a 'mail order divorce' from a Guam court in 1989. Ten years later, a question arose concerning the wife's rights concerning the matrimonial home. This question turned on the effectiveness of the Guam divorce. The wife therefore applied to the Superior Court of Guam for, in effect, a notice to set aside the divorce as invalid on the grounds that the original Guam court had lacked jurisdiction. The Superior Court of Guam denied the wife's application on the basis of estoppel: the husband had re-married, but in any event both parties had for ten years treated the divorce as though it were perfectly valid. Notwithstanding this ruling, the wife sought a divorce from the English court and the husband applied to have that petition struck out. Finding in favour of the husband, it was held that the word 'effective' in the 1986 Act imposed a less stringent test than 'valid'. Thus, although the decree may have been invalid *per se* (on jurisdictional grounds), it was nonetheless effective because of the supervening legal decision that an equitable estoppel would prevent the divorce being invalidated.

Had the Superior Court in Guam held the original divorce to be invalid, there would have been no question of it being recognised by the English courts so as to deny the wife the opportunity to petition for divorce in this country. But what would have been the position if the Superior Court of Guam had never been approached to pronounce upon the validity of the 'mail order' divorce? In such circumstances, there would have been no supervening legal decision giving rise to the *res judicata* principle which, incidentally, had prevented the mainland US courts from examining the issue.[57] On the other hand, there may still have been an estoppel based on the husband's re-marriage and the parties' conduct. What at least *seems* clear is that, where there is neither an estoppel nor a supervening court decision, a divorce that has been invalidly granted will not be regarded as effective in the country in

[56] [2000] 1 FLR 785.

[57] It seems that the US courts would not have recognised the validity of the 'mail order' divorce *per se*, but the US doctrine of 'full faith and credit' prevented them from questioning the Superior Court's ruling as to estoppel.

which it was obtained where there is every likelihood that a superior court would set aside a divorce if the decision were to be appealed.[58]

More straightforwardly, a foreign decree will not be regarded as effective where an appeal is pending,[59] where dissolution under the local law requires a specified period of time to elapse from the date of the decision[60] or where the local tribunal lacks competence to pronounce a divorce.[61]

(b) Country The fact that recognition under the 1986 Act requires the divorce in question to be effective in the 'country' in which it was obtained is a further source of complexity. This is because certain political countries, such as the United States, comprise a federation of States within which there are different systems of law relating to matrimonial causes.[62] In such cases, it is entirely feasible – though not common – for a divorce obtained in one State not to be recognised in one or more of the remaining States in the federation.[63] To meet such circumstances, section 49 of the Family Law Act 1986 makes two provisions. First, it stipulates that where recognition turns upon the habitual residence or domicile of one of the parties in the foreign country concerned, each separate territory within that country shall be treated as if it were a separate country.[64] Secondly, it provides that where nationality comprises the required connection to the State or territory from which the divorce is obtained, the divorce will still be recognised in this country so long as the divorce would have been effective throughout the whole of the country in which the divorce was obtained.[65] Thus, if man domiciled in Idaho were to obtain a divorce in New Hampshire, the divorce would be recognised in this country so long as it would be effective throughout the whole of the United States. Again, the general thrust of this provision is to treat a State divorce – a New Hampshire divorce, in our example – as though it were an 'American divorce'.

(c) Personal connections to the foreign country Each of the connecting factors listed in section 46(1) and about which a little has been said in the

[58] *D v D* [1994] 1 FLR 38. But in what sense, if there is no appeal pending, is such a divorce ineffective? Arguably, recognition might have been better denied in such a case on the basis of one of the grounds in s 51: see J. Murphy, 'The Recognition of Overseas Marriages and Divorces: Some Opportunities Missed?' (1995) 46 *Northern Ireland Legal Quarterly* 35.

[59] *Torok v Torok* [1973] 3 All ER 101.

[60] *Martin v Buret* 1938 SLT 479.

[61] *Adams v Adams* [1971] P 188.

[62] In relation to those composite countries – such as Australia and Canada – in which divorce is a federal matter, s 49 is of no moment.

[63] See, eg, *Williams v North Carolina (No 2)* 325 US 226 (1945).

[64] Family Law Act 1986, s 49(2). See *Emin v Yeldag* [2002] 1 FLR 956. But contrast *B v B (Divorce: Northern Cyprus)* [2000] 2 FLR 707.

[65] *Ibid*, s 49(3).

preceding paragraph requires a little elaboration here. The term 'habitual residence' is one that is often used as a jurisdictional criterion and its meaning can vary to some degree from one country to another. For the purposes of section 46, however, it is to be interpreted only in accordance with the English meaning of the term (notwithstanding that the habitual residence in question will have taken place in some other country). By contrast, the term 'domicile' can be understood in two different ways for the purposes of the Act. It may bear its English meaning or alternatively, the relevant foreign meaning of the word.[66] In addition, in recognition of the fact that the term 'domicile' may have more than one meaning in any one country, according to context – as indeed it does in this country – the Act further provides that the relevant foreign concept of domicile is that which obtains 'according to the law of that country in family matters'.[67]

The Act provides no definition of the word 'nationality', but extrapolating from section 54 of the Act (which deals with colonies and dependent territories of the United Kingdom), it would seem that nationality depends upon the country in question having a law of nationality or citizenship and the person in question possessing the relevant citizenship or nationality under that law. Where a person possesses dual nationality, the best indications are that so long as he is a national of the country in which the divorce was obtained, it is immaterial that he is also a national of another country.[68]

In one special case covered by section 47(2) of the 1986 Act, it is immaterial whether either of the parties had, at the time of the divorce, one of three specified connections to the relevant country. This is the case in which a legal separation is converted into a divorce in accordance with a facility for such conversion provided by the local law. Under this subsection, so long as the original separation was entitled to recognition, the subsequent divorce will be similarly recognised regardless of whether domicile or habitual residence in, or nationality of, the country concerned has been lost.

(d) Findings of jurisdictional fact Just as habitual residence, domicile and nationality are central to the English courts' determination of whether they possess jurisdiction to pronounce a divorce, so too is jurisdiction in many other foreign systems of law based on such connecting factors.[69] It follows, then, that before a foreign court will grant a divorce, it will make a prior

[66] *Ibid*, s 46(5).

[67] *Ibid.*

[68] *Torok v Torok* [1973] 3 All ER 101: a Hungarian man possessed dual nationality, and the court would have been prepared to recognise the divorce he obtained in Hungary were it not for the presence of other factors grounding a refusal of recognition.

[69] The actual basis of a foreign court's jurisdiction is, *per se*, irrelevant subject to any public policy factor that might justify non-recognition under s 51 of the 1986 Act.

determination that one or both parties are resident in, or domiciliaries or nationals of, the country concerned. Where such a finding of fact has been made by the foreign court, the English court must treat it as 'conclusive evidence of the fact found' so long as both parties to the marriage took part in the proceedings.[70] In any other case – including the one in which only one of the parties was present at the proceedings – the foreign court's finding of fact shall be 'sufficient proof of the fact [concerned] unless the contrary be shown'. The reason why in the second scenario the finding of fact is not taken to be conclusive is as follows. Where only one spouse was present, the other will have lacked the opportunity to question the relevant finding of fact during the proceedings.

(e) Proceedings The recognition requirements in section 46(1) of the 1986 Act are triggered only in respect of 'proceedings divorces'. This, of course, begs the question of what amounts to 'proceedings' for these purposes. And given that divorces can be obtained throughout the world by a wide range of mechanisms – only some of which can be recognised according to the rules in section 46(1) – the fundamentality of this question should not be underestimated.[71] The Act itself offers little guidance: it states no more than that '"proceedings" means judicial or other proceedings'.[72] However, a combined reading of two cases that were decided under the previous legislation does provide an authoritative interpretation of the related phrase, 'other proceedings', which appeared there.[73] Furthermore, this interpretation has since been held – albeit only in the context of a decision of the Immigration Appeal Tribunal[74] – to be equally applicable to the corresponding words in the 1986 Act.

The first of those cases is *Quazi v Quazi*[75] in which there was some difference of opinion among their Lordships as to just what constituted proceedings. Nonetheless, the case at least provided clear authority for the proposition that a Pakistani *talaq* divorce[76] was obtained by means of proceedings given that the Pakistan Muslim Family Laws Ordinance 1961 required that notification of the divorce be supplied to the chairman of an arbitration council and stipulated that the effect of the *talaq* would be suspended by ninety days to

[70] Family Law Act 1986, s 48(1). The subsection relates to findings of fact generally; but its chief importance, as is made clear in s 48(2), relates to findings as to domicile, habitual residence or nationality for the purposes of exercising jurisdiction.

[71] For a host of examples, see Poulter, *op cit* n 2, ch 5; *id*, 'Recognition of Foreign Divorces – the New Law' [1987] *Law Society Gazette* 253, 254; North & Fawcett, *op cit* n 3, p 798.

[72] Family Law Act 1986, s 54(1).

[73] The Recognition of Divorces and Legal Separations Act 1971, s 2.

[74] *Baig v Entry Clearance Officer, Islamabad* [2002] UKIAT 4229.

[75] [1980] AC 744.

[76] For the meaning of this term, see section 3 below.

allow conciliation proceedings to take place. In interpreting their Lordships' speeches in that case, Oliver LJ said in *Chaudhary v Chaudhary*:[77]

> Proceedings must . . . at least bear in the statute a meaning which the word would have in normal speech where, as it seems to me, no one would ordinarily refer to a private act conducted entirely by parties *inter se* or by one party alone, as a proceeding, even though the party performing it may give it an additional solemnity or even an efficacy by performing it in the presence of other persons whose only involvement is that they witness its performance. The word would not, in my judgment, ordinarily be used as being synonymous with 'procedure' or 'ritual' . . . [But where there is] a solemn change of status, it does seem to me that *the word must import a degree of formality and at least the involvement of some agency, whether lay or religious, of or recognised by the state, having a function that is more than simply probative.*[78]

Even the involvement of a court that simply records whether the divorce is revocable or not, and lacks any independent power to grant or refuse a decree, is sufficient to amount to proceedings for present purposes.[79]

Purely administrative divorces, such as those available in Denmark,[80] clearly fall within the scope of section 46(1). The involvement of State officials – albeit that they are not judges – coupled with the proper recording and certification of the divorce puts it beyond doubt that such dissolution meets the requirements of this subsection. That said, the involvement of religious figures or religious institutions should not, *per se*, be taken to make the divorce a 'proceedings divorce'.[81]

3 Overseas decrees obtained otherwise than by means of proceedings

As already noted, there exist throughout the world a great many different means by which a divorce may be obtained.[82] Some of these – especially those available in some parts of the Middle East and Asia – are highly informal. Thus, in some countries, a divorce may be obtained by nothing more than a unilateral declaration by one of the parties (usually the husband). A good example of such a divorce is the bare *talaq* that is used in a number of

[77] [1984] 3 All ER 1017.

[78] *Ibid*, at 1030–1031 (emphasis added).

[79] *El Fadl v El Fadl* [2000] 1 FLR 175.

[80] See also, eg, *Manning v Manning* [1958] P 112.

[81] Compare the designation of a Jewish *ghet* as a 'proceedings divorce' because of the necessary and active participation of the rabbinical court (*Berkovits v Grinberg* [1995] 2 All ER 681) with the religious conversion of one spouse that carries with it a repudiation of the marriage (*Viswalingham v Viswalingham* [1979] 1 FLR 15).

[82] There are far fewer instances of non-proceedings legal separations and non-proceedings annulments, but they do exist (see, eg, *Connelly v Connelly* (1851) 7 Moo PCC 438 (extra-judicial separation) and *Butterley v Butterley* (1974) 48 DLR (3d) 351 (extra-judicial annulment)) and the Family Law Act 1986 makes suitable provision for them.

Muslim countries[83] and which, unlike the *talaq* pronounced in *Quazi v Quazi*, requires no more for it to be effective than that the husband should utter the words 'I divorce you' three times with the intention of repudiating the marriage.[84] In other countries, such as Japan and Thailand,[85] consensual divorces can be obtained which require only that the spouses agree to the divorce. Whether unilateral or consensual in nature, informal divorces involve no State or religious figures so as to bring them within the category of 'proceedings divorces'.

Under section 46(2) of the Family Law Act 1986, the rules governing the recognition of non-proceedings divorces are considerably more restrictive than those applicable to proceedings divorces. There are three main reasons why this is so (although not all of them apply to consensual divorces). First, as a one-time Lord Chancellor pointed out, unilateral non-proceedings divorces tend to be 'informal [and] arbitrary' with the consequence that, being 'almost exclusively obtained by men against women . . . [they] discriminate against women'.[86] Secondly, such divorces also have the capacity to offend our sense of natural justice. For in the case of bare *talaqs*, there is no requirement that the relevant words be enunciated in the presence of the wife;[87] she has no right of reply or defence. Finally, *all* non-proceedings divorces are apt to give rise to problems of proof since there is often no requirement that the divorce be witnessed or recorded in any way.

Whether these objections constitute sufficient reasons to adopt a more stringent approach to the recognition of overseas non-proceedings divorces is, however, questionable. Indeed, we shall in due course examine the extent to which they are in fact convincing. But first, we must consider the way in which the requirements for the recognition of non-proceedings divorces differ from those applicable in relation to judicial and administrative divorces.

Under section 46(2) of the Act, the validity of an overseas divorce obtained otherwise than by means of proceedings will presumptively be recognised if two conditions are met. First, the divorce must be effective under the law of the country in which it was obtained. Secondly, on the date of the divorce, *either* both spouses must have been domiciled in that country, *or* one spouse must have been domiciled there while the other was domiciled in another country in which the divorce was recognised. Recognition will be denied

[83] Eg, Kashmir (see *Chaudhary v Chaudhary* [1984] 3 All ER 1017), Dubai (see *Zaal v Zaal* (1983) 4 FLR 284) and Iraq (see *Sharif v Sharif* [1980] *Family Law* 216).

[84] The divorce may also be in written form, but in such a case it is properly referred to as a *talaqnama*.

[85] See, eg, *Varanand v Varanand* (1964) 108 *SJ* 693; *Ratanachai v Ratanachai* [1960] CLY 480.

[86] Lord Hailsham, *Hansard*, HL Deb, Vol 473, col 1082 (22 April 1986).

[87] See *Zaal v Zaal* (1983) 4 FLR 284. See also *R v Secretary of State for the Home Department, ex p Fatima* [1986] AC 527 where the wife was in Pakistan and the husband in England.

only if one of the grounds for refusing recognition (considered below) is satisfied, or if either of the spouses was habitually resident in the United Kingdom throughout the year prior to the date on which the divorce was obtained.

For the purposes of the recognition of non-proceedings divorces, it will be noted that domicile is the sole connecting factor between the parties and the country or countries in which the divorce would be valid that is countenanced. This is the source of at least two potential problems. To begin with, just as in relation to proceedings divorces, the term 'domicile' may be interpreted either according to its English meaning or that attributed to it under the law of the country in which the divorce is obtained.[88] As such, both parties may be domiciled in country X (according to the law of domicile in country X). But what happens if one of the parties is, according to the English concept of domicile, domiciled not in country X, but in this country? According to a straightforward reading of the Act, it should be of no significance that one of the spouses was regarded as an English domiciliary under English law, so long as that party was equally regarded as a domiciliary of country X (or any other country in which the divorce would be effective) according to the relevant foreign law. It is submitted that an English judge faced with this problem ought to adopt the literal interpretation set out here, for it accords not only with the cardinal rule of statutory interpretation, but also with the most significant policy objective in this area – the avoidance of limping marriages.

The second problem associated with the requirement that the divorce be valid according to the law of both parties' domicile is that a divorce may be recognised even though the form of divorce in question would not be valid according to the law of the parties' nationality or habitual residence. Given that domicile has the capacity to comprise a less substantial connection with any particular country than either nationality or habitual residence,[89] it seems an odd connection to insist upon for the purposes of recognising non-proceedings divorces. This is especially so given that the main recognition rules contained in section 46(1) do not suggest any obvious primacy of a connection based on domicile.

4 Transnational divorces

A third class of divorces, not specifically referred to in the 1986 Act, requires discussion here. It concerns what are generally referred to as 'transnational' divorces – that is, divorces that are obtained partly in this country and partly abroad. Divorces obtained by a Muslim *talaq* of the kind that featured in *Quazi v Quazi*, or a Jewish *ghet*, are particularly apt to fall into this

[88] Family Law Act 1986, s 46(5).

[89] See, eg, *Bowie (or Ramsay) v Liverpool Royal Infirmary* [1930] AC 588.

category. This is because they can both involve a religious element[90] that takes place in one country with a further, mainly administrative element[91] that takes place in a another. The problem in such cases centres on determining the country in which the divorce is actually obtained. And this can be crucial for two reasons. First, regardless of whether the divorce is of the proceedings or non-proceedings variety, the statute requires in either case that it be 'effective under the law of the country in which it was obtained'.[92] Secondly – but only in the context of a divorce begun in this country – section 44(1) of the Family Law Act 1986 may be relevant, providing as it does that 'no divorce obtained in any part of the British Isles is regarded as effective unless it is granted by a court of civil jurisdiction'.[93] In both instances, it is critical to determine whether the country in which the divorce is begun, or the country in which it is completed, constitutes the country in which it is 'obtained'. For the purposes of further analysis of this issue, it is necessary once again, to draw the distinction between proceedings divorces and non-proceedings divorces.

(a) Transnational divorces obtained by means of proceedings So far as proceedings divorces are concerned, the problem may be confined to those divorces obtained extra-judicially. This is because no difficulty arises in identifying the country in which the divorce was obtained where it takes the form of a judicial decree. Only proceedings divorces of the kind in *Quazi v Quazi* are apt to cause difficulties in this context. Under the old law, one of the conditions of recognition of an overseas proceedings divorce was that the spouse in question must have been a national of the country 'at the date of the institution of the proceedings in the country in which the divorce was obtained'.[94] This requirement was interpreted to mean that the proceedings must have been begun and completed in the same overseas jurisdiction. It thus followed that a transnational divorce begun in this country and completed in Pakistan could not be granted recognition since the totality of the proceedings did not take place abroad, as the statute required.[95]

[90] Pronouncing the required formula of the *talaq*; writing a *ghet* in accordance with Jewish ecclesiastical law.

[91] In the case of a Pakistani *talaq*, posting the requisite Ordinance notice to the Pakistani authorities; in the case of a *ghet*, delivering the written document to the wife.

[92] *Ibid*, s 46(2)(a).

[93] Family Law Act 1986, s 44(1). For application, see *Sulaiman v Juffali* [2002] 1 FLR 479.

[94] The Recognition of Divorces and Legal Separations Act 1971, s 3.

[95] *R v Secretary of State for the Home Department, ex p Fatima* [1986] AC 527. For the argument that this decision is inconsistent with the Court of Appeal's decision in *Chaudhary v Chaudhary* [1984] 3 All ER 1017, to which no reference was made in *Fatima*, see B. Berkovits, 'Transnational Divorces: The *Fatima* Decision' (1988) 104 *Law Quarterly Review* 60, 68–72.

The wording of the equivalent provisions in the 1986 Act[96] differs somewhat from their 1971 counterparts. Under the 1986 Act, the right to have a foreign divorce recognised for the purposes of English law is in part contingent upon the parties' connection with the foreign jurisdiction – via domicile, habitual residence or nationality – at the date of the commencement of the proceedings.[97] But quite independently, the Act requires also that the divorce be effective in the country in which it was obtained.[98] It does not require, unlike its 1971 predecessor, that the proceedings should be commenced and completed in the same jurisdiction. As such, it could be argued that a transnational divorce of the kind described above could be granted recognition under the 1986 statute.[99] The matter arose directly in *Berkovits v Grinberg.*[100]

In that case, a *ghet* was written according to Jewish ecclesiastical law in London, and subsequently delivered to the wife at a district rabbinical court in Israel. Under local law, it was this formal delivery of the *ghet* that effected a valid divorce. The question of whether the divorce could also be recognised under English law was raised by a judge of the Beth Din[101] in this country who wished to know whether there were any impediments under English law such as to prevent the husband re-marrying here.[102] Notwithstanding the different wording in the 1971 and 1986 Acts, Wall J said:

> In my view, the word 'obtained' connotes a process rather than a single act. To obtain a divorce a party must go through a process, in the same way that a person obtains a university degree or any other qualification. If that process is part of a judicial process (proceedings) and therefore linked to one judicial authority, it seems to me there is logic and sense in saying that the proceedings must begin and end in the same place.[103]

[96] Family Law Act 1986, s 46(3).

[97] *Ibid*, s 46(1)(b), (3)

[98] *Ibid*, s 46(1)(a).

[99] Berkovits, *op cit* n 95, at 79–80; J. Young, 'The Recognition of Extra-Judicial Divorces in the United Kingdom' [1987] *Legal Studies* 78, 87. From a policy perspective, too, it can be argued that a failure to recognise such divorces would be to support 'a law which distinguishes very sharply between those Pakistani nationals who can afford to fly to Pakistan to pronounce a *talaq* and send out the notices there and those whose financial resources preclude such [action]' (Poulter, *op cit* n 71, at 256). Furthermore, in *Kellman v Kellman* [2000] 1 FLR 785 it was suggested (*obiter*) that postal divorces are not *per se* repugnant to the conscience of the English courts. As such, there would be little scope for refusing recognition on the basis of public policy under s 51 of the 1986 Act. As Paul Coleridge QC said (at 798): '[t]he mere fact that the decree in this case was obtained via a "mail order divorce" does not, in my judgment, automatically render it manifestly contrary to public policy'.

[100] [1995] Fam 142.

[101] An ecclesiastical court for adherents to Judaism seeking to abide by Jewish law.

[102] Under the Family Law Act 1986, s 55(1)(d) anyone may seek a declaration as to the validity of a divorce obtained outside England and Wales.

[103] [1995] Fam 142, at 157.

This decision has been interpreted to mean that, in future, no transnational divorce obtained by means of proceedings will be recognised under the Family Law Act 1986.[104] But this may be too sweeping a conclusion; for it is certainly arguable that the level and language of the decision combine to leave scope for genuine doubt. Being only a first instance decision, it is of course technically open to a future court to depart from Wall J's decision. Furthermore, the excerpted words suggest a narrow judgment. Wall J insisted that the proceedings must begin and end in the same place only where the divorce involves 'a judicial process . . . linked to one judicial authority'. Thus, while the involvement of the Israeli Beth Din would bring a transnational *ghet* within the rule, the involvement of a non-judicial body – for example, the arbitration council in *Quazi v Quazi* – would exclude from the rule Ordinance *talaqs* and other such divorces.

(b) Transnational divorces obtained otherwise than by proceedings Besides the 'bare *talaq*' described above, there are other kinds of informal marriage dissolution that would fit the description of a divorce obtained otherwise than by way of proceedings. One example is the Muslim *khula* which is a kind of consensual divorce arsing out of the wife's suggestion that the parties should separate. In such a case, it is conceivable that a wife living in country X (but domiciled in country Y) may write to her estranged husband still resident and domiciled in country Y suggesting a divorce. Since such *khula* divorces require the parties' agreement, the divorce would become effective upon the husband's acceptance of the wife's suggestion by pronouncing the word *khul*. By analogy with conventional contract law rules, the parties' agreement would be completed – and, hence, the divorce would be obtained – in the place where acceptance occurred.[105] Assuming that country Y permits such divorces, the *khula* would warrant recognition by an English court subject to its statutory discretion to refuse recognition (considered below). But assuming recognition would be granted, there would be an apparent inconsistency in the law in that a transnational *khula* would be recognised while a transnational *ghet* (involving considerably more formality) would not.[106]

5 Discretionary refusals of recognition

Outside the Brussels IIA regime, the bases on which a British Isles or overseas divorce may be denied recognition by the English courts are all contained in section 51 of the Family Law Act 1986. Each of these grounds,

[104] See A. Reed, 'Extra-Judicial Divorces Since *Berkovits*' [1996] *Family Law* 100, at 102.

[105] *Entores Ltd v Miles Far East Corporation* [1955] 2 All ER 493.

[106] The response that there would be no inconsistency – since the *ghet* is unilateral whereas the *khula* is consensual – can itself be met by the reply that even the Jewish *ghet* requires the wife's co-operation and compliance in attending her local Beth Din.

unlike their Article 22 counterparts in Brussels IIA, invests the court with a discretion (but no obligation) to refuse recognition.

(a) Recognition inconsistent with an earlier judgment Recognition of a British Isles or overseas divorce may be refused if it was obtained at a time when it was irreconcilable with a prior decision of an English court dissolving or annulling the marriage,[107] or if it was irreconcilable with any equivalent decision of a foreign court whose decree is, or would be, recognised in England.[108] Just as with the equivalent provisions in Brussels IIA considered earlier,[109] the Act here seeks to relieve the English court of the need to recognise the dissolution or annulment of a marriage that has already ceased to subsist in the eyes of English law. In practice, these are likely to be relatively uncontroversial grounds of refusal since they are premised upon the widely accepted principle of *res judicata*.

(b) No subsisting marriage in the eyes of English law Unlike the previous ground, which requires there to be a prior court decision by virtue of which the marriage in question ceased to exist in the eyes of English law, this second ground for refusing recognition relates to divorces and legal separations[110] granted or obtained at a time when, according to English law – including English private international law – there would have been no subsisting marriage to dissolve. There is obviously some overlap between this and the preceding ground, but this ground extends to the non-recognition of extra-judicial divorces as well as to cases in which the marriage was never previously annulled or dissolved but is simply void *ab initio* in the eyes of English law (for example, through lack of capacity to marry).

(c) Violation of natural justice The Family Law Act 1986 provides two natural justice-based grounds upon which an overseas divorce or legal separation obtained by way of proceedings may be denied recognition. The first of these applies where the dissolution or separation was obtained:

> without such steps having been taken for giving notice of the proceedings to a party to the marriage as, having regard to the nature of the proceedings and all the circumstances, should reasonably have been taken.[111]

As with all the grounds in section 51, this one is discretionary. Accordingly, a failure to take steps to supply notice of the relevant proceedings will not lead automatically to a refusal of recognition. And this is so even if, in all

[107] See, eg, *Vervaeke v Smith* [1983] 1 AC 145.
[108] Family Law Act 1986, s 51(1).
[109] Arts 15(1)(c), (d).
[110] But not annulments.
[111] Family Law Act 1986, s 51(3)(a)(i).

the circumstances, such steps should have been taken.[112] Indeed, case-law seems to indicate that this discretionary refusal of recognition will be exercised only sparingly, the general requirement being a *fundamental* breach of natural justice.[113] To some extent, this approach can be justified by reference to the fact that the court is specifically required to have regard to the nature of the foreign proceedings. For where the foreign law does not require much effort to be made to ensure proper provision of notice, the divorce will have been obtained in full compliance with the local law (albeit contrary to the English notion of natural justice). On the other hand, the courts must take account of all the circumstances, so even if there is compliance with the local law, the English courts may still deny recognition if the local rules are themselves considered to be unreasonable. As Balcombe J put it in *Sabbagh v Sabbagh* – a case in which a wife in England received no notice of her husband's appeal in Brazil against an initially unsuccessful application for a decree of separation there: 'it cannot be sufficient merely to comply with local procedure, otherwise the provisions of the Act would be nugatory'.[114]

The second natural justice ground for refusing recognition to an overseas divorce or legal separation may be invoked where the dissolution or separation has been obtained:

> without a party to the marriage having been given (for any reason other than lack of notice) such opportunity to take part in the proceedings as, having regard to those matters he should reasonably have been given.[115]

At the heart of this ground is the concern that the respondent has unjustly been denied the opportunity to take part in the relevant matrimonial proceedings. In practice, it is only very occasionally invoked,[116] and consequently does not require detailed discussion here. However, it is perhaps worth noting that the opportunity to participate for these purposes does not necessarily involve the respondent having the opportunity to be present in court:[117] the

[112] See, eg, *Sabbagh v Sabbagh* [1985] FLR 29.

[113] *B v B (Divorce: Northern Cyprus)* [2000] 2 FLR 707, at 715 *per* Judge Compston. However, on the facts, since the British Government did not recognise the Turkish Republic of Northern Cyprus, the English court would not recognise a divorce granted there.

[114] [1985] FLR 29, at 33. See also the *obiter dictum* in *D v D* [1994] 1 FLR 38, at 53 *per* Wall J.

[115] Family Law Act 1986, s 51(3)(a)(ii).

[116] For examples in relation to substantially the same provision in s 8 of the Recognition of Divorces and Legal Separations Act 1971, see *Joyce v Joyce* [1979] Fam 93 and *Newmarch v Newmarch* [1978] 1 All ER 1. In both cases, wives in England were denied the opportunity to participate in foreign proceedings despite receiving notice of those proceedings and communicating their desire to contest them before the relevant judicial authorities. But notwithstanding the injustice in the latter case, the court declined to exercise its discretion in favour of non-recognition.

[117] *Sabbagh v Sabbagh* [1985] FLR 29.

chance simply to have one's views put before the court may well suffice.[118] Thus, in one case, a mere five days notice of foreign nullity proceedings was held to provide the respondent with an adequate opportunity to participate.[119]

It is also worth stressing that the opportunity to participate in the proceedings is not to be construed narrowly by reference purely to temporal or geographical factors. Rather, it must be an 'effective opportunity'.[120] As such, while the opportunity for physical presence in court may not be required in every case, it may nonetheless be critical in others. Thus, the court may sometimes take account of the fact that respondent cannot afford to travel abroad to attend the relevant proceedings; and this may well be a relevant consideration in determining whether there was a sufficient lack of opportunity to participate.[121] Furthermore, where the reason why the respondent cannot afford to do this is the petitioner's default in making maintenance payments, even greater weight can be attached to this factor.[122]

The final point to note in this context is that the nature of the proceedings in question is also probably relevant.[123] As such, the lack of opportunity to participate in the essentially administrative proceedings that accompany certain non-judicial divorces (such as the Pakistani *talaq*) may well be treated differently from the want of opportunity to participate in judicial proceedings in a court of civil jurisdiction. Thus, in *El Fadl v El Fadl*[124] it was observed that even if the wife had been granted such an opportunity in the context of a *talaq* divorce, it would have made absolutely no difference to the conduct or outcome of the proceedings.

(d) Absence of official certification in non-proceedings divorces An overseas divorce, annulment or separation obtained otherwise than by means of proceedings may be denied recognition where there is no official document certifying that it is effective under the law of the country where it was obtained *or*, if appropriate, where there is no official document certifying

[118] *Joyce v Joyce* [1979] Fam 93, at 111 *per* Lane J.

[119] In *Law v Gustin* [1976] Fam 155, Bagnall J did not explain why the requirements had been met. He said simply (at 159): '[w]ith some hesitation I have reached the conclusion that I ought to find that sufficient notice was given and that the decree cannot be criticised on the basis of natural justice'.

[120] *Joyce v Joyce* [1979] Fam 93, at 111 *per* Lane J.

[121] *Mamdani v Mamdani* [1984] FLR 699.

[122] *Joyce v Joyce* [1979] Fam 93. A similar approach was taken in a case in which the wife was prevented from travelling because the husband had held onto her passport: *Sharif v Sharif* [1980] *Family Law* 216.

[123] In relation to the lack of notice provision in s 51(3)(a)(i) this is made explicit. By contrast, under the present provision (s 51(3)(a)(ii)), the court is somewhat cryptically required to have regard to 'those matters'. It seems probable that what is implied is 'those matters *adumbrated in the previous sub-paragraph*'.

[124] [2000] 1 FLR 175.

that a divorce obtained in one foreign country would be recognised as valid under the law of a second foreign country (the latter being the country in which either of the parties was domiciled).[125] In the context of this ground for non-recognition, an 'official' document is one that has been 'issued by a person or body appointed or recognised for the purpose under [the relevant] law'.[126] But it must be borne in mind that the statute confers merely a discretion to refuse recognition on this basis. It is entirely possible that expert evidence as to the validity of the divorce in question would suffice to persuade a court not to refuse recognition.[127]

(e) Divorces contrary to public policy It has already been noted at several points that the core policy consideration in the context of the recognition of foreign divorces is the desire to avoid the creation of limping marriages. Naturally, this concern points towards a strong presumption that overseas divorces should be recognised wherever possible, but does not support a rule of law according to which *all* foreign divorces will be recognised by the English courts. Indeed, there may sometimes be even stronger policy considerations that pull in the opposite direction and justify the refusal of recognition. Provision for such countervailing considerations is made in the 1986 Act in the shape of section 51(3)(c) which provides for the refusal of recognition on the basis that the divorce in question would be 'manifestly contrary to public policy'.

Because this ground is so open-textured, it is impossible to set out definitively all the kinds of case in respect of which it might be invoked. Nonetheless, some guidance as to its potential use can be gleaned from a variety of sources. To begin with, Rees J once said generally in relation to the equivalent provision in the previous law that:

> [t]his court should have regard to all the surrounding circumstances which would include a full investigation of the facts relied upon to support a refusal of recognition; the likely consequences if the petitioning spouse had been given the opportunity to take part in the proceedings; an assessment of what the legitimate objectives of the petitioning spouse are, and to what extent those objectives can be achieved if the foreign decree remains valid, and what the likely consequences to the spouses and any children of the family would be if recognition were refused.[128]

Secondly, it is also possible to make a somewhat more specific observation. This is that the qualification 'manifestly' makes it clear that this residual

[125] Family Law Act 1986, s 51(3)(b).

[126] *Ibid*, s 51(4).

[127] See, eg, *Wicken v Wicken* [1999] Fam 224: evidence of the validity of a Gambian divorce was supplied by a former Gambian Attorney-General.

[128] *Newmarch v Newmarch* [1978] Fam 79, at 95.

ground for non-recognition cannot be at all lightly invoked.[129] Minor offence to domestic standards and inhibitions are plainly an insufficient basis upon which to invoke this ground. As Carter has explained: '[t]he automatic injection of standards applicable in a domestic situation may be seen, at best as an exercise in mechanical jurisprudence, and at worst as blatant judicial chauvinism.'[130]

Thirdly, still further insight into the use of this ground may be gleaned from two illustrative cases (albeit that one of them was decided under the equivalent provision in the 1971 Act). In the leading case of *Kendall v Kendall*,[131] for example, the wife was duped into signing various documents written in Spanish that she was not proficient enough to read. She was told by both her husband and by Bolivian lawyers that the documents were to facilitate her removing her children from Bolivia. In truth, however, they conferred a power of attorney upon the Bolivian lawyers and enabled them to commence divorce proceedings on her behalf without her knowledge. The court itself was also deceived. Various witnesses supplied bogus evidence to the effect that they had seen the wife assaulted by the husband. The court duly granted a divorce to the wife, but when the wife discovered what had happened she sought a declaration as to the status of the Bolivian decree. Hollings J declined to recognise its validity on the basis that it would have been manifestly contrary to public policy to do so. In coming to this decision, he was mindful of the catalogue of deceptions and untruths in the case.

As the facts illustrate, *Kendall v Kendall* was a truly singular case. But not only is it factually unique, it is also exceptional in being the only reported case in which a foreign decree has been denied recognition on the statutory ground that it was manifestly contrary to public policy. More commonly, in other cases involving fraud, the courts have held that the decrees thereby obtained were not sufficiently offensive to public policy to warrant a refusal of recognition. For example, in *Eroglu v Eroglu*,[132] the fact that both parties had deceived the Turkish court into granting them a divorce of convenience was not enough to persuade the English court that it should be denied recognition.[133]

Finally, there are certain cases decided under the broadly equivalent, but now superseded,[134] principles of common law that may provide additional

[129] Particular stress was placed on this adverb in *Kellman v Kellman* [2000] 1 FLR 785, at 798 *per* Paul Coleridge QC (sitting as a deputy judge of the High Court).

[130] P.B. Carter, 'The Role of Public Policy in English Private International Law' (1993) 42 *International and Comparative Law Quarterly* 1, 2.

[131] [1977] Fam 208.

[132] [1994] 2 FLR 287.

[133] See also *Bater v Bater* [1906] P 209 for an equivalent approach under the old common law.

[134] The Family Law Act 1986, s 45(1), (2) provides that the statutory rules governing the recognition of foreign divorces are exclusive rules (so long as Brussels IIA does not apply).

guidance as to the kinds of circumstances in which the courts may now decline to recognise a foreign divorce on the basis of public policy.[135] In *Gray v Formosa*,[136] for example, it was held that the English courts had a discretion to refuse recognition to a Maltese nullity decree that had been granted purely on the basis that the parties had married in an English register office rather than in a Roman Catholic church. Lord Denning MR captured the offence associated with the recognition of this decree in the following passage:

> I am content to decide this case on the simple basis that the courts of this country are not compelled to recognise the decree of the court of another country when it offends against our ideas of justice and this decree, in my judgment, does so offend. I do not think these courts are bound to declare this English marriage no marriage.[137]

It is submitted that, if the English courts were in the future asked to recognise a foreign nullity decree at the heart of which was a foreign conflicts rule that denied recognition to a marriage properly contracted according to the law of this country, it is probable that recognition would now be refused under section 51 of the Family Law Act 1986. The request for recognition in this country would fail for want of 'substantial justice', an old common law concept.[138] Similarly, if a foreign decree were to be obtained by duress, it seems probable that the English court would again draw on the former common law,[139] and translate what was then another want of substantial justice into the modern requirement of an offence to public policy.[140]

In the light of the foregoing paragraphs we may conclude that the scope to refuse recognition on the basis of public policy is a sort of necessary evil. It is necessary because the recognition rules in section 46 are both rigid in nature and broad in scope making the need for an 'escape route' in exceptional cases almost inevitable. However, the public policy exception is also an evil (or, at least, a potential evil) in the sense that its use or abuse forms an obvious basis for accusations of inherent ethnocentrism and other prejudices on the part of the English judiciary.[141] Conscious of this problem, one High Court judge recently issued the reminder that 'our courts should

[135] For a host of examples, see North & Fawcett, *op cit* n 3, pp 814–816.

[136] [1963] P 259.

[137] *Ibid*, at 269.

[138] See, eg, *Gray v Formosa* [1963] P 259, at 268 *per* Lord Denning MR.

[139] *Re Meyer* [1971] P 298 (the divorce in question was forced upon the German spouses in this case by the Nazi authorities).

[140] For the argument that the two concepts are synonymous, see Carter, *op cit* n 130, at 5.

[141] See A. Mayss, 'Recognition of Foreign Divorces: Unacceptable Ethnocentrism' in J. Murphy (ed), *Ethnic Minorities, Their Families and the Law* (Oxford: Hart Publishing, 2000).

accept the conscientiously held but very different standards of another [country] where they are applied'. As such, this ground will probably remain one that is invoked far more frequently by hopeful litigants than one that is actually used to veto recognition of a foreign divorce by the English courts.[142]

6 Retrospective Foreign Annulments

As we have already noted, the rules governing the recognition of foreign nullity decrees are the same as those governing the recognition of foreign divorces and legal separations.[143] And this is so whether the relevant recognition principles are those contained in Brussels IIA or those in section 46 of the Family Law Act 1986. As such, references throughout this chapter have been made simply to foreign divorces rather than, cumbersomely, to divorces, annulments and legal separations *except* where context has required a higher level of specification. Yet notwithstanding the fact that the actual recognition rules are identical for all matrimonial causes, there is nonetheless one matter that arises in connection with the recognition of retrospectively effective foreign nullity decrees that warrants particular consideration here.

The issue centres on the fact that a foreign nullity decree with retrospective effect may lead to an unavoidable conflict within English law. The point can be clarified by reference to *Vervaeke v Smith*.[144] In that case, the petitioner (a Belgian national) married her first husband in England. The marriage was entirely contrived, being contracted simply so that the petitioner could acquire UK citizenship by virtue of the marriage and thus continue working in this country. Without ever divorcing, the petitioner married another gentleman who died intestate. In an attempt to succeed to his estate, she petitioned in this country for an annulment of the first marriage on the basis of the absence of genuine consent. The court dismissed the petition and held the first marriage to be valid under English law. Undaunted, she sought and obtained a nullity decree in Belgium,[145] and later still sought recognition of that decree before the English courts. The difficulty with these proceedings was that the English court was being asked to recognise a Belgian decree (based on the absence of consent) that would have retrospectively required the very same marriage that Ormrod J had previously held to be valid[146] to be treated as void *ab initio* for the purposes

[142] *El Fadl v El Fadl* [2000] 1 FLR 175, at 190 *per* Hughes J.

[143] One difference relating to *non-recognition* exists under s 51 of the Family Law Act 1986 (see above).

[144] [1983] 1 AC 145.

[145] Under the Belgian conflicts rules according to which Belgian (not English) law was the applicable law.

[146] But note that the marriage was only valid according to English law. Under Belgian law, a decree declaring the marriage to be void *ab initio* means that for Belgian purposes, the marriage never existed. As such, the decree occasions no change

of English law.[147] Lord Diplock captured the point succinctly when he explained:

> [the petitioner] was seeking to obtain from the High Court in England a judgment the effect of which would be to declare that her cause of action for a decree of nullity based on absence of consent was well founded despite the existence of the final and conclusive Ormrod judgment to the contrary.[148]

The solution provided in the case by the House of Lords was not entirely satisfactory, for it was premised upon a cause of action estoppel whereby the Ormrod judgment was final and prevented their Lordships recognising the decree in question. But such an approach does not lend itself to the situation in which a marriage is valid according to English law, but its validity has never been judicially confirmed. Several writers have wisely suggested that the best solution to such cases is to treat the relevant foreign decree as a valid termination of the marriage but to deny it retrospective effect. To do otherwise, they caution, would be to allow the status of the parties to be determined by a foreign rule of law rather than an equally tenable English one.[149]

While these observations may well be founded, it is important to keep a sense of practical importance in all of this. At least three reasons can be cited that tend to reduce the significance of the problem just considered. In the first place, it is important to bear in mind that divorce is nowadays nearly always the preferred means of terminating a marriage with the consequence that there are far fewer potentially problematic foreign annulments than in years gone by. Secondly, even if recognition of a foreign nullity decree would require it to be given retrospective effect by the English courts, this does not necessarily mean that any practical difficulties will arise. This is because it is only where rights contingent upon a change of status are at stake that the contradiction within the English context becomes truly significant. Finally, the potential problems associated with giving retrospective effect to a foreign nullity decree will be strictly limited to those cases in which the marriage would not also be regarded as void *ab initio* under the English conflicts rules. In *Salvesen v Administrator of Austrian Property*,[150] for example, the English court recognised a German nullity decree declaring

---

of status in Belgium whereas the *recognition of the decree in England* does imply a change of status under English law. For further analysis, see A.J.E. Jaffey, '*Vervaeke v Smith*' (1983) 32 *International and Comparative Law Quarterly* 500, esp 502–505.

[147] There can be no doubt that the English courts would normally apply retrospective effect to a foreign nullity decree that declares the marriage to be void *ab initio*: *Salvesen v Administrator of Austrian Property* [1927] AC 641.

[148] *Vervaeke v Smith* [1983] 1 AC 145, at 160.

[149] See, eg, Jaffey, *op cit* n 146, at 502; Clarkson & Hill, *op cit* n 17, p 427.

[150] [1927] AC 641.

a twenty-seven-year Austrian marriage to be void *ab initio*. But no problem arose when the English courts recognising the retrospective effect of this decree since the marriage would also have been regarded as void *ab initio* under English conflicts rules.

Conclusions and critique

As we have seen, the rules relating to the acquisition and recognition of foreign divorces fall into two broad categories: those falling within the Brussels IIA regime and those governed by domestic legislation. While the objectives of the two systems are broadly similar – to remove possible jurisdictional confusion and to provide for the general recognition of divorces obtained abroad – there is a notable contrast between them. Under Brussels IIA – whether in relation to the staying proceedings or the recognition of decrees – the relevant rules are characterised by inflexibility. By contrast, the equivalent rules under the Domicile and Matrimonial Proceedings Act 1973 and under the Family Law Act 1986 contain a good deal of discretion. One possible explanation for this divergence is that the Brussels IIA rules are as much linked to a broader European project concerning closer integration and harmonisation as they are to the desire to meet a particular need within international family law.[151] Yet even though Brussels IIA may well be welcome as a further step in the Europeanisation of family law[152] it nonetheless suffers from a number of well-documented practical defects, chief among which is the fact that it may cause spouses to race to a forum of choice rather than to devote efforts towards reconciliation or conciliation.[153]

Turning to the more specific matter of the rules governing the recognition of foreign divorces, it is to be noted that the primary rules in both Brussels IIA and the Family Law Act 1986 are rigid in nature, and point generally towards the recognition of foreign decrees. Indeed, any measure of flexibility is only observable in the secondary rules that govern the refusal of recognition. Both Brussels IIA and the Act provide for refusal of recognition on grounds of public policy. Yet the inclusion of such a ground invites the familiar objections associated with the invocation of public policy in the private international law context.[154] This is perhaps a pity since history

[151] See, eg, C. McGlynn, 'A Family Law for the European Union?' in J. Shaw (ed), *Social Law and Policy in an Evolving European Union* (Oxford: Hart Publishing, 2000), O. Remien, 'European Private International Law, the European Community and its Emerging Area of Freedom, Security and Justice' (2001) 38 *Common Market Law Review* 55 and McEleavy, *op cit* n 16.

[152] I have borrowed this phrase from C. McGlynn, 'The Europeanisation of Family Law' [2001] *Child and Family Law Quarterly* 35.

[153] See, eg, Mostyn, *op cit* n 16, Truex, *op cit* n 11 and Karsten, *op cit* n 16.

[154] See Carter, *op cit* n 130 and ch 4 of this work.

would suggest that the need for a public policy ground is at the very least questionable. In the one case in which this ground has actually been invoked successfully,[155] it is at least arguable that the same result could have been achieved on the basis that the wife was denied an opportunity to participate in the proceedings. Recalling also the reluctance with which the courts would invoke the common law equivalent – a want of substantial justice – one might seriously question whether the presence of this ground in both the statute and Brussels IIA is apt to do more harm (albeit symbolic harm) than good.

Also in relation to the grounds for refusing recognition, we might similarly ask whether there is any justification for retaining the facility to deny recognition to a foreign divorce obtained otherwise than by means of proceedings on the basis that there has been no official certification of the divorce. It has already been noted that the lack of proof of a non-proceedings divorce might offend some observers, but it is to be doubted whether this is an adequate basis on which to deny such divorces recognition altogether.[156] Indeed, what this ground seems to overlook is the fact that many of those countries in which non-proceedings divorces are available are developing nations in respect of which it may be unreasonable to expect the parties to seek institutional certification of their divorces.

Finally, it is perhaps worth remarking that the continuing insistence in this country on 'domicile' as a jurisdictional connecting factor has very little to ground it. Domicile features not only in relation to the jurisdiction rules but also, somewhat anachronistically, in relation to the recognition rules.[157] In an age in which migration is remarkably common, it seems much better to ground both jurisdictional and recognition rules primarily on the more meaningful connection of habitual residence. The replacement of domicile with habitual residence in the context of jurisdiction rules would bring this country further into line with the connecting factors used in a sizeable number of international family law instruments (not just Brussels IIA), and would in all probability make little practical difference to our substantive law.[158]

[155] *Kendall v Kendall* [1977] Fam 208.

[156] See J. Young, *op cit* n 99, at 81–83. See also North & Fawcett, *op cit* n 3, pp 799–800.

[157] For further inadequacies of 'domicile' see P.B. Carter, 'Domicil: The Case for Radical Reform in the United Kingdom' (1987) 36 *International and Comparative Law Quarterly* 713. See also R. Fentiman, 'Activity in the Law of Status: Domicile, Marriage and the Law Commission' (1986) 6 *Oxford Journal of Legal Studies* 353.

[158] This is not to say that the concepts of nationality and habitual residence are problem free: see, eg, the difficulty in establishing the country/countries of habitual residence in *Ikimi v Ikimi (Divorce: Habitual Residence)* [2001] 1 FLR 913.

6

Financial relief, matrimonial property and succession

Although in one sense financial relief, matrimonial property and succession rules are fairly distant cousins – some apply upon the breakdown of a relationship, while others apply upon death – there is also a sense in which they are connected. This link inheres in the fact that they all generally involve one family member acquiring money or property that formerly belonged to another family member. In the light of this connection, and mindful of the fact that the law relating to families is the organising theme around which the various issues covered in this book are centred, each of these sets of rules is examined in this chapter. On the other hand, there is no discussion of the more general rules concerning the transfer of property *inter vivos* and of trusts. For these rules are of much greater generality and bear only a limited connection to a book concerned with family law.[1]

Financial relief

In the first section of this chapter we are concerned with the making and recognition of orders for financial support as well as those relating to rights in the matrimonial home and other matrimonial property. For convenience, however, we shall simply refer to them all as orders for financial relief (save where context requires greater specificity). More particularly, we shall address the three main issues that arise in this context: the *general jurisdiction* of the English courts to grant such relief, the jurisdiction of the English

[1] Those interested in the private international law rules concerning these subjects should consult more general works on the conflict of laws such as P.M. North & J.J. Fawcett, *Cheshire and North's Private International Law* (London: Butterworths, 1999) Part VI and J.G. Collier, *Conflict of Laws* (Cambridge: Cambridge University Press, 2001) chs 14, 17.

courts to grant such orders *following a foreign decree* of divorce, nullity or legal separation, and the recognition of foreign financial relief orders.

In relation to the general question of jurisdiction, matters are complicated where the second State involved is a member of the European Union or EFTA. As far as the European Union is concerned, despite the long title of Brussels IIA[2] proclaiming it to be a Regulation 'concerning jurisdiction and the recognition and enforcement of judgments in matrimonial matters', it is clear that it does not apply in this context since it also specifically provides that 'this Regulation . . . should not deal with issues such as the grounds for divorce, *property consequences of the marriage or any other ancillary matters*'.[3] On the other hand, the earlier Regulation, Brussels I,[4] is applicable to 'matters relating to maintenance'; and it makes no difference whether the maintenance to be paid is maintenance during the subsistence of a marriage or following a divorce or annulment.[5]

As regards EFTA states, identical jurisdictional provision to that contained in Brussels I is made in the Lugano Convention 1989;[6] and this latter instrument received the force of law in this country by virtue of the Civil Jurisdiction and Judgments Act 1991.[7] In both Brussels I and the Lugano Convention, the term 'maintenance' is undefined. However, case law indicates that it will be construed broadly so as to encompass not only orders for periodical payments,[8] but also orders for property transfer and lump-sum payment orders *so long as* their purpose is to ensure that a former spouse is thereby maintained.[9] As such, where they apply,[10] Brussels I and the Lugano Convention supersede the traditional rules governing the jurisdiction of the English courts over most ancillary relief matters[11] as well as other financial relief sought during the currency of a marriage.

[2] Council Regulation (EC) No 2201/2003.

[3] *Ibid*, Recital 8.

[4] Council Regulation (EC) No 44/2001.

[5] *Ibid*, Art 5(2).

[6] Art 5(2).

[7] Where a European State is both a member of the EU and EFTA, Art 54B of the Lugano Convention spells out which instrument is to apply.

[8] These are clearly covered: see, eg, *De Cavel v De Cavel* [1980] 3 CMLR 1.

[9] *Van den Boogaard v Laumen* [1997] QB 759. Where a lump-sum payment arises out of a division of matrimonial property, it would probably be inapt to construe it as maintenance.

[10] Brussels I and the Lugano Convention operate only where one or both parties meet one of the specified connections with the Member State in whose courts a maintenance order is sought. These are considered below.

[11] Art 5(2) of both the Regulation and the Lugano Convention makes applicability contingent upon the existence of other 'proceedings concerning the status of a person'. This contingency presumably does not include judicial separation proceedings. Cf the view expressed in North & Fawcett, *op cit* n 1, p 842.

General jurisdiction of the English courts

English courts have the power to grant financial relief in three circumstances. They may do so wherever they possess jurisdiction to grant a decree of divorce, nullity or legal separation.[12] They may also do so during the subsistence of a marriage (where one spouse is failing properly to maintain the other), and they may finally make an order for financial relief where they are called upon to recognise a foreign decree of divorce, nullity or legal separation. We consider each of these situations in turn.

1 Relief ancillary to an English decree of divorce, etc

When an English court grants a decree of divorce, nullity or judicial separation, it also has jurisdiction to make a variety of financial relief awards for the benefit of one of the spouses and/or any children of the marriage.[13] The options include orders for periodical or lump-sum payments, orders for the transfer or settlement of property and pension-sharing orders. And since an English court will possess jurisdiction with respect to divorce, nullity or judicial separation where the applicant alone is resident or domiciled in this country,[14] it follows that it may even make an order for financial relief against a foreign spouse who is domiciled and resident abroad.[15] On the other hand, ancillary relief is granted at the court's discretion and it seems that orders will not be granted against those domiciled or resident overseas where the court believes it would be utterly ineffective to do so.[16] So, for example, where one respondent had no substantive connection with England, and the courts in the country where he lived would have refused to give effect to an English order, the English court declined to make an order for ancillary relief.[17]

2 Orders during the subsistence of a marriage

If, during the currency of a marriage, one spouse has failed to provide reasonable maintenance for the other spouse or any child of the family, the High Court has jurisdiction to order that periodical or lump-sum payments be made in order that such maintenance be provided in the future.[18] The High Court also has the power to make orders for the transfer of property

[12] For full details of when such jurisdiction exists, see ch 5.

[13] Matrimonial Causes Act 1973, ss 23, 24. For fuller discussion, see S.M. Cretney, J.M. Masson & R. Bailey-Harris, *Principles of Family Law* (London: Sweet & Maxwell, 2002) ch 14.

[14] Domicile and Matrimonial Proceedings Act 1973, s 5.

[15] See, eg, *Cammel v Cammel* [1965] P 467 (the husband in this case was both domiciled and resident in France).

[16] See, eg, *Goff v Goff* [1934] P 107 and *Wyler v Lyons* [1963] P 274.

[17] See, eg, *Tallack v Tallack* [1927] P 211.

[18] Matrimonial Causes Act 1973, s 27.

to, or for the benefit of, precisely the same persons;[19] and it can vary maintenance agreements made by the parties themselves (upon receiving an application by one of them) if their financial situation has changed, or if the maintenance provided under the agreement is inadequate to meet the needs of a child of the family.[20] In addition to this range of powers, the magistrates' court also has jurisdiction to make financial provision orders on grounds similar to those that govern the High Court's jurisdiction. Furthermore, however, the magistrates may also make a financial provision order where the respondent has either behaved in such a way that the applicant cannot reasonably be expected to live with him, or where the respondent has deserted the applicant.[21]

3 Other maintenance orders

Under the Maintenance Orders (Facilities for Enforcement) Act 1920 and the Maintenance Orders (Reciprocal Enforcement) Act 1972, provision is made for the English courts to make a maintenance order in respect of a defendant who resides in a country outside the United Kingdom, but with which there is a reciprocal agreement for the confirmation and enforcement of the English order. The mechanics of the two Acts need not be considered here.[22] It suffices to note that they relate, broadly, to reciprocal agreements that have been reached with Commonwealth countries, Ireland and most of the States in the United States.

4 The power to exercise jurisdiction

So far as jurisdiction is concerned, if the second State involved is a European State, and one or both parties are connected in one of the specified ways to the relevant European country, the applicable jurisdiction rules will be those found in either Brussels I or the Lugano Convention.[23] According to both the Regulation and the Convention, 'a court of a Member State before which a defendant enters an appearance shall have jurisdiction' except 'where [that] appearance was entered to contest the jurisdiction [of that court]'.[24]

[19] *Ibid*, s 24. Where the spouses have separated but both remain resident in this country, the financial obligations of the absent parent in respect of any qualifying child or children will be governed by the Child Support Act 1991; but for the purposes of this book we shall assume that the respondent is resident in another country. For a detailed and up-to-date account of the mechanics of the Child Support legislation see R. Bird, *Child Support – The New Law* (Bristol: Jordan Publishing, 2003); Cretney *et al*, *op cit* n 13, ch 15.

[20] Matrimonial Causes Act 1973, s 35.

[21] Domestic Proceedings and Magistrates' Court Act 1978, s 1(c), (d).

[22] For discussion of the mechanics of the two Acts, see North & Fawcett, *op cit* n 1, pp 838–839.

[23] But note that Denmark is expressly excluded from the operation of the Regulation: Brussels I, Art 1(3).

[24] Brussels I, Art 24; Lugano Convention, Art 18.

Equally, if the respondent is domiciled in England, the English courts will again have jurisdiction,[25] as they will where the petitioner is domiciled or habitually resident in this country while the respondent is domiciled in another Member State.[26] Finally, if the parties have made an agreement to the effect that the English court will have jurisdiction, and at least one of the parties is domiciled in a Member State, that agreement shall be effective to confer jurisdiction upon the English courts.[27]

A linked consideration that requires comment here relates to the English courts' power to vary (or perhaps even revoke) a prior maintenance order made in this country. Where the maintenance order was made ancillary to divorce, nullity or judicial separation proceedings, the English court will retain its jurisdiction to vary (and revoke) that order regardless of whether the original basis for the court's jurisdiction has ceased to obtain.[28] Where, on the other hand, the original jurisdiction to make the order was founded upon the habitual residence or domicile of the applicant, an English court will lose jurisdiction to alter its own prior order if the applicant ceases to be resident or domiciled here while the respondent is domiciled in another Member State.[29]

Next in this context we must consider the important staying provisions contained in both Brussels I and the Lugano Convention, for naturally these will (or may, in the case of discretionary stays) restrict the power of the English courts to exercise jurisdiction they would otherwise hold with respect to ordering financial relief. First, the courts of this country are required to stay any ancillary proceedings if 'proceedings involving the same cause of action and between the same parties' are brought before the court of another Member State so long as that other court was the one 'first seised of jurisdiction'.[30] In addition, a discretion to stay proceedings is also conferred where there are related proceedings pending before the court of another Member State.[31] Finally, where the parties have formally agreed that the courts of another Member State shall have jurisdiction to settle their dispute, the agreement will have the effect of excluding the jurisdiction of the English courts.[32]

[25] Art 2(1) of both the Regulation and the Convention. In both cases – Brussels I, Art 59; Lugano Convention, Art 52 – domicile is given a particular meaning that, in the case of foreign domiciliaries, closely resembles the English concept of habitual residence. For further detail, see Collier, *op cit* n 1, pp 138–139.

[26] Art 5(2) of both Brussels I and the Lugano Convention.

[27] Brussels I, Art 23(1); Lugano Convention, Art 17(1).

[28] Matrimonial Causes Act 1973, s 35.

[29] So much is implicit from Arts 2(1) and 5(2) of both Brussels I and the Lugano Convention.

[30] Brussels I, Art 27; Lugano Convention, Art 21.

[31] Brussels I, Art 28; Lugano Convention, Art 22.

[32] Brussels I, Art 23(1); Lugano Convention, Art 17(1).

Finally, we must consider the traditional rules which will apply where jurisdiction is not governed by Brussels I or the Lugano Convention. In this connection, the jurisdiction of each level of court must be considered separately. Turning first to the High Court, the traditional rules confer jurisdiction where one of the spouses is domiciled in England on the date of the application, *or* where the applicant has been habitually resident here for the period of one year immediately prior to the application, *or* where the respondent is resident in the United Kingdom on the date of the application.[33] For these purposes, 'the question of residence depends partly on the factual state of affairs and partly on intention'.[34] Accordingly, 'residence is not a simple question of bodily presence', because '[b]odily presence at the critical date may not involve residence . . . [while] bodily absence is not inconsistent with residence'.[35] As regards the magistrates' court, jurisdiction in relation to the making of maintenance orders affecting foreign domiciliaries is somewhat uncertain. Jurisdiction will clearly exist where the respondent is ordinarily resident in the catchment area covered by the particular court.[36] But it may also exist where that person is merely present within the United Kingdom,[37] or where that person (though domiciled and resident abroad) submits to the jurisdiction of the court.[38] What is beyond doubt, however, is that there is no jurisdiction to make financial provision orders where the respondent is resident abroad and fails to submit to the jurisdiction of the English courts. In such a case, the respondent's domicile is completely irrelevant.[39]

Financial relief following a foreign decree

There are two main reasons why the question of financial relief following a foreign decree of divorce, nullity or judicial separation needs to be considered separately. In the first place, a rather esoteric question arises as to the effect of a foreign decree on a *prior* English order for financial relief (such as one granted by the magistrates' court during the subsistence of the marriage). Secondly, there is a particular set of rules contained in Part III of the Matrimonial and Family Proceedings Act 1984 that were enacted to meet some of the hardships frequently encountered by English spouses (normally wives) whose marriages were formally terminated abroad by

[33] Matrimonial Causes Act 1973, s 27(2).
[34] *Sinclair v Sinclair* [1968] P 189, at 221 *per* Willmer LJ.
[35] *Ibid*, at 222 *per* Russell LJ.
[36] Domestic Proceedings and Magistrates' Court Act 1978, s 30(1).
[37] *Forsyth v Forsyth* [1948] P 125, at 132 *per* Tucker LJ.
[38] For an argument to this effect, based on the characterisation of an application for financial provision as an action *in personam*, see North & Fawcett, *op cit* n 1, p 838.
[39] Domestic Proceedings and Magistrates' Court Act 1978, s 30(5).

proceedings that afforded them little to no financial security following the termination of the marriage.

1 Effect of a foreign decree on a prior English order for financial relief

As regards the effect of a foreign decree on a prior English maintenance order, the law is relatively straightforward. For where an English court has already granted a maintenance order in favour of one spouse, a subsequent foreign divorce, annulment or judicial separation that is recognised in this country need not be treated as terminating that maintenance order. Statute merely provides that such orders shall cease to have effect upon the remarriage of the party in whose favour it was made.[40] But the courts have made clear that they have a discretion to continue the effectiveness of the maintenance order notwithstanding a subsequent foreign decree that is recognised in this country;[41] and they have even extended this approach to interim maintenance orders.[42]

2 Jurisdiction of the English court to grant financial relief following an earlier foreign decree

Perhaps the first point to note in relation to Part III of the Matrimonial and Family Proceedings Act 1984 is that if the country in which the marriage is terminated (or in which the parties obtain a legal separation) is a 'Brussels I country' or a 'Lugano Convention country', then the jurisdiction rules in those instruments will apply in place of those contained in the 1984 Act.[43] We have already considered these rules, but two qualifications need to be made. The first relates to the fact that the Regulation and Convention are expressly excluded from applying to 'rights in property arising out of a matrimonial relationship'. As such, jurisdiction in relation to property adjustment orders not capable of being construed as a form of maintenance[44] is governed exclusively by the 1984 Act. The second and slightly more contentious qualification that needs to be made is that Article 23 of Brussels I and its equivalent, Article 17 of the Lugano Convention, would appear to be of limited applicability in this context. This is because these provisions – loosely allowing the parties to agree that the courts of a particular Member State shall have exclusive jurisdiction with respect to their maintenance dispute – are contingent upon there being 'disputes that have arisen or which may arise in connection with a particular legal relationship'. And since the marriage will already have been validly terminated in the case of a divorce

[40] *Ibid*, s 4(2); Matrimonial Causes Act 1973, s 28(2).
[41] *Wood v Wood* [1957] P 254.
[42] *Newmarch v Newmarch* [1978] Fam 79.
[43] Matrimonial and Family Proceedings Act 1984, s 15(2).
[44] Recall *Van den Boogaard v Laumen* [1997] QB 759 discussed above.

or nullity decree, it can be argued that there no longer exists a 'legal relationship' between the parties thus rendering these Articles redundant.[45]

A second prefatory point worth making is that where the 1984 Act does apply, it does so with retrospective effect making it equally applicable to divorces, annulments and separations obtained both before and after it came into effect.[46] On the other hand, the Act is somewhat restrictive in that jurisdiction to grant relief exists only in respect of parties whose foreign decree was obtained by way of proceedings, and in any event terminates upon the re-marriage of either party.[47]

Although the orders that can be made under the 1984 Act can be dealt with very briefly – they basically reflect those that can be made where the relevant decree is obtained in this country[48] – the rules concerning jurisdiction are rather more complicated. They are set out in section 15(1) of the Act which, once unpicked, reveals three basic grounds for jurisdiction: English domicile held by one of the parties; the habitual residence in this country of one of the parties; either or both the parties having a beneficial interest in a former matrimonial home located in this country.

In respect of each of these jurisdictional grounds there are important temporal factors that must be taken into account. Thus, where jurisdiction

[45] Of course, a legal relationship will continue to exist in the case of a judicial separation and Arts 23 and 17 of the two instruments can be invoked perfectly well in such cases. For the curious argument that they may even be invoked following a foreign divorce or annulment by virtue of a somewhat spurious analogy with the relationship that is deemed to exist between the parties to a void commercial contract, see C.M.V. Clarkson & J. Hill, *Jaffey on the Conflict of Laws* (London: Butterworths, 2002) p 434. A better analogy may perhaps be the implicit legal relationship that enables the English courts to make a financial relief order following a nullity decree awarded in this country in respect of a void marriage. But even here the analogy seems strained: in the one context, the concern is with a relationship that never properly came into being; in the other, it is with a relationship that has been legally ended *specifically because* the parties do not want any ongoing legal connection to one another.

[46] See, eg, *M v L (Financial Relief After Overseas Divorce)* [2003] 2 FLR 425 (the applicant sought and was awarded an order some thirty years after the divorce in 1973).

[47] Matrimonial and Family Proceedings Act 1984, s 12.

[48] Matrimonial and Family Proceedings Act 1984, ss 17, 19, 22. Furthermore, the considerations taken into account in deciding to grant the order for financial relief sought are essentially the same as those made in connection with domestic divorces, annulments and separations: *ibid*, s 18(3)–(5). Finally, it is clear that English law is the applicable law in terms of whether and how much maintenance (or other relief) will be awarded; which is not to say that the courts will ignore the fact that the parties may well have been married in a country in which a community of property principle operates. The only, very limited, circumstances in which English law will not be the only applicable law are contained in the Maintenance Orders (Facilities for Enforcement) Act 1920 and the Maintenance Orders (Reciprocal Enforcement) Act 1972.

is founded on domicile the relevant party must have been domiciled here either 'on the date of the application' or 'on the date on which the divorce, annulment or legal separation obtained in the overseas country took effect in that country'.[49] By contrast, where jurisdiction is founded on the habitual residence of one or both parties, that residence must have occurred during 'the period of one year ending with the date of the application' or 'the period of one year ending with the date on which the [foreign decree] . . . took effect in that country'.[50] Finally, where jurisdiction exists by virtue of the presence of a former matrimonial home in this country, either or both the parties must hold a beneficial interest in that property at the date of the application.[51]

What these rules are designed to achieve is a suitable balance whereby parties who are inadequately connected to this country cannot invoke the powers of the English courts to obtain financial relief following an overseas divorce, annulment or separation, but those who are adequately connected can obtain such relief. Of course, the jurisdictional ground based on the presence in this country of a former matrimonial home says little to nothing about the personal connections of the parties to this country; yet it was felt appropriate to include it as an alternative to the grounds based on domicile and habitual residence to catch those cases where both parties had left this country, divorced abroad but not yet resolved the matter of what to do with their most significant capital asset, the former matrimonial home.[52] It would appear that, leaving aside the complex way in which section 15(1) is drafted, an appropriate balance has been struck in determining the circumstances when a court *may* make an order. That, however, is a different question to the normative one of when an English court *ought to* make a financial relief order following a foreign decree. It is to that question that we now turn.

As a preliminary filter on any attempt to obtain financial relief in this context, the 1984 Act requires all would-be applicants to first obtain the leave of the English court. Such leave is to be granted only where the court in question is satisfied that there exists a 'substantial ground for the making of an application'.[53] While the term 'substantial ground' is not defined within the Act, it is made clear that the mere fact that the foreign decree was made in conjunction with an order for financial relief will not, *per se*, be taken to

[49] *Ibid*, s 15(1)(a).

[50] *Ibid*, s 15(1)(b).

[51] *Ibid*, s 15(1)(c).

[52] See Law Com No 117, *Family Law: Financial Relief after Foreign Divorce* (London: HMSO, 1982) paras 2.7–2.8.

[53] Matrimonial and Family Proceedings Act 1984, s 13(1). In addition leave may be granted on a purely conditional basis (*ibid*, s 13(3)), and in any event, the English court will require the would-be applicant to place all the material facts of the case before it: *M v M (Financial Provision After Foreign Divorce)* [1994] 1 FLR 399.

be indicative of the absence of a 'substantial ground'.[54] This arguably suggests that a degree of generosity ought to be shown in respect of claims that there exists the requisite 'substantial ground'.

The second filter is set out in section 16(1) of the 1984 Act. There it is provided that, '[b]efore making an order for financial relief the court shall consider whether in all the circumstances of the case it would be appropriate for such an order to be made'. In reaching this decision the court is specifically required to take account of a number of factors. These include the connection of the parties to England and Wales, their connection to the country in which the foreign decree was obtained, their connection to any other country, the existence of a prior foreign order for financial relief, the prospect of a future foreign order and the prospect of any order under the 1984 Act being enforced abroad.[55] In part, these factors are intended to import into this context the familiar *forum conveniens* principle,[56] but they are also intended to encapsulate the principle that 'there should be no two bites at the one cherry'.[57] Partly this is an application of the *res judicata* principle, but it is also closely associated with the comity of nations. Thus, in *M v M (Financial Provision After Foreign Divorce)*,[58] where an order in relation to shared matrimonial property had already been refused by the French courts, Thorpe J declined to grant the order later sought in this country on the basis that the matter had already been dealt with in the 'competent jurisdiction of one of our nearest neighbouring friendly states'.[59] By contrast, however, the court in *M v L (Financial Relief After Overseas Divorce)*[60] sought to distinguish the kind of case in which payments had only ever been ordered in respect of the children of the family. In such circumstances, it was held, there was no reason for the English court to consider itself inhibited from making a subsequent order in favour of the wife herself. As Coleridge J, continuing an earlier metaphor, put it:

> I reject the suggestion that this is a case of someone seeking a second bite of the cherry after a proper foreign determination . . . This wife has scarcely had a first nibble let alone a bite of the cherry . . . Considering 'all the circumstances

[54] *Ibid*, s 13(2). Furthermore, under s 18(6) of the Act the court can take into account the degree of likelihood that a foreign order will be complied with in deciding whether to grant an order to an applicant. It may even make an award in relation to matrimonial assets held overseas: see, eg, *Hamlin v Hamlin* [1986] Fam 11.

[55] *Ibid*, s 16(2).

[56] See *Holmes v Holmes* [1989] Fam 47 where Purchas LJ said (at 57–58): 'the court must always be slow to interfere with a competent court seized of the matter'.

[57] *Lamagni v Lamagni* [1995] 2 FLR 452, at 454 *per* Butler-Sloss LJ.

[58] [1994] 1 FLR 399.

[59] *Ibid*, at 407 *per* Thorpe J. See to similar effect the *dictum* of Butler-Sloss LJ in *Hewitson v Hewitson* [1995] Fam 100, at 105, stressing the 'comity existing between courts of comparable jurisdiction'.

[60] [2003] 2 FLR 425.

> of this case' and despite the long time gap, I am quite satisfied that this is an apt application under Part III [of the 1984 Act].[61]

The recognition of foreign financial relief orders

Since many if not most overseas maintenance orders are capable of variation, they cannot be regarded as final orders. As such, they will not attract the application of the usual rules applicable to the recognition of judgments *in personam*[62] and will, according to the traditional rules, be incapable of recognition and enforcement in this country.[63] Thus, as Sankey J said of a foreign maintenance order in *Harrop v Harrop*:

> [A] judgment or order cannot be said to be final or conclusive if (1) an order has to be obtained for its enforcement, and (2) on application for such an order *the original judgment is liable to be abrogated or varied.*[64]

Given the non-finality of most maintenance orders, but recognising also their prevalence and importance, their recognition and enforcement has since been afforded special statutory treatment. And the criteria laid down for recognition need to be considered under three separate heads.

1 Maintenance orders made elsewhere in the United Kingdom

If a maintenance order is made elsewhere in the United Kingdom than in this country, it may nonetheless be registered in an English court if the person liable is resident here and it appears convenient that the order should be enforceable in this jurisdiction.[65] Registration is at the discretion of the court granting the order rather than the court requested to register it. But, once registered, the order is enforceable as though it had been made by the registering court.

2 Recognition of foreign maintenance orders

Provision is made under the Maintenance Orders (Facilities for Enforcement) Act 1920 for the reciprocal enforcement of maintenance orders granted

[61] *Ibid*, at [37]–[38].

[62] For a detailed account of these rules see North & Fawcett, *op cit* n 1, pp 407–423.

[63] *Nouvion v Freeman* (1889) 15 App Cas 1. Where the judgment is an unimpeachable *res judicata* for, say, the payment of a fixed lump sum, there is normally no problem with recognising and enforcing it according to the usual rules. However, if the order were granted in the context of divorce, nullity or separation proceedings in which the awarding court lacked jurisdiction to deal with the fundamental matrimonial cause, the ancillary relief order granted in conjunction with the decree would be denied recognition: *Simons v Simons* [1939] 1 KB 490.

[64] [1920] 3 KB 386, at 399 (emphasis added).

[65] Maintenance Orders Act 1950, Part II.

in this country and those Commonwealth countries to which the Act has been extended by Order in Council. What this means, in effect, is that on a reciprocal basis the relevant Commonwealth countries will have the facility to register a maintenance order granted here[66] while the English courts will have the facility to register a maintenance order made in one of the relevant Commonwealth countries.[67] The facility for registration in this country, however, is likely to be of use only where the respondent was initially resident in the Commonwealth country in which the order was made, but is now resident here. (The opposite is of course true in relation to registration in a Commonwealth country.) Similar provisions to those in the 1920 Act are also contained in the Maintenance Order (Reciprocal Enforcement) Act 1972.[68] But in this case the twinning arrangements extend to any reciprocating foreign country and there exists a facility, created by statutory instrument, to refuse registration (and hence recognition) of a foreign maintenance order where registration would be 'manifestly contrary to public policy'.[69]

Finally, those States that are bound by the provisions of Brussels I or the Lugano Convention must generally recognise maintenance orders made in other Member States.[70] There are, however, four circumstances in which recognition within these regimes will mandatorily be refused. First, there will be no recognition of a maintenance order granted in another Member State where it would be manifestly contrary to public policy to recognise it.[71] Secondly, there will be no recognition where the order was granted in default of appearance if the defendant was not duly served with the document instituting proceedings (or its equivalent) in time to arrange his defence.[72] Thirdly, recognition will be denied if the order is irreconcilable with a prior judgment granted in proceedings between the same parties in the Member State in which recognition is sought.[73] Fourthly, there will be no recognition if the order is irreconcilable with an earlier judgment involving the same

[66] Maintenance Orders (Facilities for Enforcement) Act 1920, s 1.

[67] *Ibid*, s 2. Where registration takes place, the order will have the same effect as if it were an order granted by the English courts: *Pilcher v Pilcher* [1955] P 318. Note also the facility under s 20 of the Act for the recognition of foreign provisional orders.

[68] See ss 2, 5, 6. There would in fact be scope for ongoing overlap were it not for the fact that the 1920 Act will be repealed when the later Act is brought fully into force: Maintenance Orders (Reciprocal Enforcement) Act 1972, s 22(2)(a).

[69] The Reciprocal Enforcement of Maintenance Orders (Hague Convention Countries) Order 1979 (SI 1979, No 1317), r 6(6).

[70] Brussels I, Art 33(1); Lugano Convention, Art 26(1).

[71] Brussels I, Art 34(1); Lugano Convention, Art 27(1). But note that under the Lugano Convention the order needs only to be 'contrary' (not 'manifestly contrary') to public policy.

[72] Brussels I, Art 34(2); Lugano Convention, Art 27(2).

[73] Brussels I, Art 34(3); Lugano Convention, Art 27(3).

cause of action given in another Member State, or in a third State provided that that judgment would itself be recognised in the Member State.[74] There is also provision made in both instruments for the discretionary refusal of recognition where there was a questionable jurisdictional basis for the original decision.[75]

Matrimonial property[76]

Unlike in England and Wales, many civil law countries (and others besides) have a system of community of property whereby both spouses are deemed to own jointly any property that each acquires separately during the subsistence of the marriage.[77] It can also mean, however, that the spouses now own jointly any property that each held prior to the marriage.[78] The fact that all matrimonial property is jointly owned has important repercussions on the occasion of divorce or death. Where the marriage is dissolved, each spouse is entitled to claim his or her share of the community without recourse to a court of law for an order to that effect. Equally, on death, the surviving spouse will not have to rely on succession laws in respect of his or her share of the matrimonial property. This may well also have beneficial tax implications for the surviving spouse.[79] Accordingly, where spouses

[74] Brussels I, Art 34(4); Lugano Convention, Art 27(5). But note that the Lugano Convention speaks only of judgments obtained in non-Contracting States in this connection.

[75] Brussels I, Arts 35, 72; Lugano Convention, Arts 28(3), 54B(3).

[76] In this section of the chapter, we are concerned only with the settled rules applicable to matrimonial property in the strict sense. Related questions to those discussed here seem an inevitable challenge for the future, especially in respect of those who have entered a registered partnership but who are not technically married. Some brief (and necessarily speculative) consideration of these matters is deferred until the concluding section of this chapter.

[77] It is arguable that English law bears a very limited notion of community of property in so far as spousal status will give rise to certain inheritance rights (under the Administration of Estates Act 1925 and the Inheritance (Provision for Family and Dependants) Act 1975) and certain rights of occupation (under the Family Law Act 1996).

[78] These illustrations embrace the two main varieties of community of property: full community of property (whereby both ante-nuptial and post-nuptial assets fall into the community) and partial community (whereby only post-nuptial acquisitions fall into the community). For details of further varieties which exist by virtue of either spousal election or rule of law, see A. Barlow, T. Callus & E. Cooke 'Community of Property – A Study for England and Wales' [2004] *Family Law* 47.

[79] See, eg, *Frankel's Estate v The Master* 1950 (1) SA 220. The existence of a community of property regime does not, of course, preclude an application on divorce for *additional* financial relief, or a claim on death to succeed to the deceased spouse's share of the community.

relocate across national borders prior to death or divorce, or where they are domiciliaries of different countries with different rules as to matrimonial property, it becomes critical to decide which system of law governs the parties' matrimonial property rights. The remainder of this section of the present chapter addresses just these matters, but it does so according to a necessary dichotomy that must be drawn between matrimonial property rights fixed by a rule of law and those fixed by a valid ante-nuptial agreement regulating the property rights.[80]

Property rights in the absence of a valid ante-nuptial agreement

Where spouses who married abroad move to this country prior to the death of one of them, or prior to their divorce here, an English court may subsequently be called upon to decide their respective matrimonial property rights. Where the parties have not made a valid ante-nuptial agreement making clear who owns what, the task can be far from easy. The rules are both complex and uncertain of meaning. That said, it is generally agreed that a fundamental distinction must be drawn between movable and immovable property.[81] The reasons for this distinction will become clear in the following pages (although it might be noted that the distinction may cease to be important within the European Union once Brussels III is finalised and implemented[82]).

1 Movable property

Historically, the rule in relation to movable matrimonial property was that the consequences of marriage for that property were to be determined by the law of the husband's domicile at the date of the marriage.[83] Over time, case law added an important but complicated gloss to this rule. In *Re Egerton's Will Trusts*,[84] a testator domiciled in England married in England a French woman domiciled in France. Prior to their marriage they agreed to settle in France but did not actually do so until two years later. When, some

[80] Under English law, such contracts are not generally enforceable: see, eg, *N v N (Jurisdiction: Pre-nuptial Agreement)* [1999] 2 FLR 745.

[81] The distinction between movable and immovable property is one that is generally accepted throughout the world in the context of conflicts of law. The notion of movable property equates broadly (but not perfectly) to the English concept of personalty. Similarly, the conflicts notion of immovable property corresponds loosely (but not perfectly) to the English concept of realty. As to the differences between movable property and personalty, and immovable property and realty, see North & Fawcett, *op cit* n 1, ch 28.

[82] Brussels III is a proposed EU Regulation on the harmonisation of private international law rules relating to matrimonial (and analogous) property.

[83] *Re Martin* [1900] P 211, at 233 *per* Lindley MR.

[84] [1956] Ch 593.

years beyond that, the testator died, the question arose as to which law should be applied to the matrimonial property. In relation to the movable property Roxburgh J said:

> In my judgment, it is reasonably plain that there is a presumption that the law of the husband's domicile applies to a marriage, and that the presumption can be rebutted. It can certainly be rebutted by express contract, and, in my judgment, it could also be rebutted by what is loosely called a tacit contract, if the circumstances warrant the inference of such a tacit contract.[85]

In the light of this decision, it is tolerably clear that the husband's domicile at the date of the marriage provides no more than a strong presumption as to the applicable law and that this presumption may be ousted where a subsequent domicile of choice is established on the basis of either an express or implied agreement to adopt the law of another country.[86] Yet while the establishment of a matrimonial home abroad will provide some indication of the requisite intention, it will not *per se* suffice. What is required is an intention that the law of the husband's domicile of choice rather than his domicile of origin should govern the spouses' rights in relation to the movable matrimonial property.

Leaving aside the objection to this rule based on its inherent chauvinism – it attributes no significance the possibility that the wife's domicile may differ from that of her husband[87] – it also fails to answer the question of which law should be applied to determine matrimonial property rights when a change in domicile occurs (for example, where spouses both married and domiciled in France later move to this country and acquire a domicile of choice here).

Where a change of matrimonial domicile occurs, there are two conflicting theories as to the applicable law in relation to movable matrimonial property. The first rests on the idea of immutability; the second, on that of mutability. According to the immutability theory, the applicable law in respect of property acquired *after* the change of domicile remains that of the regime that was operative prior to the change of domicile. Conversely, the mutability theory holds that property acquired after the change in domicile should be subject to the new regime. There is no authoritative ruling favouring either

[85] *Ibid*, at 607.

[86] It was held on the facts that the spouses' agreement to move to France as soon as possible after the wedding did not amount to an agreement that French law would determine their matrimonial property rights. As such, Roxburgh J's comment in relation to the rebuttal of the presumption that the law of the husband's domicile will apply is technically *obiter*.

[87] In so doing, does it fall foul of Art 8 of the European Convention on Human Rights requiring respect for the private lives of all citizens? Certainly, one's domicile could be viewed as integral to one's very identity, and thus one's private life.

one of these approaches.[88] The stronger case, however, can probably be made in favour of the mutability doctrine since the traditional argument in favour of immutability – that the husband could cheat his wife out of her share of post-nuptial acquisitions by recourse to the simple expedient of changing domicile – no longer applies.[89]

Notwithstanding the conflicting theories briefly outlined in the preceding paragraph, there seems a good deal to be said for the popular hybrid approach[90] that hinges upon the distinction between vested and inchoate property rights. According to the suggested compromise, the mutability theory is to be applied, in tempered form, so that only those rights in relation to movables acquired after the change of domicile are governed by the new regime. If, then, a husband and wife begin their married life in Sweden where the husband purchases movables A, B and C, this will be subject to the Swedish community regime notwithstanding the later acquisition of an English domicile. Only the movables X, Y and Z that the husband acquires after obtaining an English domicile will be subject to the English separation of property rules. This hybrid approach seems broadly fair and sensible: there is no good reason why the husband should be permitted to dispossess his wife of her vested rights by making a will that purports to leave everything he owns to a third party; and there is no good reason why he should be able to claim the application of Swedish rules to movable property acquired by an English domiciliary in England.[91]

[88] Ostensibly favouring mutability is the ancient decision of the House of Lords in *Lashley v Hogg* (1804) 4 Paton 582. But the case has been convincingly shown to be concerned with succession rather than community of property: see G.D. Goldberg, 'The Assignment of Property on Marriage' (1970) 19 *International and Comparative Law Quarterly* 557, 580–584 (a separate Appendix devoted to *Lashley v Hogg*) and *De Nicols v Curlier* [1900] AC 21. Apparent (but not unproblematic) support for the immutability principle can be discerned in *Chiwell v Carlyon* (1897) 14 SC 61.

[89] By virtue of the Domicile and Matrimonial Proceedings Act 1973, the wife no longer simply acquires a domicile of dependency based on her husband's domicile and thus the consequences of a husband's change of domicile need not result in adverse consequences for her.

[90] See, eg, the support supplied in North & Fawcett, *op cit* n 1, pp 1020–1021 and Collier, *op cit* n 1, p 284.

[91] A further rejection of the immutability theory may be suggested on the basis of the European Convention of Human Rights, Art 14 and Art 1 of the First Protocol. It runs thus: the idea that movable property rights are determined by reference to the husband's domicile at the time of the marriage is a form of discrimination against women. This is an argument of limited application, however, for it could realistically be invoked only in the relatively infrequently occurring scenario in which the husband alone changes his domicile and acquires further movable property prior to a divorce or his death. And here it is uncertain whether the immutability principle would apply in any case since it is normally suggested that it applies (if at all) where both the husband *and* the wife change their domicile.

The main difficulty associated with this modified mutability rule is that it may well confound the expectations of the parties. Consider the case in which, say, a French married couple migrate to this country and obtain a domicile of choice here. Imagine further that the husband acquires a fortune in movable property before predeceasing his wife. In such a case, it may well be that the wife would be liable to inheritance tax because she is deemed to have inherited all of her husband's movable property rather than just half of it. Conversely, an English wife that moved abroad together with her husband may be equally surprised to learn that she was free to dispose in her will of only half the movable property she had acquired since the change of domicile. In each case, the problem is one of ignorance of the various matrimonial property regimes that exist in different countries. There may also be a problem with contracting out of the new regime, for if the couple migrate *after marriage* they will, by definition, have no opportunity to make a valid *antenuptial* contract to govern their respective proprietary entitlements.

To some extent, the difficulties outlined in the preceding paragraphs are mitigated by legislation. Under the Inheritance (Provision for Family and Dependants) Act 1975, a spouse will be entitled to make a claim for financial provision notwithstanding the fact that all the deceased's property may have been left in his will to a third party. The surviving (former) spouse's surprise at the separation of property regime in this country in the case of a mutability rule will thus be tempered by this legislation.[92] Similarly, even if the immutability rule were to be applied, other dependants of the deceased would still be able to claim under the 1975 Act.[93]

2 Immovable property

The general rule in relation to immovable property is that the proper law for determining rights in that property is the law of the country in which that property is situated (the *lex situs*). This, according to the decision of the House of Lords in *Welch v Tennent*,[94] is as true of matrimonial property as any other immovable property. (The ostensibly aberrant case of *Re De Nicols*,[95] in which a home purchased in this country by a French couple was

[92] Inheritance (Provision for Family and Dependants) Act 1975, s 1(1)(a), (b). Furthermore, s 17 of the Married Women's Property Act 1882 grants an English judge the power to 'make such order . . . as he thinks fit' in any dispute between a husband and wife concerning title to, or possession of, property. This discretionary power exists regardless of whether the parties are domiciled abroad under a community regime or whether the property is in this country: see *Re Bettinson's Question* [1956] Ch 67. It is equally immaterial that the parties are foreign domiciliaries and that the property in question is held abroad so long as it has at some point been under the control of one of the spouses in this country: see *Razelos v Razelos (No 2)* [1970] 1 WLR 392.

[93] *Ibid*, s 1(1)(ba)–(e).

[94] [1891] AC 639, at 645 *per* Lord Herschell.

[95] [1900] Ch 210.

dealt with according to the French community principles, can be explained away on the basis of a valid implied contract to that effect between the spouses.) It has been suggested that the *lex situs* rule is unsatisfactory in that it can lead to juridical fragmentation of an estate whereby various items of immovable property in different countries are potentially subject to different matrimonial property regimes.[96] While this is true, it is reducible, in essence, to an argument for juristic neatness and simplicity. Yet seldom do simple rules provide good justice in hard cases. What might be better is a general recognition of the validity of ante-nuptial agreements that specify clearly the respective entitlements of the spouses.[97]

Property rights under an ante-nuptial agreement

We explored in the preceding section the mitigating effect of the Inheritance (Provision for Family and Dependants) Act 1975 and the Married Women's Property Act 1882 on the uncertainty that surrounds the question of whether the English courts will adopt the mutability or the immutability rule in connection with movable matrimonial property in the context of couples who change their domicile during a marriage. A further possible mitigating factor to bear in mind is the existence of an ante-nuptial agreement that seeks to regulate the respective rights of the spouses in relation to their matrimonial property. That said, the validity of such agreements cannot be taken for granted; nor is their validity a straightforward matter.[98] This is partly because there is an important distinction to be made between ante-nuptial *contracts* and ante-nuptial settlements. It is also because, although ante-nuptial *contracts* are not binding on the English divorce courts, they may nonetheless nowadays be influential when the court is exercising its jurisdiction in relation to financial relief on divorce.

1 Ante-nuptial contracts and ante-nuptial settlements

The basic difference between an ante-nuptial settlement and an ante-nuptial contract was well captured by Wall J in *N v N (Jurisdiction: Pre-nuptial Agreement)*.[99] He said:

[96] Clarkson & Hill, *op cit* n 45, pp 502–503. The authors advocate the application of the law of the matrimonial domicile. But this itself can be opposed (not just because it is chauvinistically determined) but also because it would make matrimonial immovable property subject to different rules of law than other immovable property, such as that owned by cohabitants (and maybe even registered partners). In the end, the law becomes no less untidy and unsatisfactory.

[97] See *Chiwell v Carlyon* (1897) SC 61.

[98] For detailed, recent consideration of their status in this country, see G. Miller, 'Pre-Nuptial Agreements in English Law' [2003] *Private Client Business* 415.

[99] [1999] 2 FLR 745.

> The difference between an antenuptial settlement and an antenuptial contract . . . is that the former seeks to regulate the financial affairs of the spouses on and during their marriage. It does not contemplate the dissolution of the marriage. By contrast, an agreement made prior to the marriage which contemplates the steps the parties will take in the event of divorce or separation is perceived as being contrary to public policy because it undermines the concept of marriage as a life-long union.[100]

Distilling out the critical points in this *dictum* we discover that ante-nuptial settlements may be recognised as valid since they do not purport to impinge upon the matrimonial relief jurisdiction of the English courts:[101] their focus is purely upon the rights and obligations of the spouses during the subsistence of the marriage. By contrast, ante-nuptial contracts are seen to be objectionable for two reasons: first, because they represent an endeavour to undermine a particular power granted to the divorce courts by Parliament;[102] and secondly because they are seen as contracts contrary to public policy in so far as they contemplate divorce and thus run counter to the idea that marriage is (or should be) a union of two persons for life. There is little to contest the first of these objections, but the second seems relatively groundless. Indeed, as Connell J has observed: '[t]he public policy objection to such agreements, namely that they tend to diminish the importance of the marriage contract, seems to me to be of less importance now that divorce is so commonplace'.[103]

2 The potential influence of an ante-nuptial contract

(a) General considerations Even though the English divorce court is not technically bound by the terms of an ante-nuptial agreement it may nonetheless be relevant for three reasons. Two of these are rooted in the Matrimonial Causes Act 1973 (the source of the courts' divorce jurisdiction), while the third stems from the general principles of private international

[100] *Ibid*, at 752.

[101] Even where they are recognised as valid they remain open to variation by the courts on the occasion of death or divorce: Inheritance (Provision for Family and Dependants) Act 1975, s 2(1)(f); Matrimonial Causes Act 1973, s 24(1)(c), (d).

[102] In *F v F (Ancillary Relief: Substantial Assets)* [1995] 2 FLR 45 Thorpe J said (at 66): 'The rights and responsibilities of those whose financial affairs are regulated by statute cannot be much influenced by contractual terms which were devised for the control and limitation of standards that are intended to be of universal application throughout our society'.

[103] *M v M (Prenuptial Agreement)* [2002] 1 FLR 654, at 661. See also the similar conclusions of a present Law Lord (writing extra-judicially) in B. Hale, 'The Family Law Act 1996 – The Death of Marriage?' in C. Bridge (ed), *Family Law Towards the Millennium: Essays for P.M. Bromley* (London: Butterworths, 1997) and S. Poulter, 'The Definition of Marriage in English Law' (1979) 42 *Modern Law Review* 409.

law. Under the 1973 Act, when the court makes an order for financial relief it is specifically required to have regard to *all the circumstances of the case*[104] and to any *conduct of each of the parties* that it would be inequitable to disregard.[105] It seems clear that making an ante-nuptial agreement could be considered as both a relevant circumstance and relevant conduct. Thus, Connell J conceded in the case of *M v M (Prenuptial Agreement)*:[106]

> In my view it matters not whether the court bears such an agreement in mind as part of the circumstances of the case (a very important factor) or as an aspect of the parties' conduct. Under either approach the court should look at any such agreement and decide in the particular circumstances what weight should, in justice, be attached to it.[107]

The third (private international law) factor to bear in mind was implicit in what Wilson J had to say in *S v S (Divorce: Staying Proceedings)*:[108] 'Where other jurisdictions . . . have been persuaded that there are cases where justice can only be served by confining the parties to their rights under prenuptial agreements, we should be cautious about too categorically asserting the contrary'.[109] In so saying, his Lordship was clearly mindful of the central role of tolerance and pluralism in the English conflicts of law rules.

Just because a pre-nuptial contract *may* nowadays be taken to be influential in proceedings for matrimonial relief on divorce does not mean that the contract automatically *will* be influential. In deciding the extent to which the ante-nuptial agreement should be taken into account, the courts will look to several factors.[110] First, it may well be material that the agreement in question was concluded abroad by foreign domiciliaries. Such an agreement may be relevant in terms of determining the appropriate forum and the reasonable expectations of the parties.[111] Secondly, the courts will look to the length of the marriage; and here, the longer the marriage, the less the degree of

[104] Matrimonial Causes Act 1973, s 25(1) (emphasis added).

[105] *Ibid*, s 25(2)(g) (emphasis added).

[106] [2002] 1 FLR 654.

[107] *Ibid*, at 661. See also *K v K (Ancillary Relief: Prenuptial Agreement)* [2003] 1 FLR 120 where, again, the existence and terms of an ante-nuptial contract was considered relevant to the court's decision-making with respect to financial relief. A pre-echo of these cases is to be observed in the *dictum* of Wilson J in *S v S (Divorce: Staying Proceedings)* [1997] 2 FLR 100. He predicted (at 103) that: 'there will come a case . . . where the circumstances surrounding the prenuptial agreement and the provision therein contained might, when viewed in the context of the other circumstances of the case, prove influential or even crucial'.

[108] [1997] 2 FLR 100.

[109] *Ibid*, at 103.

[110] See Miller *op cit* n 98, at 418–424.

[111] See, eg, *N v N (Foreign Divorce: Financial Relief)* [1997] 1 FLR 900, at 912–913 *per* Cazalet J; *R v R (Divorce: Stay of Proceedings)* [1994] 2 FLR 1036, at 1043 *per* Ewbank J.

influence the ante-nuptial agreement is likely to have.[112] Thirdly, the courts will take note of the source of the family wealth: if only one party has contributed to its acquisition, the courts will be far less prepared to divide the property equally.[113] Fourthly, the courts will consider relevant the degree of financial provision for the less well-off spouse as *per* the parties' agreement as well as the circumstances in which the agreement was signed (including the absence or presence of full knowledge and/or undue influence).[114]

(b) Particular requirements Thus far we have merely noted the change in attitude on the part of the English courts: the fact that there is now a general preparedness to pay regard to the terms of an ante-nuptial agreement without considering themselves to be bound by it. Yet in all of this we have merely assumed the validity of the ante-nuptial agreement according to its proper law. In truth, however, any such assumption may be unwise since there are several hurdles – namely capacity, formal validity and essential validity – that must first be surmounted before any ante-nuptial agreement will carry the least weight with the English courts. In relation to the first of these, capacity, it is useful to recall that people nowadays generally marry at a later stage in their lives than formerly. As such, the significance of incapacity to enter into an ante-nuptial agreement (generally through minority) is much less a practical consideration than in bygone years. It thus suffices to note here that, though the case law is unclear, the governing law would seem to be the law of matrimonial domicile (rather than the law of the parties' respective domiciles at the time of the marriage).[115]

As to the formal validity of an ante-nuptial agreement or settlement, it seems that the test is whether the agreement satisfies the requirements of *either* the proper law[116] *or* the law of the country where it was made.[117] By contrast, the essential validity of an ante-nuptial agreement is to be gauged solely by reference to its proper law. In the absence of express choice by the spouses, the proper law will be presumptively the law of the matrimonial

[112] See, eg, *M v M (Prenuptial Agreement)* [2002] 1 FLR 654. Cf *K v K (Ancillary Relief: Prenuptial Agreement)* [2003] 1 FLR 120.

[113] *M v M (Prenuptial Agreement)* [2002] 1 FLR 654, at 668 *per* Connell J; *K v K (Ancillary Relief: Prenuptial Agreement)* [2003] 1 FLR 120, at 132 *per* Rodger Hayward-Smith QC.

[114] *K v K (Ancillary Relief: Prenuptial Agreement)* [2003] 1 FLR 120, at 131–132 *per* Rodger Hayward-Smith QC; *M v M (Prenuptial Agreement)* [2002] 1 FLR 654.

[115] The three leading authorities – *Re Cooke's Trusts* (1887) 56 LJ Ch 637, *Cooper v Cooper* (1888) LR 13 App Cas 88 and *Viditz v O'Hagan* [1900] 2 Ch 87 – are rather unclear. They are also very dated, which tends to bear out the contention made here that capacity is more of theoretical than practical significance. For analysis of just what these cases do and do not decide see North & Fawcett, *op cit* n 1, pp 1025–1027, Collier, *op cit* n 1, pp 279–280 and Clarkson & Hill, *op cit* n 45, pp 504–505.

[116] *Van Grutten v Digby* (1862) 31 Beav 561.

[117] *Guépratte v Young* (1851) De G & Sm 217.

domicile;[118] but the presumption may be displaced where the parties hold different domiciles in favour of a test based on a combination of their separate domiciles and the place with which the contract has its closest connection (judged by reference to the location of the property, the form and contents of the agreement and the place where the title deeds are kept).[119]

Succession[120]

The only persons entitled to distribute or administer[121] the estate of a deceased person are his[122] executors (appointed by will) or an administrator (who deals with his property upon intestacy or where a testamentary appointment fails). Since this chapter is presented from a family law perspective, we are not concerned with the mundane aspects of administration – such as the payment of debts and taxes – but rather with the rights of family members to succeed to their deceased relative's estate on death. We analyse both the applicable rules where the deceased made an effective will and those that apply where he died intestate. In the course of this analysis, we shall again distinguish between movable and immovable property.[123]

Testate succession

1 Movable property

Five distinct questions need to be addressed in connection with testamentary succession to movable property. These are discussed in turn.

(a) Capacity So far as capacity to make a valid will is concerned, non-age and mental incapacity are the most likely invalidating factors, and they are clearly to be treated alike. For as Scarman J once put it: 'I know of no distinction drawn between lack of capacity due to immaturity or status and

[118] *Duke of Marlborough v A-G* [1945] Ch 78.

[119] *Re Bankes* [1902] 2 Ch 333.

[120] For comprehensive treatment see G. Miller, *International Aspects of Succession* (Aldershot: Ashgate, 2000).

[121] Administration can be distinguished from disposition in that it includes, among other things, the power to pay/collect debts owed by/to the deceased (see, eg, *Re Kloebe* (1884) 28 Ch D 175) and to pay maintenance to minor beneficiaries (see, eg, *Re Kehr* [1952] Ch 26).

[122] For convenience of exposition it will be assumed throughout that the deceased is male.

[123] This distinction will become redundant once Brussels IV – an EC Regulation to harmonise private international law rules with respect to succession throughout the EU – becomes operative. But at the time of writing it is matter of pure speculation as to when this will be.

incapacity arising from ill-health' since either way 'a will must express the true will of a free and capable testator'.[124] In terms of the law by which the testator's capacity is to be judged, it seems preferable if this were to be referred to the law of his domicile at the time of making the will rather than the law of his domicile on the date of his death.[125] Although the matter has never been settled authoritatively, taking the date of the will allows for consistency with the English domestic approach, but more significantly prevents a once valid will becoming invalid upon the testator acquiring, and dying under, another domicile that is more restrictive in terms of its capacity rules. In connection with the related question of the capacity of a legatee to take a bequest under a will, an authoritative ruling has been supplied. In *Re Hellmann's Will*[126] it was held that the legatee is capable of taking a bequest if he had capacity either according to the law of the testator's domicile on death, or by the law of his own domicile on the date that he claims the legacy.

(b) Formal validity The second question in relation to wills concerns formal validity. And it is statute that provides the relevant rules in this context. By section 1 of the Wills Act 1963 it is provided that:

> A will shall be treated as properly executed if its execution conformed to the internal law in force in the territory where it was executed, or in the territory where, at the time of its execution or of the testator's death, he was domiciled or had his habitual residence, or in a state of which, at either of those times, he was a national.

What this somewhat convoluted provision means, once unpicked, is that apart from a will being formally valid if it is so regarded by the law of the country in which it is made,[127] it will also be formally valid if it satisfies the requirements of the law of the testator's domicile, nationality or habitual residence at the time of execution or death. In fact, a moment's reflection reveals that this section, in providing so many ways in which a will can achieve formal validity, makes formal *invalidity* a highly unlikely (if not altogether impossible) event. This is not to say, however, that the matter is entirely problem-free. To the contrary, where nationality forms the putative basis of formal validity, difficulties might well arise where a testator holds dual nationality. Here a will may have been invalid at the time of making in country X, but valid according to the law of country Y (in which country the testator died). Clearly, assuming the testator to be a national of

[124] *In the Estate of Fuld (No 3)* [1968] P 675, at 696.

[125] It is beyond doubt that the question is referable to the law of the testator's domicile: *Re Lewal's Settlement Trusts* [1918] 2 Ch 391, at 396 *per* Peterson J.

[126] (1866) LR 2 Eq 363.

[127] For these purposes, it is irrelevant that the testator was only on a temporary visit to the country in question: *Re Wynn* [1983] 3 All ER 310.

both X and Y, a choice must be made as to which country should be taken to govern. There are arguments both ways,[128] but given that the original common law rules were too rigid in this regard,[129] and given also the fact that the 1963 Act was designed to liberalise the English approach, it seems more in the spirit of the legislation to choose that nationality which is conducive to the formal validity of the will.[130] Certainly, section 6(3) of the Act is indicative of this legislative intent in so far as it provides that a will shall be formally valid if it complied with the requirements of *any* of the laws set out above either at the time of execution, or subsequently if the law in question was later changed with retrospective effect.

(c) Essential validity The third question that arises in this context concerns the essential validity of a will: that is, whether in substance it meets with certain domestic requirements of the governing law (such as leaving a fixed proportion of one's estate to certain relatives, or whether a witness can also be a beneficiary[131]). For these purposes, the essential validity is referable to the testator's domicile on death.[132] But it is important to note that the will shall only be held invalid to the extent that it does not comply with the relevant domestic requirements. It need not be regarded as wholly invalid so that once the required provision for, say, a widow and dependant children has been made, the remaining bequests in the will can be distributed as the testator intended.[133] English law imposes no fixed requirements of this kind, but it does grant certain dependants the right to apply for financial provision under the Inheritance (Provision for Family and Dependants) Act 1975.[134]

(d) Interpretation The penultimate question that may arise in connection with a will concerns the matter of its construction. In many cases, there will be no problem as long as its wording is clear and unequivocal. But problems can arise in relation to legacies left to beneficiaries who are unnamed but referred to generically by phrases such as 'next of kin'[135] which may bear a

[128] See North & Fawcett, *op cit* n 1, p 989.

[129] For illustrations of how it was too rigid, see *Bremer v Freeman* (1857) Moo PCC 301.

[130] For an analogous argument, based largely on the Parliamentary draftsman's intention to conform with the approach taken in the Hague Convention on the Formal Validity of Wills 1961, see F.A. Mann, 'The Formal Validity of Wills in Case of Dual Domicile' (1986) 35 *International and Comparative Law Quarterly* 423.

[131] Ostensibly this is a matter of form, but it is treated as one of substance: *Re Priest* [1944] Ch 58. For criticism, see O. Kahn-Freund 'Inconsistencies and Injustices in the Law of Husband and Wife' (1952) 15 *Modern Law Review* 238.

[132] *Groos v Groos* [1915] 1 Ch 572; *Re Ross* [1930] 1 Ch 377; *Re Cohn* [1945] Ch 5.

[133] *Re Annesley* [1926] Ch 692.

[134] For details, see Cretney *et al*, *op cit* n 13, pp 201–215.

[135] See, eg, *Re Fergusson's Will* [1902] 1 Ch 483.

different meaning from one country to the next. In such a case it becomes imperative to determine which law governs the interpretation of the will and the rule is that it is presumptively to be construed according to the law of the country in which the will was made.[136] The presumption can, however, be ousted where the will is framed in terms that make it clear that a particular law other than that operative in the country in which the will was made is to apply.[137]

(e) Revocation The final, by no means simple, question that arises in relation to wills concerns revocation. But since the rules on revocation vary from one country to the next, the issue that surfaces is which set of rules should determine whether the will has been revoked. Under English domestic law, a will may be revoked by the testator's subsequent marriage, by making a new will or by an act of revocation (such as destroying the original will with the intention that destruction should result in revocation). These are common (though not universal) means by which wills might be revoked. They therefore provide a useful organising structure against which the relevant conflicts rules might be considered.

Where a testator domiciled in this country makes a will, then later *both* marries *and* changes his domicile, the critical matter is whether he marries before or after changing his domicile for the law of the domicile at the time of the marriage will be the applicable law. Thus, if he changes his domicile before marrying, the will may or may not be revoked (depending on the new domiciliary law); but if he marries here before changing his domicile, revocation will occur.[138] If an English domiciliary enters into a voidable marriage it will suffice to revoke the will;[139] but a void marriage will have no effect upon it.[140]

As regards making a new will, statute provides that a subsequent will shall be effective (and thus revokes any earlier will) so long as it complies with the requirements as to formal validity under *any* of the laws by which the formal validity of the earlier will could be governed.[141] Thus, a will made in England (the testator's second domicile) will revoke an earlier will made in, say, Germany (the testator's original domicile) even if the second will would be regarded as formally valid only under English law. Finally, there is no clear rule in relation to acts of revocation. However, on principle, it would seem that an act of revocation – such as deliberate destruction of the

[136] *Re Cunnington* [1924] 1 Ch 68.
[137] *Re Price* [1900] 1 Ch 442.
[138] *Re Martin* [1900] P 211, at 240 *per* Vaughan-Williams LJ. Since the marriage occurred before revocation, the matter was dealt with as a matter of English matrimonial law.
[139] *Re Roberts* [1978] 3 All ER 225.
[140] *Mette v Mette* (1859) 1 Sw & Tr 416.
[141] Wills Act 1963, s 2(1)(c).

will – shall revoke a will only where the act in question constitutes an effective means of revocation under the law of the testator's domicile *at the time of the act*.[142]

2 Immovable property

The same five issues of capacity, formal and essential validity, interpretation and revocation that we considered in connection with movable property are pertinent to dispositions of immovable property. However, in the interests of economy of exposition, only the differences between the rules in respect of immovable and movable property will be noted. Otherwise, it may be taken that the rules are the same.[143]

So far as immovable property is concerned, it seems probable that, just as the *lex situs* governs both intestate succession and the capacity to take under a will,[144] so does it also govern the capacity to make a will in this regard.[145] In relation to formal validity, the statutory rules that apply in relation to movable property also apply in relation to immovable property except that compliance with the rules of the *lex situs* will also suffice.[146] Essential validity in relation to immovable property is governed by the *lex situs*.[147] The law of the testator's domicile will again be presumed to be the intended governing law, but where this renders construction of the will illegal or impossible, the canons of interpretation under the *lex situs* will apply.[148]

Intestate succession

Intestate succession occurs not just where a person dies without having left a valid will, but also where he dies leaving property that is not accounted for by, and disposed of under, the will. In either case, the intestacy rules require us to make the usual distinction between movable and immovable property.

1 Movable property

It has long since been settled that the distribution of movable property on intestacy is governed by the domiciliary law of the deceased at the time of

[142] See F.A. Mann, 'The Time Element in the Conflict of Laws' (1954) 31 *British Yearbook of International Law* 217.

[143] For a detailed account of the law, see North & Fawcett, *op cit* n 1, pp 1001–1008.

[144] *Birtwhistle v Vardill* (1839) 7 Cl & F 895.

[145] For the analogy with the capacity to contract with respect to foreign land (certainly governed by the *lex situs*: *Bank of Africa Ltd v Cohen* [1902] 2 Ch 129) see Collier, *op cit* n 1, p 275. For the contrary view that it should be the law of the testator's domicile that governs, see Clarkson & Hill, *op cit* n 45, p 516.

[146] Wills Act 1963, s 2(1)(b).

[147] *Freke v Lord Carbery* (1873) LR 16 Eq 461; *Re Miller* [1914] 1 Ch 511; *Re Ross* [1930] 1 Ch 377.

[148] *Philipson-Stow v IRC* [1961] AC 727.

his death.[149] But the clarity and simplicity with which this rule may apparently be stated is somewhat misleading in that two qualifications need to be added. The first of these is necessary to accommodate one potential problem turning on a change in the applicable law between the date of the intestate's death and the date on which his estate falls to be distributed. In short, is it the rules on death or the rules at the date of distribution that must be applied? There is some indication in the case law that it is the rules on death that govern;[150] but the relevant authorities are not beyond criticism.[151] The second qualification relates to the situation in which the intestate dies with no relatives left who are eligible to succeed to his movable property on intestacy. In such a circumstance, if the property is located in England, it will pass to the Crown regardless of whether under the foreign law the foreign government or treasury would be entitled to acquire the property by way of *bona vacantia* (that is, that it is no-one's property).[152] On the other hand, if the foreign country's *succession* laws would allow the foreign government or treasury to *succeed* to the intestate's movable property, that foreign law will be respected and the Crown will not acquire the property in question.[153]

2 Immovable property

The applicable law in relation to an intestate's immovable property is always that of the *lex situs*.[154] This rule, like many simple rules, is apt to give rise to questionable outcomes where the intestate who has movable property in this country dies domiciled in another country. This is because his widow stands to gain the benefit of two statutory legacies: one relating to his movable property abroad, and one based on immovable property here. In *Re Collens*,[155] the intestate died domiciled in Trinidad and Tobago leaving property not just there, but also in England. Under the law of his domicile, the intestate's widow had a claim to $1 million in settlement of any claim located in Trinidad and Tobago. But by English intestacy laws, she was also entitled to the immovable property situated in England. The then Vice-Chancellor expressed his misgivings about her double succession, yet felt bound to apply the separate laws, clear as they were, with respect to the intestate's movable and immovable property. He said:

> I think there is much force in the trenchant criticism contained in *Dicey & Morris: The Conflict of Laws* pp 613–614 as to the illogicality of requiring

[149] *Pipon v Pipon* (1744) Amb 25.
[150] *Lynch v Provisional Government of Paraguay* (1871) 2 P & D 268; *Re Aganoor's Trust* (1895) LJ Ch 521.
[151] See Collier, *op cit* n 1, pp 270–271.
[152] *Re Barnett's Trusts* [1902] 1 Ch 847.
[153] *Re Maldonado* [1954] P 223.
[154] *Duncan v Lawson* (1889) 41 Ch D 394; *Re Collens* [1986] Ch 505.
[155] [1986] Ch 505.

> English immovable assets to be regulated for the purpose of succession by the *lex situs* rather than by the law of the domicile. However, that is the law as it stands at present . . . [and] it is my job to administer the law as it is now.[156]

Conclusions and critique

In common with other areas of private international law affecting families, the rules on jurisdiction in relation to financial relief have become a veritable morass over the past few decades due largely to European initiatives in the shape of Brussels I and the Lugano Convention 1989. The Maintenance Orders (Facilities for Enforcement) Act 1920 and the Maintenance Orders (Reciprocal Enforcement) Act 1972 merely add another layer of complexity to an already confused area of the law. There is, regrettably, little prospect of rationalising or consolidating these various sets of rules since they apply to different geographic regions and there is no single legislative body with the necessary competence to effect such rationalisation. As if this were not complicated enough, things are set to get a good deal more complex when Brussels III and Brussels IV (concerning the harmonisation of 'matrimonial' property and succession rules, respectively) are implemented. The content of these Regulations is yet to be finalised; but a few tentative words about the scope and possible ramifications of Brussels III can, at least, be offered.[157]

It seems certain that the final version of Brussels III will not be confined to issues surrounding matrimonial property *in the narrow sense*. For as one of the authors of a background study undertaken on behalf of the European Commission has explained, his remit was 'the rules governing conflicts of jurisdiction and laws on matrimonial property regimes and the implications for property issues of the separation of unmarried couples in the member states'.[158] In other words, Brussels III looks destined to extend beyond the proprietary relations of married couples to those of registered partners. That it should do so is perfectly in line with the proliferation throughout continental Europe of the facility to enter such partnerships which will, as often as not, entail proprietary consequences akin to community of property for the partners concerned.[159] So the English courts, assuming the familiar

[156] *Ibid*, at 512–513 *per* Browne-Wilkinson VC.

[157] At the time of writing, I was unable to garner any practical information on the probable content of Brussels IV.

[158] C.M.V. Clarkson, 'Brussels III – Matrimonial Property European Style' [2002] *Family Law* 683, at 683.

[159] This is true of Belgium, Denmark, Germany, Iceland, The Netherlands, Norway and Sweden: see the statistics on the effects of registered partnerships as of 3 March 2003 in 'Recognition of Same-Sex Relationships in Europe' [2003] *Focus on the Family*, available at www.fotf.ca/familyfacts/takeaction European Laws Regarding Same-Sex Relationships.pdf-Sex_Relationships.pdf.

recognition and enforcement provisions get included in Brussels III, may find themselves required not only to recognise a foreign community of property regime applicable to spouses but also one applicable to registered partners. No longer will it be a matter of presumptions and rebuttals in relation to 'matrimonial property', or of discretion in relation to ante-nuptial agreements. The fact that a couple married or registered their partnership abroad will almost always lead to a clear choice of law rule and an equally clear obligation to recognise any judgment given in accordance with that choice of law. Parallel issues and problems will doubtless arise in connection with Brussels IV on succession.

Almost inevitably, there will be those who will resent this further intrusion of Brussels into the arena of English private international law.[160] Yet on the other hand, if these Regulations serve to eradicate within the EU the application of chauvinistic rules – such as that which dictates the consequences of marriage on movable matrimonial property by reference to the law of the husband's domicile – it will be no bad thing. Nor will it be a bad thing if Brussels III frees the courts from making a choice between the mutability theory, the immutability theory and the modified mutability approach; for none of these is clearly just in all cases. If there are to be unsatisfactory outcomes – to some extent unavoidable – it is arguably better that they are not attributable to individual judges who may be seen as personally responsible for the perceived injustices.

In the meantime – for it is presently unclear when we might expect Brussels III and Brussels IV to be implemented – there is at least a positive sign that a more open-minded approach will now be taken by the English courts towards the status of ante-nuptial agreements. It is to be hoped that the lead shown by the inferior courts in this regard will receive the approval of the appellate courts should the opportunity arise. To nullify meticulously drafted agreements founded on careful foresight and realism on the basis that they confound assumptions linked to a bygone age seems unwarranted in the extreme. Of course, evidence of undue influence, or of duress or of any of the usual factors that might be invoked to set aside an otherwise binding agreement should not be overlooked; but as a general principle – and consonant with the modern-day favouring of the private over the public in family law[161] – there should no longer be presumptive abhorrence shown to a form of matrimonial property regulation that is popular and effective on a close-to global basis.

[160] For an example of 'offence' being taken in the past, see D. Hodson, 'Brussels III: Financial Provision – The Next Generation' [2002] *Family Law* 30.

[161] See M. Neave, 'Private Ordering in Family Law – Will Women Benefit?' in M. Thornton (ed), *Public and Private Feminist Legal Debates* (Melbourne: Oxford University Press, 1995); A. Bainham, 'The Privatisation of the Public Interest in Children' (1990) 53 *Modern Law Review* 206.

Part III

Children in international families

7

Intercountry adoption

Adoptions with an international element fall into two broad categories: those that are afforded more or less automatic recognition by virtue of statute[1] or regulation,[2] and those that must satisfy the rules of private international law in order to achieve recognition.[3] Within the first category of cases there are two subcategories. The first of these comprises those adoptions that are afforded presumptive recognition because they fall within the regime established by the Hague Convention on Protection of Children and Co-operation in Respect of Intercountry Adoption 1993. The second embraces those cases that are afforded similar presumptive recognition on account of the fact that they were designated adoptions – that is, adoptions obtained in a country that appears on a list designated by the Secretary of State in which the legal system is thought to sanction acceptable forms of adoption.[4] Given that the recognition of adoptions falling within this second subcategory

[1] Adoption and Children Act 2002, s 66(1).

[2] Adoption (Designation of Overseas Adoptions) Order 1973 (SI 1973, No 19).

[3] Technically, a third category could be introduced: namely, that of adoptions obtained elsewhere in the British Isles than in England and Wales. But this is in practical terms of no significance since adoptions obtained in Scotland and Northern Ireland receive automatic recognition in this jurisdiction under ss 105–106 of the Adoption and Children Act 2002. And under s 108 of that Act, provision is made for regulations to be made to extend similar automatic recognition to adoptions obtained in the Isle of Man and Channel Islands.

[4] This category – referred to by statute as 'overseas adoptions' (see Adoption and Children Act 2002, s 87) – describes adoptions obtained in most of the Commonwealth, the United States, all Western European countries and some of the countries in the Balkans. (For a full list of countries, see the Adoption (Designation of Overseas Adoptions) Order 1973 (SI 1973, No 19), Sched 1.) There are several preconditions that must be satisfied for an adoption to qualify as an 'overseas adoption', so it is technically possible that an adoption obtained in a country on the designated list might not receive automatic recognition: Adoption (Designation of Overseas Adoptions) Order 1973 (SI 1973, No 19). For details see p 201 below.

turns mainly on the question of whether the country in which the adoption was obtained is one on the specified list of designated countries, such adoptions are generally unproblematic and do not require very detailed discussion in this chapter.[5] Accordingly, elaboration of, and comment upon, the relevant legal principles will be confined to just those cases falling under either the Convention regime or under the rules of private international law.

Adoption within the Intercountry Adoption Convention

Background to the Convention

The annual number of intercountry adoptions was relatively insignificant in Britain until about 1990.[6] It was about this time, however, that our television screens brought into our living rooms images of the appalling conditions under which orphaned and abandoned children were living in Romania (especially) and other former communist countries in Eastern Europe. Shortly thereafter, similar television exposure of almost equally pitiful conditions in certain Central and South America countries merely served to fuel the considerable interest in the prospect of intercountry adoption that had already sprung up in the immediate wake of the Eastern European revelations.

This growth in the desire to adopt from abroad was not, however, merely driven by the altruism of childless couples around the world,[7] sympathetic towards the plight of these children. Rather – perhaps even in greater measure – it was also spurred by the dire shortage of desirable babies and infants that were available for domestic adoption.[8] Moreover, and alarmingly, in this clamour to overcome their childlessness, many of these couples removed

[5] A useful description can be found in Department of Health, *Intercountry Adoption Guide* (London: Department of Health, 2003). One difficulty that could conceivably arise is whether the adoption was valid by the law of the country in which it was obtained. But this problem exists more in theory than reality, for all the countries on the designated list impose proper legal safeguards to prevent 'wrongful' adoptions.

[6] According to one account, there were as few as fifty per annum: see the White Paper, *Adoption: The Future* Cm 2288 (London: HMSO, 1993) para 6.2. By contrast, the estimate in a 1992 review of adoption law was of roughly 100–120 per year: see Department of Health and Welsh Office, *Review of Adoption Law*, Discussion Paper No 4 (London: HMSO, 1992) para 27.

[7] For the history of the growth in intercountry adoption up to the drafting of the Intercountry Adoption Convention, see M. Humphrey & H. Humphrey (eds), *Intercountry Adoption: Practical Experiences* (London: Routledge, 1993). For the history since, see C. Bojorge, 'Intercountry Adoptions: In the Best Interests of the Child' [2002] *Queensland University of Technology Law and Justice Journal* 266, at 267–268.

[8] This shortage can be attributed to a range of factors including wide use of easily available contraceptives, liberalisation of abortion laws, de-stigmatisation of single motherhood and falling fertility rates.

children from their State of origin with little or no formality,[9] while others obtained foreign adoption orders that were not afforded legal recognition by English law.[10] Neither the continuance of clandestine and underhand adoptions nor an absence of any proper international regulatory framework could be tolerated for long.[11] For the problem was not confined to couples in Western Europe 'exploiting' the new availability of children for adoption from their Eastern European neighbours. Similar intercountry practices were becoming established in the United States,[12] and in Australia and New Zealand.[13] Indeed, in 1994, it was estimated that the global annual figure for intercountry adoptions stood at between 15,000 and 20,000 children.[14]

The growth in popularity of intercountry adoptions coupled with the absence of any satisfactory international standard practice[15] led almost inevitably to frequent abrogation of the extant Immigration Rules. It rapidly became apparent that a proper system of regulation was required.[16] And since both sending and receiving States had a keen interest in this matter, it was widely agreed throughout both the developed and the developing world that international co-operation over the regulation and recognition of intercountry adoptions was desirable.[17] A conference was duly convened at The

[9] See C. Bridge, 'Reforming Intercountry Adoption' [1992] *Journal of Child Law* 116 and the sources cited therein at nn1–3.

[10] See, eg, *Re C (Adoption: Legality)* [1999] 1 FLR 370 where a Guatemalan adoption order was not recognised under English Law and *Re Adoption Application (Non-Patrial: Breach of Procedures)* [1993] 2 WLR 110 where an order obtained in El Salvador was held invalid.

[11] See W. Duncan, 'The Hague Convention on the Protection of Children and Co-operation in Respect of Intercountry Adoption' (1993) 17 *Adoption and Fostering* 9; P.H. Pfund, 'Intercountry Adoption: The 1993 Hague Convention: Its Purpose, Implementation and Promise' (1994) 28 *Family Law Quarterly* 54.

[12] In 2002, there were 20,099 intercountry adoptions in which the United States was the receiving State: see W.L. Pierce, 'Finding American Homes' [2002] *National Review Online* at www.nationalreview.com/comment/comment-pierce102402.asp.

[13] See Bojorge, *op cit* n 7, at 268.

[14] J. Couchman, 'Intercountry Adoption in New Zealand – A Child Rights Perspective' (1997) 27 *Victoria University of Wellington Law Review* 421, at 422.

[15] The Hague Convention on Jurisdiction, Applicable Law and Recognition of Decrees Relating to Adoption 1965, having only three signatories, was of nugatory effect.

[16] Duncan has highlighted a variety of bad and illicit practices associated with privately arranged intercountry adoptions: namely, 'poor selection and matching of adoptive parents, pressure on biological parents, failure to explore alternatives in the child's country of origin, failure to determine a child's adoptability, falsification of documents, improper financial gain, trafficking and sale of children': W. Duncan, 'Regulating Intercountry Adoption – An International Perspective' in A. Bainham *et al* (eds), *Frontiers of Family Law* (Chichester: John Wiley, 1995) p 46.

[17] For details of early signatories, see P. Nygh, 'Australia Joins Another Hague Convention' (1998) 12 *Australian Journal of Family Law* 212. Some twelve years after the Hague Conference, there is still a fairly even mix of countries that have

Hague on the Private International Law on Intercountry Adoption in 1993, and by May of that year, a Convention to *regulate*[18] intercountry adoption had been drawn up. This Convention – the Convention on Protection of Children and Co-operation in Respect of Intercountry Adoption – has now come into force not just in the United Kingdom,[19] but also in sixty-one other States around the world.[20]

Objectives of the Convention

It is clear from the Preamble to the Convention that it is intended to be consistent with the principles embodied in both the United Nations Convention on the Rights of the Child and the United Nations Declaration on Social and Legal Principles relating to the Protection and Welfare of Children with special reference to Foster Placement and Adoption Nationally and Internationally. In general terms, this signals the fact that the Intercountry Adoption Convention is intended to operate in a manner consistent with the best interests of the child;[21] and, indeed, this point is amplified in subsequent Articles.[22] This overarching objective is complemented by two subsidiary objectives. The first of these is to establish a system co-operation amongst Contracting States to ensure that the various safeguards built into the Convention are properly respected so as to minimise the incidence of child

---

ratified/acceded to the Convention: see Hague Conference on Private International Law, *Status Table*, available at http://hcch.e-vision.nl/index_en.php?act=conventions status&cid=69.

[18] It is important to note that the Convention was designed to be regulatory in nature rather than simply a means of facilitating intercountry adoptions. As such, in the Preamble to the 1993 Convention there is a clear statement that the emphasis should lie with finding acceptable homes for children rather than with finding children for childless couples. It signals 'the necessity to take measures to ensure that intercountry adoptions are made in the best interests of the child . . . and to prevent the abduction, the sale of, or traffic in children'.

[19] The Convention was incorporated into English law as Sched 1 to the Adoption (Intercountry Aspects) Act 1999. This in turn was brought into effect on 1 June 2003 by the Adoption (Intercountry Aspects) Act 1999 (Commencement No 8) Order 2003 (SI 2003, No 189). Most of the 1999 Act has now been re-enacted in the Adoption and Children Act 2002. Sections 1, 2, 7 and Sched 1 are the exceptions.

[20] Figures accurate as of 23 August 2004. For regular updates on the status of the Convention, see Hague Conference on Private International Law, *op cit* n 17.

[21] Art 21 of the UN Convention on the Rights of the Child provides: 'States Parties that recognize and/or permit the system of adoption shall ensure that the best interests of the child shall be the paramount consideration.' Contrast the very parent-centred understanding of the Convention proffered (extra-judicially) by Judge Heald that 'foreign adoptions should be encouraged to help those childless couples who want as near to normal a child as possible': 'W(h)ither Adoption: Present and Future Developments' [1992] *Family Law* 29, at 30.

[22] Intercountry Adoption Convention, Arts 1(a), 4(b).

trafficking, as well as the sale and abduction of children.[23] The second subsidiary objective is to seek to establish a uniform system of recognition of adoptions obtained in accordance with the principles and procedures contained in the Convention.[24]

Adoption under the Convention

In terms of its day-to-day operation, the Convention works according to a system of safeguards and procedures that take the form, largely, of duties that are ostensibly incumbent upon Contracting States, but which in reality are performed by national, designated Central Authorities[25] (or accredited bodies[26]). As regards procedure, Chapter IV of the Convention details a series of functions that are to be performed by the Central Authorities (or other authorised bodies) of each Contracting State. These functions relate, loosely, to the preparation and transmission of reports and other information between Central Authorities,[27] ensuring that the safeguards set out in the Convention have been properly observed[28] and facilitating the smooth transfer of the child from the State of origin to the receiving State.[29] But before exploring these safeguards and procedures in greater depth, it is useful to say a word or two about the scope of the Convention.

1 Scope

In terms of scope, the Convention is limited in its application by reference to the residency requirements built into its provisions. So, apart from the more or less self-evident point that the Convention applies only as between Contracting States,[30] Article 2(1) also makes it clear that, more narrowly still, the Convention applies only 'where a child habitually resident in one

[23] *Ibid*, Art 1(b).

[24] *Ibid*, Art 1(c).

[25] This is consistent with Art 21(e) of the United Nations Convention on the Rights of the Child which favours the placement of children for intercountry adoption by 'competent authorities or organs'. In England and Wales, the Central Authority is the Department of Health.

[26] Although the functions of a Central Authority may be performed by an accredited body, Arts 10 and 11 of the Intercountry Adoption Convention make it clear that accreditation may be granted only upon demonstration of competence to carry out the various tasks in accordance with non-profit objectives and only subject to proper supervision. Oddly, the functions of the Central Authority may also be performed by non-accredited bodies to which the non-profit condition does not apply. This gives rise to the possible difficulties discussed below.

[27] Intercountry Adoption Convention, Arts 7(2), 9, 15, 16, 20.

[28] *Ibid*, Arts 8, 17.

[29] *Ibid*, Arts 18, 19, 21.

[30] The point is nonetheless made clear in the Intercountry Adoption Convention, Art 41.

state ("the state of origin") has been, is being, or is to be moved to another Contracting State ("the receiving state")'. What this means in practice is that, since the country in which the child is habitually resident is by implication necessarily different to the country in which the prospective adopters reside,[31] the Convention cannot apply where the would-be adopters reside in the same country as the child. This would mean, for example, that a refugee-orphan residing in country X could not be adopted by sympathetic would-be parents also residing in country X. Furthermore, the Convention has no application to a case in which a child, though a national of a Contracting State is now residing in a non-Contracting State. As such, a refugee-orphan who has crossed a national border in order to avoid, say, civil war may well lose the benefits of the Convention's regime if he or she has moved to, and become habitually resident in, a non-Contracting State. These are arguably serious shortcomings in a Convention that is avowedly concerned with the best interests and protection of children.[32]

2 Safeguards

The safeguards built into the Intercountry Adoption Convention centre around three fundamental concerns. The first of these is that both the child and the would-be parents involved should be assessed for their eligibility and suitability for intercountry adoption.[33] The second is the need for proper counselling which must be provided for the birth parents, the child concerned (in the case of an older child adoption) and the would-be parents.[34] The third concern centres on the principle that intercountry adoptions must take place only once all the relevant parties have given their free consent to the adoption.[35] At a descriptive level these safeguards appear fairly straightforward. But closer analysis reveals a number of interpretational and other problems.

[31] This is not spelled out in the Convention, but it is clearly intended that there should be two different countries involved in order to give meaning to the 'intercountry' nature of the adoption: see G. Parra-Aranguren, *Explanatory Report on the Convention on Protection of Children and Co-operation in Respect of Intercountry Adoption* (1992) para 73, available at www.hcch.net/e/conventions/expl33e.html.

[32] For sustained criticism, see K. Beevers, 'Intercountry Adoption of Unaccompanied Refugee Children' [1997] *Child and Family Law Quarterly* 131 and Bojorge, *op cit* n 7. For the suggestion, however, that such children should be regarded as adoptable only once a two-year search for the child's biological family has been carried out, see United Nations High Commissioner for Refugees, *Inter-Office Memorandum No 59/95* (Geneva: UNHCR, 1995).

[33] Intercountry Adoption Convention, Arts 4(a), (b), 5(a).

[34] *Ibid*, Arts 4(c)(1), (d)(1), 5(b). There is a strong case that such counselling should be provided by specialists not only before the adoption takes place but also afterwards because of the particular difficulties that can be presented in the context of intercountry adoption.

[35] *Ibid*, Arts 4(c)(2)–(4), (d)(3).

(a) Eligibility and suitability There is a measure of difficulty associated with the Article 4 duty on the part of the State of origin to determine whether the child is suitable for adoption in both general terms and for the purposes of an intercountry adoption. The first problem here is that the Convention provides no definition of the term 'adoptable'. Does this connote that the child is merely capable of being adopted or that the child ought to be adopted? This is an important point for, as Celica Bojorge has argued, 'children should not be "adoptable" immediately following a socio-political upheaval or natural disaster, where children may only temporarily be separated from their parents'.[36] Rather, since '[t]he Convention covers only adoptions which create a permanent parent–child relationship',[37] it would be preferable if it were spelled out that the child must either have been orphaned or abandoned before an intercountry adoption may be sanctioned.[38] It is, of course, open to individual Contracting States to make more specific provision as to the criteria that will determine adoptability;[39] but this is not a step that has been taken in this country.

A second difficulty with Article 4 is the requirement in Article 4(b) that the Central Authority in the State of origin must begin its assessment of the child's adoptability by giving 'due consideration' to the possibility of a domestic placement. Again, the Convention is silent on the meaning of the key phrase 'due consideration'. On one interpretation, this might be viewed as a presumption in favour of a State of origin placement. And the basis for this interpretation would be the contention that Article 4(b) must be read in the light of Article 21(b) of the United Nations Convention on the Rights of the Child. Recalling that the Preamble to the Intercountry Adoption Convention States that it is intended to 'establish common provisions' with 'the principles set forth in . . . the United Nations Convention on the Rights of the child', it can plausibly be argued that Article 4(b) must be read consistently with Article 21(b) of the United Nations Convention. And since that latter provides that that an intercountry adoption should be countenanced only 'if the child cannot be placed in a foster or an adoptive family or cannot be cared for in the child's country of origin', it would seem to imply that 'due consideration' of domestic alternatives really means that those alternatives must always be used in preference to an intercountry adoption.[40]

[36] Bojorge, *op cit* n 7, at 271.

[37] Intercountry Adoption Convention, Art 2(2).

[38] Unicef advocates intercountry foster placements and respite care in such cases and cites the statistic of some 60,000 children being thus accommodated in Italy alone in 1997: see Unicef (1998) 4 *Innocenti Digest* 1, at 9–10.

[39] See Parra-Aranguren, *op cit* n 31, para 119.

[40] This interpretation of Art 4(b) seems consistent with the 'subsidiarity principle of intercountry adoption' described in Parra-Aranguren, *op cit* n 31, paras 120–124. See also the powerful support in A. Bainham, 'International Adoption from Romania' [2003] *Child and Family Law Quarterly* 223, at 229–231.

On the other hand, it can also be argued that since the overriding best interests principle applies to Article 4(b), there need only be *some* (but not necessarily prioritised) consideration given to possible domestic options for the child. This interpretation would recognise that a foreign adoption might frequently supply the most beneficial solution given the social realities that frequently attend intercountry adoptions: namely, high levels of poverty and unsanitary conditions in the State of origin.[41] As Johnson J noted in one case involving a Mayan Indian adoptee from Guatemala:

> Anyone who has seen the conditions in which some children are brought up in some Central and South American countries, in the shanty towns and favelas alongside the great cities, will feel an urgent desire that [these] children be given the opportunities represented by adoption into an English family.[42]

While it may plausibly be thought preferable that the latter interpretation should triumph over the former – it does, after all, hold at its core the best interests of the child rather than the arguably myopic strictures of Article 21 of the United Nations Convention – this may not be the reality. This is because of an important political dimension that cannot be ignored and which is likely to have a bearing on the interpretation adopted judicially. Article 4(b) was inserted into the Intercountry Adoption Convention quite deliberately with Article 21 of the United Nations Convention in mind. What was intended was that the Convention should not become a mere instrument to *facilitate* intercountry adoptions, but rather one to *regulate* the practice and one to encourage the establishment of better child care services in the developing nations. William Duncan has explained the anti-exploitative content of Article 4(b) in the following terms:

> [I]n intercountry adoptions, there is concern lest the principle of giving priority to the child's interests be used as an excuse for social engineering, that is to justify a more generalised transfer of children from poor to wealthy parents or from developing to rich economies.[43]

[41] For more detailed discussion on this point see J. Murphy, 'Rhetoric and Reality in Inter-Country Adoptions: Divergent Principles and Stratified Status' in J. Murphy (ed), *Ethnic Minorities, Their Families and the Law* (Oxford: Hart Publishing, 2000) and Beevers, *op cit* n 32, at 135–137.

[42] *Re C (Adoption: Legality)* [1999] 1 FLR 370, at 376–377. Other problems that make domestic adoption impossible include intolerance to certain types of children (such as mixed-race children in Vietnam: see R.R. Carlson, 'Transnational Adoption of Children' (1988) 23 *Tulsa Law Journal* 317, 318) and artificially high numbers of children (such as the children that fertile couples were economically forced to have in Ceausescu's Romania: see H.E. Bogard, 'Who are the Orphans? Defining Orphan Status and the Need for an International Convention on Intercountry Adoption' (1991) 5 *Emory International Law Review* 571, 581).

[43] Duncan, *op cit* n 16, p 42.

In the light of Duncan's explanation, it would seem probable that the first of the two interpretations of Article 4(b) suggested here will be preferred. Yet this may be unfortunate, since in terms of the quality of housing, sanitation, education, state support, access to health care, quality of health care and other such factors not generally associated with the developing nations (usually constituting States of origin), it is difficult to see how the child's best interests can realistically be secured by a provision that creates a presumption in favour of a State of origin placement.[44] As Beevers has observed, the political arguments that surface in this connection 'highlight the conflict that can arise between consideration of the best interests of the individual and the best interests of the community'.[45]

In relation to would-be adopters, the Convention again sets a minimal requirement. It states that 'the competent authorities of the receiving State [should] have determined that the prospective adoptive parents are eligible and suited to adopt'.[46] Beyond this, it is open to Contracting States to put in place more elaborate criteria relating to both eligibility and suitability.[47] In this country, this has been done by regulations that stipulate a range of conditions (relating to minimum age,[48] residency in the jurisdiction[49] and particular forms of non-criminality[50]) before a prospective adopter will be considered eligible for an intercountry adoption. What the regulations do not appear to do, however, is make the crucial distinction between eligibility and suitability. While eligibility is a necessary precondition for adoption, it should not, without more, be taken to be a sufficient one. Under Article 5 of the Convention, suitability of the adoptive parents is also required. Thus,

[44] This is not to deny that a State of origin placement may sometimes be preferable; for example, where the child concerned is no longer an infant, has acquired a particular cultural identity, has learnt to speak a language other than English or formed a close bond with individuals living in his or her country of birth. There is a wealth of literature on the importance of racial and cultural matching: see, eg, J.W. Rojewski & J.L. Rojewski, *Intercountry Adoption from China: Examining Cultural Heritage and Other Postadoption Issues* (New York: Bergin & Garvey, 2001); J. Murphy, 'Child Welfare in Transracial Adoption: Colour-blind Children and Colour-blind Law' in Murphy (ed), *op cit* n 41; P. Hayes, 'Giving Due Consideration to Ethnicity in Adoption Placements – A Principled Approach' [2003] *Child and Family Law Quarterly* 255; E. Bartholet, 'Where do Black Children Belong? The Politics of Race-Matching in Adoption' (1991) 139 *University of Pennsylvania Law Review* 1163.

[45] Beevers, *op cit* n 32, at 134.

[46] Intercountry Adoption Convention, Art 5(c).

[47] See Parra-Aranguren, *op cit* n 31, paras 109, 113.

[48] Intercountry Adoption (Hague Convention) Regulations 2003 (SI 2003, No 118) r 4. The minimum age specified is twenty-one years.

[49] *Ibid*. The prospective adopter(s) must have been habitually resident within the British Isles for a period of at least one year prior to being considered eligible.

[50] *Ibid*, r 6. The person cannot be regarded as eligible if he or she has been convicted or cautioned in relation to certain types of offence specified in Sched 2 to the Adoption Agencies Regulations 1983 (SI 1983, No 1964): *ibid*, r 6(2).

while eligibility governs the general question of whether *in principle* X and Y may qualify as prospective adopters, suitability goes beyond this and requires, further, that X and Y might also be regarded as appropriate parents for the particular child, Z.

The Convention is silent on what constitutes suitability; but in only countenancing adoptions by 'spouses or a person habitually resident in the receiving State',[51] it is clear that both same-sex partners and unmarried opposite-sex cohabitants were originally regarded as unsuitable adopters. However, since the Convention was finalised some countries have begun to permit same-sex marriage making it possible for gay and lesbian married couples to fall within the Convention's requirement that joint adopters be 'spouses'. In this country, however, regulations continue to prohibit intercountry adoptions by same-sex spouses.[52] And in imposing such a prohibition, they are not only out of step with the way in which the Convention must now arguably be understood, but also with domestic adoption legislation, which permits adoption by unmarried couples of whatever sexual orientation.[53] Given that the English regulations were drafted after same-sex marriage became possible in a number of countries, it seems regrettable that they should impose such a bar, especially since they are designed to facilitate the operation of a Convention that has the best interests of children as its primary concern. For as Bojorge has argued:

> De facto couples and same-sex couples . . . can provide a child with a family environment in an atmosphere of happiness, love and understanding as required by the Hague Convention . . . The focus should be on whether the person is suitable to meet and promote the child's best interests and not on stereotypes and assumptions about homosexuality and marital status.[54]

And as Andrew Bainham has pointed out (although not specifically in relation to the Intercountry Adoption Convention), 'it is illogical that one member of an unmarried couple, whether heterosexual or homosexual, should be allowed to achieve singly what that couple cannot achieve together'.[55]

(b) Counselling As regards the counselling safeguard, it is incumbent on the competent authorities of both States to ensure that all relevant parties 'have been counselled as may be necessary'.[56] In reality, what this means is that

[51] Intercountry Adoption Convention, Art 2(1).

[52] Intercountry Adoption (Hague Convention) Regulations 2003 (SI 2003, No 118) r 3(1).

[53] Under the Adoption and Children Act 2002, s 50, provision is made for adoption by 'couples'; and the term 'couples' is defined in s 144(4) in terms of stable cohabiting partners whether of the same or different sex.

[54] Bojorge, *op cit* n 7, at 278.

[55] A. Bainham, *Children – The Modern Law* (Bristol: Jordan Publishing, 1998) p 212.

[56] Intercountry Adoption Convention, Arts 4(c)(1), 5(b).

prior counselling of the birth parents, the (sufficiently mature) child and the adoptive parents is seen as an important precursor to an intercountry adoption. But what is lacking in the Convention is any mention of the kinds of persons that must provide such counselling. For instance, ought they to hold particular qualifications in relation to intercountry adoption? Equally, the Convention is silent on the matter of what constitutes counselling 'as may be necessary'. It fails to specify any minimal understanding that must be achieved, or any minimum time period that must be devoted to such counselling, just as it omits to identify who is to judge what level of counselling is 'necessary'.

Despite these gaps in the Convention, the Intercountry Adoption (Hague Convention) Regulations 2003 do elaborate a little on the matter. Where this country is the receiving State, the regulations require generally that there must be a counselling service for the prospective adopter(s) and that the legal implications and procedures associated with a Convention adoption are properly explained.[57] They also require, more specifically, that once the relevant information concerning the *particular child* has been received, that information should be sent to the would-be adopters and that it should be discussed with them with supplemental counselling made available.[58] It might sensibly be asked, then, whether the regulations go far enough, given the duty in Article 9(c) of the Convention for the Central Authorities to 'promote the development of adoption counselling and post adoption services within their States'. Certainly, one might have expected some elaboration of the minimum Convention requirements regarding counselling since it is clear that the counselling envisaged by Article 4 is necessarily of a limited nature: it implies that counselling will take place only prior to an adoption.[59]

(c) Free consent Before an intercountry adoption can take place, the Convention requires that the birth parents (and/or any relevant institutions and authorities[60]) must 'consent freely, in the required legal form' to that adoption.[61] It also states that a freely given consent on the part of the child

[57] Intercountry Adoption (Hague Convention) Regulations 2003 (SI 2003, No 118) r 5(1)(a), (b).

[58] *Ibid*, r 12(2).

[59] Art 29 of the Intercountry Adoption Convention prohibits any contact between the birth and adoptive parents until after the counselling requirements of Arts 4 and 5 have been fulfilled. This suggests that counselling may stop at a relatively early stage.

[60] In the case of a child who has been orphaned or abandoned, the child is probably in some form of state or institutional care, and it is from these authorities or institutions that the appropriate consent must be obtained. Such consent on the part of these authorities must be given before the child reaches eighteen years of age otherwise the Convention ceases to apply: Intercountry Adoption Convention, Art 3.

[61] Intercountry Adoption Convention, Art 4(c)(2). This subsection also requires, for evidentiary purposes, that the consent be 'expressed or evidenced in writing'.

is required 'having regard to the age and degree of maturity of the child'.[62] It does not state explicitly that the child must beyond a certain level of maturity – a level at which, presumably, he or she would understand the nature and effects of an intercountry adoption – but it seems tolerably clear that this is what is intended.[63] Nor does the Convention state what is meant by freely given consent. But this is unlikely to prove a problematic notion for the English courts since it is a familiar concept present in both the Adoption and Children Act 2002[64] and the Matrimonial Causes Act 1973 (in relation to the quality of consent required to contract a valid marriage).[65] Nonetheless, the significance of this requirement should not be downplayed, for it is central to the Convention's endeavour to eliminate the trafficking or sale of children.

In relation to both the consent of the birth parents and (in appropriate cases) of the child concerned, it is clear that the Convention sets its face against financially induced adoptions. More specifically, it requires the competent authorities of the State of origin to ensure that the consents of both the birth parents and (where appropriate) the child should not have been 'induced by payment or compensation of any kind'.[66] Ostensibly, this would appear to rule out any kind of monetary transactions in connection with Convention adoptions. But in fact this is not the case, for Articles 8 and 32 have an important bearing on the proper construction on this prohibition. Under Article 8, Central Authorities are required to take 'all appropriate measures to prevent *improper financial or other gain* in connection with an adoption'.[67] While under Article 32 '[n]o one shall derive *improper financial or other gain* from an activity related to an intercountry adoption', it is also provided that '[o]nly costs and expenses, including reasonable professional fees . . . may be charged or paid'.[68] It is thus clear that so far as the parents and children are concerned, there shall be no monetary (or money's worth) payments or compensation paid in order to secure a consent. What is specifically proscribed under Article 4 is that the relevant consents have not been *induced* in this way. Once the consents have been given free from any

[62] *Ibid*, Art 4(d)(3). This subsection also requires that the consent be 'expressed or evidenced in writing'.

[63] Recalling the fact that the Intercountry Adoption Convention purports in its Preamble to be at one with the principles enshrined in the United Nations Convention on the Rights of the Child, it is worth recalling that Art 12(1) of that latter stipulates that any child able to form his or her own views ought to have due weight accorded to those views in the light of his or her age and maturity.

[64] Under s 52(5) of that Act, 'consent' is defined as being 'consent given unconditionally and with full understanding of what is involved'. The notion of full and free consent also appeared in the previous legislation, the Adoption Act 1976, s 16(1).

[65] Under the 1973 Act, s 12(c) provides helpful guidance as to the kinds of factors that will vitiate consent, eg, duress, mistake and unsoundness of mind.

[66] Intercountry Adoption Convention, Arts 4(c)(3), (d)(4).

[67] Emphasis added.

[68] Intercountry Adoption Convention, Art 32(1), (2) (emphasis added).

financial incentive or guarantee, certain, payments may be made, so long as they are not 'improper'.

Here, again, a problem of interpretation arises in connection with a key word. In deciding whether any cash (or other valuable) payments fall foul of the Convention everything turns on the meaning of the word 'improper' within Articles 8 and 32. Yet there is no definition of what constitutes an improper payment, and opinion is likely to be divided. What amounts to a reasonable sum by way of, say, professional legal fees in this country may well be seen as exorbitant by those in an impoverished, developing nation. Equally, a request by the orphanage from which the child comes in, for example, Ecuador, might be seen as a relatively small sum by the adoptive parents asked to pay it, but hugely – perhaps exploitatively – gainful on the part of those making the request. One thing is for certain, and that is that intercountry adoption is anything but a non-commercial phenomenon, at least if the Romanian example is anything to go by.[69]

A final point of note in relation to consent is that a birth mother is not permitted to give her consent to an intercountry adoption until after the birth of the child. This provision displays both merits and flaws. On the one hand, it clearly helps to avoid the possibility of pressure being applied to a pregnant woman to encourage her to surrender her child for adoption while she is confined in hospital. But on the other hand, it arguably does not go far enough. For, in allowing the mother to consent very shortly after the birth, it runs the risk that she may make a hasty and ill-considered decision to allow her child to be adopted. A useful contrast may be drawn here with domestic adoption legislation which stipulates that the birth mother cannot give an effective consent to adoption until at least six weeks after the birth of the child concerned.[70] The rationale for this provision is clearly to allow the mother to recover properly from the birth and the depression that can frequently attend the immediate post-natal period.

3 Procedural matters

In addition to the various safeguards built into the convention, there are a number of minimum procedural requirements that must be observed.[71] These, again, are designed to promote the best interests of the child. They centre on the twin objectives of ensuring that there is the proper gathering and transmission of information between the relevant Central Authorities and the removal in advance of any obstacles that might otherwise arise in the actual migration process.

[69] See Bainham, *op cit* n 40, at 227. See also the alarming facts of *Re M (Adoption: Interactional Adoption Trade)* [2003] 1 FLR 1111.

[70] Adoption and Children Act 2002, s 52(3).

[71] Intercountry Adoption Convention, Art 39(2) specifically envisages bilaterally agreed derogations from the duties of Central Authorities where those derogations are aimed at 'improving the application of the Convention in their mutual relations'.

(a) Reports and checks Under Articles 15 and 16 of the Convention, respectively, the Central Authorities of the receiving State and State of origin must prepare and exchange reports on the eligibility and suitability of the prospective adopters and on the adoptability of the child.[72] Before reaching any final decision on a proposed adoption, the Central Authorities must also carry out various checks on the relevant consents[73] and the particular match between the child and prospective adoptive parents (in terms of special needs, medical history, religious and cultural background, etc).[74] Only once these final checks have been made may an adoption proceed.

(b) Smooth migration Once the Central Authorities are satisfied that an intercountry adoption may proceed, they must also take the necessary steps to ensure the smooth transmission of the child between the State of origin and the receiving State. Accordingly, the central authorities of *both* States are required to take 'all necessary steps to obtain permission for the child to leave the State of origin and to enter and reside permanently in the receiving state'.[75] Furthermore, it is also incumbent upon the receiving State to have determined that the child is or will be authorised to enter that State and reside there permanently.[76] These two provisions seek to make sure that proper migration clearance has been obtained in order to eliminate any potential distress to the child caused by migration bureaucracy. Article 19 of the Convention goes still further by focusing on the actual passage of the child, as opposed to the legal matters associated with crossing national borders. It requires the Central Authorities to ensure that the transfer of the child takes place in secure and appropriate circumstances, if possible with the accompaniment of the adoptive parents.[77]

Recognition of Convention adoptions

Although the general rule is that an adoption made in compliance with the principles and provisions contained in the Intercountry Adoption Convention

[72] Parts 2 and 3 the Intercountry Adoption (Hague Convention) Regulations 2003 (SI 2003, No 118) elaborate considerably upon these minimal requirements stating, eg, the exact information that should be contained in the reports. Detailed guidance is also available in Department of Health, *op cit* n 5, Parts I and II.

[73] Intercountry Adoption Convention, Arts 16(1)(c), 17(a).

[74] *Ibid*, Art 16(1)(b), (d).

[75] *Ibid*, Art 18.

[76] *Ibid*, Art 5(c). In view of this requirement, by virtue of an amendment to the British Nationality Act 1981, s 1(5) wrought by the Adoption (Intercountry Aspects) Act 1999, s 7, elaborate provision is made for foreign children to acquire British citizenship automatically – sometimes in advance of the actual adoption order. For details: see C. Bridge & H. Swindells, *Adoption – The Modern Law* (Bristol: Jordan Publishing, 2003) pp 304, 307–309.

[77] *Ibid*, Art 19(2).

will trigger automatic recognition of that adoption among all other Contracting States,[78] the legal status of the child may nonetheless be uncertain in some cases. Under the Convention, adoptions need not necessarily take place in the receiving State; they may equally well occur in the State of origin.[79] And as Rainer Frank has explained, adoptions often will take place there, for many such '[s]tates of origin want to protect the interests of their children, especially against the traffic in children'.[80] In such circumstances, two types of difficulty can arise: one relates to a discretion to refuse recognition to a State of origin adoption, the other stems from the fact that recognition may in any event be difficult because of different juridical notions of what an adoption entails.

Article 24 of the Convention permits a Contracting State to refuse to recognise an adoption 'if the adoption is manifestly contrary to its public policy, taking into account the best interests of the child'.[81] The Convention does not specify any examples of what might be a suitable policy consideration for these purposes. Possibly it would be sufficient if the adoption obtained in State X had been sanctioned by a non-judicial authority, while the receiving State, in the interests of proper public records and solemnity, adhered to a policy whereby only judicially sanctioned adoptions should be valid.[82] Alternatively, it may well be that after an adoption has taken place but before the child has been transferred to the receiving State, certain violations of the Convention come to light – for example, wrongful cash payments to the birth parents or authorities in the State of origin. In such circumstances the receiving State may refuse to recognise the adoption. Finally, and perhaps most likely, difficulties could also arise where a third Contracting State refused to recognise an adoption.[83] It may well be that a country would seek to refuse recognition of an adoption where the adoptive

[78] *Ibid*, Art 23(1). For the purposes of the Convention, recognition primarily involves recognition of the legal parent–child relationship between the adoptee and his or her adopter(s) and the parental responsibility of the adoptive parent(s) for the child: *ibid*, Art 26(1).

[79] *Ibid*, Art 2(1).

[80] R. Frank, 'The Recognition of Intercountry Adoptions in the Light of the 1993 Hague Convention on Intercountry Adoptions' in N. Lowe & G. Douglas (eds), *Families Across Frontiers* (Amsterdam: Kluwer Academic Publishers, 1996) p 591.

[81] Even after a Convention adoption has been granted, the English courts have the power to annul it on the ground of public policy: Adoption and Children Act 2002, s 89(1).

[82] Art 23(1) of the Convention requires only that a Convention adoption be certified by a competent authority; it does not insist that the competent authority be a court. Yet it has long been a condition of the validity of an 'overseas adoption' that the relevant order is made by a court: see Adoption (Designation of Overseas Adoptions) Order 1973 (SI 1973, No 19) r 3(3).

[83] Under Art 23(1), all Contracting States are *prima facie* bound to recognise a Convention adoption.

family wished to migrate to the objecting country in whose eyes the adoption was offensive either because the adoptive parents were too young, or because they were unmarried, or because they were same-sex spouses.

The second source of uncertainty concerning the status of an intercountry adoption is Article 26 which seeks to specify the *effects* of recognition.[84] More particularly, there are three uncertainties to which Article 26 gives rise. The first of these stems from Article 26(2) which provides:

> In the case of an adoption having the effect of terminating a pre-existing legal parent–child relationship, the child shall enjoy in the receiving State, and in any other Contracting State where the adoption is recognised, rights equivalent to those resulting from adoptions having this effect in each such State.

The intention behind this provision was to make the child's rights in the receiving State the same as those of any other child adopted in the receiving State *so long as* the receiving State permits adoptions whereby there is complete severance of the legal relationship between the child and the birth parents. This provision was considered important because not all countries have only the 'absolute' form of adoption (that is, an adoption whereby the legal link to the child is transferred entirely from the birth parents to the adoptive parents). France, for example, has both the *adoption plénière* and the *adoption simple*. According to the latter model, the adoption does not sever altogether the legal tie between the child and the natural parents. Article 26(2) attempts to make it clear that, if the adoption granted in the State of origin is an absolute adoption, it should also be viewed as having this effect in the receiving State even though the receiving State may also permit simple adoptions.

But in solving one problem, this 'half-baked' provision would appear to suggest another: namely, that of a legal limbo for the child where the State of origin allows only the open form of adoption (the *adoption simple*, to use the French term). Article 26(2) cannot be invoked in such circumstances because it is a condition precedent of its applicability that there is an 'adoption having the effect of terminating a pre-existing legal parent–child relationship'.[85] As such, if the receiving State does not provide for the *adoption simple* (in which case it is an unfamiliar juridical entity in that State) it is difficult to envisage just what *effects* the simple adoption obtained in the first State will be granted in the receiving State.

A possible solution to this problem – but a somewhat problematic one – may inhere in the *tenor* of Article 26(3), for this subparagraph allows the

[84] As to the difference between recognition *per se*, and the *effects* of recognition, see Frank, *op cit*, n 80.

[85] Recognising the fact that different States have different models of adoption, domestic legislation makes special provision allowing 'partial Convention adoptions' to have the same effects as in the country of origin: Adoption and Children Act 2002, s 87.

receiving State (or any other Contracting State in which the question of recognition arises) to ignore Article 26(2) and apply 'any provision more favourable for the child' so long as it is a provision that is 'in force in the Contracting State [in question]'. The gist of this provision is to allow the juridical character of the original adoption to be overlooked in the receiving State so as to better promote the interests of the child. Extrapolating from this provision, it could be argued that an *adoption simple* ought to be treated in the same manner as its *nearest comparator* (full adoption) under the domestic law of the receiving State in order to avoid the limbo situation described above. Yet if this were done, and if the *adoption simple* obtained in the State of origin were to be treated as though it were an *adoption plénière* in the receiving State, would the receiving State thereby sever any succession rights that may otherwise have accrued *vis-à-vis* the birth parents, and would any siblings that the adoptee may have had cease to be regarded as such?

A second problem with Article 26(2) arises where the State of origin in which the adoption is obtained purports to apply a model of full adoption, but in fact, in truth applies a model closer to the French *adoption simple* which allows the birth parents to retain a range of residual rights in respect of the child concerned. Rainer Frank has identified a number of such States;[86] and it simply not clear whether Article 26(2) applies in these circumstances. This in turn means that the child's legal link to both the adoptive and birth families is somewhat hazy, even though there is no question that the child is formally an adoptee within the Convention. In such a situation, perhaps the best approach would be to repeat the adoption in the receiving State in order to put beyond doubt its juridical character. But the problem with this is Article 27(1) of the Convention which provides for such repeat adoptions only '[w]here an adoption granted in the State of origin does not have the effect of terminating a pre-existing legal parent–child relationship'. The remainder of the Convention is totally silent on whether repeat adoptions are permissible in other circumstances.[87] That said, it would seem contrary to the spirit of the Convention to allow free and easy use to be made of repeat adoptions in the receiving State. For so doing would tend to undermine Chapter V of the Convention, which is specifically designed to provide for the recognition of any adoption obtained in a Contracting State.[88] As such Article 27 is probably better understood as laying down the *only* circumstances in which repeat adoptions will be permissible. And its applicability is unclear in this context.

[86] See Frank, *op cit* n 80, p 601.

[87] Cf Rainer Frank's interpretation that 'Article 27 states that the repetition of an intercountry adoption domestically is excluded if the adoption leads to a termination of the natural parent–child relationship': Frank, *op cit* n 80, p 603.

[88] There would be far less point in having a Convention to regulate intercountry adoptions if it failed to reduce to a minimum the need for repeat adoptions.

The third uncertainty to which Article 26 gives rise stems from the wording of Article 26(1), for this does no more than stipulate that the newly established parent–child relationship (together with parental responsibility) is to be recognised among other Contracting States. It does not, however, indicate which law governs the nature of that parent–child relationship, the law of the receiving State or the law of the State of origin. The matter might be important, for at least two reasons. First, it would be important to know the extent of the adopter's parental responsibility for the purposes of decision-making with respect to the child in cases where the State of origin adoption did not completely sever the initial parent–child relationship. Secondly, there would be the potential problem of the child growing up without a proper sense of belonging to the adoptive family. The acquisition of an incomplete self-image of this kind can hardly be viewed in terms of the child's best interests. Of course, the remedy in this situation would be to repeat the adoption in this country under Article 27. But some adoptive parents, now perhaps thousands of miles from the State of origin, might not perceive the need to do this. Indeed, they might well consider the matter not to be an issue at all until it is too late and the birth parents have, some years down the line, already sought to re-establish contact with their child.

To a large extent the problems outlined in relation to the recognition provisions of the Convention stem from the fact that this part of the Convention was drafted by way of a political compromise between the developed nations (primarily as receiving States) and the developing nations (most commonly, States of origin). It favours neither receiving nor sending States. But in having been drafted with this attempt at compromise in mind, it is unsurprising that the various provisions considered here should give rise to interpretational uncertainty; for legislative compromise often comes at the cost of high levels of specificity. But the real pity is that, amidst the legal disputes to which these uncertainties may well give rise, the best interests of children are in danger of being compromised.

Non-Convention adoptions

Intercountry adoptions obtained outside the regime established by the Intercountry Adoption Convention fall into three categories. By statute, the first of these categories is labelled 'overseas adoptions'. And the relevant rules governing the recognition of such adoptions are entirely statutory. They create a strong presumption (but not a guarantee) of recognition. The second category comprises cases in which the adoption in question concerns a foreign child adopted abroad. Here, the main rules governing recognition are to be found in the common law, although some statutory provisions also apply. Finally, the third category embraces cases in which a child of foreign domicile is brought to this country for adoption here. In this context, the bulk of the relevant law is to be found in the Adoption and Children Act 2002 as well as regulations made under both that Act and the Adoption (Intercountry Aspects) Act 1999.[89] We consider each category in turn.

Overseas adoptions

Under section 87 of the Adoption and Children Act 2002, the Secretary of State is empowered to designate 'overseas adoptions' which, by virtue of this status, will presumptively have the same effect in law as adoptions obtained within England and Wales. This power is not a new one, and a great many adoptions throughout the world – especially adoptions obtained in most of the Commonwealth, the United States, Western Europe and parts of the Balkans – have already been designated 'overseas adoptions' for these purposes under corresponding powers in previous legislation.[90] It is important to stress, however, that designation refers to adoptions rather than countries. This can be significant because a number of conditions must be satisfied before any given adoption may qualify for 'overseas adoption' status: the adoption must have been effected under statutory provisions (not common law or customary law), and the adoption must be in respect of an unmarried person who was under the age of eighteen at the time of the application.[91] If, then, for the sake of argument the adoption of an adult occurs in a country that is named on the list, the adoption cannot be treated as an overseas adoption.

Furthermore, even if the adoption meets these conditions, it may still be annulled subsequently on the grounds of public policy.[92] We have already seen in the context of Convention adoptions that public policy provides a basis for refusal of recognition; and the kinds of considerations discussed there could also (presumably) be invoked to invalidate an overseas adoption. Finally, an overseas adoption may also be denied recognition on the alternative basis that the authority that purported to authorise it was not competent to do so.[93]

Other non-Convention adoptions effected abroad

In this context we are concerned with non-Convention adoptions that take place abroad, involve foreign children and do not qualify as 'overseas adoptions'. Although in reality most adoptions that take place abroad are likely to be either Convention adoptions or overseas adoptions, this third category

[89] Adoption of Children from Overseas Regulations 2001 (SI 2001, No 1251).
[90] Adoption (Designation of Overseas Adoptions) Order 1973 (SI 1973, No 19).
[91] *Ibid*, r 3(3).
[92] Adoption and Children Act 2002, s 89(2)(a).
[93] *Ibid*.

of foreign adoptions is not wholly unimportant. For example, the recognition of such an adoption may well be critical to determining a child's right to migrate to this country when the adoptive family seeks to move here from abroad.[94] And more commonly – at least according to the reported cases – the question of recognising such an adoption will be central in resolving certain property claims, such as the right of an adoptive child to take property upon intestacy,[95] or under a will,[96] or according to a settlement.[97] And it will be equally central to determining the right of an adoptive parent to succeed upon the adoptive child's intestacy.

At common law, the recognition of such adoptions turns upon the adoptive parents being domiciled in the country in which the adoption took place at the time of the adoption. One basis for the Court of Appeal's decision to this effect in *Re Valentine's Settlement*[98] was that, since adoption concerns status – a matter usually referable to domiciliary law – the validity of any such foreign adoption ought to be judged according to the law of the parents' domicile. A second reason for the court adopting this approach was the fact that the private international law rule would be analogous to the domestic jurisdictional rule according to which an adoption in this country could be sanctioned only if one or both of the adoptive parents were domiciled here. However, since the Adoption and Children Act 2002 now permits domestic adoptions both by parents who are domiciled in this country and by parents who are merely habitually resident here (and have been for at least one year ending with the date of the adoption application),[99] it is arguable that the rule in *Re Valentine's Settlement* should be extended to cover foreign adoptions by parents habitually resident in the country in which the adoption takes place. This would certainly preserve the analogy between the recognition rules and the domestic jurisdictional rules. But it would also mean that certain English domiciliaries who become habitually resident in a non-Convention country would be able to adopt in that country without, as is currently required under the common law, surrendering their English domicile.

In other words, if the rule in *Re Valentine's Settlement* were to be extended in this way, it may create a facility by which a wealthy, childless person or couple might seek to circumvent the usual immigration controls. There can be no doubt that such practice would be contrary to the spirit of the modern

[94] See, eg, *Secretary of State for the Home Department v Lofthouse* [1981] Imm AR 166.

[95] See, eg, *Re Wilson* [1954] Ch 733.

[96] See, eg, *Re Marshall* [1957] Ch 507.

[97] See, eg, *Re Valentine's Settlement* [1965] Ch 831.

[98] [1965] Ch 831.

[99] Adoption and Children Act 2002, s 49(2), (3). One difference that remains between applications made on the basis of domicile and habitual residence is that whereas only one of the couple needs to be domiciled here, both the would-be adoptive parents must have been habitually resident here.

legislation. Indeed, section 83 of the Adoption and Children Act 2002 was inserted into the legislation in response to the much-publicised 'internet adoption' case of *Flintshire County Council v K*[100] – a case in which, after the payment of money, an English couple brought twins to this country following their adoption of the twins in Arkansas. Under section 83, it is now an offence to bring a child into the United Kingdom within six months of his or her adoption abroad if there has been no compliance with the prescribed regulations.[101]

Even as it stands, the rule in *Re Valentine's Settlement* might be thought inadequate since it refers only to the domicile of the adoptive parents.[102] It pays no heed to the domicile of the child although the status of the child is just as much an issue as the status of the would-be adoptive parents. There is some judicial support for the view that the child should at least have been habitually resident in the country in which the adoption takes place.[103] Such an approach might be commended in practical terms because it at least acknowledges the significance of the child's interests in the adoption, yet it also has the flexibility to permit adoptions of orphaned refugee children that may have crossed national frontiers and established a new habitual residence. Nonetheless, *Re Valentine's Settlement* remains the pre-eminent authority in this context. And it was resolutely held in that case that an adoption in South Africa by a couple domiciled in Southern Rhodesia could not be recognised on the basis that the parents were not domiciled in South Africa. In the words of Lord Denning MR: 'we should recognise an adoption order made by another country when the adopting parents are domiciled there.'[104]

Finally, it is again important to note the potential relevance of public policy. In *Re Valentine's Settlement*, Lord Denning MR expressed the view that a foreign adoption which passes the threshold test discussed above may nonetheless be denied recognition by the English courts on the basis of public policy.[105] This rule mirrors the approach of both the Intercountry Adoption Convention[106] and the domestic legislation in relation to 'overseas adoptions',[107] and an obvious instance in which this discretion to refuse recognition might be invoked is where the adoption was designed to circumvent immigration laws. Another possible scenario would be where the

[100] [2001] 2 FLR 476.

[101] Adoption (Bringing Children into the United Kingdom) Regulations 2003 (SI 2003, No 1173).

[102] It is not clear from the case whether one parent being domiciled in the country in which the adoption takes place would suffice. But if the analogy with the domestic jurisdictional rule is to be complete, it ought to suffice.

[103] See *Re Valentine's Settlement* [1965] Ch 831, at 842–843 *per* Lord Denning MR (*obiter*) and *Re B (S) (An Infant)* [1968] Ch 204, at 209–210 *per* Goff J.

[104] [1965] Ch 831, at 842.

[105] *Ibid*. But contrast the view of Salmon LJ: *ibid*, at 854.

[106] Art 24.

[107] Adoption and Children Act 2002, s 89(2)(a).

adoption was of an adult (which is permissible under some systems of law). On the other hand, it might be argued that recognising the adoption of an adult is no more antithetical to public policy than the recognition of a polygamous marriage,[108] or even the recognition of a non-judicial divorce.[109] And since these are both possible, why should recognition of an adoption involving an adult adoptee be treated any differently?

Other non-Convention adoptions effected in this country

The final category of non-convention adoptions to be considered comprises those adoptions of *foreign* children that take place in this country. Because such adoptions are effected here, the English courts must abide by the elaborate provisions of the Adoption and Children Act 2002 which apply equally to purely domestic adoptions before any order can be made.[110] The fact that the same legislative provisions apply regardless of the nationality of the child serves to dilute the significance of the child's foreign nationality. However, four distinguishing factors can be identified between adoptions involving foreign children and children born here. First, there are fixed procedures set out in regulations that must be adhered to before any child can be brought into the United Kingdom for the purpose of adoption.[111] Secondly, in making its assessment of whether an adoption would be conducive to a foreign child's welfare (as is required by statute[112]), the court may need to take account of the fact that the adoption may not be recognised by the law of the child's domicile; for granting an adoption application may create a situation in which a child has two sets of parents (according to the two systems of law), both of whom have a valid claim to parental status. Thirdly, dispensing with the birth parents' consent to an adoption on the grounds that they cannot be found may acquire a special significance in this context.[113] And finally, where the motive behind an adoption is an endeavour to

[108] See ch 3.

[109] See ch 5.

[110] For details, see S.M. Cretney, J.M. Masson & R. Bailey-Harris, *Principles of Family Law* (London: Sweet & Maxwell, 2002) ch 23.

[111] Adoption (Bringing Children into the United Kingdom) Regulations 2003 (SI 2003, No 1173). Failure to abide by these regulations amounts to a criminal offence punishable by imprisonment, or a fine, or both: Adoption and Children Act 2002, s 83(7), (8).

[112] Adoption and Children Act 2002, s 1.

[113] Such dispensation is permitted under s 52(1)(a) of the Adoption and Children Act 2002. But case-law suggests that rather strenuous efforts should be made to find the birth parents including unmarried fathers who have played a significant part in the child's life: *Re H; Re G (Adoption: Consultation of Unmarried Fathers)* [2001] 1 FLR 646. On the other hand, where there has already been a foreign adoption, and the local law prohibits the tracing of birth parents, the English courts will have to treat those parents as untraceable: *Re A (Adoption of a Russian Child)* [2000] 1 FLR 539.

circumvent immigration controls rather than a *bona fide* transfer of parental responsibility, the English courts may treat the application as a sham and decline to grant an order.[114]

Effect of non-Convention adoptions

The effects of non-Convention adoptions are always the same.[115] It makes no difference whether a foreign child is adopted in this country, whether the adoption is an 'overseas adoption', or whether it is simply a foreign adoption recognised as valid in this country by virtue of the rules of private international law. All foreign adoptees are treated as legitimate and as if they had been born to the adoptive parents. They will no longer be regarded as the children of the birth parents.[116] As such, the adoption can serve to confer British nationality upon a foreign child, and it may also have legal repercussions in terms of succession or social security laws (such as eligibility for child tax credits). Social security legislation is far too complex to warrant discussion here. But in terms of succession, it may briefly be noted that an adopted child will enjoy virtually the same rights as any other child.[117] The only exceptions in this context relate to titles of honour. Thus, adoption 'does not affect the descent of any peerage or dignity or title of honour'.[118] Nor, in the absence of contrary intention, is property that is limited to devolve along with a title of honour affected by adoption.[119]

Conclusions and critique

There can be no doubt that many of the concerns voiced at the Hague Conference convened in connection with the largely unregulated growth in intercountry adoption have been endorsed by the widespread ratification of, and accession to, the 1993 Convention. However, notwithstanding this extensive implementation of the Convention among wealthy, industrialised States and developing nations alike, there remain, in intercountry adoption terms, some very important countries that continue to fall outside its regime.

[114] See *Re B (Adoption Order: Nationality)* [1999] 1 FLR 907.

[115] It will be noted that provision is made for recognition of partial adoptions, which will have a more limited effect under s 87 of the Adoption and Children Act 2002.

[116] Adoption and Children Act 2002, s 67(1)–(3).

[117] If the succession in question is a foreign one, the applicable law is the foreign law. But English law may still be relevant in determining the initial question concerning the adoptive status of the child.

[118] Adoption and Children Act 2002, s 71(1).

[119] *Ibid*, s 71(2), (3).

At the time of writing, for example, both China and the United States – respectively very significant sending and receiving States – were among those States that had merely signed but not yet ratified the Convention.[120] The imperfections in the Convention regime do not, however, end there. Many of these we noted in passing, such as the fact that orphaned, refugee children that flee to another country where prospective adopters exist are, by definition, excluded from the compass of the Convention.[121] There are other flaws, too. For instance, the key concept of an 'adoptable' child is nowhere defined in the Convention; yet the child's adoptability is central to the operation of the Convention.[122] Similarly, although Central Authorities are required to take all appropriate measures to prevent improper financial gain being made in connection with intercountry adoptions, the term 'improper financial gain' is, again, undefined. This may well prove to be a significant shortcoming since adoptions may still be co-ordinated by non-accredited bodies or persons[123] who are not limited (in contrast to their accredited counterparts) to pursue non-profit objectives. In such circumstances, the demarcation between proper and improper financial gain becomes critical.

In related vein, the requirement that the competent authorities of a State should ensure that the relevant consents 'have not been induced by payment or compensation of any kind'[124] may prove to have the least force where it is most needed. This is because Article 8 of the Convention imposes no higher duty upon Central Authorities than to take 'all appropriate measures' to ensure that the consents were obtained free of any financial or other inducement. Since the 'appropriate measures' are to be determined by the Central Authorities themselves, the danger here is that in relatively poor, sending States, the threshold of what amounts to 'appropriate' might be set a level that does not correspond to what wealthier States would consider to be appropriate.

In terms of omissions, a serious shortcoming in the Convention is its failure to put in place any enforcement mechanism or complaints procedure.[125] This is in stark contrast to precisely this approach taken under the Optional Protocol to the UN Convention on the Rights of the Child on the

[120] See Department of Health, *op cit* n 5, Annex B.

[121] For two alternative suggestions as to how the plight of such children might better be dealt with, see Beevers, *op cit* n 32, at 137–147.

[122] Bojorge, *op cit* n 7, at 271 has argued that it ought to mean that 'children are declared abandoned or orphaned' before they will be regarded as adoptable, and that they should not be regarded as adoptable 'immediately following a socio-political upheaval or natural disaster, where children may only be temporarily separated from their parents'.

[123] Art 22(2) of the Intercountry Adoption Convention permits such adoptions, and even demands the usual standards of integrity, professional competence and experience.

[124] *Ibid*, Art 4(c)(3).

[125] Bojorge, *op cit* n 7, at 287.

Sale of Children, Child Prostitution and Child Pornography 2000.[126] Indeed, it has been suggested elsewhere that it was a mistake not to take the opportunity in this Convention to create international crimes associated with the sale and trafficking of children.[127]

Outside the Convention regime, the system of 'overseas adoptions' seems to be working well. This should come as no surprise, however, for the nations appearing on the designated list are overwhelmingly associated closely with this country either by virtue of Commonwealth or EU membership. At the very fringes, by contrast, the rules of private international law – so far as they relate to the recognition of foreign adoptions – seem a little dated in continuing their insistence on the centrality of domicile rather than habitual residence.[128] They also seem not to be especially well geared towards meeting the challenges that may well be posed by immigrating same-sex spouses that may have adopted abroad.[129] At the very least, it is hard to see why, if same-sex marriages should be recognised by English conflicts rules,[130] adoptive parenting by such persons should not.

[126] The same enforcement mechanism exists in the Optional Protocol to the UN Convention on the Rights of the Child on the Involvement of Children in Armed Conflict 2000.

[127] See M. Eade, 'Inter-Country Adoption: International, National and Cultural Concerns' (1993) 57 *Saskatchewan Law Review* 381, at 389–390.

[128] As noted above, the conflicts rules were originally devised to be analogous with domestic jurisdiction rules. But domestic jurisdiction rules, as we also noted, have now accommodated the more meaningful test of habitual residence by virtue of the Adoption and Children Act 2002.

[129] For the argument that, on principle, such adoptions should be recognised by the courts of this country, see J. Murphy, 'The Recognition of Same-Sex Families in Britain: The Role of Private International Law' (2002) 16 *International Journal of Law, Policy and the Family* 181.

[130] See ch 3.

8

International child abduction

One unfortunate corollary to the marked growth in transborder family formation has been the corresponding growth in the potential for, and incidence of, international child abduction. Predictably enough, when marriages and other relationships of a transnational nature break down, there is often a desire on the part of one of the parents to return with the children of the family to his or (more commonly) her State of origin. Often, the left-behind parent will object to any such removal; yet it is in just such circumstances that many international child abductions take place. In recognition of this danger, the United Nations Convention on the Rights of the Child requires that 'States Parties shall take measures to combat the illicit transfer and non-return of children abroad' and that they 'promote the conclusion of bilateral or multilateral agreements or accession to existing agreements'.[1]

For the majority of this chapter, we shall concern ourselves with the civil law concerning child abduction; and in particular with the way in which it accommodates various international instruments that meet the UN ideal and contain provisions designed to facilitate and secure the return of internationally abducted children.[2] But there is also a criminal law perspective from which international child abduction can be viewed and domestic legislation in fact provides for two kinds of offence based on either sending or taking children out of the United Kingdom. These offences will also be considered in this chapter, albeit in the context of a more general account of

[1] Art 11.

[2] These mechanisms are contained in two international Conventions and one EC Regulation which is of direct effect in this country. The Conventions are the Hague Convention on the Civil Aspects of International Child Abduction 1980 and the European Convention on Recognition and Enforcement of Decisions Concerning Custody of Children and on Restoration of Custody of Children 1980. Both were incorporated into the Child Abduction and Custody Act 1985 (as Schedules 1 and 2, respectively). The Council Regulation is the so-called Brussels IIA Regulation (Council Regulation (EC) No 2201/2003).

the range of domestic deterrents that exist in order to dissuade would-be abductors from removing children in the first place.

Domestic deterrence in respect of outgoing abductions

Given the low prosecution rates associated with the common law offence of kidnapping,[3] the chief deterrents relating to the abduction of children *from* the United Kingdom are now to be found in the two offences created by the Child Abduction Act 1984. These offences turn upon the wrongful taking or wrongful sending a child out of the United Kingdom without having first obtained the appropriate consent.[4] For these purposes, 'the appropriate consent' means the consent of the child's mother or father (if he has parental responsibility), the child's guardian[5], any person in whose favour a residence orders exists (or who otherwise has custody of the child), or the consent of the court.[6] The Act is somewhat restrictive, however, in that these offences can be committed only by persons who are connected to the child in one of a series of prescribed ways.[7] Anyone who does not fall within the list of specified connections cannot be caught by these offences. They were designed only to catch abductions by those who, by one means or another, stand in *loco parentis* to the child. On the other hand, where prosecutions are secured, the penalties are potentially severe.[8]

The offences created by the Act are made subject to a number of qualifications that warrant brief description here. First, no offence is committed if a person in possession of a residence order[9] removes the child for less than

[3] See Criminal Law Revision Committee, *Offences Against the Person*, Cmnd 7844 (1980); G. Williams, 'Can Babies Be Kidnapped?' [1989] *Criminal Law Review* 473.

[4] Child Abduction Act 1984, s 1(1).

[5] Including any 'special guardian' as created by Adoption and Children Act 2002.

[6] *Ibid*, s 1(3).

[7] The prescribed connections are that the abductor is (i) the child's parent, (ii) anyone, in the case of unmarried parents, who may reasonably be believed to be the child's father, (iii) the child's guardian, (iv) a person in whose favour there exists a residence order, or (v) a person who otherwise possesses custody of the child: Child Abduction Act 1984, s 1(2). So far as persons who do not possess the specified connections to the child are concerned, there are two separate offences turning on the wrongful taking or detention of a child: *ibid*, s 2. Case-law has added the requirement that the removal or retention must be in the knowledge that some third party has lawful control: *O v Governor of Holloway Prison and Government of USA* [2000] 1 FLR 147.

[8] Provision is made for imprisonment for up to seven years: Child Abduction Act 1984, s 4(1)(b). Partly because of this, prosecutions may only be instituted with the consent of the Director of Public Prosecutions: *ibid*, s 4(2).

[9] This is an order 'settling the arrangements to be made as to the person with whom a child is to live' made under the Children Act 1989, s 8.

one month *and* the removal is not in breach of an order made under Part II of the Children Act 1989.[10] Secondly, there is no offence where the person removing or sending the child abroad does not have the appropriate consent but honestly believes that the person with lawful control either does consent or would consent if he or she was aware of all the relevant circumstances.[11] Thirdly, there can be no conviction if the person removing the child has taken all reasonable steps to communicate with the person whose consent is required but has in fact failed to make contact with that person.[12] Finally, there is generally no criminal liability if the reason that the child is removed or sent abroad without an appropriate consent is that the person whose consent is required is unreasonably withholding it.[13] There are, however, three exceptions to this last exemption: the removal remains culpable if there exists a residence order in favour of the person whose consent is required; if that person is otherwise invested with the custody of the child; or if the removal would be in breach of a court order.[14]

What is apparent from some of the above provisions is the comparatively strong position that is held by anyone in whose favour a residence order exists. Under the first exemption, the residence order will generally entitle the person holding it to take the named child abroad for anything up to a month.[15] At the same time, a residence order grants the person in whose favour it has been made the power to impose a veto on the child's removal by anyone else. And this is a veto that cannot even be imposed by the child's parents *qua* parents. In this connection, there is a real danger that the acquisition of a residence order may be used as the first step towards a permanent removal abroad. Thus, as Carol Bruch has written:

> The Children Act 1989 and the Child Abduction Act 1984 normally permit the holder of a residence order to take a child abroad for up to one month without the other parent's consent . . . It is, therefore, possible that even if a parent in whose favour a residence order has been entered moves abroad lock, stock and barrel, clearly indicating no intention to return, the removal may not be wrongful at the time of the departure.[16]

[10] Child Abduction Act 1984, s 1(4), (4A). The most likely kind of order under the Children Act 1989 that must not breached in this context is a prohibited steps order (defined in n 22, below).

[11] *Ibid*, s 1(5)(a).

[12] *Ibid*, s 1(5)(b).

[13] *Ibid*, s 1(5)(c).

[14] *Ibid*, s 1(5A).

[15] In practice this may be of limited importance since the residence order represents a prior court's determination of which parent is the preferable carer for the child and the loser of that 'contest' may be less inclined to challenge a removal from the jurisdiction than otherwise might be the case.

[16] C.S. Bruch, 'Child Abduction and the English Courts' in A. Bainham & D. Pearl (eds), *Frontiers in Family Law* (London: John Wiley, 1993) p 55.

Of course, the Child Abduction Act 1984 like any criminal law statute is a less than perfect tool to effect deterrence. As such, other domestic measures are also available to assist in the prevention of international abductions. The police, for example, may become involved on the basis of their statutory power to remove a child into police protection where there is reasonable cause to believe that the child would otherwise suffer significant harm.[17] Where such a removal into protection takes place – on the grounds that there is sufficient risk of a prospective abduction – the statute also requires that this removal be communicated to the parents or other person with parental responsibility or custody.[18]

In addition to police involvement, various kinds of passport control can be exercised to help prevent international abductions.[19] These may well be linked to the police instituting what is known as an 'All Ports Warning' which would work in the following way. Upon being satisfied that there is a real and imminent danger of a removal, the police may put all ports and airports on the alert by way of a computerised broadcast in respect of a suspected potential abduction. Such warnings typically take the form of a police bulletin containing information such as the passport numbers of the adult and the child concerned together with further identification details including gender, age, height, etc. However, to minimise the associated administrative difficulties, these details only remain on the 'stop-list' for a maximum of four weeks.[20]

Finally, the assistance of the civil courts may also be invoked to help avert the prospect of a potential abduction. In the first place, these courts might issue various kinds of restraining order that can be useful where a would-be abductor is simply unaware of the criminality of his or her intended removal of a child. In general, such orders may be obtained in one of two ways: either under the High Court's wardship jurisdiction,[21] or under the Children Act 1989 in the shape of either a residence order or a prohibited steps order.[22] As an alternative, the civil courts might also require the person

[17] Children Act 1989, s 46(1), (2).

[18] *Ibid*, s 46(4).

[19] For further details, see S.M. Cretney, J.M. Masson & R. Bailey-Harris, *Principles of Family Law* (London: Sweet & Maxwell, 2002) pp 671–672.

[20] For a more detailed account of the All Ports Warning system, see N. Lowe & G. Douglas, *Bromley's Family Law* (London: Butterworths, 1998) pp 480–481.

[21] Such orders are particularly attractive since their breach constitutes a contempt of court and as such they carry an added criminal deterrent. On Wardship generally, see Lowe & Douglas, *op cit* n 20, ch 16.

[22] A prohibited steps order is an order by which 'no step which could be taken by a parent in meeting his parental responsibility for a child, and which is of a kind specified in the order, shall be taken by any person without the consent of the court': Children Act 1989, s 8.

taking the child abroad on holiday to provide security,[23] or sign an undertaking,[24] as to the child's safe return by a specified date.

Notwithstanding this array of deterrents, there remains a significant annual number of international abductions from England and Wales.[25] And the way in which the courts respond to such abductions will depend on whether or not the case can be dealt with under the provisions of the three international instruments relating to child abduction by which this country is bound. These are the Hague Convention on the Civil Aspects of International Child Abduction 1980 (hereafter, 'the Hague Convention'), the European Convention on Recognition and Enforcement of Decisions Concerning Custody of Children and on Restoration of Custody of Children 1980 (hereafter, 'the European Convention')[26] and the Brussels IIA Regulation.[27] Where cases cannot be dealt with according to one or other of these instruments (because the other State is not bound by their terms), the courts are forced to resort to a miscellany of other, often limited, options. We shall consider these in due course. But first we must examine the two main Conventions, noting in passing the extent to which their operation is either amended or superseded by Brussels IIA in certain contexts.

The Hague Convention

Although there are two Abduction Conventions to which the United Kingdom is a contracting party,[28] the Hague Convention is the more significant

[23] See, eg, *Re L (Removal from Jurisdiction: Holiday)* [2001] 1 FLR 241 (a holiday providing the child with a chance to meet his extended family in the United Arab Emirates was in the best interests of the child, but the court required a deposit of £50,000 as security for his return).

[24] See, eg, *Re S (Leave to Remove from Jurisdiction: Securing Return from Holiday)* [2001] 2 FLR 507 (the mother was required to sign an undertaking as to her children's return from Pakistan by a specified date and as to the surrender of their passports thereafter).

[25] For some (albeit slightly dated) indication of the modern numbers, see the statistics for 1999 in S. Armstrong, 'Is the Jurisdiction of England and Wales Correctly Applying the 1980 Hague Convention on the Civil Aspects of International Child Abduction?' (2002) 51 *International and Comparative Law Quarterly* 427, at 427, 432.

[26] The basic differences between the two Conventions, apart from the obvious geographical limits to which the latter is subject, are, first, that the European Convention works according to a system of recognition and enforcement of court orders whereas the Hague Convention is geared towards international co-operation in the return of children *regardless* of whether such prior judgments have been entered and, secondly, that the European Convention is not limited to cases falling within a definition of wrongful removal or wrongful retention.

[27] Council Regulation (EC) No 2201/2003.

[28] A tertiary role is also fulfilled by Brussels IIA which 'amends' the Hague Convention and ousts the European Convention in cases involving two EU States. For details, see below.

from a practical point of view since the majority of Convention cases are dealt with according to its provisions. This is not only because the Hague Convention enjoys a wider geographic sphere of operation than its European counterpart,[29] but also because, unlike the European Convention, there is no requirement that the applicant should have in his or her favour a prior court order conferring custody or access rights in respect of the abducted child. Furthermore, since virtually all those states that are Parties to the European Convention are also Contracting Parties to the Hague Convention,[30] there is little need, even in the context of abductions between two European countries, to invoke the former.

Scope of the Convention[31]

The Hague Convention is designed to protect children from the presumptive harmful effects of international abduction by securing, via means of inter-country co-operation, their speedy return to their country of habitual residence. This system of co-operation is administered by administrative bodies known as Central Authorities that each Contracting State is obliged to establish.[32] In England and Wales, the Lord Chancellor is the designated Central Authority.[33] However, the relevant functions are in practice discharged on his behalf by the Child Abduction Unit, located in the Official Solicitor's office in London. These functions are in fact rather limited and purely administrative in nature.[34] Thus, in the case of children abducted from this country, the responsibility of the Unit will be to transmit to the relevant Central Authority abroad the application for the child's return; and in respect of children abducted to this country, it will instruct an experienced solicitor to act on the applicant's behalf within a very short time of receiving the application.[35]

[29] As of 20 August 2004 there were a total of seventy-five Contracting States: for periodic updates, see www.hcch.net/e/status/abdshte.html#ratifications.

[30] The exceptions are Belgium and Liechtenstein.

[31] For a good general account of the history, and basic workings, of the Convention, see A.E. Anton, 'The Hague Convention on International Child Abduction' (1981) 30 *International and Comparative Law Quarterly* 537, esp at 543–555.

[32] Hague Convention, Art 6.

[33] Child Abduction and Custody Act 1985, s 3(1)(a).

[34] For details see C.S. Bruch, 'The Central Authority's Role under the Hague Child Abduction Convention: A Friend in Deed' (1994) 28 *Family Law Quarterly* 35; N. Lowe, M. Everall & M. Nicholls, *International Movement of Children: Law, Practice and Procedure* (Bristol: Jordan Publishing, 2004) ch 13.

[35] Art 1 of the Hague Convention makes 'the prompt return of children wrongfully removed' one of the objects of the Convention while Art 11 stipulates that 'judicial or administrative authorities . . . shall act expeditiously in proceedings for the return of children'. For a critique, see Armstrong, *op cit* n 25.

In terms of substance, the Convention applies only in relation to children under the age of sixteen who have been wrongfully removed from, or retained in, another Contracting State.[36] For these purposes a wrongful removal or retention occurs where the removal or retention is in breach of custody rights conferred by the law of the State in which the child was habitually resident prior to the abduction so long as those rights were actually being exercised (or would have been but for the removal or retention) at the time of the removal or retention.[37] This somewhat convoluted definition of wrongfulness requires some unpicking. In particular, there are esoteric meanings attached to the terms 'custody rights', 'habitual residence' and 'removal and retention' and we thus consider each in turn.

1 Custody rights

The term 'custody rights' corresponds broadly to the English concept of parental responsibility,[38] and such rights may inhere not only in people but also in 'an institution or . . . other body'.[39] However, the correlation between custody rights and parental responsibility should not be supposed to be an exact one. As Waite LJ cautioned in *Re B (A Minor) (Abduction)*:

> The Convention is to be construed broadly as an international agreement according to its general tenor and purpose, without attributing to any of its terms a specialist meaning which the word or words in question may have acquired under the domestic law of England.[40]

Thus, in that case the *de facto* parenting of the child by his unmarried father and maternal grandmother was regarded as sufficient to qualify as 'custody rights' for the purposes of the Convention.[41] Similarly an unmarried father

[36] *Ibid*, Art 4.

[37] *Ibid*, Art 3.

[38] They include 'rights relating to the care of the person of the child and, in particular, the right to determine the child's place of residence': Hague Convention, Art 5(a). These rights must be contrasted with mere 'rights of access' which are stated (in Art 5(b)) to include 'the right to take a child for a limited period of time to a place other than the child's habitual residence': see *S v H (Abduction: Access Rights)* [1997] 3 WLR 1086 (an unmarried father had only access rights, therefore the mother was free to take the child out of the jurisdiction). For full discussion of the concept of custody rights see Lowe *et al*, *op cit* n 34, pp 256–265.

[39] Hague Convention, Art 3(a). For an example of such rights being held by a court of law, see *Re H (A Minor) (Abduction: Rights of Custody)* [2000] 2 AC 291; and for an example of such rights being held by an adoption agency, see *Re JS (Private International Adoption)* [2000] 2 FLR 638.

[40] [1994] 2 FLR 249, at 257. This sentiment has since been echoed in *Practice Note (CAEW: Hague Convention: Applications by Fathers Without Parental Responsibility)* [1998] 1 FLR 491.

[41] See also, to like effect, *Re O (Abduction: Custody Rights)* [1997] 2 FLR 702. Cf *Re J (A Minor) (Abduction: Custody Rights)* [1990] 2 AC 562 where the unmarried father was held not to possess custody rights where he had been exercising *de facto*

granted interim care and control in wardship proceedings has been treated as having custody rights for the purposes of the Hague Convention even though those rights would be held only for a limited period of time and in any event shared with the High Court.[42] Custody rights have even been held to have vested in a paternal grandmother on the sole basis of the length of the child's placement with her by the mother.[43] By contrast, a divorced father with a mere right of contact, coupled with the right to be informed of any important steps taken concerning his children, does not possess custody rights. The right to be informed of where the children would be living could not be equated with a right to determine a child's place of residence (which latter was taken to be inherent within the notion of custody rights).[44]

In addition to the requirement that there be an infringement of custody rights, Article 3 of the Hague Convention also stipulates that those rights must emanate from 'the law of the State in which the child was habitually resident immediately before the removal or retention'. This naturally requires the courts to be clear about the child's country of habitual residence. This is something which has proved to be problematic on many occasions, not least because the term 'habitual residence' is defined in neither the Convention nor the statute giving effect to it.[45]

2 Habitual residence

Although the term 'habitual residence' was deliberately left undefined in the Hague Convention, it does at least seem clear that it is to be regarded as a question of fact,[46] determined on a case-by-case basis. In reaching this

---

joint custody with the child's mother. She alone possessed *de jure* custody rights. For subsequent confirmation that the sharing of custody with the mother, under the same roof, is fatal to an unmarried father's claim to custody rights (in the absence of *de jure* parental responsibility on his part), see *Re C (Child Abduction) (Unmarried Father: Rights of Custody)* [2002] EWHC 2219, at [43] *per* Munby J.

[42] *Re S (A Minor) (Custody: Habitual Residence)* [1997] 4 All ER 251.

[43] *Re G (Abduction: Rights of Custody)* [2002] 2 FLR 703.

[44] *Re V-B (Abduction: Rights of Custody)* [1999] 2 FLR 192.

[45] For an account of several divergent understandings of this concept and an argument in favour of an 'independent child centred' notion, see R. Schuz, 'Habitual Residence under the Hague Abduction Convention – Theory and Practice' [2001] *Child and Family Law Quarterly* 1. For an insight into some of the problems to which this absence of clear definition can lead see J.L. Schiratzki, 'Friends at Odds – Construing Habitual Residence for Children in Sweden and the United States' (2001) 15 *International Journal of Law, Policy and the Family* 297.

[46] In *Re J (A Minor) (Abduction: Custody Rights)* [1990] 2 AC 562, at 578 *per* Lord Brandon; *Re M (Abduction: Habitual Residence)* [1996] 1 FLR 887, at 890 *per* Balcombe LJ. For a contrasting approach according to which habitual residence is to be regarded as a mixed question of fact and law, see the American case of *Feder v Evans-Feder* 866 F Supp 866 (criticised staunchly in M. Kelly, 'Taking Liberties: The Third Circuit Defines "Habitual Residence" under the Hague Convention on International Child Abduction' (1996) 41 *Villanova Law Review* 1069).

determination the courts will initially be mindful of three key factors. First, the child's place of residence must be a voluntarily chosen abode; secondly, it must be for a settled purpose; thirdly, it can be lost with a change of intention regarding country A, but only acquired over time in respect of country B.[47]

In respect of the first of these touchstones – that the place of abode must be voluntarily chosen – an obvious difficulty arises in connection with young children who are not themselves able to formulate the requisite intention.[48] To meet this difficulty the English courts have held that the relevant intention in such cases is to be observed in the person who has parental responsibility for the child. As Waite J put it in *Re B (Minors: Abduction) No 2*: '[t]he habitual residence of the young children of parents who are living together is the same as the habitual residence of the parents themselves and neither parent can change it without the express or tacit consent of the other or an order of the court.'[49] As a rider to this, it has also been stated that the child must have been resident in the relevant country for at least some period of time. This additional requirement can be justified on the basis that, without it, a child might be deemed habitually resident in a country with which he or she has little to no practical connection.[50]

In relation to the second requirement – that the residence in question must be for a settled purpose – there has again been a considerable amount of case-law. The requirement itself can be traced to the decision of the House of Lords in *R v Barnet London Borough Council, ex p Shah (Nilish)*.[51] This was a case dealing not with child abduction but with some foreign students' applications for local education authority grants based on the contention that they were 'ordinarily resident' in the appropriate borough. Notwithstanding these somewhat distant origins, the requirement of 'settled purpose' espoused there has since established itself firmly in the context of Hague Convention case law. In general it is to be observed where the relevant intention as to the chosen abode is formed with 'a sufficient degree of continuity . . . to be properly described as settled'.[52] Thus it has been held that the intention to remain in Germany until a suitable place to live had been found was sufficient even though the duration of the residence was relatively

[47] *Re M (Abduction: Habitual Residence)* [1996] 1 FLR 887, at 890 *per* Balcombe LJ.

[48] There is, presumably, no such problem where the child in question is sufficiently mature and intelligent to make up his or her own mind.

[49] [1993] 1 FLR 993, at 995. For the argument that it would be preferable to adopt a child-centred approach turning on 'the child's connections with the country in question and not the parents' connections or intentions' see Schuz, *op cit* n 45, at 13.

[50] *Re M (Abduction: Habitual Residence)* [1996] 1 FLR 887; *Re A (Abduction: Habitual Residence)* [1998] 1 FLR 497.

[51] [1983] 2 AC 309.

[52] *Re B (Minors: Abduction) No 2* [1993] 1 FLR 993, at 995 *per* Waite J.

short.[53] Similarly, a limited period of residence for educational purposes,[54] or temporary work placement[55] purposes, will suffice.

By contrast, residence in a particular place for the purposes of a holiday while a decision as to permanent future arrangements is reached is not sufficient to ground habitual residence. Thus, in *Re A (Abduction: Habitual Residence)* there was no habitual residence in Greece after just three weeks of a six week holiday on the part of a child who had been taken there partly to enable his mother and father 'to discuss in greater depth than they had achieved [previously] how they were going to order their lives and that of their child in the future'.[56] Accordingly, when the mother took the child back to England before the planned six-week holiday had expired, there was no wrongful removal of the child so as to constitute an abduction.

The third consideration that the courts take into account when identifying the place in which a child is habitually resident is the fact that such residence can be lost much more quickly in relation to one country than it can be acquired in relation to another. A good illustration of this principle is provided by *Re J (Abduction: Custody Rights)*.[57] In that case, the mother was a British citizen who took her child to England from Australia without the father's knowledge or consent. The mother had left Australia with the express intention of living permanently in England. The unmarried father who remained in Western Australia only obtained a court order granting him custody rights *after* the mother and child had begun living in England. Naturally enough, the question of the child's habitual residence arose during the proceedings, and it was held that the mother and child had lost their habitual residence in Australia immediately upon their departure, yet the three weeks spent in England were not enough to have acquired a new habitual residence in that country.[58] As Lord Brandon explained:

> [T]here is a significant difference between a person ceasing to be habitually resident in country A, and his subsequently becoming habitually resident in country B. A person may cease to be habitually resident in country A in a single day if he or she leaves it with a settled intention not to return to it but to take up long-term residence in country B instead. Such a person cannot, however, become habitually resident in country B in a single day. An appreciable period of time . . . will be necessary to enable him or her to become so.[59]

[53] *Ibid.*

[54] This was sufficient in *R v Barnet London Borough Council, ex p Shah (Nilish)* [1983] 2 AC 309, but this, it will be recalled, was not a Hague Abduction Convention case.

[55] *Re R (Abduction: Habitual Residence)* [2003] EWCH 1968.

[56] [1998] 1 FLR 497, at 505 *per* Stuart-White J.

[57] [1990] 2 AC 562.

[58] On the facts, this did not matter, since the father had never possessed custody rights at the same time that child had been habitually resident in Western Australia.

[59] [1990] 2 AC 562, at 578–579.

Notwithstanding these general touchstones for assessing the habitual residence of young children, there are at least two situations for which they fail to supply an unequivocal determination. The first concerns the circumstance in which there is no holder of parental responsibility with whose habitual residence the child's own habitual residence may be associated. *Re S (A Minor) (Custody: Habitual Residence)*[60] provides a good illustration. There, the sole holder of parental responsibility for the child in question was his unmarried mother. She died in hospital while the boy was just one year old. And the day after her death, the boy's maternal grandmother and maternal aunt took him to Ireland. His father objected to this removal and obtained custody rights from the English court in the shape of an order granting him interim care and control. The question that arose was whether the child's retention in Ireland was wrongful within the meaning of the Hague Convention. In deciding this matter, the House of Lords had first to identify the child's habitual residence. In the event, their Lordships held that his habitual residence was to be determined by the place in which he had been habitually resident immediately prior to the retention called into question. Lord Slynn explained the matter thus:

> Neither defendant had parental rights over the child, who was too young to form any intention as to his own future residence, and two days with the defendants in Ireland is not sufficient of itself to result in his existing habitual residence being lost and a new one gained. The position is quite different in the case of a mother with parental rights and on whose habitual residence the child's habitual residence depends . . . Such is not the present case where no parental rights were involved and where S's habitual residence did not depend on and automatically change with those of the defendants.[61]

The second circumstance in which it will not be possible clearly to identify the child's place of habitual residence is where the child is born in a country in which no-one in possession of custody rights is habitually resident.[62]

3 Removal and retention

Probably the best starting point for an understanding of the twin terms 'removal' and 'retention' is the decision of the House of Lords in *Re H, Re S*.[63] In that case, Lord Brandon began by observing that 'both removal and retention are events occurring on a specific occasion, for otherwise it would

[60] [1998] AC 750.

[61] *Ibid*, at 762–763 *per* Lord Slynn.

[62] See, eg, the rather unusual facts of *W v H (Abduction: Surrogacy) (No 1)* [2002] 1 FLR 1008.

[63] [1991] 2 AC 476.

be impossible to measure a period of one year from their occurrence [as *per* Article 12 of the Convention]'.[64] He then set out what he perceived to be the difference between these mutually exclusive concepts:[65]

> [Whereas] removal occurs when a child, which has previously been in the State of its habitual residence, is taken away across the frontier of that State . . . retention occurs where a child, which has previously been for a limited period of time outside the State of its habitual residence, is not returned on the expiry of such limited period.[66]

While his Lordship's definition of 'removal' is straightforward and self-contained, the same cannot be said of his explanation of 'retention'. To begin with, there was no mention of the fact that, for there to be a wrongful retention, there must first have been a prior legitimate removal (either by virtue of a rule of law,[67] or because there was consent to the removal by the non-removing parent). However, it is clear that this must be the case, since otherwise there would be a prior wrongful removal (bearing in mind his Lordship's view that the two concepts are mutually exclusive). Secondly, his definition of 'retention' has since been extended by subsequent case law. In *Re S (Minors) (Child Abduction: Wrongful Retention)*,[68] a mother came to study in England along with her husband and two children. The parents agreed to stay in England for at least one year, but before the year expired the father returned to Israel and began divorce proceedings. The wife not only made an application in those proceedings for maintenance for the children, but also made it plain that she had no present or future intention to return the children despite what she and her husband had agreed. In holding there to be a wrongful retention – notwithstanding the fact that the agreed one-year period had not yet expired – Wall J remarked that the mother could not have 'the benefit of the agreement without the burden'.[69] Thus, 'by announcing her intention not to return the children to Israel at all . . . the mother [had] wrongfully retained the children in England as at the date of that announcement'.[70] Indeed, it has even been held that the mere application for a court order will suffice for these purposes so long as

[64] *Ibid*, at 499. As to the significance of the one-year period, see p 222 *et seq* below.

[65] Lord Brandon opined that 'Article 3 [which refers to 'the removal or the retention'] . . . seems to me to predicate that removal and retention are mutually exclusive concepts': *ibid*, at 488.

[66] *Ibid*, at 500.

[67] Eg, a removal for up to one month by someone with a residence order under the Child Abduction Act 1984, s 1(4), (4A).

[68] [1994] 1 FLR 82.

[69] *Ibid*, at 93.

[70] *Ibid*.

its effect would be inconsistent with the custody rights of the non-removing parent.[71]

4 Applicants

So long as the child in question is under the age of sixteen,[72] 'any person, institution or other body claiming that a child has been removed or retained in breach of custody rights may apply . . . for assistance in securing the return of the child'.[73] The fact that the Convention states that 'any person' may lodge an application for a child's return would seem broad enough to encompass the permissibility of an application by the child concerned (always assuming that he or she possessed sufficient maturity and understanding). Equally, the fact that the Convention countenances applications by an 'institution or other body' means that bodies such as an English local authority or a foreign equivalent may apply for the return of a child. Thus, in *Re JS (Private International Adoption)*,[74] a child was returned to an adoption agency in the United States after the agency in question had been informed by an English local authority of the unsuitability of the English would-be parents with whom the children had been placed.

In order to facilitate an application for the return of a child – particularly one made by a person in possession of custody rights – section 8 of the Child Abduction and Custody Act 1985 affords the High Court jurisdiction to issue a declaration that any given removal or retention was wrongful where the applicant for that declaration appears to the court to have an interest in the matter and if the application is made for the purposes of Article 15 of the Convention.[75] Perhaps surprisingly, it has been held that such a declaration can be made even if there are proceedings to determine the child's habitual residence still pending in another Contracting State.[76] Indeed, it has even been said that the proper function of such a declaration

[71] In *Re B (Minors) (Abduction) (No 2)* [1993] 1 FLR 993 Waite J said (at 999): '[f]ull and sensible effect can only be given to [the Convention] . . . if the term "retention" is construed as wide enough to comprehend not only acts of physical restraint on the part of the retaining parent but also juridical orders obtained on his initiative.'

[72] The Convention ceases to apply once a child attains the age of sixteen: Hague Convention, Art 4.

[73] *Ibid*, Art 8.

[74] [2000] 2 FLR 638.

[75] Under Art 15, the judicial or administrative authorities in the returning State *may* require an applicant to seek such a declaration before they will make an order for the return of the child. The intention is plainly to ensure that, in cases of doubt, the facts and law upon which an application hinges can be verified locally before any return is actually ordered. Since in most cases the relevant facts and law are not in dispute, it is more often than not unnecessary for a returning State to request that a declaration be sought. For a full discussion of Art 15, see Lowe *et al*, *op cit* n 34, ch 15.

[76] *Re P (Abduction: Declaration)* [1995] 1 FLR 831.

is to inform the foreign court of the English court's stance with respect to the removal or retention.[77]

Mechanics of the Convention

1 Procedure

In terms of its day-to-day operation, the Hague Abduction Convention depends heavily (though not exclusively) upon the functions performed by designated Central Authorities[78] in each of the Contracting States. In broad terms, it falls to such Central Authorities to ensure a system of co-operation between Contracting States in the discovery and prompt return of abducted children.[79] As such, where a person seeks the return of a child who has been abducted, he or she will typically begin the process by making an application for the assistance of the Central Authority in his or her own State.[80] The application will disclose identification information about the abductor, the abductee and the place at which, and person with whom, the child is now believed to be.[81]

In the usual case in which an application for assistance in relation to an abducted child is made to the applicant's domestic Central Authority, it is the duty of that Central Authority to transmit the application to the Central Authority in the country to which it is alleged that the child has been taken (so long as the Authority has reason to believe that the child has been taken there).[82] This transmission of the application must take place both directly and without delay,[83] suggesting that the Central Authority in the requesting State may quite legitimately be far from *convinced* that the child has been taken to the other Contracting State. Indeed, if a prompt return must be secured, it would seem logical that even fairly minimal evidence in relation to the removal should suffice in this context.

[77] *Re L (Children) (Abduction: Declaration)* [2001] 2 FCR 1.

[78] Each Contracting State must designate a Central Authority to discharge the various duties laid down in the Convention: Hague Convention, Art 6. In England and Wales the designated Central Authority is the Lord Chancellor: Child Abduction and Custody Act 1985, s 3(1)(a).

[79] Hague Convention, Art 7. For these purposes, co-operation includes exchanging relevant information pertaining to abducted children (Art 7(d)), providing up-to-date information on relevant matters of law (Art 7(e)) and keeping each other informed as to how the Convention operates in the various Contracting States (Art 7(i)).

[80] *Ibid*, Art 8. While an application to the Central Authority of the returning State is equally within the terms of Art 8, standard practice is heavily influenced by the advantages of language and the relative ease with which one can normally contact one's own Central Authority.

[81] *Ibid.*

[82] *Ibid.*

[83] *Ibid.*

Once an application has been transmitted to the Central Authority in the returning country, it will be incumbent upon that Central Authority to take all appropriate steps to trace and secure the return of the child.[84] Moreover, this must be done with a view to obtaining the voluntary return of the child.[85] At this point, an inherent conflict within the objectives of the Convention becomes apparent. For while the Preamble to the Convention makes it clear that the 'prompt return' of children is one of the stated objectives, and while Article 11 amplifies this objective by requiring Contracting States to 'act expeditiously in proceedings for the return of children', it is difficult to reconcile speedy, compulsory measures with the ideal of securing voluntary returns where possible.[86]

2 The presumptive duty to return an abducted child

Subject to the exceptions in Article 13 (considered below), once a child has been located, it is normally incumbent upon the judicial or administrative authorities of the State in which the child is being held to order the immediate return of the child if that child was wrongfully removed or retained less than one year previously.[87] Even if a period of more than one year has elapsed between the date of wrongful removal or retention and the date on which proceedings for the child's return were commenced, the duty to return the child still applies *unless* it is shown that the child 'is now settled in his or her new environment'.[88] In either case, there is a very strong presumption that an abducted child shall be returned to the country of his habitual residence. And this presumption is founded largely upon a familiar private international law principle of allowing the underlying dispute between the child's parents to be resolved in the country most closely connected to that dispute: the country of the child's habitual residence.[89] Consonant with this, Article 16 of the Convention prevents the judicial or administrative authorities of the returning State from making any decision on the merits of custody rights

[84] *Ibid*, Art 7(a).

[85] *Ibid*, Art 10.

[86] For full elaboration of this point see Armstrong, *op cit* n 25.

[87] Hague Convention, Art 12.

[88] *Ibid*. In *Re N (Minors) (Abduction)* [1991] 1 FLR 413 Bracewell J explained (at 417–418) that the word 'now' should be taken to refer to the time that the proceedings were commenced rather than the date of the hearing. She also explained that the word 'settled' involves both a physical and an emotional element, so that the child should feel secure in his or her new home. (To similar effect see *Re M (A Minor) (Abduction: Acquiescence)* [1996] 1 FLR 315.) Finally, her Ladyship said that the term 'new environment' should be understood broadly so as to encompass the child's home, friends, school, opportunities, etc.

[89] See R. Schuz, 'The Hague Child Abduction Convention: Family Law and Private International Law' (1995) 44 *International and Comparative Law Quarterly* 771, arguing (at 774) that the underlying rationale for a presumptive return of the child is no more than the familiar private international law principle of *forum non conveniens*.

until it has been determined that the child is not to be returned or unless an application is not lodged within a reasonable time of that authority receiving notice of the removal or retention.

3 Exceptions to the presumptive return of a child

The range and extent of the exceptions to the presumptive return of a child depend on whether or not Brussels IIA applies. Where it does not apply, Article 13 provides a set of grounds that, if proven on the balance of probabilities,[90] will allow the English court to depart from the presumption that a child must be returned forthwith. Where it does apply, however, the situation is considerably more complex since the general impact of Brussels IIA is to dilute the Article 13 exceptions. Brussels IIA is dealt with only after consideration of the various Article 13 defences. But even before we consider those defences, it should be noted that their successful invocation never amounts to an outright prohibition on the court ordering the return of a child. Article 13 goes no further than to provide that, in the case of them being invoked, 'the State is not bound to order the return of the child if the person, institution or other body which opposes its return establishes [one of the grounds]'. However, in practice, being able to prove one of the listed exceptions in a non-Brussels IIA case will almost always lead to the court refusing to order the child's return. Indeed, prior to Brussels IIA coming into force, the only instance in which demonstration of one of the Article 13 exceptions would *not* lead to a return was where the requested State exercised its residual discretion under Article 18 to order the child's return notwithstanding the successful demonstration of one of the Article 13 defences.[91] Article 18 is also considered in due course.

(a) Article 13(a) Article 13(a) comprises a complex, composite ground for ousting the application of the general rule that the abducted child should be returned forthwith. It contains three distinct bases upon which the obligation to return the child can be negated: namely, that 'the person, institution or other body having the care of the person of the child was not actually exercising the custody rights at the time of the removal or retention, or had consented to or subsequently acquiesced in the removal or retention'. In relation to the first of these – the non-exercise of custody rights – there is precious little English authority. But some useful guidance as to the import of this provision may be gleaned from the decision of the Scottish Outer

[90] Although child abduction can result in criminal liability, the application of the Convention is a civil law matter hence the application of the civil law standard of proof: see *Re C (Abduction: Consent)* [1996] 1 FLR 414. See also the House of Lords' endorsement of this approach in *Re H (A Child) (Abduction: Habitual Residence: Consent)* [2000] 2 FLR 294.

[91] See, eg, *Re D (Abduction: Discretionary Return)* [2000] 1 FLR 24.

House in *S v S (Child Abduction: Custody Rights: Acquiescence)*.[92] In that case, the father of two children applied for their return to Western Australia. His wife, who had removed the children, contended (among other things) that the father had failed to exercise his custody rights while he was compulsorily detained in hospital through mental illness. It was held that it would be contrary to the spirit and purpose of the Convention construed as a whole to hold that a person so detained was not actually exercising his custody rights. It was not that the father had abandoned his custody rights; and in any event the mother had the onus to show that the father was not actually exercising those rights.

As regards the second sub-ground – that there was consent to the removal or retention – there is a wealth of relevant English case-law. But perhaps the best analytical starting point when considering it is the decision in *Re K (Abduction: Consent)*[93] where Hale J made it clear that 'consent must be real' and that '[i]t must be positive and unequivocal'.[94] So far as the reality of consent is concerned, it is well established that there is no genuine consent if that consent 'has been obtained through a calculated and deliberate fraud on the part of the absconding parent'.[95] Accordingly, in one case in which the mother had left Greece to study a language course in England, there was no genuine consent to her taking her son with her when the father's consent to his removal had only been procured by the mother concealing the twin facts that she had begun a relationship with another man and that she intended to make the move a permanent one.[96] As Charles J put it: 'by not telling the father of her relationship with Mr G she deceived him and there was therefore no consent for the purposes of the Hague Convention.'[97]

What is slightly more contentious is what the courts require by way of clear and unequivocal consent. In *Re W (Abduction: Procedure)*, Wall J expressed the view that the absconding parent would normally be required to produce written evidence (or other supporting documentary material) of the other parent's consent.[98] However, subsequent to that decision, two further judges of the High Court have doubted the rigidity of his Lordship's approach highlighting the fact that, while written evidence of consent is undoubtedly helpful, it is not specifically required under the Convention.[99]

[92] 2003 SLT 344.
[93] [1997] 2 FLR 212.
[94] *Ibid*, at 217.
[95] *Re B (A Minor) (Abduction)* [1994] 2 FLR 249, at 261 *per* Waite LJ.
[96] *T v T (Abduction: Consent)* [1999] 2 FLR 912.
[97] *Ibid*, at 920.
[98] [1995] 1 FLR 878, at 888.
[99] See *Re C (Abduction: Consent)* [1996] 1 FLR 414, at 418 *per* Holman J, *Re H (A Child) (Abduction: Habitual Residence: Consent)* [2000] 2 FLR 294, at 301 *per* Holman J and *Re K (Abduction: Consent)* [1997] 2 FLR 212, at 217 *per* Hale J. See also Wall J's retraction of his earlier view (in the interests of eradicating a difference

With respect, this latter view seems preferable, for as Wall J has himself observed, 'parents do not necessarily expect to reduce their agreements and understandings about their children to writing'.[100] What seems equally sensible is the rider added by Hale J, in *Re K*, that once consent has been given and subsequently acted upon by the absconding parent, it cannot be retracted by a simple change of mind on the part of the non-removing parent.[101]

As regards implied consent, it was held in *Re M (A Minor) (Abduction: Consent or Acquiescence)*[102] that if a parent's overall conduct is such that genuine consent can be inferred from it, it is not necessary to show that that parent has made an actual unequivocal statement of consent. Accordingly, in that case, where the father was fully aware that the mother intended permanently to leave Greece with their child and had adopted the attitude that the mother could do as she liked, there was sufficient material evidence from which the court could infer his consent to the removal from Greece. As Wall J explained in relation to the father in that case:

> [H]is overall attitude – that the mother could do what she wished and that she could go to England with [the child] if she wished – combined with his conduct in standing by whilst she openly made preparations to leave, and the statements he made . . . are sufficient to demonstrate a course of conduct from which his consent can properly be inferred.[103]

The final Article 13(a) ground upon which the absconding parent may seek to resist the child's return is acquiescence on the part of the objecting parent. The leading authority on this ground is *Re H (Abduction: Acquiescence)*.[104] In that case, the parties were Orthodox Jews living in Israel. The mother took their three children to England without obtaining the father's consent. To begin with, the father sought relief through the religious court in Israel, but the mother ignored the return summons issued by that court. According to his religion, the father was prohibited from engaging the secular courts without having obtaining the permission of the religious court. Some six months therefore passed before the father was able to make an application under the Hague Convention. In response to that application, the mother argued that the father's inaction for the previous six months constituted acquiescence. The House of Lords held that there had been no acquiescence since there was nothing acquiescent about trying to obtain a return through the religious court and obeying the strictures of one's religion before invoking

---

of judicial opinion) in *Re M (A Minor) (Abduction: Consent or Acquiescence)* [1999] 1 FLR 171, at 187.

[100] *Re C (Abduction: Consent)* [1996] 1 FLR 414, at 418–419.

[101] [1997] 2 FLR 212, at 218.

[102] [1999] 1 FLR 171.

[103] *Ibid*, at 189.

[104] [1998] AC 72. For analysis, see D. McClean, 'International Child Abduction – Some Recent Trends' [1997] *Child and Family Law Quarterly* 387, 395–398.

the Hague Convention. But more importantly for present purposes, Lord Browne-Wilkinson set out a series of guiding principles to be applied in cases involving acquiescence.

To begin with, his Lordship made clear the fact that acquiescence involves a state of mind on the part of the non-absconding parent.[105] He then said: 'the subjective intention of the wronged parent is a question of fact for the trial judge to determine in all the circumstances of the case' with 'more weight [attaching] to the contemporaneous words and actions of the wronged parent than to his bare assertions in evidence of his intention'.[106] To this general approach, Lord Browne-Wilkinson envisaged just one exception:

> Where the words or actions of the wronged parent clearly and unequivocally show and have led the other parent to believe that the wronged parent is not asserting or going to assert his right to the summary return of the child and are inconsistent with such return, justice requires that the wronged parent be held to have acquiesced.[107]

To fall within the exception, the wronged parent must have acted in such a clear and unequivocal fashion that the usual requirement of proof as to his or her subjective state of mind can be waived. But once waived, 'the wronged parent . . . cannot be heard to go back on what he has done and seek to persuade the judge that all along he has secretly intended to claim the summary return of the children'.[108] *Re AZ (A Minor) (Abduction: Acquiescence)*[109] provides a good example of the kind of rare case that will in fact fall within this exception. In that case, the mother brought the child in question to England from Germany where the father, an American serviceman, was based. The father consented to the child being taken to England in the first place, and he also later consented to the boy's maternal aunt looking after him after the mother had left him with her. Indeed, the father even asked the aunt to look after the child. Later, the aunt applied for a residence order and the relevant papers were served upon the father. He overtly indicated that he had no intention of contesting that application. After a further three months, the father signalled his intention to have the child returned to him. The case was one in which the father's conduct was sufficiently clear and unequivocal to oust the requirement that his acquiescence must be proved.[110]

[105] Authority for this proposition already existed in *Re S (Minors) (Abduction: Acquiescence)* [1994] 1 FLR 819, at 838 *per* Neill LJ.

[106] *Ibid*, at 90.

[107] *Ibid.*

[108] *Ibid*, at 89.

[109] [1993] 1 FLR 682.

[110] See also *Re D (Abduction: Acquiescence)* [1998] 2 FLR 335 (acquiescence where an Australian father both consented to the mother obtaining residence orders in this country and expressed a personal intention to move here himself); *Re R*

More commonly, there will be some measure of ambiguity associated with the conduct and statements of the wronged parent so as make the usual approach applicable. Thus, if a wronged father begrudgingly accepts that his child should remain in the country to which it was taken, but only on the condition that he should retain regular access to the child, it will be far from clear that he has acquiesced, and it will be no mean feat for the absconding parent to prove the necessary acquiescence.[111] Similarly, actions that ostensibly suggest acquiescence may in truth turn out to be nothing of the sort. For instance, if a parent demurs for a long time before taking action under the Convention, his delay will not be treated as acquiescence where it is attributable to erroneous legal advice,[112] or a long period of mental illness.[113] And if the aggrieved parent was unaware of his or her rights under the Convention, that, too, may provide a suitable explanation for a lengthy delay in taking action. As Stuart-Smith LJ explained in *Re A (Minors) (Abduction: Custody Rights)*:[114]

> A party cannot be said to acquiesce unless he is aware, at least in general terms, of his rights against the other parent. It is not necessary that he should know the full or precise nature of his legal rights under the Convention: but he must be aware that the other parent's act in removing or retaining the child is unlawful.[115]

In short, each case must be assessed according to its own particular facts. The presence of factors that would tend to suggest acquiescence cannot normally be taken as conclusive of the matter. All other relevant evidence must also be placed in the balance. Thus, the fact that the wronged parent does not immediately invoke the Convention suggests acquiescence, but this must be weighed against the countervailing fact that the very same parent continues to debate with the absconding parent the place where their child or children should ultimately live.[116] And the fact that there is a suggestion of acquiescence on the part of a parent who does not invoke the Convention for eight months must be weighed against the fact that the absconding

---

(Abduction: Acquiescence) [1999] 2 FLR 818 (acquiescence where a father took the wife and children to the airport knowing they were making a one-way flight); *Re A (Minors) (Abduction: Custody Rights)* [1992] Fam 106.

[111] See *P v P* [1998] 2 FLR 835. On the stated facts, the trial judge considered that the case was a difficult and borderline one, but held on balance that there was not sufficiently clear evidence of the father's acquiescence.

[112] See, eg, *Re S (Minors) (Acquiescence)* [1994] 1 FLR 819 (the father's delay of eight months was not taken to be acquiescence where two separate law firms failed to provide him with advice as to his rights under the Convention). Cf *W v W* [1993] 2 FLR 211 where a father's ten-month delay was taken to amount to acquiescence.

[113] *S v S* 2003 SLT 344.

[114] [1992] Fam 106.

[115] *Ibid*, at 119–120.

[116] See, eg, *Re I (Abduction: Acquiescence)* [1999] 1 FLR 778.

parent attempts to hide the whereabouts of herself and the children. For continuing to conceal one's whereabouts is inconsistent with a belief in the acquiescence on the part of the aggrieved parent,[117] and any such doubt would hardly conduce to the abducting parent *proving* acquiescence, as she must.

(b) Article 13(b) Under Article 13(b), the judicial or administrative authorities need not order the child's return where 'there is a grave risk that his or her return would expose the child to physical or psychological harm or otherwise place the child in an intolerable position'. The Law Reports reveal a great many cases in which an attempt has been made to invoke this provision in so far as it relates to a grave risk of harm, but there are comparatively few instances of it succeeding. This is because the courts have consistently emphasised the very high threshold involved[118] and the fact that the primary purpose of the Convention is to secure the return of abducted children in order that the underlying parental dispute can be resolved in the courts of the country of habitual residence.[119] Perhaps the best explanation of the stringent interpretation of the requirements of Article 13(b) is that provided by the Court of Appeal in *Re S (A Child) (Abduction: Custody Rights)*.[120] There, the mother resisted a child's return to Israel where she believed there was a continuing threat of terrorism which would make that country an unsafe environment for the child. She also gave evidence of the anxiety disorder that she herself had developed as a consequence of her ongoing fear of such an attack. On the facts, it was held that while terrorism did pose a risk to the child it was not a grave risk that would make it intolerable for the child to be raised there. It was only intolerable from the perspective of the mother. In summing up the appropriate test, Ward LJ said:

> [T]he proper approach for the court considering a defence alleging a grave risk of exposure to physical or psychological harm should be to consider the grave risk of that harm as a discrete question but then stand back and test the conclusion by looking at the Article in the round, reflecting whether the risk of harm is established to an extent which would lead one to say that the child will be placed in an intolerable situation if returned.[121]

[117] *Re H (Abduction: Child of 16)* [2000] 2 FLR 51.

[118] In *Re N (Minors) (Abduction)* [1991] 1 FLR 413 Bracewell J said (at 419): '[I]t is plain that it is not a trivial risk and it is not a trivial psychological harm which is envisaged and which has to be justified and . . . the intolerable situation envisaged has to be something extreme and compelling.' In similar vein, see *Re H (Abduction: Grave Risk)* [2003] EWCA Civ 355; *TB v JB (Abduction: Grave Risk of Harm)* [2001] 2 FLR 515; *Re M (Abduction: Undertakings)* [1995] 1 FLR 1021; *Re O (Child Abduction: Undertakings)* [1994] 2 FLR 349.

[119] See, eg, *Re C (A Minor) (Child Abduction)* [1999] 2 FLR 478; *N v N (Abduction: Article 13 Defence)* [1995] 1 FLR 107.

[120] [2002] EWCA Civ 908.

[121] *Ibid*, at [41].

What is clear from this test is that, whether one relies on a risk of psychological harm or a risk of physical harm, the child's predicament upon his or her return must be intolerable. With rather more subtlety, however, it also suggests a fairly narrow interpretation of the term 'grave risk'. In the abstract, the phrase might be understood to refer simply to the likelihood of the risk materialising. But it might also be capable of embracing a relatively moderate risk of a quite drastic form of harm; for even a low probability of a life-threatening danger might legitimately be considered a grave risk. Given the facts of *Re S*, there can be no doubt that a grave form of physical harm was in issue. But the fact that there was a low probability of it occurring led the invocation of Article 13(b) to fail.[122] Furthermore, this narrow interpretation is consistent with the vast majority of decided cases in which it has been repeatedly asserted that there is an insufficiently grave risk where the courts in the country of the child's habitual residence are able to issue injunctions against, or obtain undertakings from, those individuals thought to pose a grave threat to the child.[123] And the judges are certainly less willing to refuse a return where the threat of violence is aimed at the abducting parent rather than the child itself.[124]

Another point that has been made on several occasions is that an absconding parent cannot artificially create a risk of psychological harm by adamantly refusing to return with the child so that the return would cause the parent and child to be separated. In *Re C (A Minor) (Abduction)*,[125] for example, a mother was refusing to return to Australia and then arguing that if she did not return with the child, there would thereby be created a grave risk of psychological harm. In rejecting that argument Butler-Sloss LJ said: '[i]f the grave risk of psychological harm to a child is to be inflicted by the

[122] This is not to suggest that the kind of harm in issue is irrelevant so long as there is a sufficiently high prospect of it materialising. Indeed, in *Re H (Abduction: Grave Risk)* [2003] EWCA Civ 355, at [30], it was specifically stated by Butler-Sloss P that, 'the risk must be grave and the harm must be serious'. The point is that the accepted understanding of Article 13(b) is that the word 'grave' qualifies the 'risk' (not the 'harm') involved.

[123] See, eg, *Re H (Abduction: Grave Risk)* [2003] EWCA Civ 355; *TB v JB (Abduction: Grave Risk of Harm)* [2001] 2 FLR 515; *Re M (A Child) (Abduction: Intolerable Situation)* [2001] 1 FLR 930; *Re C (Abduction: Grave Risk of Psychological Harm)* [1999] 1 FLR 1145; *Re M (Abduction: Undertakings)* [1995] 1 FLR 1021; *Re O (Child Abduction: Undertakings)* [1994] 2 FLR 349. For criticism, see M. Kaye, 'The Hague Convention and the Flight from Domestic Violence: How Women and Children are being Returned by Coach and Four' [1999] *International Journal of Law, Policy and the Family* 191.

[124] See B. Hale, 'The View from Court 45' [1999] *Child and Family Law Quarterly* 377, 379–380. A similar stance is taken where the threat pertains to the step-brother or step-sister of the child whose return has been ordered: see *Re C (A Child) (Abduction: Grave Risk of Physical or Psychological Harm) (No 2)* 1999 WL 982473.

[125] [1989] 1 FLR 403.

parent who abducted him, then it would be relied upon by every mother of a young child who removed . . . and refused to return [the child] . . . [This would] . . . drive a coach and four through the Convention.'[126] On the other hand, if a sufficiently mature older sibling objects to being returned, a defence based on the risk of psychological harm to the younger sibling (who is not mature enough to object to a return) may succeed where the source of harm is attributable to the separation from the older sibling.[127]

Notwithstanding the relative infrequency with which Article 13(b) has been raised successfully, there are a few reported cases in which it has succeeded. One such case involved a child whose return would have necessitated a separation from two older brothers who were old enough to resist their own return.[128] Another case involved a child who had a history of being the victim of the applicant's violence.[129] And this was in spite of the settled approach according to which violence will not, *per se*, be taken to suffice; for where such a threat exists it is usually felt that that the domestic courts can offer adequate protection and a return may still be ordered.[130]

(c) The child's objections As an independent rider to Article 13,[131] it is provided that the judicial and administrative authorities in the returning State are invested with the discretion not to return the child if that child is of sufficient age and maturity for his or her objection to a return to be taken into account. The fact that non-return is discretionary in these circumstances means that that a child's objection is not conclusive; and the Court of Appeal has twice confirmed this.[132] On the other hand, the courts have shown considerable generosity in terms of what amounts to sufficient age and maturity. In *Re R (Child Abduction: Acquiescence)*,[133] for example, the court was prepared to respect the objections of brothers aged six and

[126] *Ibid*, at 410. Cf *Re G (Abduction: Psychological Harm)* [1995] 1 FLR 64. See also, eg, *Re L (Child Abduction) (Psychological Harm)* [1993] 2 FLR 401.

[127] See, eg, *Re T (Abduction) (Abduction: Child's Objections to Return)* [2000] 2 FLR 192.

[128] *B v K (Child Abduction)* [1993] 1 FCR 382.

[129] *Re F (A Minor) (Abduction: Custody Rights Abroad)* [1995] 3 All ER 641.

[130] See, eg, *Re H (Abduction: Grave Risk)* [2003] EWCA Civ 355; *TB v JB (Abduction: Grave Risk of Harm)* [2001] 2 FLR 515; *Re C (Abduction: Grave Risk of Psychological Harm)* [1999] 1 FLR 1145.

[131] The independence of this part of Art 13 was confirmed by *Re S (Minors) (Abduction: Custody Rights)* [1993] Fam 242, at 250 *per* Balcombe LJ.

[132] *Re A (Foreign Access Order: Enforcement)* [1996] 1 FLR 561, at 567 *per* Waite LJ; *Re S (A Minor) (Abduction: Custody Rights)* [1993] Fam 242, at 251–252 *per* Balcombe LJ. On the other hand, where the aggrieved parent delays unnecessarily in making an application for the child's return so as to strengthen the child's preference for remaining where it is, the court will take this into account in giving greater weight to the child's view: see *Re L (A Child) (Abduction: Child's Objections to Return)* [2002] 2 FLR 1042.

[133] [1995] 1 FLR 716.

seven.[134] This apparent leniency is possibly explicable in terms of the fact that the issue at stake is arguably understood more straightforwardly than some of those arising in cases involving controversial medical procedures or aspects of religious faith in which a demonstrably stricter test has been applied.[135] That said, even in the present context, the maturity criterion must on principle be satisfied as a question of fact in each particular case.[136]

In terms of the child's objection, it has been made clear that what the child must be opposed to is the return that would otherwise be ordered under Article 12. It is insufficient for the purposes of this defence if what the child objects to is merely a compulsory separation from the abducting parent.[137] On the other hand, the child's objection need not be purely referable to the country from which he or she was abducted: the court is perfectly at liberty to take account of the fact that the objection centres largely on the perceived undesirability of resuming residence with the non-abducting parent.[138] Yet what the court must, of course, be cautious of is the danger that the view expressed is not genuinely that of the child but rather a view expressed under the influence of the abducting parent who has encouraged the child to say that he or she objects to a return.[139]

4 The residual discretion to order a return

Article 18 of the Hague Convention provides that '[t]he provisions of . . . [Article 13] do not limit the power of a judicial or administrative authority to order the return of the child at any time'. Thus, even where the abducting parent can establish one of the exceptions discussed in the preceding paragraphs, the court may still order the child's return. In exercising this discretion, the court will be mindful of the following factors set out by Waite J in *W v W (Child Abduction: Acquiescence)*[140] (and subsequently approved by the Court of Appeal in *H v H* (*Abduction: Acquiescence*[141]):

[134] According to one research finding, a four-year-old's objection held sway before a German court: see N. Lowe & A. Perry, 'The Operation of the Hague and European Conventions on International Child Abduction between England and Germany: Part II' [1998] *International Family Law* 52.

[135] For the stringent maturity test applicable in cases involving controversial medical procedures see M Brazier, *Medicine, Patients and the Law* (London: Penguin, 2003) ch 14.

[136] *Re S (A Minor) (Abduction: Custody Rights)* [1993] Fam 242.

[137] *Ibid.*

[138] See, eg, *Re T (Children) (Abduction: Child's Objections to Return)* [2000] 2 FLR 192; *Re M (A Minor) (Child Abduction)* [1994] 1 FLR 390.

[139] For judicial recognition of this point, see *Re T (Abduction: Child's Objections to Return)* [2000] 2 FLR 192; *Re P (A Minor) (Abduction: Minor's Views)* [1998] 2 FLR 825; *Re S (A Minor) (Abduction: Custody Rights)* [1993] Fam 242; *Re R (A Minor) (Abduction)* [1992] 1 FLR 105.

[140] [1993] 2 FLR 211.

[141] [1996] 2 FLR 570.

(a) the comparative suitability of the forum in the competing jurisdictions to determine the child's future in the substantive proceedings;
(b) the likely outcome (in whichever forum they be heard) of the substantive proceedings;
(c) the consequences of the acquiescence [where present], with particular reference to the extent to which the child may have become settled in the requested State;
(d) the situation which would await the absconding parent and the child if compelled to return to the requesting jurisdiction;
(e) the anticipated emotional effect upon the child of an immediate return order (a factor which is to be treated as significant but not as paramount);
(f) the extent to which the purpose and underlying philosophy of the Hague Convention would be at risk of frustration if a return order were to be refused.[142]

Beyond the general observation that the courts in the State of origin are clearly presumed to provide a more suitable forum for resolving outstanding residence issues (thus implying the appropriateness of a return[143]), little can be added to Waite J's relatively straightforward guidance. This is largely because there are very few reported cases dealing with the Article 18 discretion. However, one such case worth noting was *Re S (Child Abduction: Delay)*[144] in which it was held that, in addition to the factors listed by Waite J, a court may also take account of any delay there may have been on the part of the aggrieved parent in his or her pursuit of a return under the Convention. The only other decision worthy of note is that in *Re D (Abduction: Discretionary Return)*.[145] There, a mother had consented to her two children leaving France to live with their father in England even though, prior to their divorce, she had been granted residence by a French court. When she later objected, it was held that despite her earlier consent, her present retraction should hold sway since the English court felt it inappropriate to sanction the children's continued residence in England where so doing would necessarily entail issuing an order that would be inconsistent with the earlier French order concerning residence. In short, the court was minded to invoke Article 18 to avoid a conflict of laws.

5 Access rights

Although the Hague Convention is primarily concerned with securing the return of abducted children to aggrieved parents whose custody rights have been abrogated, it does make some residual provision with respect to access

[142] *Ibid*, at 574–575.
[143] For detailed consideration of the significance of the *forum conveniens* principle in this context see Schuz, *op cit* n 89, at 780–792.
[144] [1993] Fam 1.
[145] [2000] 1 FLR 24.

rights.[146] Article 21 permits applications to Central Authorities for arrangements to be made with respect to 'organizing or securing the effective exercise of rights of access . . . in the same way as an application for the return of a child' (and for the purposes of English law, the term 'access' equates closely to the domestic term 'contact'[147]). Furthermore, the Central Authorities of each Contracting State are required to promote the peaceful enjoyment of access rights in cases where the child will remain in the new country.[148] This duty is to be fulfilled by the removal, so far as possible, of any obstacles – including those created by the abducting parent – that may be encountered in the exercise of those access rights.[149]

Since the duty in Article 21 is limited to making 'arrangements for organizing or securing the effective exercise of rights of access', it is clear that any subsequent court proceedings remain formally independent. This is important, for at least two reasons. First, any legal right to access can be granted by the courts alone: thus, anyone seeking contact with a child in this country must obtain a court order to that effect under section 8 of the Children Act 1989. The Central Authority's obligation goes no further than arranging for suitably qualified solicitors to act on the applicant's behalf.[150] Secondly, applications in respect of access rights do not attract the automatic entitlement to legal aid that applies (by virtue of Article 7(g) of the Hague Convention) in respect of returns. On a happier note, however, it has been held that the Article 21 facility continues to operate even once the child has become habitually resident in the new country.[151]

6 The impact of Brussels IIA

Although according to its long title Brussels IIA concerns jurisdiction and the recognition and enforcement of judgments in matrimonial and parental responsibility matters, it also contains a number of provisions that relate exclusively to cases of child abduction between two Member States of the European Union.[152] Indeed, one of its chief political objectives has been

[146] See N. Lowe, 'Problems Relating to Access Disputes under the Hague Convention on International Child Abduction' (1994) 8 *International Journal of Law and the Family* 374.

[147] Under s 27(4) of the Child Abduction and Custody Act 1985, 'a decision relating to rights of access . . . means a decision as to the contact which a child may, or may not, have with any person'.

[148] Hague Convention, Art 21.

[149] *Ibid.*

[150] *Re T (Minors) (Hague Convention: Access)* [1993] 2 FLR 617.

[151] *Re G (A Minor) (Enforcement of Access Abroad)* [1993] Fam 216.

[152] The Regulation applies to all Members of the European Union with the exception of Denmark: Brussels IIA, Art 2(3). It takes precedence (by virtue of Arts 60(a), (d) and 1(b)) over both the Hague and European Conventions in so far as they concern civil matters relating to the attribution, exercise, restriction or termination of parental responsibility. The extent to which Brussels IIA affects the European Convention is considered on p 00 of this chapter.

identified as being 'to provide a Community remedy for European child abduction cases'.[153] A useful starting point to understanding the impact of Brussels IIA on the Hague Convention is Article 10 of the former which sets out the circumstances in which a requesting Member State will retain jurisdiction with respect to a child who has yet to acquire a habitual residence in another Member State. It is a lengthy and complex Article, but its general thrust is that jurisdiction should not be lost in the State of origin simply by virtue of the fact that an abduction has occurred. More specifically, yet almost impenetrably, it provides that jurisdiction will be retained until the child acquires a new habitual residence in another Member State *and* (a) the aggrieved parent (or other relevant body) has acquiesced in the removal or retention,[154] *or* (b) the child has lived in the new State for a period of one year since the holder of custody rights had actual or constructive knowledge of the child's whereabouts *and* the child is now settled in the new environment *and* a request for return has been withdrawn (with no new request being made within a specified time-frame) *or* such a request has failed in an attempt to secure his return, *or* the chance to contest the child's custody has been time-barred in the originating State.[155]

The fact that jurisdiction is retained by a State of origin in these various circumstances means that the courts in that State are free to decide substantive issues relating to parental responsibility (including custody and access). And since any judgment entered by such a court is entitled to recognition in accordance with Chapter III of the Regulation,[156] this in effect means that a decision that has already been reached in the requested State to the effect that a child need not be returned can be overridden by a subsequent State of origin decision.[157] McEleavy has pithily captured the effect of such subsequent orders by calling them 'trumping orders'. He has also astutely noted that these trumping orders are difficult to reconcile with the general comity of nations principle since they comprise orders available in one Member

[153] P. McEleavy, 'Brussels II *bis*: Matrimonial Matters, Parental Responsibility, Child Abduction and Mutual Recognition' (2004) 53 *International and Comparative Law Quarterly* 503, 505. For further discussion of the impact of Brussels IIA on the Hague Convention, see N. Lowe, 'Regulating International Parental Child Abduction – Brussels Style' [2004] *Contemporary Issues in Law* 315.

[154] *Ibid*, Art 10(a).

[155] *Ibid*, Art 10(b)(i)–(iv).

[156] Brussels IIA, Art 40(2) provides that '[a] judgment given in a Member State shall be recognised and enforceable in another Member State without the need for a declaration of enforceability and without any possibility of opposing its recognition if the judgment has been certified in the Member State of origin'. For critique based on the undermining of trust between Member States, see McEleavy, *op cit* n 153, at 510–512.

[157] As much is spelled out in Art 11(8) of Brussels IIA. On the concerns about the overuse of the Art 13 defences that prompted the inclusion of this provision, see McEleavy, *op cit* n 153, at 509; Lowe, *op cit* n 153, at 335–336.

State that are *specifically designed* to overrule previous orders obtained in other Member States. As he rightly observes:

> [I]f courts are acting responsibly and only using the safety valve [in the Hague Convention] when required, there is no justification to allow courts in another Member State to go behind such findings and in essence have a rehearing. If 'trumping orders' are made as a matter of course it will undoubtedly give rise to a body of ill-feeling and resentment between courts in Member States.[158]

In addition to the fact that decisions on non-return can effectively be challenged in such a way, Brussels IIA further provides that a court 'cannot refuse to return a child on the basis of Article 13(b) . . . if it is established that adequate arrangements have been made to secure the protection of the child after his or her return'.[159] To a large extent, this merely lends legislative authority to the existing approach of the English courts developed by way of judicial exegesis.[160] More novel, however, is the provision in Article 11(5) whereby a court cannot refuse to return a child unless the requesting parent has been given the opportunity to be heard.[161] Similarly novel are the twin provisions in Article 11(6) and (7) that require a court refusing a return to send all the documentation relating to the non-return to the relevant judicial or administrative authorities in the requesting State so that the aggrieved parent can, if he or she desires, institute proceedings questioning the child's custody in the courts of that country. If the applicant's case is viewed favourably, these proceedings may lead to a 'trumping order' being made that must then be recognised and enforced in the State to which the child was taken,[162] and generally without the need for a declaration of enforceability and without the scope for future challenge by the requested State.[163]

One final matter worthy of mention is the fact that access decisions will be afforded the same treatment as custody decisions: that is, they too will be afforded automatic recognition and enforcement so long as they were issued

[158] McEleavy, *op cit* n 157, at 510.

[159] *Ibid*, Art 11(4).

[160] See, eg, *Re H (Abduction: Grave Risk)* [2003] EWCA Civ 355; *TB v JB (Abduction: Grave Risk of Harm)* [2001] 2 FLR 515; *Re C (Abduction: Grave Risk of Psychological Harm)* [1999] 1 FLR 1145.

[161] Brussels IIA, Art 11(5). Note also that under Art 11(2) there is a change of emphasis on the views of the child: these now *must* be heard unless it is inappropriate to do so because of the child's lack of age or maturity. Cf Hague Convention, Art 13(2) (and for critique see Lowe, *op cit* n 153, at 334). In similar emphasis-changing vein is the requirement in Brussels IIA, Art 11(3) that a court seised of jurisdiction *must* issue judgment within six weeks unless exceptional circumstances prevail.

[162] *Ibid*, Art 11(8).

[163] *Ibid*, Art 42(1). The only exception is where the return order is not certified in the Member State of origin as having been granted in compliance with the requirements of natural justice.

and properly certified in one Member State and due to take effect in another.[164] In addition, by Article 48 of Brussels IIA, the courts in the Member State of enforcement 'may make practical arrangements for organising the exercise of rights of access'. As such, the need to invoke Article 21 of the Hague Convention will be much reduced between Member States of the European Union.[165]

The European Convention[166]

Comparison with the Hague Convention

As noted in passing, beyond the obvious different geographical application of the two Conventions, the European Convention differs in two further principal respects from the Hague Convention. First, the European Convention is not limited to cases of wrongful removal or retention. To this extent, it is wider in scope than the Hague Convention. Secondly, since the European Convention works according to a system of recognition and enforcement of judgments, it is narrower in scope than the Hague Convention; for the latter does not require the applicant to be in possession of a court order[167] relating to the custody of the abducted child.

A third notable difference, however, relates to the relative emphasis placed upon the child's welfare within the two Conventions. Whereas the Preamble to the Hague Convention speaks of signatory States being '[f]irmly convinced that the interests of children are of paramount importance in matters relating to their custody', the equivalent prefatory statement in the European Convention is that 'the welfare of the child is of overriding importance in reaching decisions concerning his custody'. The difference in language is subtle but significant. For while the Hague Convention refers generally to the best interests of *children*, it contains no reference to the best interests of the *individual child*.[168] Instead, by allowing for the non-return of an individual

[164] *Ibid*, Art 41(1). For discussion of the magnitude of this change, see Lowe, *op cit* n 153, at 336–337.

[165] For scepticism as to the likely efficacy of this provision, see Lowe *op cit* n 153, at 337.

[166] The full title of the Convention is the European Convention on Recognition and Enforcement of Decisions Concerning Custody of Children and on Restoration of Custody of Children. For a good general account see Lowe, *et al*, *op cit* n 34, ch 19.

[167] Strictly, the European Convention envisages decisions entered by both judicial and administrative authorities; but in practice this almost always means court orders – only in Denmark, Norway and Switzerland are child custody decisions taken by administrative authorities.

[168] See E. Pérez-Vera, *Explanatory Report, Hague Conference on Private International Law, Acts and Documents of the Fourteenth Session, Vol III* (The Hague: HCCH Publications, 1982) para 23: 'the dispositive part of the Convention contains no explicit reference to the interests of the child . . . [mindful of] the Convention's

child where he or she has become settled in his or her new environment,[169] and by allowing for the retention of the child where the child's return would entail a grave risk of physical or psychological harm,[170] the Hague Convention merely hints at a commitment to the welfare of individual children. However, in emphasising speedy returns, the Hague Convention also jeopardises the prospect of voluntary returns, and this in turn may lead to acrimonious legal proceedings in the State of origin which would have a predictably disruptive and detrimental effect upon the child concerned.[171] By contrast, as Waite LJ has pointed out, '[t]he European Convention seeks to spare children the unsettling effect of a conflict of orders for custody or contact in different jurisdictions'.[172] Furthermore, the language in which the paramountcy of individual child's welfare is expressed under the European Convention is unequivocal.

Notwithstanding these differences between the Hague and European Conventions, there are number of fundamental similarities. For a start, the European Convention also works according to system of Central Authorities whose initial tasks involve the receiving and transmitting of information concerning incoming and outgoing requests (including any necessary explanations of aspects of domestic law).[173] In addition, it also requires these Central Authorities to undertake (or, at least, initiate) the discovery of an abducted child's whereabouts,[174] to eliminate obstacles to the operation of the Convention[175] and to secure the recognition and enforcement of decisions[176] (including securing the physical return of the child to the applicant[177]). In short, the functions of Central Authorities under the European Convention are essentially similar to those contained in the Hague Convention.

Secondly, although the Convention is centrally concerned with the recognition and enforcement of custody orders,[178] it does have built into it the concept of "improper removal". This is defined in terms broadly in line with the twin Hague Convention concepts of wrongful removal and wrongful retention.[179] Yet, for the most part, it is not the impropriety of the removal

stated objective, which is to secure the prompt return of children who have been wrongfully removed or retained.' See also, M. Freeman, 'In the Best Interests of Internationally Abducted Children? – Plural, Singular, Neither or Both?' [2002] *International Family Law* 77.

169 Hague Convention, Art 12.

170 *Ibid*, Art 13(b).

171 See Armstrong, *op cit* n 25, at 434.

172 *Re A (Foreign Access Order: Enforcement)* [1996] 1 FLR 561, at 567.

173 European Convention, Art 3(2).

174 *Ibid*, Art 5(1)(a); Art 8.

175 *Ibid*, Art 3(2)(c)

176 *Ibid*, Art 5(1)(c).

177 *Ibid*, Art 5(1)(d).

178 *Ibid*, Art 7.

179 *Ibid*, Art 1(d).

per se that is significant, it is the fact that the applicant is in possession of an enforceable decision relating to custody. The exceptional case in which an applicant will also have to show an unlawful removal is governed by Article 12. This in essence provides that, where at the time of the child's removal there was no enforceable decision relating to his custody, any subsequent decision to that effect and which declares the removal to have been unlawful[180] will entitle the applicant to invoke the Convention and secure the child's return.[181] Furthermore, the term 'decision relating to custody' is defined broadly in terms of a judgment that 'relates to the care of the person of the child, including the right to decide on the place of his residence, or the right of access to him'.[182] This is a sufficiently wide definition to embrace not only those in possession of parental responsibility, but also those holding either a residence order or a contact order under the Children Act 1989.[183]

Mechanics of the Convention

The first step for an aggrieved parent seeking to secure the return of his or her child is to make a formal application to a Central Authority.[184] The applicant is entirely free as to which Central Authority is contacted,[185] but there will frequently be logistical and linguistic advantages associated with contacting the Central Authority in the country from which the child has been abducted since the application must be accompanied by a set of specified documents.[186] Once received, it is incumbent upon the Central Authority to take appropriate steps to secure the prompt recognition and enforcement of the relevant custody decision.[187] There is one situation, however, in which the Central Authority addressed will not be obliged to register the custody decision with a court in that country, and this where the child has been further removed to a third Contracting State. In such circumstances, the

[180] Under English law, a declaration as to the impropriety of a removal can be obtained under the Child Abduction Act 1985, s 23(2).

[181] See, eg, *Re S (A Minor) (Custody: Habitual Residence)* [1997] 4 All ER 251; *Re S (Abduction) (European Convention)* [1996] 1 FLR 660.

[182] European Convention, Art 1(c).

[183] A residence order is 'an order settling the arrangements to be made as to the person with whom a child is to live'; a contact order is 'an order requiring the person with whom a child lives, or is to live, to allow the child to stay with or visit the person named in the order, or for that person and the child otherwise to have contact with each another': Children Act 1989, s 8(1).

[184] European Convention, Art 2(1).

[185] *Ibid*, Art 4(1).

[186] *Ibid*, Art 4(2). Under Art 13 this documentation includes a copy of the order in question, written authorisation for the Central Authority to act on the applicant's behalf and suggestions as to how custody of the child might be restored.

[187] *Ibid*, Art 5(1).

Central Authority addressed is obliged to transmit the documentation 'directly and without delay to the Central Authority of that State'.[188]

Once registered with a court in the Contracting State to which the child has been removed and is currently being held,[189] a custody decision will usually be recognised and enforced as though it were an order made directly by the court affording such recognition.[190] The fact of registration does not, however, guarantee recognition and enforcement[191] because Articles 9 and 10 of the Convention set out various grounds on which recognition may be refused by the courts of the State addressed.

Refusal of recognition and enforcement

The starting point for any consideration of the scope for refusing recognition and enforcement of judgments under the Convention is Article 8.[192] This is an optional provision[193] that, if implemented by a Contracting State, ousts the availability of the grounds for refusal of recognition in cases where an application for the child's return was made within six months of the child's removal from a country of which he and his parents were nationals at the time of the application being made (or at the time of the judgment being entered in the applicant's favour, if later).[194] In practice, however, Article 8 has not proven popular and the majority of States Parties have not implemented it.

Where Article 8 does not apply, the grounds for refusal of recognition that may be invoked are located in Articles 9 and 10 of the Convention. Broadly, the objections contained in Article 9 centre upon procedural irregularities associated with the acquisition of the custody order for which recognition is sought. The premise for the operation of the various (rather narrow) grounds for non-recognition located within this provision is that an application to a Central Authority has been made within six months of an improper removal. Where such an application has been made, a custody decision may be refused recognition where the abducting parent, through no fault of her own, failed to receive notice of the proceedings in which the order was obtained,[195] *or*,

[188] *Ibid*, Art 5(3).

[189] In England and Wales, this is the High Court: Child Abduction and Custody Act 1985, s 16.

[190] European Convention Art 7; Child Abduction and Custody Act 1985, s 18.

[191] See, eg, *Re H (A Minor) (Foreign Custody Order: Enforcement)* [1994] Fam 105.

[192] While recognition and enforcement will normally go hand in hand, they may nonetheless be treated separately under the Convention so that recognition need not necessarily be accompanied by enforcement: see *Re H (Foreign Custody Order: Enforcement)* [1994] Fam 105.

[193] Article 8 is made optional under Art 17(1) of the Convention.

[194] European Convention, Art 8(2).

[195] *Ibid*, Art 9(1)(a).

where the court granting the custody decision did not ground its jurisdictional competence on either the habitual residence of the parents or the child,[196] *or*, where the decision conflicts with an enforceable prior decision granted in the State addressed.[197]

Under Article 10, the grounds on which recognition and enforcement may be refused are (at least ostensibly) somewhat broader in scope.[198] Thus, a refusal of recognition is permitted where the effects of the decision for which recognition is sought is 'manifestly incompatible with the fundamental principles of the law relating to the family and children in the State addressed'.[199] However, in reality, although the grounds for manifest incompatibility are theoretically numerous, there is only limited scope for the invocation of this ground given that the European Convention operates only among European democracies with broadly similar (if not congruent) family law principles. *T v R (Abduction: Forum Conveniens)*[200] provides a useful insight into the kind of approach the English courts will adopt in such cases. There, a mother had been granted custody of the child while the father had been granted access. The mother refused to honour the father's access rights and removed the child from Sweden to England without the father's knowledge or consent. In the light of this abrogation of the father's access rights, a Swedish court changed the original order and awarded sole custody to the father. The father sought recognition and enforcement of this order. The mother countered by arguing, among other things, that the English court would never reverse a residence order without a full investigation of all the circumstances, and that it certainly would not do this on the mere basis that the father's contact rights had been denied. In holding that the Swedish approach was not manifestly incompatible with what would have been done in England, Charles J said:

> a change of residence to a father who the court considers is capable of caring appropriately for the child in circumstances where the mother is refusing contact and to take a full and proper part in the court process is not incompatible with the approach taken in England . . . [since the father's custody order] is within the range of orders that would have been open to an English court.[201]

A more promising basis on which to ground a refusal of recognition is that there has been 'a change of circumstances, including the passage of time . . .

[196] *Ibid*, Art 9(1)(b).

[197] *Ibid*, Art 9(1)(c).

[198] But for the argument that they must be construed very narrowly in order to ensure the attainment of the Convention's primary goals, see R.L. Jones, 'Council of Europe Convention on Recognition and Enforcement of Decisions Relating to the Custody of Children' (1981) 30 *International and Comparative Law Quarterly* 467, 474–475.

[199] *Ibid*, Art 10(1)(a).

[200] [2002] 2 FLR 544.

[201] *Ibid*, at [115]–[116].

after an improper removal, [such that] the effects of the original decision are manifestly no longer in accordance with the welfare of the child'.[202] Yet even here the court is required to ascertain the views of the child concerned (unless this is impracticable in the light of his or her age and understanding) before reaching a conclusion on this ground.[203] Curiously, the European Convention is silent on the matter of whether the court must attribute any particular weight to the child's views. But this must be implicit, for the provision would otherwise be pointless.[204] However, in line with the general assumption that a return is presumptively in the child's best interests, the English courts have taken a restrictive approach to this ground. They have repeatedly insisted that there is a very high hurdle to cross in order to establish that the decision in question is 'manifestly no longer in accordance with the child's welfare'.[205] That said, there have been successful invocations of this defence.[206] For example, in one case, a delay of twenty-one months in the lives of two very young children (aged two and four) could not be ignored. Accordingly, Booth J refused to recognise and enforce the father's French custody order relying chiefly upon 'the passage of time during which the children have continued to live with the mother who has always been their primary carer and the dangers inherent in now removing them'.[207] Similarly, in another case where the abducting mother had re-married and established a new, emotionally and financially secure home for the child, it was held that there had been a sufficient change of circumstances to justify non-recognition and non-enforcement of the custody order in question.[208]

What must be borne in mind in relation to this ground is the fact that the court has only a discretion (not an obligation) to refuse to recognise and enforce a custody order. It therefore follows that a judge may take account of broader considerations that may well point towards the child's return notwithstanding a fundamental change of circumstances. In *Re D (Abduction:*

[202] *Ibid*, Art 10(1)(b).

[203] *Ibid*, Art 15(1)(a).

[204] In *Re A (Foreign Access Order: Enforcement)* [1996] 1 FLR 561 Waite LJ held (at 567) that those views are not 'conclusive', although in *Re H (A Minor) (Foreign Custody Order)* [1994] Fam 105 the views of a thirteen-year-old who was implacably hostile to any further contact with her father held sway.

[205] See, eg, *T v R (Abduction: Forum Conveniens)* [2002] 2 FLR 544, at 121 *per* Charles J; *Re H (A Minor) (Foreign Custody Order: Enforcement)* [1994] 105, at 110 *per* Sir Stephen Brown P; *Re L (Child Abduction: European Convention)* [1992] 2 FLR 178, at 182 *per* Ward J; *Re G (A Minor) (Abduction: Enforcement)* [1990] 2 FLR 325.

[206] Note also that a court may recognise a judgment but decline to enforce it: see *Re H (A Minor) (Foreign Custody Order: Enforcement)* [1994] Fam 105; *Re G (Foreign Contact Order: Enforcement)* [2004] 1 FLR 378.

[207] *F v F (Minors) (Custody: Foreign Order)* [1989] Fam 1.

[208] *Re R (Abduction: European and Hague Conventions)* [1997] 1 FLR 663. See also *Re L (Abduction: European Convention: Access)* [1999] 2 FLR 1089.

Discretionary Return),[209] for example, the trial judge felt that although the children in question had settled well with their father after he had kept them in England following a holiday spent there with the mother's consent, it was nonetheless in the children's best interests to be returned to France so that the French courts could resolve the residence dispute that had arisen when the mother later sought to invoke the Convention. Wilson J held that not to have done so would have jeopardised any future visits to France by the children because the French courts may have enforced the existing French residence order in favour of the mother that the parents had chosen to ignore.

Thirdly, recognition and enforcement of a foreign custody decision may be refused if, at the time the Convention proceedings were instituted in the State of origin, the child was either exclusively a national of, or habitually resident in, the State addressed *or* a joint national of the State addressed and the State of origin but habitually resident in the State addressed.[210] Finally, recognition and enforcement may be refused if the order in question is incompatible with some prior decision (either issued in the State addressed or enforceable there after having been issued in a third State), and refusal of recognition would be in accordance with the welfare of the child.[211]

Access applications under the European Convention

In much the same way that the Hague Convention makes secondary provision with respect to access rights, so too does the European Convention. However, under the latter regime there is considerably more scope for the enforcement of such rights. For a start, access decisions 'shall be recognised and enforced subject to the same conditions as other decisions relating to custody'.[212] Secondly, the legal aid that is available under the European Convention in respect of securing the recognition and enforcement of custody rights extends equally to rights of access.[213] By contrast, under the Hague Convention, as we have already observed, considerably less assistance can be expected from a Central Authority with respect to one's access rights than with one's custody rights. The considerably better protection of access rights under the European Convention is best explained by reference to the statement in the Preamble that it is 'desirable . . . to emphasise that the right of access of parents is a normal corollary to the to the right of custody'.

Notwithstanding the fact that there exists a very strong presumption in favour of the recognition and enforcement of access decisions, the practicalities of access can nonetheless become complex where it is to be exercised

[209] [2000] 1 FLR 24.
[210] European Convention, Art 10(1)(c).
[211] *Ibid*, Art 10(1)(d).
[212] *Ibid*, Art 11(1).
[213] *Ibid*, Art 5(3).

across national borders.[214] To meet these difficulties, Article 11(2) of the Convention permits the courts in the State addressed to 'fix the conditions for implementation and exercise of the right of access taking into account, in particular, undertakings given by the parties on this matter'. What this provision achieves, therefore, is a facility whereby the court in the State addressed can make practical modifications to access orders that were granted in a State of origin before the difficulties now associated with access existed. What Article 11(2) does not permit, however, is any substantive review, and Article 9(3) makes this abundantly clear.[215] Nor, seemingly, will a court exercise its discretion under Article 11(2) to facilitate transnational contact in the absence of constructive suggestions as to how this can be achieved.[216]

The proper construction of Article 11(2) was most recently considered in *Re G (Foreign Contact Order: Enforcement)*.[217] There, Thorpe LJ began by noting that '[a]ccess orders can seldom be written on stone tablets . . . [because they] are peculiarly vulnerable to change of circumstance . . . [thus making] enforcement, not only after lapse of time but after relocation and in a foreign court . . . always likely to be problematic'.[218] He then concluded that '[t]hese realities . . . demand a liberal construction of Art 11(2) in order to achieve the overriding objectives of the European Convention, one of which is to ensure that the act of relocation does not avoid the orders for contact made by the court [in the State of origin]'.[219] In short, his Lordship's view was that Article 11(2) should be construed broadly enough to enable the courts of the addressed State to fix conditions that make transnational contact feasible and workable.[220]

In cases in which access rights, *per se*, have not hitherto been raised – either because the applicant never obtained such rights in the State of origin, or because he asserted custody rights that the State addressed refused to recognise – the Central Authority in the State addressed may, under Article 11(3) apply to its own courts for rights of access on the aggrieved parent's

[214] A further prospective layer of complication may emerge if the European Convention on Contact Concerning Children 2003 becomes applicable. At the time of writing, this has not occurred. Accordingly, the Convention (so far as it has cross-border implications) is not discussed here. For a detailed account of the Convention, however, see ch 10.

[215] Article 9(3) provides that '[i]n no circumstances may the foreign decision be reviewed as to its merits'. See also the judicial endorsement of this caveat in *Re A (Foreign Access Order: Enforcement)* [1996] 1 FLR 561, at 565 *per* Leggatt LJ.

[216] *Re L (Abduction: European Convention: Access)* [1999] 2 FLR 1089.

[217] [2004] 1 FLR 378.

[218] *Ibid*, at [27].

[219] *Ibid*.

[220] On the other hand, his Lordship also recognised, and added as a rider, the fact that the whole question of contact may need to be revisited in the future and that this may require direct international judicial co-operation as to the tricky matter of *forum conveniens*: *ibid*, at [29].

behalf where that parent so requests. This level of proactive involvement by the Central Authority in the State addressed is markedly more beneficial to non-abducting parents than the equivalent provision in the Hague Convention, considered earlier. Taken in tandem with the point, also made earlier, that legal aid is available in relation to access applications under the European Convention, it becomes clear that it is in this context that the infrequently invoked European Convention is a much more advantageous instrument than the its Hague counterpart. That said, the utility of the European Convention must now be read subject to Brussels IIA, which very significantly circumscribes its sphere of operation.

The impact of Brussels IIA on the European Convention

A useful starting point for understanding the impact of Brussels IIA on the European Convention is paragraph 5 of the Recital to that Regulation which states that '[i]n order to ensure equality for all children, this Regulation covers all decisions on parental responsibility'.[221] The next points of note are that, for the purposes of Brussels IIA, the term 'parental responsibility' is defined so as specifically to 'include rights of custody and rights of access', and that it applies to all 'civil matters relating to . . . the attribution, exercise, delegation, restriction or termination of parental responsibility' including, in particular, 'rights of custody and rights of access'.[222] What this means, then, is that, because Brussels IIA takes precedence over the European Convention in such matters,[223] any decisions as to custody or access must be dealt with according to the former, not the latter, instrument. And this applies both at the level of the attribution of jurisdiction and at the level of the recognition and enforcement of such decisions. The jurisdiction provisions of Brussels IIA were considered earlier, in the context of the discussion of its impact on the Hague Abduction Convention. As such, they need not be revisited here. What does need to be considered here, however, is the profound effect of Brussels IIA in so far as it covers the recognition and enforcement of custody decisions.

It will be recalled that a major difference between the Hague and European Conventions is that the former works according to a system of international co-operation in directly securing the return of abducted children whereas the latter works according to a more indirect system whereby the return of abducted children is dependent upon the recognition of judicial orders conferring custody rights. Since Brussels IIA also works according to

[221] Under the previous Regulation, Brussels II, parental responsibility matters were covered only to the extent that they were an adjunct to matrimonial proceedings. This gave rise to severe interpretational difficulties: see *Re G (Foreign Contact Order: Enforcement)* [2004] 1 FLR 378, at [39]–[41] *per* Thorpe LJ.

[222] Brussels IIA, Art 1(1)(b), (2).

[223] *Ibid*, Art 60(d).

a system of recognition and enforcement of judgments,[224] there is no scope for the European Convention to be read side by side with it. Thus, while the impact of Brussels IIA on the Hague Convention is largely limited to diluting the significance of the Article 13 defences,[225] it has the effect of completely ousting the operation of the European Convention so long as the two States involved are both Members States of the European Union and so long as what is in issue is the recognition of *any* custody judgment obtained in a Member State. Indeed, any attempt to invoke the European Convention in cases involving two such States would be treated as a nullity.[226]

While this means that the European Convention ceases to operate as an alternative to the Hague Convention in most European abduction cases, it does not cease to operate in its entirety, for there remain a number of States that lie outside the European Union but which are Parties to the European Convention. In respect of such States, Brussels IIA is of no significance.[227] Accordingly, European abductions involving these States may still be dealt with on the basis of the European Convention (subject to the child having acquired an habitual residence in a European Union State of which he or she is not a national or domiciliary[228]).

In respect of those cases in which the European Convention can no longer be invoked, however, the effect of Brussels IIA is likely to be significant. Most importantly, a considerable advantage will accrue to aggrieved parents by virtue of the fact that it provides that '[a] judgment given in a Member State shall be recognised and enforceable in another Member State without the need for a declaration of enforceability and without any possibility of opposing its recognition if the judgment has been certified in the Member State of origin'.[229] This 'fast track regime',[230] which applies equally to custody and access decisions,[231] marks an endeavour to accommodate the Tampere

[224] Brussels IIA, Ch III.

[225] It also provides guidance on how the Hague Convention should be applied *as between Member States*: Brussels IIA, Art 11. This guidance, discussed earlier, suggests mainly changes in emphasis within current practice. For a more detailed discussion see Lowe, *op cit* n 153, at 333–334.

[226] For a clear statement to this effect (albeit in relation to the equivalent provisions of the previous Regulation, Brussels II), see *Re G (Foreign Contact Order: Enforcement)* [2004] 1 FLR 378, at [48] *per* Thorpe LJ.

[227] The relevant States, at the time of writing, are: Bulgaria, Denmark, Iceland, Liechtenstein, Macedonia, Moldova, Norway, Serbia & Montenegro and Turkey.

[228] Brussels IIA, Art 10.

[229] *Ibid*, Arts 41(1) and 42(1) in relation to access orders and return orders, respectively. As regards certification, the judgment must have been certified in the Member State of origin as having been granted in compliance with the requirements of natural justice: *ibid*, Arts 41(2), 42(2).

[230] I have borrowed this term from McEleavy, *op cit* n 153, at 511.

[231] The access provisions of the European Convention will remain operative only as between those Member States set out in n 227. For further details of the impact of

European Council[232] view that 'judgments in the field of family litigation should be "automatically recognised throughout the Union without any intermediate proceedings or grounds for refusal of enforcement"'.[233] Another notable feature of Brussels IIA is that, even in cases where fast-track recognition does not apply, there will remain a facility to engage the assistance of a specially designated Central Authority that must, among other things, 'provide information and assistance to holders of parental responsibility seeking the recognition and enforcement of decisions'.[234] Perhaps of equal importance is the fact that Central Authority assistance will be provided free of charge. More negatively, however, the court's power under the European Convention to fix conditions to access rights will be lost.

Non-Convention abductions

Every year there is a significant number of child abductions that take place outside the scope of the Hague Convention, the European Convention and Brussels IIA.[235] In respect of such 'non-Convention cases', the extent to which there is in place a helpful, legal machinery to secure the return of an abducted child varies greatly depending on whether the abduction is an incoming or outgoing one, on which non-Convention country is involved, and on whether the child has actually been born at the time of the birth mother's sudden departure from a particular country.[236] For analytical neatness, we shall employ here only the incoming/outgoing abduction dichotomy.

Inward abductions from a non-Convention country

Where a child is abducted to the United Kingdom from a non-Convention country, it is typically the English High Court exercising its wardship jurisdiction[237] that will decide the question of whether the child should be returned

Brussels IIA on the access provisions of the European Convention, and for details, also, of its prospective impact on the European Convention on Contact Concerning Children 2003, see Lowe *et al*, *op cit* n 34, pp 596–605.

[232] 16 October 1999, see http://presidency.finland.fi/frame.asp.

[233] Brussels IIA, Recital, para 23. But note – by analogy with *Re B (Children) (Abduction: New Evidence)* [2001] 2 FCR 531 – the scope for complications associated with the fact that the fast-track regime relates only to recognition and not enforcement.

[234] *Ibid*, Art 55(b).

[235] For statistics as recent as June 2002, see Lowe *et al*, *op cit* n 34, p 430.

[236] See *W and W v H (Child Abduction: Surrogacy) (No 2)* [2002] 2 FLR 252 for an example of a mother 'abducting' unborn twins and being dealt with on a non-Convention basis even though the two countries involved were Parties to the Hague Convention.

[237] On wardship, see Lowe & Douglas, *op cit* n 20, ch 16.

to its State of origin. This is because of the speed with which a child can be made a ward of court, and because the invocation of wardship provides a useful safeguard against the child's further removal. An alternative to engaging the wardship jurisdiction of the court is to apply for the court to exercise its powers with respect to children under the Children Act 1989. But in either case, the English court cannot dispose of the case unless it possesses jurisdiction in the first place.[238] Where such jurisdiction does exist – and this will normally be the case because the child's presence in this country will usually suffice[239] – the child's welfare will be the court's paramount consideration. And this is so regardless of whether the case is heard under the wardship jurisdiction or under the Children Act 1989.[240]

In the context of wardship proceedings, the court will normally have to consider whether to order the summary return of the child in order that the full merits of the case can be heard before a court in the country from which the child was removed or whether it would be preferable to explore the full merits of the case itself. According to one Court of Appeal decision, it is inappropriate for the English courts to start from what is essentially a *forum conveniens* presumption that it is generally preferable for the merits of any given case to be decided in the child's country of origin.[241] Rather, the court should seek to satisfy itself, first, that ordering a return would not expose the child to any obvious danger to his or her physical or psychological well-being and secondly, that the applicable law in the country of origin embodies legal principles that would be acceptable to an English court. In considering whether the standards are acceptable for these purposes, the English courts will shy away from seeking to impose English standards *per se.* They will instead apply a more pluralistic approach that is neatly exemplified by *Re S (Minors) (Abduction)*.[242]

In this case, children born and brought up in Pakistan by parents who had both been born in Pakistan (although the mother had been raised in

[238] The relevant rules are contained in the Family Law Act 1986 (as amended). For a detailed account of these rules, see Lowe *et al*, *op cit* n 34, ch 3.

[239] Family Law Act 1986, s 3(1)(b).

[240] See, respectively, Children Act 1989, s 1(1) and *Re P (A Minor) (Child Abduction: Non-Convention Country)* [1997] Fam 45 where Ward LJ said (at 54): 'welfare is the only consideration which governs the court's decision.' For a helpful discussion of much of relevant case law, see K. Beevers, 'Non-Convention Child Abduction – Consideration of Welfare and Undertakings' [2004] *Contemporary Issues in Law* 303 and D. McClean & K. Beevers, 'International Child Abduction – Back to Common Law Principles' (1995) 7 *Child and Family Law Quarterly* 128.

[241] *Re F (A Minor) (Abduction: Jurisdiction)* [1991] Fam 25. On the other hand, it is possible to regard the appropriate forum in terms that are consistent with the child's welfare; for the most informed, best-positioned court is most likely to arrive at the most suitable decision: see *Re Z (A Minor) (Abduction: Non-Convention Country)* [1999] 1 FLR 1270.

[242] [1994] 1 FLR 297.

England since the age of five and acquired British citizenship) were brought to England by their mother without the father's consent. The mother instituted proceedings under the Children Act 1989 to obtain an order formally sanctioning the children's residence with her. The father sought the return of the children to Pakistan. In the course of those latter proceedings the English court was required to consider whether alternative proceedings brought in Pakistan would apply principles that were acceptable to the English courts. In a pluralistic judgment that noted the fact that the Pakistani courts would apply principles reflecting a Muslim point of view, Nolan LJ opined that the first instance judge had been 'fully entitled to take the view that, for Muslim children of Muslim parents whose home hitherto has been in Pakistan, the principles of Pakistani law are appropriate by English standards'.[243]

In terms of making the determination that the standards applicable in the relevant non-Convention country are acceptable and appropriate by English standards, some degree of evidence of the foreign law will be required. In *Re JA (Child Abduction: Non-Convention Country)*,[244] Ward LJ suggested that, '[i]t is only when this court is satisfied that the child's welfare will be protected by the foreign court that this court can entrust the decision to that foreign court'.[245] Yet while his Lordship's dictum may have be applauded in so far as it insisted that the English court should make its decision on an informed basis, it arguably displayed shades of cultural imperialism (or intolerance, at the very least) in its requirement that the foreign court must decide cases on the basis of the English welfare principle, and that it must do this regardless of the cultural values of the parties actually concerned. It came as little surprise, then, when a subsequent Court of Appeal resiled from this approach with Pill LJ asserting:

> I have no difficulty in accepting the judge's conclusion that the application of Muslim law to this Muslim family is appropriate and acceptable . . . These are Sudanese children. Their welfare may be well served by a decision in accordance with Sudanese law which may be taken to reflect the norms and values of the Sudanese society in which they live.[246]

It is suggested that Pill LJ's approach, echoing as it does that espoused by Nolan LJ in *Re F (A Minor) (Abduction: Jurisdiction)*,[247] is the preferable

[243] *Ibid*, at 305.
[244] [1998] 1 FLR 231.
[245] *Ibid*, at 242.
[246] *Re E (Abduction: Non-Convention Country)* [1999] 2 FLR 642, at 651. In similar vein, see *Re S (Child Abduction: Asylum Appeal)* [2002] 2 FLR 465. Cf *Al Habtoor v Fotheringham* [2001] 1 FLR 951 at [44] where Thorpe LJ appears to have been driven by concerns of cultural relativism rather than cultural pluralism. On the critical differences between relativism and pluralism, see M. Freeman, 'Images of Child Welfare in Child Abduction Appeals', in J. Murphy (ed), *Ethnic Minorities, Their Families and the Law* (Oxford: Hart Publishing, 2000).
[247] [1991] Fam 25.

one to adopt in this context. But a much-needed, final clarification of the law by the House of Lords in this connection would certainly be welcome.

Where the courts of this country are unsatisfied as to the standards or principles of justice applied in the country from which the child has been removed, they may refuse to order the child's return. This, indeed, is what happened in *Re JA* where it transpired that the courts in the United Arab Emirates did not apply the welfare principle and were in fact constrained by a deeply patriarchal system of law. According to recent *obiter dicta*, the English courts may even refuse to order a child's return on these grounds if the effect of that refusal is to ride roughshod over the terms of a custody order granted in the State of origin.[248]

Outward abductions to a non-Convention country

Where a child is abducted from this country to a non-Convention country, there is little by way of legal machinery to secure the child's return. The aggrieved parent can attempt to institute proceedings in the country to which the child was taken or in which he or she was wrongfully retained, but so doing may well involve a lengthy, costly and somewhat hit-and-miss process.[249] An alternative is to obtain a domestic remedy – either by virtue of wardship, or under the Children Act 1989 – which may, on occasion, be sufficiently influential to persuade the authorities in the country to which the child was taken to order the child's return notwithstanding the absence of any reciprocal agreement between the two countries to recognise and enforce one another's judicial decisions.[250]

A final possibility – though it targets the abducting parent rather than the child, and therefore provides no guarantee of the child's ultimate return to this country – is extradition. This centres on the criminality of the abductor's conduct and depends for success upon an extradition treaty with the relevant non-Convention country. However, the complexity and cost involved in extradition proceedings should not be underestimated and, combined with the general reluctance towards punishing the criminal conduct of abducting mothers,[251] this may serve to dissuade many aggrieved fathers from initiating such proceedings.

[248] See *Al Habtoor v Fotheringham* [2001] 1 FLR 951, at [44] *per* Thorpe LJ.

[249] For details of the kinds of practical and legal difficulties involved as well as of the limited assistance that can be expected in overcoming them, see Lowe *et al*, *op cit* n 34, pp 457–459.

[250] See, eg, the persuasive effect on the Indian authorities of an order obtained in wardship in *Re KR (Abduction: Forcible Removal by Parents)* [1999] 2 FLR 542.

[251] See Lowe *et al*, *op cit* n 34, p 461.

Conclusions and critique

The law relating to international child abduction is now extremely complicated. There is a range of international instruments – sometimes overlapping, sometimes conflicting – which may need to be consulted in order to determine whether any given child ought to be returned to his or her State of origin. Worse still, things are set to get even more confusing once the Hague Convention on the Protection of Children 1996[252] and the European Convention on Contact Concerning Children 2003 acquire the force of law in this country. It is difficult to see how things can be simplified, however, since the various international instruments emanate from a variety of sources with no single body possessing the competence to consolidate them into a unitary body of rules.[253]

Arguably, the criticism that the disparate sources of law are as likely to confuse as they are to produce satisfactory outcomes for abducted children pales into relative insignificance beside the point that the welfare of children is not made paramount under the Hague Convention. Furthermore, Sarah Armstrong has convincingly argued that the emphasis on speed within the Hague Convention comes at the significant cost of making voluntary returns less likely;[254] and if a return takes place only because it has been ordered, it is more probable that any subsequent dispute as to the custody of the child will be contested bitterly with negative repercussions for the child concerned. It is therefore highly questionable whether the emphasis on speed is appropriate in the first place, and doubly questionable whether the strengthening of this emphasis under Art 11(3) of Brussels IIA is a step in the right direction. At the heart of all of this lies a *forum conveniens* presumption.[255] Yet the grounds for this presumption are certainly contestable; and it is perhaps telling that no equivalent presumption exists in non-Convention cases.[256]

[252] Although Art 50 of this Convention declares that it shall not affect the application of the Hague Child Abduction Convention, it will, as Lowe and his co-authors point out, provide 'a wholly independent means of dealing with abductions': see Lowe *et al*, *op cit* n 34, p 558. See also G.F. De Hart, 'The Relationship Between the 1980 Child Abduction Convention and the 1996 Protection Convention' (2000) 33 *New York Journal of International Law and Politics* 83.

[253] One commentator has suggested, however, that the provisions in Brussels IIA which relate to the operation of the Hague Convention among EU States may have been unnecessary given that the Convention was operating fairly successfully in any event: see N. Lowe, 'Article 5(3) of the Draft EU Regulation on Parental Responsibility – Dealing with Child Abduction' [2002] *International Family Law* 36.

[254] Armstrong, *op cit* n 25.

[255] The official *Explanatory Report* states that 'the Convention rests implicitly upon the principle that any debate on the merits . . . should take place before the competent authorities in the State where the child had its habitual residence prior to its removal': see Pérez-Vera, *op cit* n 168, para 19.

[256] *Re F (A Minor) (Abduction: Jurisdiction)* [1991] Fam 25.

There are, however, those who would defend the Hague Convention approach and argue, further, that rapid, compulsory returns are generally entirely consistent with the welfare of children. Gloria F. De Hart, for instance, has expressed the view that, if the Hague Abduction Convention is read in conjunction with the Child Protection Convention of 1996, the child's best interests will necessarily be protected since:

> [t]he combined effect of the two Conventions is to make it completely clear that wrongful behaviour should not be rewarded, and that the best interests of the child are served by following the [Abduction] Convention's mandate and returning the child. No-return is the last resort, not the acceptable alternative.[257]

This argument is not devoid of merit,[258] but it perhaps overlooks the fact that the quality of justice in some Convention cases is highly suspect on natural justice grounds. As such, some amendment to the Convention to make clear the centrality of the *individual* child's welfare would certainly be welcome. The view that the underlying problems in abduction cases can best be resolved in the State of origin should (if anything) be the empirically grounded conclusion, rather than the presumptive starting point.

Most codified sources of law suffer from some element of terminological uncertainty, and the Hague Convention is no exception. What is particularly problematic with that instrument, however, is the fact that nearly all the pivotal Articles contain terms that are undefined and uncertain of meaning. Indeed, the official *Explanatory Report* expressly concedes the quite deliberate omission of any definition of legal concepts contained in the Convention.[259] In consequence, key concepts such as habitual residence, wrongful retention and custody rights, to name but a few, have been richly litigated and, at times, given rise to some curious interpretations. To take just one example, the notion that courts of law can possess custody rights (as opposed to parental responsibility) is a somewhat odd one. Yet as we saw earlier, the English courts have deemed themselves capable of possessing such rights for the purposes of the Convention where the removing parent is the sole holder of parental responsibility and proceedings in which residence or a prohibition against a threatened removal are pending at the time of the removal. Whether this can be described as a meaningful possession of custody rights is highly doubtful, however, for, as Nigel Lowe and his co-authors have pointed out,

[257] De Hart, *op cit* n 252, at 94. The argument is expressly predicated on the fact that the 1996 Convention makes it clear that primary jurisdiction is to rest with the authorities in the child's country of habitual residence.

[258] Perhaps for this reason, return orders under the Hague Convention have been recognised to be congruent with Art 8 of the European Convention on Human Rights which confers a right to respect for one's family life: see *Sylvester v Austria* [2003] 2 FLR 210 and *Maire v Portugal* Application No 48206/99 EctHR.

[259] Pérez-Vera, *op cit* n 168, at para 83.

'courts do seem unlikely holders of rights of custody and less likely litigants. Unlike other bodies or institutions, they can neither sue nor be sued'.[260]

A final point worth making in connection with the Hague Convention is that it seems somewhat half-hearted insofar as it makes provision with respect to rights of access. Not only does the Convention fall short of providing a means to enforce access rights, it also fails to confer upon those who engage the help of a Central authority the automatic right to legal aid when it comes to undertaking the appropriate legal proceedings to acquire or enforce a right of access. At least from a European perspective – given the recent production of the European Convention on Contact Concerning Children 2003 – the Hague Convention appears to be much less helpful than perhaps it could and should have been with respect to rights of access.

In relation to non-Convention cases involving children abducted *to* this country, there is considerable scope for the courts to develop a more pluralistic approach to the question of whether the children concerned should be returned to their State of origin in order that the underlying custody dispute between the parents can be resolved. It is one thing – and an admirable one at that – to recognise that foreign courts may apply 'alien' standards in child custody disputes, and that these standards may well be acceptable to the litigants involved. But is quite another – and arguably hypocritical (given that the readily applied Hague Convention contains no such contingency) – to require a foreign court to abide by the paramountcy principle in resolving child custody disputes.

[260] Lowe *et al*, *op cit* n 34, p 279.

Part IV

Other child-centred conventions

9

The United Nations Convention on the Rights of the Child

This country adopts a dualist (as opposed to monist) conception of international Conventions according to which Conventions and municipal law are seen as capable of dealing with the same subject matter, but not within the same sphere of operation. What this means in practical terms is that mere ratification of a Convention does not suffice to create individual rights that are enforceable before the national courts of this country. In order to do this, a Convention must be actively incorporated into domestic legislation, for example as a Schedule to an Act of Parliament. Where no such incorporation takes place – and this is the case in relation to the United Nations Convention on the Rights of the Child (UNCRC) – any conflict between municipal law and international law is to be resolved by the English courts in favour of the municipal law. In other words, if a child is denied a right guaranteed under UNCRC, he or she has no right to enforce that right before a domestic tribunal. This does not however mean that UNCRC is a useless instrument.

The very act of ratification does serve to make the Convention binding as an instrument of public international law, and in so far as it imposes a range of obligations on States Parties, these ought to be fulfilled and are technically subject to the Convention's inbuilt enforcement machinery (albeit that, in practice, this suffers from a number of imperfections). Secondly, since UNCRC is the most widely ratified international instrument specifically pertaining to family law it now 'exerts an increasingly powerful influence on the developing law and is often used as an international template against which to measure domestic standards'.[1] Finally, it is not just the English courts that are mindful of its provisions,[2] there is also a strong political

[1] J. Fortin, *Children's Rights and the Developing Law* (London: Butterworths, 2003) p 31.

[2] The courts have invoked UNCRC in a variety of circumstances: see, eg, *R v Westminster City Council, ex p G* [2003] ELR 73 (regarding educational needs); *R v*

incentive on the part of the government (and Parliament more generally[3]) to take heed of its many aspirations and standards. Against this background it can hardly be denied that the Convention is significant. And it certainly warrants detailed consideration in this chapter with particular emphasis on the way in which it compares with English domestic law.

The political incentive to comply with the Convention derives only partly from the innate willingness to do so manifest in the act of ratification.[4] For, in addition, it can also be attributed to the work of the Committee on the Rights of the Child established under Article 43. This is because the Committee is required periodically to examine 'the progress made by States Parties in achieving the realization of the obligations undertaken in the present Convention';[5] and each Contracting State is obliged, in turn, to 'submit to the Committee . . . reports on the measures they have adopted which give effect to the rights [in the Convention]'.[6] But even beyond this, there is still further political motivation to abide by the Convention that is fuelled by the desire of all States to avoid the shame or embarrassment associated with non-compliance.[7] And non-compliance can scarcely be justified when one

---

Secretary of State for the Home Department, ex p Ahmed [1998] Imm AR 375 (regarding immigration); *Re R (A Minor) (Contact: Biological Father)* [1993] 2 FLR 762 (regarding contact rights). Moreover, not only did a *Westlaw* search reveal no fewer than forty-nine domestic cases in which the Convention had been cited; there is also evidence that both the European Commission and Court of Human Rights have considered it to be influential: see, eg, *A v United Kingdom (Human Rights: Punishment of Child)* [1998] 2 FLR 959, at [22]; *V v United Kingdom* (1999) 30 EHRR 121, at [73].

[3] Government ministries are immediately responsible for securing so-called first-generation human rights (that is, negative liberties which take the form of protection from oppressive State action). By contrast, Parliament (as the legislature) is concerned with the furtherance of second-generation human rights (namely, positive rights designed to safeguard children's welfare and promote their development into happy, healthy adulthood). Parliament was undoubtedly influenced when drafting Part III of the Children Act 1989 by the then broadly known, but not yet finalised, contents of UNCRC, Arts 19, 20 and 23–27.

[4] Note, however, that the United Kingdom's ratification is subject to reservations concerning immigration and the care of young offenders.

[5] UNCRC, Art 43(1).

[6] UNCRC, Art 44(1). For the view that the contents of such reports may sometimes present a rosier picture of compliance than is truly warranted, see M. Freeman, 'The Future of Children's Rights' (2000) 14 *Children and Society* 277, 278–279 and C.M. Lyon, 'Children and the Law – Towards 2000 and Beyond: An Essay in Human Rights, Social Policy and the Law' in C. Bridge (ed), *Family Law Towards the Millennium: Essays for P.M. Bromley* (London: Butterworths, 1997) pp 59–60.

[7] See U. Kilkelly, 'The UN Committee on the Rights of the Child – an Evaluation in the Light of Recent UK Experience' [1996] *Child and Family Law Quarterly* 105; G. Douglas, 'The Significance of International Law for the Development of Family Law in England and Wales' in Bridge (ed), *op cit* n 6, esp pp 92–93; G. Van Bueren, 'Annual Review of International Family Law' in A. Bainham (ed), *The International Survey of Family Law 1997* (The Hague: Kluwer Academic Publishers, 1999) p 1.

considers that the objective, when drafting the Convention, was to produce an instrument of universal application containing standards to which all States can reasonably aspire: they lie somewhere between the minimum acceptable and the optimum achievable (in recognition that the highest standards could realistically be achieved only by the developed nations).[8]

Contents of the Convention[9]

There can be no question that UNCRC is a most ambitious Convention: it embraces the full gamut of first- and second-generation human rights from the civil and political,[10] to the (perhaps more predictable) social welfare[11] and education rights[12] of all children under the age of eighteen (save where majority is attained earlier under the relevant domestic law).[13] Somewhat irksome, however, is the fact these various rights are not set out according to any kind of logical structure within the Convention. There are in fact just two parts to it. Part I contains all the substantive rights and freedoms. These are inconsistent in terms of content[14] and somewhat irritatingly jumbled together in a manner that tends to obscure themes within the Convention.

If a golden thread linking all the various rights and freedoms is discernible, it is that the child's best interests 'shall be a primary consideration' in relation to 'all actions concerning children, whether undertaken by public or private social welfare institutions, courts of law, administrative authorities or legislative bodies'.[15] This was a deliberately lower standard than the familiar

[8] See S. Detrick (ed), *The United Nations Convention on the Rights of the Child: A Guide to the Travaux Préparatoires* (Dordrecht: Martinus Nijhoff, 1992).

[9] For a more detailed account than is provided here, see D. McGoldrick, 'The United Nations Convention on the Rights of the Child' (1991) 5 *International Journal of Law and the Family* 132.

[10] Eg, the rights to freedom of expression (Art 13), freedom of thought, conscience and religion (Art 14) and freedom of association (Art 15).

[11] Eg, the rights to the highest attainable standards of health and medical treatment (Art 24), State support in connection with child protection, coupled with periodic review of that support (Arts 25–27).

[12] UNCRC, Arts 28, 29.

[13] *Ibid*, Art 1.

[14] Some Articles – most notably Article 12, which ensures respect for a child's views – are vague and perhaps hopelessly aspirational (for critique, see Douglas *op cit* n 7, pp 104–105). Others, by contrast, are highly detailed, spelling out very specific requirements, such as Art 21(a) which imposes the need to ensure that 'adoption is permissible in view of the child's status concerning parents, relatives and legal guardians . . . [and that] the persons concerned have given their informed consent to the adoption on the basis of such counselling as may be necessary'.

[15] UNCRC, Art 3.

paramountcy principle that dominates English child law.[16] For as Dominic McGoldrick notes, '[t]he "best interests" of the child . . . is only *a* and not *the* primary consideration [since] [t]here were strong reservations . . . to a proposal to make the best interests of the child *the* primary consideration'.[17] And as Jane Fortin has explained further, this lower standard is 'comprehensible, given that the [best interests] formula was intended to govern all the articles contained in the Convention, including those applicable to young offenders' whose needs 'it would be difficult to claim . . . should always be *paramount* to those of society'.[18] On the other hand, if the Convention had been structured according to themes or types of rights, the best interests principle could have been elevated to the level of paramountcy where appropriate, and left as the mere first consideration elsewhere.[19]

Part II of the Convention is a good deal more straightforward. It contains just six Articles, and each of them relates in one way or another to the implementation of the Convention. They are relatively straightforward.

For present purposes – and cognisant of the fact that this book is essentially concerned with family law – it might be assumed that we should not be so concerned with the civil, political or even education rights that the Convention enshrines, but rather with its social welfare and child protection provisions. Yet this would be a misguided assumption. For it is a not uncommon mistake on the part of family law jurists to overlook (or at least downplay) the importance of children's civil and political rights. The civil and political rights of children – not least in the relation to the way they are dealt with as young offenders and autonomous human agents – are inextricably bound up with the central objective of the Convention, to ensure that children achieve through their childhood a smooth and rounded passage into adulthood. Eekelaar has called this the 'developmental interest' of children, and explained it thus:

> within certain overriding constraints created by the economic and social structure of society (whose extent must be open to debate), all children should have

[16] The child's best interests are made paramount under both the Children Act 1989, s 1 and the Adoption and Children Act 2002, s 1.

[17] McGoldrick, *op cit* n 9, at 136. For an illustration of the difficulties associated with this rather lower weighting given to the child's best interests than under domestic law, see *Hendriks v Netherlands* UN Doc A/43/40, 230.

[18] Fortin, *op cit* n 1, p 38.

[19] This is precisely the approach taken under the Children Act 1989. For the s 1 paramountcy principle does not apply outside the context of courtroom litigation, nor even within the context of courtroom litigation if the child's upbringing or the administration of his or her property is not *directly* in issue (eg, in applications by 'remote' adults for leave to apply for private law orders in respect of children: see, eg, *Re A (Minors) (Residence Orders: Leave to Apply)* [1992] 3 All ER 872). Nor does it apply in respect of the support services that must be arranged for children in need and their families under Part III of that Act: *Re M (A Minor) (Secure Accommodation Order)* [1995] Fam 108.

> an equal opportunity to maximize the resources available to them during their childhood . . . so as to minimize the degree to which they enter adult life affected by avoidable prejudices during childhood.[20]

In short, it is about steering the ship of childhood successfully into balanced adulthood. Thus, given the inclusion of both first- and second-generation rights within the Convention, the following discussion covers not just the social welfare rights afforded to children, but also their civil and political rights. More particularly, we consider their rights under three heads: rights to State support and protection,[21] membership rights[22] and autonomy rights. Admittedly, there is some overlap between these categories; but the achievement of a taxonomy that avoids all overlap appears to be unattainable.[23]

State support and state protection

Although Parts IV and V of the Children Act 1989 are centrally concerned with child protection, they are by no means as specific as UNCRC in spelling out the kinds of abuse, maltreatment, exploitation or risk from which children should be protected. For whereas Part IV of the 1989 Act is based upon on a general and rather loose concept of 'significant harm',[24] and whereas Part V is based on the equally opaque notion of children 'at risk',[25] the Convention spells out the right to be protected from economic exploitation,[26] sexual exploitation,[27] child trafficking and being sold[28] as well as from more familiar

[20] J. Eekelaar, 'The Emergence of Children's Rights' (1986) 6 *Oxford Journal of Legal Studies* 161, 170. This somewhat hedged 'development' right finds expression in UNCRC, Arts 4 and 6(2).

[21] That is, their right to the prevention of harm and the protection from neglect, and their right to State support in the form of the provision of assistance in cases of basic and developmental need.

[22] Here, we mean membership not just of their families, but also of the society in which they live.

[23] See, eg, the equally overlapping categories in T. Hammarberg, 'The UN Convention on the Rights of the Child – and How to Make it Work' (1990) 12 *Human Rights Quarterly* 97; Fortin, *op cit* n 1, pp 36–41; M. Freeman, *op cit* n 6, at 277–278.

[24] Children Act 1989, s 31. There is some definition of the term in s 31(9)–(10) of that Act, but the notion remains far from clear: see M.D.A. Freeman, 'Care After 1991' in D. Freestone (ed), *Children and the Law: Essays in Honour of Professor H.K. Bevan* (Hull: Hull University Press, 1990). Cf A. Bainham, 'Care After 1991 – A Reply' [1993] *Journal of Child Law* 99.

[25] For details, see S.M. Cretney, J.M. Masson & R. Bailey-Harris, *Principles of Family Law* (London: Sweet & Maxwell, 2002) ch 22.

[26] UNCRC, Art 32.

[27] *Ibid*, Art 34. In terms of reform, Lyon (*op cit* n 6) suggests the need (at p 65) for 'an overhaul of the relevant legislation . . . [coupled with] guidance such as that issued by the Department of Health in the form of *Working Together – A Guide to Inter-Agency Co-operation in Child Protection* . . . [so as] to take account of the difficulties posed by the problem of child prostitution'.

[28] *Ibid*, Art 35.

forms of physical and emotional abuse sometimes suffered domestically at the hands of parents or other primary carers.[29] Yet while it may be comforting to suppose that these inclusions in the Convention – especially in relation to the prevention of child prostitution and economic exploitation – were made primarily in order to set benchmarks for the many developing nations that have ratified UNCRC, it is somewhat embarrassing to note that they seem equally warranted in respect of this country. According to Christina Lyon, there is 'a high incidence of abuse amongst those who ran away and resorted to prostitution and an over-representation of young people from residential care amongst those working on the streets of London'.[30] Yet notwithstanding this,

> in the area of prostitution, attention has focused rather more on the criminal law provisions which treat both the abused and the abuser as criminal offenders. Many apparent difficulties stand in the way of social services and the police acting together to ensure that even very young children are not criminalised at a very early age by reason of their involvement in prostitution.[31]

Apart from the alarming prevalence of child prostitution in this country, matched by an equally alarming incidence of it among at least some of our continental neighbours,[32] it seems highly questionable whether the conviction of such children is in the spirit of UNCRC. Under Art 40(3), States Parties are required 'to promote the establishment of laws, procedures, authorities and institutions specifically applicable to children alleged as, accused of, or recognized as having infringed, the penal law'. More particularly, the Convention requires States to implement an equivalent of the *doli incapax* rule,[33] as well as a forum other than a court of law to deal with such children where appropriate.[34] Furthermore, the Convention also suggests a variety of sanctions in place of routine criminal convictions such as 'care, guidance and supervision orders; counselling; probation; foster care; education and vocational training programmes'.[35] These alternatives are recommended with a view to ensuring 'that children are dealt with in a manner appropriate to their well-being and proportionate to their circumstances'.[36] So it is little wonder that the Committee on the Rights of the child should, in response to the United Kingdom's second periodic report on the implementation of the

[29] *Ibid*, Art 19(1).
[30] Lyon, *op cit* n 6, p 61.
[31] *Loc cit.*
[32] See J. van der Bloeg, 'Homelessness – A Multi-Dimensional Problem' (1989) 11 *Children and News Services Review* 1.
[33] UNCRC, Art 40(3)(a).
[34] *Ibid*, Art 40(3)(b).
[35] *Ibid*, Art 40(4).
[36] *Ibid.*

Convention, recommend that 'the State Party . . . should review its legislation not to criminalise children who are sexually exploited'.[37]

As regards the rights of a child to State support and the provision of assistance in respect of his or her basic and developmental needs, the provisions of UNCRC are again more detailed than their counterpart provisions located in Part III of the Children Act 1989. Whereas section 17 of the 1989 Act merely imposes a general duty on local authorities 'to safeguard and promote the welfare of children in their area who are in need' (and although this duty undergoes some degree of elaboration in the ensuing provisions[38]), the Convention is altogether more particular and ambitious in spelling out a number of rights that fall into this broad category but which are difficult to identify within the Children Act 1989.[39] So, for example, the Convention elevates to the level of general principle the right of an ethnic minority child to be nurtured and to develop according to his or her cultural, religious or ethnic heritage.[40] The language is slightly vague, but the spirit of the provision is abundantly clear.[41] The Children Act, by contrast, recognises the significance of race and ethnicity in only two contexts. First, and somewhat speciously, it requires any local authority that is looking after a child to 'give due consideration to the child's religious persuasion, racial origin and cultural and linguistic background'.[42] Secondly, and even more remotely, where a local authority is making arrangements for the provision of day care, or arrangements designed to encourage people to act as foster parents, it has the duty 'to consider racial groups to which children in need belong'.[43] Martin Parry has argued that these occasional and obscure references in Part III of the Children Act to race, ethnicity, culture and so on are to some extent remedied by the role played by Department of Health practice

[37] Committee on the Rights of the Child, *Concluding Observations of the Committee on the Rights of the Child: United Kingdom of Great Britain and Northern Ireland* CRC/C/15 188 (Geneva: Centre for Human Rights, 2002) para 56(b). These observations are available at www.crights.org.uk/pdfs/UNCRC_conc_obs_2002.pdf.

[38] Children Act 1989, ss 18–30 (and Sched 2). For a detailed critique of Part III of the Act, see J. Murphy, 'Children in Need – the Limits of Local Authority' [2003] *Legal Studies* 102.

[39] These are in addition to the familiar kinds of provision dealing with basic supply, where needed, of food, clothing, shelter and health care: see UNCRC, Arts 23–27.

[40] UNCRC, Art 30.

[41] For some insight into the precise meaning of the provision see *Lovelace v Canada* UN Doc A/36/40 166 in which the import of the virtually identical words of the International Covenant on Civil and Political Rights 1966, Art 27 were considered. See also, D. McGoldrick, 'Canadian Indians, Cultural Rights and the Human Rights Committee' (1991) 40 *International and Comparative Law Quarterly* 658 and A. Bayefsky, 'The Human Rights Committee and the Case of Sandra Lovelace' (1982) 20 *Canadian Yearbook of International Law* 244.

[42] Children Act 1989, s 22(5)(c).

[43] *Ibid*, Sched 2, para 11.

guidance.[44] This may be true, but it is important to appreciate that the guidance, too, has its limitations. It applies only to the conduct of local authorities, and not to the disposal of cases by the courts. The guidance therefore has no bearing on private law proceedings in which the nearest the 1989 Act comes to recognising the significance of ethnicity, etc is the general welfare checklist in section 1 of the Act. And the checklist itself does no more than make a broad reference to the relevance of a child's 'background' in making any given decision.[45]

In similar highly aspirational vein is the Convention right 'to rest and leisure, to engage in play and recreational activities appropriate to the age of the child and to participate freely in cultural life and the arts'.[46] Again it is unclear just what this right entails – or even whether it is appropriate to describe it as a 'right'[47] rather than an 'interest'. Nonetheless, it is certainly more positive in its thrust than the nearest comparator in the Children Act 1989: the less-than-concrete duty on the part of local authorities to provide, where resources permit, recreational activities to children in need.[48]

Membership rights

The membership rights contained in the Convention recognise the child's *prima facie* right to be brought up as a member of a family,[49] but also as part of the broader community.[50] The Children Act 1989 tends to emphasise

[44] M.L. Parry, 'Local Authority Support for Ethnic Minority Children' in J. Murphy (ed), *Ethnic Minorities, their Families and the Law* (Oxford: Hart Publishing, 2000) p 30.

[45] Children Act 1989, s 1(1)(g).

[46] UNCRC, Art 31.

[47] According to Joseph Raz, 'law creates a right if it is based on and expresses the view that someone has an interest which is sufficient ground for holding another to be subject to a duty': see J. Raz, 'Legal Rights' (1984) 4 *Oxford Journal of Legal Studies* 1, 13. Whether it could be said, as would be necessary according to this plausible formulation, that society at large recognises the leisure interest of children to this extent is questionable. On the other hand, play and aesthetic experience would be regarded as 'basic forms of human flourishing' for the purposes of founding natural rights according to John Finnis' *natural rights* theory: see J. Finnis, *Natural Law and Natural Rights* (Oxford: Oxford University Press, 1980) pp 87–88.

[48] Children Act 1989, Sched 2, para 8.

[49] The Preamble to UNCRC recognises that 'the child, for the full and harmonious development of his or her personality, should grow up in a family environment, in an atmosphere of happiness, love and understanding'. Art 7(1) provides further for the child's 'right to know and be cared for by his or her parents' while Art 8(1) refers to the right of the child to the preservation of 'family relations as recognized by law'. See also Arts 9–10 (enshrining, respectively, the right of children not to be separated from their parents against their will and the duty on States to facilitate and promote family re-unification across national borders).

[50] The Preamble to UNCRC again recognises that 'the child should be fully prepared to live an individual life in society'.

only the former. Thus, in the context the support obligations contained in Part III of the Act, there is acknowledgement that a child should, where possible, be accommodated with relatives or friends,[51] as near to his or her home as practicable,[52] and together with siblings if more than one child is in need of accommodation.[53] The Convention goes much further, however, since it makes plain, for example, the right of a disabled child to 'special care',[54] which includes 'effective access to . . . education, training, health care services, rehabilitation services, preparation for employment and recreation opportunities *in a manner conducive to the child's achieving the fullest possible social integration and individual development*'.[55] This approach is clearly geared towards ensuring that all children have the capacity to maximise their potential and, so far as they can do so, integrate themselves into society.[56] This is a principle that receives general expression in Article 2 of the Convention where it is provided that all the rights in the Convention should be extended to every child 'without discrimination of any kind, irrespective of . . . race, colour, sex, language, religion, political or other opinion, national, ethnic or social origin, property, disability, birth or other status'.[57] Although this Article does not enshrine any free-standing right on behalf of the child, it may nonetheless be infringed when read in conjunction with any of the more concrete rights contained in the Convention.[58]

Autonomy rights

By virtue of Article 12(1) of the Convention, the child capable of forming his or her own views is afforded the 'the right to express those views freely in all matters'[59] with due weight being given to those views 'in accordance with the age and maturity of the child'. This right largely mirrors the so-called '*Gillick*-competence' principle that operates domestically to empower

[51] Children Act 1989, s 23(6)(b).

[52] *Ibid*, s 23(7)(a).

[53] *Ibid*, s 23(7)(b).

[54] UNCRC, Art 23(2).

[55] *Ibid*, Art 23(3) (emphasis added).

[56] See also UNCRC, Art 7(1) embracing the still wider 'right to acquire a nationality'. Cf the traditional stance in international law whereby children have historically been treated 'in a similar vein to aliens': G. Van Bueren, *The International Law on the Rights of the Child* (Dordrecht: Martinus Nijhoff, 1995) p 141.

[57] *Ibid*, Art 2(1). For criticism of the non-inclusive nature of this provision, see Freeman, *op cit* n 6, at 282.

[58] Partly for this reason, it seems questionable whether one critic, in his analysis of Art 23, is right to claim that '[b]y using the language of anti-discrimination rather than the principle of inclusion, it legitimates segregation': see Freeman, *op cit* n 6, at 282–283.

[59] UNCRC, Art 12(2) makes clear that this extends to 'any judicial and administrative proceedings affecting the child'.

adolescents and mature children to make medical and other important decisions on their own behalf[60] (at least where their lives are not in jeopardy[61]). But, much as the content of Article 12 already exists in English law, it has been argued that Article 12 has served the additional function of raising 'awareness among policy-makers of the importance, or at least the relevance of, children's wishes and feelings'.[62]

Beyond Article 12, the Convention also enshrines a child's right to freedom of expression,[63] freedom of thought, conscience and religion,[64] as well as the right to freedom of association (which can readily be linked to the formation and dissemination of one's moral and religious views)[65] and the right to privacy.[66] In these respects, the Convention goes much further – at least in terms of explicit language – than English law.

Enforcement

Even before it was substantially incorporated into English domestic law, the European Convention on Human Rights was enforceable by way of complaints against States[67] lodged with both the European Commission on Human Rights and the European Court of Human Rights, which latter

[60] See *Gillick v West Norfolk and Wisbech Area Health Authority* [1986] AC 112 (discussed in J. Eekelaar, 'The Eclipse of Parental Rights' (1986) 102 *Law Quarterly Review* 4). See also the reflection of Art 12(1) in the Children Act 1989, s 1(3)(a) which requires courts bound by the welfare principle to have regard to the 'ascertainable wishes and feelings of the child concerned (considered in the light of his age and understanding)'. For detailed comparison of the similarities between UNCRC and domestic law, see B. Walsh, 'The United Nations Convention on the Rights of the Child: A British View' (1991) 5 *International Journal of Law and the Family* 170, 184–188.

[61] See, eg, *Re W (A Minor) (Medical Treatment: Court's Jurisdiction)* [1992] 4 All ER 627 (discussed in J. Murphy, 'W(h)ither Adolescent Autonomy?' [1992] *Journal of Social Welfare and Family Law* 529).

[62] Douglas, *op cit* n 7, p 105.

[63] UNCRC, Art 13.

[64] *Ibid*, Art 14. This right ought to be read in conjunction with the (again aspirational) Art 17 right to 'access to information and material from . . . national and international sources', since information is often critical to the production and refinement of thought.

[65] *Ibid*, Art 15.

[66] *Ibid*, Art 16.

[67] Now that the European Convention on Human Rights forms part of the domestic law of England and Wales, it arguably gives rise to actions against fellow citizens and not just Contracting States: see M. Hunt, 'The "Horizontal Effect" of the Human Rights Act 1998' [1998] *Public Law* 423 and N. Bamforth, 'The Application of the Human Rights Act 1998 to Public Authorities and Private Bodies' [1999] *Cambridge Law Journal* 159.

passed final judgment on those complaints.[68] Though equally a human rights instrument, UNCRC has no comparable enforcement mechanism. Instead, compliance is secured either by diplomatic good will or by political pressure. Arguably, this is not entirely a bad thing. As we have noted at several junctures, certain Articles in the Convention are couched in the language of optimistic aspiration rather than that of concrete rights. As such, even if there were a fixed forum for holding States Parties to account, it would be enormously difficult for litigants to succeed in their actions. How, for example, would one ever be able to demonstrate a failure to ensure adequate rest, leisure and play *per* Article 31?[69]

Recognising the opacity of many of the Convention's rights is essential. For it is important to grasp that just because certain rights are incorporated into the text of a Convention does not mean that such incorporation will guarantee a range of fixed, beneficial consequences for children. The more opaque the language in which a right is couched, the greater the scope for Contracting Parties to decide for themselves what it entails and how far they will go in securing it. Hunt has neatly captured this limitation of written-down rights in his observation that:

> Rights . . . have the capacity to be elements of emancipation, but they are neither a perfect nor an exclusive vehicle for . . . emancipation. [Rather, they] can only be operative as constituents of a strategy for social transformation as they become part of an emergent 'common sense'.[70]

In other words, rights are can be useful things to have[71] but only so as long as those who owe the corresponding obligations take those obligations seriously. Accordingly, the Convention's success or failure arguably turns as much upon this issue as it does upon the oft-criticised absence of an international tribunal for children's rights. Indeed, it may not even be by conscious

[68] For the impact of the Convention on domestic child law, see J. Fortin, 'Rights Brought Home for Children' (1999) 62 *Modern Law Review* 350; *id*, 'Children's Rights and the Impact of Two International Conventions: The UNCRC and the ECHR' in The Rt Hon LJ Thorpe & C. Cowton (eds), *Delight and Dole: The Children Act 10 Years on* (Bristol: Jordan Publishing, 2002); H. Swindells, '"Crossing the Rubicon" – Family Law Post the Human Rights Act 1998' in S. Cretney (ed), *Family Law: Essays for the New Millennium* (Bristol: Jordan Publishing, 2000).

[69] For criticism of the Convention on the basis of its vagueness, see Freeman, *op cit* n 6. See also the altogether more pessimistic critique in M. King, 'Children's Rights as Communication: Reflections on Autopoietic Theory and the United Nations Convention' (1994) 57 *Modern Law Review* 385.

[70] A. Hunt, 'Rights and Social Movements: Counter-Hegemonic Strategies' (1990) 17 *Journal of Law and Society* 309.

[71] For the highly contestable contention that 'listing 40 substantive "legal rights" . . . *certainly* contributes to [a] process of rights devaluation', see Fortin, *op cit* n 1, p 43 (emphasis added). In similar vein, see M. Minow, 'Interpreting Rights: An Essay for Robert Cover' (1987) 96 *Yale Law Journal* 1860.

choice that certain States have a tendency to fall short of the ideal in the minds of the draftsmen. It could simply be attributable to a genuine, yet culturally imbued interpretation.

On the other hand, a sense of perspective is important at this juncture. For it would be fanciful to suppose that, had the language of many of the Convention rights been tightened up, and had there been a specialist court devoted to their enforcement, children across the world would somehow cease to be uneducated, homeless, conscripted into fighting civil wars or made the objects of sex tourism.[72] Given, then, that the success of the Convention depends in large measure on both political good will and political pressure, it is worth reflecting at some length on each of these factors, and in particular on what might generate that good will or pressure.

Political good will

Any lengthy consideration of UNCRC would be incomplete without at least some mention of its genesis. Widespread recognition of certain fundamental human rights first appeared in the wake of the Second World War.[73] In 1948, mindful of the wartime atrocities perpetrated by the Nazis, the United Nations General Assembly adopted the Universal Declaration of Human Rights, which amounted to little more than a statement of recognition of certain inalienable rights of all human beings. The Declaration was perhaps more notable for its rhetoric than for any substantive rights, and as the President of the General assembly once admitted, the Declaration fell short of being a Treaty 'by which States would be bound to carry out and give effect to fundamental human rights, nor would it provide for enforcement; yet it was a step forward'.[74] So a seed had been sown, and other international human rights instruments steadily followed.[75] But it was not until the 1970s with a heightened awareness of the worldwide abuse of children and the violation of their rights that the political will to establish a document guaranteeing their rights really gathered impetus. The year 1979 was to be declared the International Year of the Child, and aware of this forthcoming declaration, the Polish government tabled before the United Nations Commission on Human Rights a document that comprised, loosely speaking, a very early draft of what was to become UNCRC.

[72] There is troubling evidence that the quality of children's lives has in fact deteriorated worldwide: see G.B. Sgritta, 'Childhood on the Economic and Political Agenda' (1997) 4 *Childhood* 375.

[73] Natural law theorists had long since posited rights of man, but their theories were not part of every-day speech.

[74] President of the General Assembly of the United Nations speaking in 1948 (cited in Douglas *op cit* n 7, p 97).

[75] For details, see Fortin, *op cit* n 1, pp 32–33.

What was so singular about the Convention, once it was eventually finalised in 1989, was its popularity. As Michael Freeman records, there were over sixty signatories immediately; and by 2000 there were only two countries – Somalia and the United States – that had not ratified the Convention.[76] Given this near-universal support for the Convention, it seems fair to conclude that there is (or should be) a very significant political desire to make it work, notwithstanding its inherent deficiencies. Certainly, one might reasonably read such commitment into the fact that a country produces a clear, well-structured and helpful report for the purposes of monitoring by the Committee on the Rights of the Child. (Whether the opposite is also true is debatable, for an ambiguous report may simply be symptomatic of a misunderstanding of the relevant obligations.[77])

Political pressure

It would doubtless be naïve to assume that every country that has ratified UNCRC has done so out of a sense of wholehearted commitment and goodwill. There are surely some States that have done so for diplomatic reasons: namely, to avoid isolation and to avoid being viewed as uncommitted to the principles and rights UNCRC embodies. In short, negative political pressure from without plays its part in securing compliance with the Convention. Bernadette Walsh has even claimed that 'the Convention is largely designed to pressurize governments into observing certain common standards';[78] and to assist in the application of such pressure, the Committee on the Rights of the Child was created under Article 43.

The starting point in understanding the capacity of the Committee to exert political pressure is the obligation for all States Parties to submit reports every five years to the Committee on the 'measures they have adopted which give effect to the rights recognised . . . and on the progress made on the enjoyment of those rights'.[79] The reports must also highlight any particular factors that make the fulfilment of obligations under the Convention difficult together with 'sufficient information to provide the Committee with a comprehensive understanding of the implementation of the Convention'.[80] The Committee now comprises eighteen experts[81] of high moral standing

[76] Freeman, *op cit* n 6, at 278.

[77] The United Kingdom has twice been criticised for the lack of transparency in its periodic reports; but it is probably stretching the truth to say that this is because of a genuine attempt to conceal its failings: see, eg, Committee on the Rights of the Child, *op cit* n 37.

[78] B. Walsh, *op cit* n 60, at 171.

[79] UNCRC, Art 44(1)(b).

[80] *Ibid*, Art 44(2). Where relevant, the Committee is entitled to request further particulars in relation to implementation.

[81] Formerly, there were just ten.

who are elected by secret ballot from among the nationals of States Parties, and who have recognised competence in the field covered by the Convention.[82] Although the Committee has no power to issue formal sanctions in cases of non-compliance, it can issue recommendations to individual States (and the General Assembly) on the basis of concerns it may have in the light of their reports,[83] as well as make the report widely available to the public so that the democratic process may play its part.[84] This potential shaming of individual States is not, however, designed to be part of a confrontational or antagonistic system of accountability. Rather, it must be seen as a system of reporting on the one hand, and of feeding back suggestions on the other. It is, as Kilkelly has explained, designed to function as a system of:

> dialogue with States Parties [which] aims to be mediatory rather than adversarial in nature and the Committee sees constructive dialogue as the vehicle through which better understanding and implementation of the Convention can be achieved . . . [For] the promotion of public debate is more fruitful than condemning the culpable behaviour of individual States.[85]

Notwithstanding this ideal, and without denying the influence that the Committee potentially wields, it is arguable that a panel of just eighteen experts has just too great a task on its hands if it is properly to scrutinise all States Parties' reports and provide suitable feedback on them. Certainly, punctual submission will not necessarily result in a rapid response. This means that if a State is guilty of non-compliance or inadequate implementation, it may well be that the children suffering in consequence may have to wait some years before the State in question is prompted to address these shortcomings.[86] And even then, there is no guarantee that the matters identified will be adequately addressed. As regards the United Kingdom's second report, submitted in 1999, the Committee noted with regret that:

> notwithstanding the legal obligation inherent to [*sic*] the ratification of the Convention, many of the concerns and recommendations it made upon consideration of the State Party's initial report have been insufficiently addressed . . . Those concerns and recommendations are reiterated in the present document.[87]

Moreover, the Committee was mindful of the way in which the European Convention on Human Rights had been incorporated into domestic law. It was particularly impressed by the fact that the Human Rights Act 1998 had

[82] UNCRC, Art 43(2), (3).

[83] *Ibid*, Art 45(d).

[84] *Ibid*, Art 44(6). The Committee also produces a set of *Concluding Observations* which are read by human rights activists, policy-makers and governments alike: see, eg, Committee on the Rights of the Child, *op cit* n 37.

[85] Kilkelly, *op cit* n 7, at 107–108.

[86] The United Kingdom's second report submitted in 1999 was not fully considered until 2002: see Committee on the Rights of the Child, *op cit* n 37.

[87] *Loc cit*, para 4.

sought to ensure the compatibility of domestic legislation with the European Convention. In the light of this experience, the Committee invited the United Kingdom to incorporate into domestic law the rights, principles and provisions of the United Nations Convention so as to ensure the compliance of all domestic legislation with the Convention.[88] This, of course, has not yet happened.

In the light of the above observations, it is clear that the reporting system falls a long way short of effective accountability. The Convention has perhaps aptly been described, therefore, as a mere 'beginning'.[89] Furthermore, there seems no doubt that '[i]f international children's rights are to have a [rosier] future, the Convention must be more intensively policed'.[90] And it may well be that it will ultimately require 'enforcement procedures to be grafted onto it'.[91] At the very least, without an extra push in the direction of effective accountability, we may be forced to sympathise with Michael King's observation that 'at the level of international law the mechanisms do not exist to force governments to comply with [those] demands which may involve the massive redeployment of resources and major changes in policy'.[92] And this is so whether or not we share his somewhat pessimistic (perhaps, even, cynical) view that '[r]econstructing children's rights as law has the additional advantage for governments . . . of [merely] giving the impression that something is being done for children'.[93]

One step short of a specialist tribunal akin to the European Court of Human Rights, and more in the nature of a compromise solution, might be an additional Protocol providing for inter-State complaints whereby one State may be permitted to complain to the United Nations about shortcomings in the implementation of the Convention on the part of another State. This is not an unknown model of accountability in international law. Indeed, a facility for inter-State complaints already exists under the International Covenant on Civil and Political Rights and the Optional Protocol to that Covenant.[94] And while such a step would in no way amount to an abrogation of Article 2(7) of the Charter of the United Nations 1945,[95] it would be

[88] *Loc cit*, para 9.
[89] Freeman, *op cit* n 6, at 290.
[90] *Loc cit.*
[91] Fortin, 'Children's Rights and the Impact of Two International Conventions: the UNCRC and the ECHR', *op cit* n 68, p 19; *id*, *op cit* n 1, pp 48–49.
[92] King, *op cit* n 69, at 401.
[93] *Loc cit.*
[94] For detailed discussion, see D. McGoldrick, *The Human Rights Committee: Its Role in the Development of the International Covenant on Civil and Political Rights* (Oxford: Oxford University Press, 1991) ch 3.
[95] This provides that '[n]othing . . . shall authorise the United Nations to intervene in matters which are essentially within the domestic jurisdiction of any State'. But whether this principle is a true reflection of UN policy is doubtful: see Van Bueren, *op cit* n 7, p 1.

perfectly consistent with the intention that UNCRC should work primarily through a system of diplomatic and peer pressure.

Conclusions and critique

The United Nations Convention on the Rights of the Child is a far from perfect document.[96] To begin with, there is a problem within its provisions of a certain amount of internal inconsistency and contradiction. To some extent, this is explicable by reference to the fact that the Convention is loosely, non-thematically structured. So, for example, if we take the child's right to a secure upbringing, we find at least three Articles that must be read alongside this right. Article 3(2) recognises that in ensuring provision necessary for a child's protection, it is nonetheless crucial to take into account 'the rights and duties of [the child's] parents, legal guardians or other *individuals* legally responsible for him or her'.[97] But then Article 5 goes on to provide that States Parties shall respect not just the rights and responsibilities of parents, but *alternatively* those of the 'community . . . or other persons legally responsible for the child'. This immediately begs a question about the degree of commitment within the Convention to the primacy of the parental role.[98] Yet this question is not remotely answered until one reaches Article 18 where there is again implicit support for the primacy of parental care-giving.[99] But this support is itself diluted in Art 27(2) which refers to the primary responsibility of '[t]he parents *or others* responsible for the child'.[100] The fairest conclusion on all of this would therefore seem to be that the Convention is fundamentally ambivalent (even though, on balance, a discernible preference perhaps exists in favour of the child's parents).[101]

[96] For thorough criticism, see Freeman, *op cit* n 6 and R.L. Barsh, 'The Convention on the Rights of the Child: A Re-Assessment of the Final Text' (1989–1990) 7 *New York Law School Journal of Human Rights* 142.

[97] Emphasis added.

[98] Under English law this is not in doubt. Under s 3 of the Children Act 1989, parental responsibility is defined narrowly as 'all the rights, duties, powers, responsibilities, and authority' held by a child's parent. Furthermore, this responsibility is made immutable under s 2(6), (9) of the Act: see J. Eekelaar, 'Parental Responsibility: State of Nature or Nature of the State?' [1991] *Journal of Social Welfare and Family Law* 37.

[99] UNCRC Art 18 requires States to use their best efforts to 'ensure recognition of the principle that both parents have common responsibilities for the upbringing and development of the child'.

[100] Emphasis added.

[101] Russel Barsh reaches a similar conclusion on the basis of his consideration of all the relevant Articles referring to the respective rights of parents, the child, relatives, guardians and the community: see R.L. Barsh, *op cit* n 96, at 144–146. His view on this matter is further explored in R.L. Barsh, 'The Draft Convention on the Rights

Further inconsistencies are also discernible within the Convention. For example, the emphasis on the centrality of care-giving and nurturing responsibilities – whether performed by parents, relatives, a community to which the child belongs or even the State – are not immediately reconcilable with the principle of child autonomy enshrined in Article 12.[102] Jane Fortin has explained why this particular inconsistency appears in the Convention,[103] but to understand its genesis is not necessarily to justify its appearance in the final text. Even *within* Article 5 – requiring respect for the rights of parents to provide guidance to the child – there are problems. For as Dominic McGoldrick has commented:

> [a]lthough the purpose of such a provision is obvious, its implementation is fraught with difficulty because those charged with providing 'appropriate direction and guidance' to the child on the exercise of its rights may well have an interest, personal or institutional, in ensuring that the child does not exercise its rights.[104]

On reflection, what the above tensions reveal is a profound dichotomy within UNCRC between the treatment of civil and political rights on the one hand, and social welfare and cultural rights on the other. For it is demonstrably the case that civil and political rights are given a higher priority within the Convention than social or cultural rights. As Jane Fortin observes, unlike the Article 3(2) obligation to protect a child, which, in its own terms, can be fulfilled only subject to 'taking into account the rights and duties of his or her parents':

> neither Article 12, which requires States to ensure that children's opinions are sought, nor Article 13 regarding a child's right to freedom of expression, contains any qualifying phrase requiring States to take account of parental wishes. Indeed, Article 12(1) makes it very clear that *every* child who is capable

---

of the Child: A Case of Eurocentrism in Standard-Setting' (1989) 58 *Nordic Journal of International Law* 24. See also Walsh, *op cit* n 60, at 173–174. It is contestable, however, whether the Convention is dominated by Eurocentricism to the extent that is sometimes alleged: Art 5, after all, does make provision (with emphasis added) for respect to be afforded to 'the members of the extended family or community *as provided for by local custom*'. This is clearly not Eurocentric. For a full account of the influence of non-western opinion on the text of UNCRC, see S. Harris-Short, 'Listening to "The Other"? The Convention on the Rights of the Child' (2001) 2 *Melbourne Journal of International Law* 305, 321–332.

[102] Some measure of reconciliation is, however, possible: see Eekelaar, *op cit* n 20, at 171; *id*, 'The Interests of the Child and the Child's Wishes: The Role of Dynamic Self-Determinism' in P. Alston (ed), *The Best Interests of the Child* (Oxford: Clarendon Press, 1994) pp 53–57; M. Freeman, 'The Rights and Wrongs of Children' (London: Frances Pinter, 1983) p 97.

[103] Fortin, *op cit* n 1, p 41.

[104] McGoldrick, *op cit* n 9, at 138–139.

> of forming his or her own views should have the right to express them freely over all matters affecting him or her.[105]

Moreover, Bernadette Walsh has noted the fact that 'the obligation [on States] in respect of civil and political rights is an immediate one', that is, one that takes effect without the need for domestic legislation to give effect to the relevant Convention right. By contrast, she continues, '[w]ith respect to economic, social and cultural rights, Article 4 clearly suggests that States are under an obligation to take measures to secure the rights [only] *where the necessary resources are available*'.[106] The italicised words highlight still further the fact that there is no guarantee of the Convention's social and cultural rights. This tends, therefore, to endorse and amplify the points made by Fortin, albeit at a more general level.

Fortunately, where tensions such as the one just considered pose practical difficulties, there is at least some scope for the Committee on the Rights of the Child to provide guidance to States on how best to resolve them.[107] And further refinement of the Convention, by way of additional Protocols, is always a possibility (as will be seen below). There is certainly no case for abandoning either the political or the social welfare rights on the basis of this internal antagonism, even if it is true, as Purdy has urged, that political rights count for little to nothing in the case of the World's most wretched and deprived children.[108]

Leaving to one side the inconsistencies within UNCRC, there remains the question of enforcement. For all its influence and popularity with lobbyists and policy-makers, and for all that the Convention is beginning to be cited in more and more domestic child-centred litigation, there remains the problem that '[t]he overall impression created by the United Kingdom's first and second reports to the Committee on Human Rights was that the government was relatively untroubled by fear of its criticism'.[109] In other words, there is still a glaring need for a more effective method of enforcement and accountability. We canvassed earlier the possibility that, by Optional Protocol, a facility for inter-state complaint (akin to the one that operates with

[105] Fortin, *op cit* n 1, p 42. She also identifies (at pp 42–43) a certain amount of inconsistency between the Art 14 right to freedom of thought, religion and conscience and the Art 29 right to a broad-based education.

[106] Walsh, *op cit* n 60, at 189 (emphasis added).

[107] For examples, see K. Marshall, *Children's Rights in the Balance: The Participation–Protection Debate* (London: Stationery Office Ltd, 1997) p 17 *et seq.*

[108] Rejecting the worth of political rights on the part of children, she argues that '[e]ven women have been relatively unsuccessful at improving their position by these means, and there are fewer morally relevant differences between women and men than between children and adults': L.M. Purdy, 'Why Children Shouldn't Have Equal Rights' (1994) 2 *International Journal of Children's Rights* 223, 224, n 9. But is not the grant of rights at the very least of symbolic (and therefore some) value?

[109] Fortin, *op cit* n 1, p 48.

respect to other human rights instruments) may be created to potential good effect. It has also been suggested that an Optional Protocol might be introduced to allow individual petitions to be lodged with the Committee which would then have the power to conduct an investigation of the complaint.[110] It remains to be seen whether either of these initiatives will be taken.

Finally, it is arguable that the Convention needs to be strengthened in terms of the rights it confers upon certain minority groups. In an insightful study, Michael Freeman has identified weaknesses in the Convention in respect of disabled children, gay children, girls, homeless 'street' children and child refugees. As regards disabled children, his criticism is founded on the fact that so far as it currently provides for such children, the Convention does so on the basis of 'non-discrimination, rather than [positive] inclusion'.[111] For example, '[t]here is no requirement of inclusive educational or social policies'.[112] In relation to gay children, he is perhaps on less solid ground. He identifies, correctly, that the general non-discrimination provision in the Convention (Article 2) does not make explicit reference of the wrongfulness of discrimination based on sexual orientation – it mentions only sex discrimination. Yet this may be an omission of no consequence since it has been ably demonstrated by Robert Wintemute that sexual orientation discrimination is perfectly capable of being recast as a form of sex discrimination.[113] And if this analysis is correct, as it seems to be, sexual orientation discrimination is in fact already covered. But even if it is not, it might simply be seen as too ambitious or contentious to expect near-worldwide consensus on the inclusion of a special provision relating to the sexual orientation of children. To do so might be seen in many quarters as condoning or encouraging sexual activity on the part of children. And since the Convention is designed to protect children, such condonation may be perceived as antithetical to its central aims given that sexual activity among children is generally discouraged.[114]

As regards girls (or 'girl children', as Freeman refers to them), the concern is that, worldwide, a huge number of girls die needlessly from pregnancy and suffer genital mutilation.[115] To these concerns Freeman could well have added the alarming rate of HIV/AIDS infection among many of the African nations. There can be no doubt, therefore, that provisions designed to improve the availability of contraception and sex education would make

[110] See Van Bueren, *op cit* n 56, pp 410–411.

[111] Freeman, *op cit* n 6, at 282.

[112] *Loc cit*, at 283.

[113] R. Wintemute, 'Recognizing New Kinds of Direct Sex Discrimination: Transsexualism, Sexual Orientation and Dress Codes' (1997) 60 *Modern Law Review* 334, 344–353.

[114] See Purdy, *op cit* n 108, at 226.

[115] Freeman, *op cit* n 6, at 284.

valuable additions to the Convention.[116] Similarly, there is much to commend Freeman's suggestion that there ought to be greater focus in the Convention on the plight of street children and child refugees.[117] The sheer numbers of such children in modern times – especially of the former group in Central and South America – is reason enough to take this approach.

Taken together, the various criticisms and inherent weaknesses in UNCRC make it clear that the suggested additional Protocols may well be needed. But there is not just scope for addition to the extant Convention. There is ample room, also, for careful restructuring and redrafting so that key themes can be highlighted, so that some of the tensions that exist between certain of the social and cultural rights, and some of the civil and political rights can be eliminated. There is also scope for increasing the input of non-Western States into the text of the Convention which has been convincingly shown – in both substance and in terms of the way its implementation is monitored – to be in need of a greater degree of cultural pluralism.[118]

[116] But see the argument that Art 36 – providing general protection against 'all . . . forms of exploitation' – is capable of being read so as to embrace the particular needs of street children: see Van Bueren, *op cit* n 56, p 284.

[117] Freeman, *op cit* n 6, at 285.

[118] Harris-Short, *op cit* n 101.

10

Other international conventions concerning children

In this chapter we consider two Conventions that have not yet received the force of law in this country but which look likely to do so in the future. The first of these is what can conveniently be called the Hague Child Protection Convention 1996,[1] and the second is the European Convention on Contact Concerning Children 2003. We examine each of them in turn.

Hague Child Protection Convention 1996

Introduction

In its abbreviated form, the title of this Convention fails to convey fully the variety of matters with which it is actually concerned. Furthermore, even the two principal Articles in the Convention that deal with its scope are somewhat vague on this. While one merely illustrates (non-exhaustively) the kinds of matters dealt with,[2] the other simply states what is not covered.[3] This makes it impossible to provide a definitive statement as to the remit of the Convention. Nonetheless, it is possible to say with certainty that it is concerned with private international law issues connected with parental responsibility and measures for the protection of children; and, more particularly, that judgments granted by courts possessing jurisdiction under the Convention ought normally to receive automatic recognition and enforcement among all other Contracting States.

[1] The rather unwieldy, full title is the Convention on Jurisdiction, Applicable Law, Recognition, Enforcement and Cooperation in Respect of Parental Responsibility and Measures for the Protection of Children (hereafter, 'Child Protection Convention'). At the time of writing, nine States had either ratified or acceded to this Convention: Australia, the Czech Republic, Ecuador, Estonia, Latvia, Lithuania, Monaco, Morocco and the Slovak Republic.

[2] The Child Protection Convention, Art 3.

[3] *Ibid*, Art 4.

The idea of having a child protection Convention is not a novel one. Indeed, the 1996 Convention was designed to improve upon, and replace, the Hague Convention Concerning the Powers of Authorities and the Law Applicable in Respect of the Protection of Infants 1961.[4] This latter instrument never proved popular,[5] however, especially because of its jurisdiction provisions that were intrinsically flawed so as to give rise to almost inevitable conflicts of jurisdiction.[6] As we shall see, the 1996 Convention seeks to address this problem by founding jurisdiction overwhelmingly upon the child's habitual residence. And while it is true that the Convention contains a number of subsidiary grounds upon which jurisdiction may be taken, these tend to be of such limited scope and duration as not to undermine significantly the main rule. As such, the Convention reflects the reality of modern-day living whereby many families may contain members who are nationals or domiciliaries of one country, habitually resident in another and perhaps even temporarily located in still another. In seeking to put in place a set of uniform private international law rules, the Convention aims to eliminate both conflicts of jurisdiction and conflicts of judgments.

On the whole, and as we shall see, the Convention seems well intentioned, refreshingly pluralistic and wisely minimalist in terms of the introduction of substantive rules of law.[7] It is therefore likely to attract a sizeable number of Contracting Parties even if, as we shall also see, it is a far from being a problem-free instrument.

Purposes and scope

The 1996 Convention contains a fairly long Preamble setting out its various aims and objectives. In essence, and in common with Article 1 of the Convention, it enumerates the kinds of aims that are common within this kind of international instrument. It seeks to establish a common set of rules for the attribution of jurisdiction and for the identification of the applicable law. It also aims to ensure a common system of recognition and enforcement of judgments. Finally, it seeks to establish co-operation between the relevant authorities of the Contracting States in securing the achievement of these aims.

[4] It also replaces the original Convention – the Hague Convention on the Guardianship of Minors 1902: Child Protection Convention 1996, Art 51.

[5] It was only ever ratified by eleven States: Austria, France, Germany, Italy, Luxembourg, The Netherlands, Poland, Portugal, Spain, Switzerland and Turkey.

[6] Since the 1961 Convention relied on two *alternative* jurisdictional bases – nationality and habitual residence – conflicts of jurisdiction were highly likely. It was also inconsistent with the Hague Child Abduction Convention 1980. For further problems with which it was beset, see N. Lowe, M. Everall & M. Nicholls, *International Movement of Children: Law, Practice and Procedure* (Bristol: Jordan Publishing, 2004) pp 536–537.

[7] Arts 16–18 of the 1996 Convention do lay down some substantive rules in relation to parental responsibility; but substantive rules are very much exceptional.

In terms of its scope, Article 2 makes it clear that it applies to all children 'from the moment of their birth until they reach the age of 18 years'.[8] And this is so regardless of whether according to the domestic law of any given Contracting State a child will acquire majority at a lower age than this. However, as the official *Explanatory Report* explains:

> This does not mean that the Convention sets at 18 years . . . the age of majority in all of the Contracting States . . . [it] simply means that the Convention's rules for jurisdiction, conflict of laws, etc apply to children up to that age, even in cases where before that age they have acquired capacity under their personal law.[9]

Article 3 details (non-exhaustively) the protective measures to which this Convention applies. It lists a total of seven kinds of measures that fall into one of three broad categories: private measures associated with the protection of children,[10] public measures associated with the protection of children[11] and any other measures relating to the 'administration, conservation or disposal of the child's property'.[12] While the kinds of measures enumerated in Article 3 are diverse, Article 4 does go on to place some important constraints on the scope of the Convention. It supplies an exhaustive list of

[8] Child Protection Convention, Art 2. This is notably out of step with the Hague International Child Abduction Convention which operates with respect to children under the age of sixteen. Equally, it is only superficially in step with the United Nations Convention on the Rights of the Child which does operate with respect to children up to the age of eighteen *unless* under the applicable law the child attains majority at an earlier age: UNCRC, Art 1.

[9] *Lagarde Report* (Hague: Hague Conference, 1997), para 16. The report is available at http://hcch.e-vision.nl/index_en.php?act=publications.details&pid=2943.

[10] These include measures concerning the attribution, exercise, termination or restriction of parental responsibility, measures dealing with custody and access and measures dealing with guardianship, curatorship and analogous institutions: Child Protection Convention, Art 3(a), (b), (c).

[11] These include measures concerning the designation and functions of any person or body having charge of the child's person or property, representing or assisting the child; measures concerning foster care, institutional care or care provided by *kafala* or an analogous institution; and measures concerning a public authority's supervision of a person having charge of a child: Child Protection Convention, Art 3(d), (e), (f). (*Kafala* is an institution of Islamic law under which, in the words of the *Lagarde Report*, *op cit* n 9 (at para 23), 'a child in need of protection may be entrusted either by a decision of the guardianship judge or by an administrative commission to a public or social institution or to a Muslim family which will care for the child's person'.)

[12] Child Protection Convention, Art 3(g). It is important to note here, however, that two types of reservation are available under Art 55(1) which allow a Contracting State to reserve (i) the jurisdiction of its own authorities to take measures directed to the protection of property of a child situated on its territory and (ii) the right not to recognise any parental responsibility or measure in so far as it is incompatible with any measure taken by its authorities in relation to that property.

those matters that are not within its compass: namely, the existence and contesting of legal parenthood, adoption (including preparatory matters), the name of a child, emancipation, maintenance obligations, trusts and succession, social security rights, public education and health rights, penal sanctions and asylum and immigration rights.

Various justifications exist for the exclusion of the matters listed in Article 4. Some are excluded because they have nothing to do with child protection. The naming of a child is perhaps the most obvious example here, although the same is also true of his or her inheritance rights and, arguably, contests about legal parenthood. Other matters – such as adoption and maintenance obligations – are excluded in order to avoid overlap and conflict with other international Conventions that already deal with these matters.[13]

Read together, Articles 3 and 4 do in truth provide a reasonably comprehensive, if not immediately transparent, view of which matters are, and which are not, covered by the Child Protection Convention. That said, some doubt does exist with respect to ordinary private law remedies awarded to a child in contract and tort. For at one level these may be seen as protective of a child, and some of the matters listed in Article 3 – particularly those which have nothing to do with coercive steps for the physical protection of a child – make it clear that the term 'protective measures' is to be construed broadly. Yet as Eric Clive has convincingly argued, normal civil law remedies ought better to be considered tacitly excluded on the basis that:

> The Convention is impliedly limited to matters which would be thought of as child protection or child law matters, rather than matters relating simply to ordinary laws of general application which have their own private international law rules.[14]

His argument is certainly consistent with the official rationale for excluding adoption and maintenance obligations from the remit of the Child Protection Convention. The final word, however, will of course rest with the courts if and when they are called upon to decide the precise limits of the Convention.

Jurisdiction

1 Habitual residence

In order to avoid the potential problems arising out of conflicts of jurisdiction with which the 1961 Convention was beset, Article 5 of the Child Protection Convention makes the child's habitual residence the predominant basis upon which jurisdiction is conferred. And although this is not the exclusive basis for jurisdiction, it enjoys such pre-eminence that one commentator has even

[13] See *Lagarde Report*, *op cit* n 9, para 26.

[14] E. Clive, 'The New Hague Convention on Children' [1998] *Juridical Review* 169, 172.

gone so far as to describe the child's habitual residence as a 'clear dominant theme which runs right through the convention'.[15]

The only circumstances in which habitual residence is likely to prove problematic as the basis for the acquisition of jurisdiction is where a change in the child's habitual residence occurs. In such circumstances, it is the authorities in the second State that will normally have jurisdiction.[16] There are only two exceptions to this rule. First, where the change in habitual residence occurs following an international abduction of the child, the State of former habitual residence will retain jurisdiction unless there has either been acquiescence in the child's abduction by all those holding custody rights, or unless the child has been resident and settled in the second State for a period of at least one year since those with custody rights had actual or constructive knowledge of the child's whereabouts.[17] Secondly, the new State of habitual residence must abstain from exercising jurisdiction (other than an emergency or temporary jurisdiction[18]) if, at the time of the commencement of proceedings, corresponding measures have been sought from another Contracting State possessing jurisdiction under the Convention and that State has neither declined jurisdiction nor disposed of the request for protective measures.[19] In short, where concurrent jurisdiction exists in relation to the same measures, the court second seised must relinquish jurisdiction in favour of the court first seised *so long as* the court first seised has been asked to take corresponding measures to those sought from the court second seised. Thus, for example, if the court second seised is asked to take measures to protect a child's property and the court first seised was asked merely to take measures with respect to the protection of the child's person, there will be no need for the second court to abstain from exercising jurisdiction.[20]

A further problem associated with a change in habitual residence is that proceedings may be on foot (but not concluded) in State A at the very time that the child's habitual residence shifts to State B. If the authorities in State B then also wish to make a protective order in respect of the child concerned, a nice question arises as to which State has jurisdiction. Because the Convention is silent on whether jurisdiction must exist at the time of the commencement of proceedings or at the time at which an order is made, it is technically unclear whether State A loses its jurisdiction before it gets round to issuing protective measures. The solution to this conflict of jurisdictions

[15] Clive, *op cit* n 14.

[16] Child Protection Convention, Art 5(2). But note that any measures taken by the authorities in the original State of habitual residence continue in force even if a change of circumstances has eliminated the jurisdictional basis for those measures: *ibid*, Art 14.

[17] *Ibid*, Art 7.

[18] These exist under Arts 11 and 12 of the Convention and are discussed below.

[19] Child Protection Convention, Art 13(1), (2).

[20] See *Lagarde Report*, *op cit* n 9, para 79.

will, no doubt, have to be resolved in line with the principle and spirit of co-operation built into the Convention. But on its face, the Convention offers no solution.

2 Secondary bases of jurisdiction

The Convention contains a number of secondary rules according to which jurisdiction may be taken. The first of these is dealt with by Article 6 and refers to jurisdiction based on presence within a particular Contracting State. But this jurisdictional ground is specifically limited to child refugees and children whose habitual residence cannot be established. As regards child refugees, the *Lagarde Report* explains that is only children that have been 'temporarily or definitively deprived of their parents' that are envisaged by this provision.[21] It is not, therefore, applicable to international runaways, nor, seemingly, to children who have been abandoned on foreign soil. As regards those children in respect of whom habitual residence cannot be determined, Article 6 provides for a 'jurisdiction of necessity'[22] based on the child's presence within a Contracting State. Although Article 6(2) of the Convention does not say so explicitly, it is understood that a jurisdiction of necessity will cease to exist if the child's habitual residence can subsequently be identified in another Contracting State.[23] Jurisdiction will lie exclusively with that second State. If, on the other hand, the child is later identified as being habitually resident in a non-Contracting State, the authorities of the State in which the child is currently present ought, on principle, to relinquish their jurisdiction of necessity, but may nonetheless take a limited jurisdiction based on Articles 11 and 12.

Article 11(1) allows a State in whose territory a child (or his property) is present to take jurisdiction based on urgency. Urgency differs from necessity in that the former presupposes the need for some immediate protective measure, whereas the latter merely confers the power to take such a measure should it be required. Given this basis of urgency, it is further provided that any measures taken on an emergency basis lapse as soon as measures required by the situation are taken in the proper State (be that another Contracting State or a non-Contracting State whose measures are recognised in the State exercising a jurisdiction of urgency).[24]

By contrast, Article 12 provides for jurisdiction to take 'provisional measures' with respect to a child (or his property) present within the territory of a Contracting State. Such provisional measures do not attract automatic recognition among all other Contracting States,[25] and are really only

[21] *Loc cit*, para 44.
[22] *Loc cit*.
[23] *Loc cit*, para 45.
[24] Child Protection Convention, Arts 11(2), (3).
[25] *Ibid*, Art 12(1).

stop-gaps designed to deal with children such as those on exchange visits or working on a seasonal harvest.[26] This jurisdiction is also made subject to Article 7 (dealing with jurisdiction in abduction cases[27]), as well as the requirement that the measures in question must not be incompatible with any protective measures taken within the State in which the child is habitually resident.[28] In line with Article 11, jurisdiction lapses under this provision once a decision as to protective measures required by the situation have been taken by the proper State, whether that be a Contracting State or non-Contracting State whose decision is recognised in the State making the provisional measures.[29]

The final alternative basis upon which jurisdiction may be grounded is governed by Article 10(1). It is a convoluted provision that permits jurisdiction to be taken by a court dealing with a divorce, nullity or legal separation application so that it can make any suitable protective measures in relation to the person or property of a child of the separating spouses. The jurisdiction, where it exists, is not an exclusive one: it is held concurrently with the authorities in the State in which the child is habitually resident. But it is not imposed automatically on the divorce court. Rather, there are three prerequisites that must be satisfied before this jurisdiction will actually vest.

First, it may be taken only if the internal law of the State in which the matrimonial proceedings are brought so permits.[30] Secondly, at the time of the commencement of the proceedings, one of the child's parent's must be habitually resident in the State in which the matrimonial proceedings are being heard *and*, at the same point in time, at least one parent must be in possession of parental responsibility.[31] Thirdly, both parents (and anyone else holding parental responsibility) must agree to the matrimonial proceedings court taking child protection jurisdiction and, in any event, it must be in the best interests of the child for the divorce court to possess such jurisdiction.[32]

[26] *Lagarde Report*, *op cit* n 9, para 74.

[27] This provision deals with the allocation of jurisdiction following a child's abduction from a Contracting State to some other State. It provides that the Contracting State that held jurisdiction prior to the abduction is to retain jurisdiction until the child acquires an habitual residence elsewhere and *either* those holding rights of custody acquiesce in the abduction, *or* the child resides in the new State for a period of at least one year after the custody rights holder became actually or constructively aware of the child's new whereabouts. For closer analysis, see P. Nygh, 'The New Hague Child Protection Convention' (1997) 11 *International Journal of Law, Policy and the Family* 344, 348–349.

[28] Child Protection Convention, Art 12(1).

[29] *Ibid*, Art 12(2), (3).

[30] *Ibid*, Art 10(1).

[31] *Ibid*, Art 10(1)(a). As has been officially explained, it was thought that 'the divorce court of two parents, both of whom have been deprived of parental responsibility, would have no basis on which to exercise protective jurisdiction in respect of the child': *Lagarde Report*, *op cit* n 9, para 64.

[32] *Ibid*, Art 10(1)(b).

An obvious objection to Article 10 inheres in the fact that it provides for concurrent jurisdictions, albeit with respect to different aspects of marital breakdown. This is an alien idea in this country, and compliance with the Child Protection Convention would require an amendment to the current domestic legislation that governs this jurisdiction. As it stands, English law is predicated upon the principle that the court with jurisdiction over the child and the divorce shall be one and the same so long as the 'the child concerned is a child of both parties to the matrimonial proceedings'.[33] Furthermore, the Convention approach may be opposed on the basis that it is 'unprincipled and adult-centred rather than child-centred to give jurisdiction to a court which might have no real connection with the child' since '[a] parent might have chosen the divorce court for tactical or financial reasons that have nothing to do with the child'.[34]

The concurrency of jurisdiction under the Convention, constrained as it is by the several preconditions to the divorce court taking jurisdiction, reveals the compromise upon which Article 10 was founded. It in fact favours neither an exclusive jurisdiction on the part of the State of the child's habitual residence nor an exclusive jurisdiction on the part of the divorce court. But whether the indirect links with the child that are implicit in the preconditions for Article 10(1) are sufficient for the purposes of a supposedly child-centred Convention seems unlikely. For beyond the objection that the child need not have any meaningful connection with the divorce State, we might also note that a divorce, annulment or separation need not have any *necessary* consequences for a child of the family. This is because post-divorce maintenance of children is commonly secured by a set of rules formally independent of those deployed by the divorce court. Furthermore, there is the additional practical consideration that a child habitually resident in a State other than the one in which the matrimonial proceedings have been brought may in practice be unable to appear and supply evidence in those proceedings precisely because he or she is resident in some other country. This obviously raises important questions about the quality of any decision reached by the divorce court affecting the child.[35]

Given the controversial nature of the Article 10 divorce jurisdiction which has the potential to create a conflict of jurisdictions, the Convention seeks to keep its lifespan to the mimimum period required. Accordingly, the jurisdiction ceases 'as soon as the decision allowing or refusing the application for

[33] Family Law Act 1986, s 2(1)(a).

[34] Clive, *op cit* n 14, at 176.

[35] There is, of course, a final objection based on the fact that the objective of removing conflicts of jurisdiction – something that bedevilled the 1961 Convention – is to some extent undermined by Art 10. As discussed below, Art 13 endeavours to deal with this and related problems.

divorce, legal separation or annulment . . . has become final, or [as soon as] the proceedings have come to an end for another reason'.[36]

3 Forum non conveniens

Notwithstanding the fact that a State may possess jurisdiction according to any of the jurisdictional rules so far discussed, it is nonetheless possible for that State to surrender jurisdiction in favour of some other State that is considered by its authorities to be 'better placed in the particular case to assess the best interests of the child'.[37] The decision need not be reached unilaterally since the Convention's endeavour to foster co-operation in relation to matters of jurisdiction permits discussion of the matter between the two States concerned prior to any transfer of jurisdiction being sanctioned.[38] The stipulated triggers for a transfer of jurisdiction under this Article are that the child in question is a national of the second State, that he or she has property situated there, that there is some form of matrimonial cause between the child's parents which is being dealt with there and that child has some other form of substantial connection with the State in question.[39]

In cases where the State seised of jurisdiction according to any of the bases discussed earlier fails to take the initiative in transferring jurisdiction to a second, better-placed State, Article 9(1) allows that second State to begin the process by requesting such a transfer. This Article also provides for a prior exchange of views and likewise makes clear that no transfer of jurisdiction can occur without the agreement of the requested State.[40] One of the virtues of Article 9 lies in the fact that the concept of *forum non conveniens* is alien to the authorities in civil law States which may not, for this reason, be inclined to initiate a transfer of jurisdiction under Article 8. But even beyond this scenario, Article 9 is likely to prove useful where protective measures in respect of a child within the territory of the requesting State are considered desirable by that State, but where there is not sufficient urgency to invoke jurisdiction under Article 11, and where provisional protective measures (under Article 12) would be considered inadequate.

4 Conflicts of jurisdiction

Although the Child Protection Convention provides for a number of alternative bases according to which jurisdiction can be taken, the practical scope for any conflicts of jurisdiction are kept to a minimum. As Clive neatly puts it:

[36] Child Protection Convention, Art 10(2). Cf Family Law Act 1986 which treats divorce proceedings as continuing until the child(ren) of the family attain eighteen years of age.

[37] *Ibid*, Art 8(1), (4).

[38] *Ibid*, Art 8(3).

[39] *Ibid*, Art 8(2).

[40] *Ibid*, Art 9(3).

> The urgency and presence jurisdictions are inherently temporary and subsidiary and must yield to the habitual residence jurisdiction once it takes the measures required by the situation. The transferred jurisdiction requires co-operation between the authorities concerned. The 'refugee' jurisdiction is, of its nature, unlikely to involve conflict with any other authority. The 'wrongful removal' [that is, 'abduction'] jurisdiction is so framed as to prevail over any jurisdiction, other than on the ground of urgency, of the State to which the child has been removed.[41]

Yet however much the potential for conflicts of jurisdiction are in practice kept to a minimum, they may nonetheless exist in at least two telling scenarios. The first arises by virtue of the way in which Article 7 is framed. There, it will be recalled, the jurisdiction of a Contracting State from which a child has been wrongfully removed will be preserved until *either* all those in possession of custody rights acquiesce in that removal, *or* one year elapses from the date on which the custody rights holder(s) became aware of the child's new whereabouts. In such circumstances, the State in which the child is now resident may claim a jurisdiction of urgency under Article 11(1). If the court seised with the jurisdiction of urgency makes an order sanctioning the retention of the child by the abducting parent, but the court of habitual residence subsequently makes an order in favour of the aggrieved parent, a genuine conflict of jurisdiction may arise. For while in theory the court of original habitual residence would be entitled to have its subsequent order recognised in the State to which the child was removed,[42] that court of urgency may seek to invoke Article 23(2)(d) of the Convention permitting non-recognition of the order in favour of the aggrieved parent on the grounds that it would be manifestly contrary to public policy to do so. The gist of this approach would be that, since the first order was necessarily made according to the court's perception of where the child's best interests lay, it would clearly be seen as at loggerheads with the second order (in favour of the aggrieved parent) that order being at variance with its own. Not until the one-year period securing an exclusive jurisdiction on the part of the new State has elapsed would a final solution to this conflict of jurisdiction be provided.

The second scenario in which a genuine conflict of jurisdiction may occur is perhaps less likely in practice. It would arise in the context where the divorce jurisdiction discussed earlier is taken. In such a circumstance, the scope for a genuine conflict of jurisdiction is minimised by the fact that both parents must have agreed to the divorce court taking jurisdiction with respect to the child.[43] This will of course go a long way to ensuring that concurrent applications in respect of the child are not lodged in two separate jurisdictions. But it does not entirely eradicate this possibility since one parent may

[41] Clive, *op cit* n 14, at 178, n 35.
[42] Child Protection Convention, Art 23(1).
[43] *Ibid*, Art 10(1)(b).

change his or her mind, before the conclusion of the matrimonial proceedings, as to the appropriate forum in which the child-centred issues should be heard. In these circumstances, the staying provision contained in Article 13(1) must be invoked. For it is there provided that, where two courts are simultaneously seised of jurisdiction under the Convention, the court from whom protective measures are sought second in time must abstain from exercising its jurisdiction with respect to corresponding measures so long as the proceedings first initiated are still under consideration.[44] There is, however, no obligation to decline jurisdiction where the second court is petitioned in relation to *non-corresponding measures.* Thus, if a divorce court is requested to make an order as to the custody of a child, there is nothing to prevent the court in the child's State of habitual residence from making an order with respect to the *property* of the child.[45] Similarly, there is no need to abstain from the exercise of jurisdiction on the part of the second court where the court first approached has declined jurisdiction.[46]

Applicable law

1 The general rule

The general rule with respect to applicable law is that the State exercising jurisdiction will apply its own internal law when deciding whether or not to sanction measures designed to protect the person or property of the child.[47] This is an eminently sensible approach since not only will it be the law best known to the authorities of that State, it will also be the most appropriate law for the reason that jurisdiction will normally be founded on the habitual residence of the child making this legal system the one with which the child has the closest connection. Where, however, jurisdiction is founded on either the urgency of the situation or the mere presence of the child, this close connection will be absent. To meet such circumstances, the Convention provides that 'in so far as the protection of the person or the property of the child requires, [the relevant authorities] . . . may exceptionally apply or take into consideration the law of another State with which the situation has a substantial connection'.[48] There is no requirement that the State whose law may be applied must be a Contracting State, but then neither is there a formal obligation to apply or even consider its law. One might therefore expect that where jurisdiction is taken on the basis of presence, and the child in question has fled a country with oppressive laws, the option to consider or apply the laws of the oppressive State may well be declined.

[44] *Ibid*, Art 13(1).
[45] *Lagarde Report*, *op cit* n 9, para 79.
[46] Child Protection Convention, Art 13(2).
[47] *Ibid*, Art 15(1).
[48] *Ibid*, Art 15(2).

If the child's habitual residence changes to State B after measures have been taken in State A, then although State B will be bound to continue in force those measures, it will be the law of State B that subsequently governs the fulfilment of those measures.[49] An example gleaned from the *Lagarde Report* helps to clarify what is meant here. It states:

> If, for example, a guardian was designated for the child in the country of his former habitual residence, with the obligation to ask the judge for authorisation to carry out certain acts, it would seem that, according to [this provision] . . . this guardian could carry out these acts all alone if the law of the new habitual residence permitted him or her to do so.[50]

2 The rules in relation to parental responsibility

The general rule concerning the applicable law is, strictly, concerned with the question of which law should govern the exercise of jurisdiction to take *protective measures*. Thus, if the law of a given State requires that a sufficiently mature child's wishes and feelings ought to be heard prior to making any protective order, those views must receive due consideration. What the general rule does not strictly cover is certain prior questions such as who holds parental responsibility for any given child. Thus, where parental responsibility is determined either by the operation of a rule of law, or by a recognised agreement,[51] or by a unilateral act,[52] the general rule does not apply. Instead, the Convention provides that, in such circumstances, the attribution or extinction of parental responsibility is to be governed by the law of the child's habitual residence.[53] And this is so even if the relevant State is a non-Contracting State.[54]

Where, by contrast, parental responsibility is created, modified or extinguished by court order, or by some equivalent order made by a competent administrative authority, the attribution of parental responsibility can be characterised as a kind of protective measure since it establishes a relationship of authority over the child and his or her property. As such, the attribution or extinction of parental responsibility by an order emanating from a judicial or administrative authority is governed by the general rule.

During the process of drafting the Convention, it was noted that a potential problem might arise concerning parental responsibility in that not all States have the same rules concerning the automatic attribution of parental responsibility. Views were divided on how to deal with this. First, there were some States that argued that any parental responsibility acquired by the

[49] *Ibid*, Art 15(3).

[50] *Lagarde Report*, *op cit* n 9, para 91.

[51] Eg, an agreement between unmarried parents as to the parental responsibility of the father.

[52] Eg, the recognition of an unmarried father's paternity.

[53] Child Protection Convention, Art 16(1), (2).

[54] *Ibid*, Art 20.

operation of a rule of law in the State of first habitual residence should be immutable and therefore not subject to possible extinction in the second State of habitual residence. Secondly, there were those States that argued that parental responsibility created otherwise than by a judicial or administrative order should be mutable: that is, the automatic attribution of parental responsibility should be governed exclusively by the law of the *current* habitual residence.[55]

In the end, the Convention steers a compromise between the two extreme positions. Under Article 16(3), any parental responsibility conferred by a rule of law in the first State is not lost by the holder of that responsibility upon a change of habitual residence to a Contracting State in which an equivalent rule does not exist. For English purposes, this will mean most significantly that an unmarried father who acquired automatic parental responsibility in the original State of habitual residence will continue to hold it upon family relocation to this country.[56] Conversely, however, where a person does not possess parental responsibility as a matter of law in the first State, but would under the law of the second, it is the law of the second State that prevails so that the person in question will henceforth be treated as being in possession of such responsibility.[57] Taken together, these provisions reveal a very father-friendly Convention since automatic attributions of parental responsibility will not generally be lost upon a change of habitual residence but may nonetheless be acquired in such circumstances.

One possible danger that arises from the immutability of parental responsibility under Article 16(3) is that third parties may not know precisely who has parental responsibility for a child. If such third parties were to engage in transactions with Parent A, without consulting Parent B, on the assumption that it is only Parent A who holds parental responsibility, there is the prospect of conducting an unlawful and invalid transaction that may well give rise to potential liability towards Parent B. To meet this circumstance, Article 19(1) states that the transaction shall be valid and that no liability will be incurred *unless* the third party knew or ought to have known of the rights of Parent B.[58] Sensibly, the *Lagarde Report* suggests that what one may expect third parties to know and discover about those who may hold parental responsibility ought to vary in proportion to the significance of the transaction in question.[59]

[55] For details of the supposed advantages and disadvantages of each argument see the *Lagarde Report*, *op cit* n 9, para 105.

[56] For further examples of the practical implications of these provisions see Clive, *op cit* n 14, at 181–182.

[57] Child Protection Convention, Art 16(4).

[58] This provision only applies so long as the third party and the person with whom he or she conducts the transaction are 'on the territory of the same State': *ibid*, Art 19(2).

[59] *Lagarde Report*, *op cit* n 9, para 113.

Importantly, also, the Convention treats differently the mere possession of parental responsibility and its actual content (that is, what may be done in the exercise of parental responsibility). In all cases – including those in which there has been a change of habitual residence – the rights and powers possessed by those who hold parental responsibility are determined by the law of the current State of habitual residence.[60] Accordingly, matters such as the power to discipline a child – perhaps even by recourse to physical chastisement – will be governed by the State in which the child is habitually resident. In addition, the authorities of the current State of habitual residence may terminate or modify parental responsibility according to the legal principles in force under its domestic law.[61] This is a rule of substantive law that may be invoked in cases where there has been a change in habitual residence in order to modify the effects of that change in residence in terms of those who should be treated as possessing parental responsibility.

Recognition and enforcement

1 The general rule

Under Article 23(1) of the Convention, the basic rule is that any protective measures taken by the judicial or administrative authorities of a Contracting State must be granted automatic recognition in all other Contracting States. Where, however, measures taken in one State and enforceable there actually require subsequent *enforcement* in a second State – an example might be an order for the compulsory sale of property[62] – that second State must, at the request of an interested party, either declare those measures to be enforceable, or register them for the purposes of enforcement as the case may be.[63] Once such a declaration or registration has occurred, the measures in question become enforceable in the second State 'as if they had been taken by the authorities of that [second] State'.[64] In both cases – that is, whether what is sought is recognition or enforcement – Article 27 imposes a prohibition upon any review of the merits of any measures taken in the first State.

[60] Child Protection Convention, Art 17.

[61] *Ibid*, Art 18.

[62] *Lagarde Report*, *op cit* n 9, para 132.

[63] Child Protection Convention, Art 26(1). Furthermore, under Art 26(2), the declaration or registration must be performed swiftly, and may be refused only on the basis of the grounds set out in Art 23(2). These grounds apply equally to the refusal of recognition and are considered in detail below.

[64] *Ibid*, Art 28. This provision goes on to state that such enforcement must take place 'in accordance with the law of the requested State to the extent provided by such law, taking into consideration the best interests of the child'.

2 Refusals of recognition or enforcement

Article 23(2) of the Child Protection Convention provides the only six grounds on which protective measures taken by one Contracting State may be denied recognition or enforcement in another such State. First, recognition may be denied where the measure in question 'was taken by an authority whose jurisdiction was not based on one of the grounds provided for [by the Convention]'.[65] This is a straightforward and uncontroversial provision. Secondly, recognition may be denied where the measure 'was taken, except in a case of urgency . . . without the child having been provided with the opportunity to be heard' where such a failure constitutes a fundamental violation of proper procedure in the State concerned.[66] Thirdly, and in similar vein, recognition may also be refused where, except in urgency cases, the measure concerned infringes the parental responsibility of the person claiming non-recognition *and* that person was not afforded the opportunity to be heard.[67] Again, these two grounds are relatively uncontroversial. They largely reflect a commonly held understanding of what natural justice entails; but in addition, the former seeks to achieve conformity with the self-determination principle enshrined in Article 12 of the United Nations Convention on the Rights of the Child.

Fourthly, recognition and enforcement may be refused where the measure in question would be manifestly contrary to public policy in the requested State, taking into account the best interests of the child.[68] This basis for the refusal of recognition appears in other private international law Conventions of this kind and seems, in one context at least, to require that the person seeking to invoke it must cross a very high evidentiary threshold.[69] It seems probable that a similarly restrictive interpretation would be applied in relation to this Convention – by the English courts at least.

The two final grounds on which recognition may be refused are somewhat esoteric and, in any event, Convention-specific. The first of these is that a measure may be denied recognition where it 'is incompatible with a later measure taken in the non-Convention State of the child's habitual residence, where this later measure fulfils the requirements for recognition in

[65] *Ibid*, Art 23(2)(a).

[66] *Ibid*, Art 23(2)(b).

[67] *Ibid*, Art 23(2)(c).

[68] *Ibid*, Art 23(2)(d).

[69] A similar phrase appears in the European Child Abduction Convention 1980, Art 10. In that context, the inclusion of the word 'manifestly' has led to a restrictive interpretation of when the ground will be available: see, *T v R (Abduction: Forum Conveniens)* [2002] 2 FLR 544, at 121 *per* Charles J; *Re H (A Minor) (Foreign Custody Order: Enforcement)* [1994] 105, at 110 *per* Sir Stephen Brown P; *Re L (Child Abduction: European Convention)* [1992] 2 FLR 178, at 182 *per* Ward J.

the requested State'. What this means, in effect, is that where there are 'two measures [that] are incompatible, preference will be given to the second, taken by an authority closer to the child and in a better position to assess the child's best interests'.[70] This ground for non-recognition might well be invoked in the following scenario. Imagine that Contracting State A makes a protective measure in relation to a child. Imagine further that the non-Contracting State of the child's habitual residence later sanctions a protective measure that is in conflict with the one taken in State A. If the child then relocates to Contracting State B, State B would ordinarily be required to recognise the measure taken in State A. But if the domestic conditions for the recognition of a court order made in the non-Contracting State are satisfied, State B is hereby given the option to disregard the measure taken in State A and recognise, instead, the measure adopted in the non-Contracting State.

Clearly, the aim of this provision is the promotion of the child's best interests. And underpinning it is the assumption (based on the greater connection with the child) that these best interests are more likely to have been promoted by the second, not the first, protective measure. If, however, this assumption is obviously misplaced – say, because the State of habitual residence is in fact not committed to the welfare principle – there is no obligation on the part of the requested State to refuse recognition to the protective measure taken in State A.

Finally, recognition may be denied if there has been a failure on the part of Contracting State A to comply with the procedure contained in Article 33 of the Convention.[71] This is an important ground, since Article 33 sets out the procedure to be followed where the authorities in Contracting State A contemplate the placement of a child in foster or institutional care in State B.[72] Naturally, this procedure requires State A to obtain the agreement of State B to the proposed measure;[73] for quite apart from the serious issue of principle at stake, it would clearly be a step too far to allow State A to make an order that could well have serious financial implications for the authorities of State B without State B being granted the final word.

Although there are six independent bases upon which protective measures taken in one Contracting State may be denied recognition and enforcement in a second Contracting State, they should not to be assumed to be of great practical significance. In most cases they are narrowly drawn and, for that reason, incapable of being invoked in anything other than unusual, if

[70] *Lagarde Report*, *op cit* n 9, para 126.

[71] Child Protection Convention, Art 33(1).

[72] The procedure envisages the transmission of a background report on the child (including the reasons why care is required) by State A as well as proper consultation and dialogue with State B.

[73] Child Protection Convention, Art 33(2).

not exceptional, circumstances.[74] In any case, to meet the concerns that may arise in connection with the possible non-recognition of measures taken in the first State, Article 24 provides for a facility whereby any interested party may request in advance a declaration from the second State as to whether or not a measure taken in the first State will be recognised or enforced.[75]

Co-operation between Contracting States

The Child Protection Convention contains a range of obligations dealing with inter-State co-operation that are to be performed, for the most part, by the Central Authorities that each Contracting State is obliged to create under Article 29. In this respect, the Convention adopts the same operational medium as its sister Hague Conventions on international child abduction and intercountry adoption. The chief functions of the Central Authorities established under this Convention concern the promotion of inter-State co-operation and the provision of information about the content of domestic laws and children in respect of whom protective measures have been taken or proposed.[76] These duties are generally diluted to the extent that the relevant Central Authorities need do only what is reasonable in order to fulfil them. Furthermore, the actual content of these duties is far from burdensome.[77] Article 31 provides a good example of the limited nature and content of these obligations. It requires Central Authorities to do no more than '*facilitate* [both] communications . . . and agreed solutions for the protection of the . . . child'[78] and to provide '*assistance* in discovering the whereabouts of a child'.[79] There is, it will be noted, no absolute obligation to do any of the listed things which, in any event, anticipate the assistance of some other body.

Notwithstanding the somewhat limp nature of the obligations aimed at co-operation that are imposed under this Convention, two particular duties

[74] Cf the view (in respect of which no supporting examples are given) that 'some of the grounds set out by Art 23(2) . . . are too loosely drawn . . . [in that they] are not prescriptive enough': Lowe *et al*, *op cit* n 6, p 553.

[75] There is no explicit statement in Art 24 that such clarification may be sought in advance, but it is implicit that this is the case; and in any event such advance notice features in the example supplied in the official commentary: see *Lagarde Report*, *op cit* n 9, para 129.

[76] Child Protection Convention, Arts 30, 31.

[77] The 'diluted' nature of these duties were considered politically expedient in that more burdensome duties, couched in absolute terms, would have been likely to dissuade some States – principally developing nations – from ratifying: see *Lagarde Report*, *op cit* n 9, para 136. Art 38 further allays such concerns by permitting reasonable charges to be made for the provision of the Central Authority's services.

[78] Child Protection Convention, Art 31(a), (b) (emphasis added).

[79] *Ibid*, Art 31(c) (emphasis added).

do call for closer scrutiny. The first is Article 32, the operation of which is triggered by the transmission of a request by the Central Authority of one Contracting State with which the child has a substantial connection to the Central Authority of the State of habitual residence. Upon receiving such a request, the latter is permitted (but not obliged) to provide a report on the child's situation and to request its own competent authorities to take protective measures. The Article is likely to be of most use where a child has been abducted from one Contracting State to another. For, here, in the wake of requesting the return of the child to the State of his or her habitual residence, the Central Authority in that State can be invited to ensure the child's protection upon his return.[80]

Article 35 also warrants particular note since it is concerned with safeguarding regular cross-border contact with a child where the person entitled to contact and the child in question are resident in two different Contracting States. The facility to promote such contact is aimed primarily at the 'competent authorities' (not Central Authorities) of the respective States.[81] But it is also possible for a request for assistance in the maintenance of such contact rights to come directly from the holder of those rights.[82] Furthermore, the provision anticipates more than mere physical contact, for it refers both to 'rights of access as well as of the right to maintain [other] direct contacts'.[83]

Article 35 is therefore a most welcome inclusion in the Child Protection Convention. It bears a broad notion of contact and even provides for direct assistance in the enjoyment of access and contact rights. This contrasts favourably with the very limited duty incumbent on the Central Authorities that operate the Hague Child Abduction Convention 1980. For there the obligation is merely one to make arrangements with respect to 'organizing or securing the effective exercise of rights of access'.[84] In practice, the Hague Convention duty seems to involve no more than the arrangement by the Central Authority for a suitably qualified solicitor to act on the applicant's behalf.[85] The Child Protection Convention also compares favourably with the European Child Abduction Convention in this respect.[86]

[80] This provision is complemented by Art 36 which further provides for the transmission of information concerning specific serious dangers to which the child and/or his family may be exposed (except, *per* Art 37, where such transmission would itself create a threat to the child, his property or his family). Notably, the Art 36 obligation is couched in peremptory terms.

[81] Child Protection Convention, Art 35(1).

[82] *Ibid*, Art 35(2).

[83] *Ibid*, Art 35(1).

[84] Hague Child Abduction Convention, Art 21.

[85] See *Re T (Minors) (Hague Convention: Access)* [1993] 2 FLR 617.

[86] For details of the assistance available under this Convention, see ch 8.

Relationship with the Hague Child Abduction Convention

Unsurprisingly, there is scope for potential overlap between the Child Protection Convention and its stable-mate, the Hague Child Abduction Convention. In recognition of this overlap, Article 50 of the former states that it 'shall not affect the application of the [latter]'. This would seem ostensibly capable of solving any potential conflicts between the two Conventions; but in fact unresolved clashes do remain.

In the first place, Article 50 goes on to state that, notwithstanding the general position, '[n]othing . . . precludes provisions of this Convention from being invoked for the purposes of obtaining the return of a child who has been wrongfully removed or retained'. In other words, it creates a function for the Child Protection Convention that is essentially the same as that ascribed to the Child Abduction Convention: securing the return of abducted children. And while it is true that it merely envisages a different way of securing the same objective – having custody rights awarded in State A recognised and enforced in the State of wrongful removal or retention, State B – the potential for conflict does exist. Two situations in particular need to be considered.

First, imagine that an application for the return of a child wrongfully removed to State B is made *per* the Abduction Convention and that the domestic authorities decline to order a return. In such circumstances, the aggrieved parent may seek to invoke the 1996 Convention in order to have his custody rights recognised and enforced. In such a scenario there would be a conflict between the duty to recognise the custody order in State A, and the domestic decision not to return the child reached in State B. Probably the only way in which the conflict could be resolved is on the basis of the non-recognition of the custody order by reason of it being manifestly contrary to public policy in State B.[87]

Secondly, a conflict may arise following an abduction where a child is removed to State B, but not in abrogation of any extant order conferring custody rights in State A. In such a situation, the Abduction Convention procedure may still be invoked even though the aggrieved parent does not posses a formal court order investing him with custody rights. *Re B (A Minor) (Abduction)*[88] is an example of a case in which *de facto* parenting of the child by his unmarried father was regarded as sufficient to qualify as 'custody rights' for the purposes of the 1980 Abduction Convention.[89] If,

[87] As *per* the Child Protection Convention, Art 23(2)(d).

[88] [1994] 2 FLR 249, at 257. This sentiment has since been echoed in *Practice Note (CAEW: Hague Convention: Applications by Fathers Without Parental Responsibility)* [1998] 1 FLR 491.

[89] See also, to like effect, *Re O (Abduction: Custody Rights)* [1997] 2 FLR 702. Cf *Re J (A Minor) (Abduction: Custody Rights)* [1990] 2 AC 562 where the unmarried father was held not to possess custody rights where he had been exercising *de facto*

following the invocation of the Abduction Convention a return of the child were to be refused, State B would then be in the position to make a provisional protection order on the basis of Article 12 of the 1996 Convention. And such provisional protection may well take the form of a temporary custody order granted in favour of the abducting parent. In this scenario, despite Article 7 (which seeks to prioritise the operation of the Abduction Convention), there would again be scope for a conflict of orders – assuming that the aggrieved parent eventually obtained a formal custody order from the proper authorities in State A.

European Convention on Contact Concerning Children 2003

Introduction

Recognising that the 'continuing internationalisation of family relationships . . . [was making] the question of transfrontier access to children . . . more and more topical',[90] and recognising, too, the limitations in the Hague and European Child Abduction Conventions (and even the Child Protection Convention) in this respect, the Council of Europe produced a Convention to deal specifically with this matter.[91] Its provisions were drafted in full recognition of the fact that Articles 9 and 10(2) of the United Nations Convention on the Rights of the Child expressly provide for the right of a child to maintain direct contact with both parents, even across national frontiers where this is possible. In short, it seeks to go beyond the facilities currently provided by various international instruments in supporting the enjoyment of parent–child contact rights.

Purposes and scope

Article 1 of the Contact Convention sets out its three abiding objectives. These are first, 'to determine general principles to be applied to contact orders', secondly 'to fix appropriate safeguards and guarantees to ensure the proper exercise of contact and the immediate return of children at the end of the period of contact', and thirdly, 'to establish co-operation between central authorities, judicial authorities and other bodies in order to promote and

joint custody with the child's mother who alone possessed *de jure* custody rights. For subsequent confirmation that the sharing of custody with the mother, under the same roof, is fatal to an unmarried father's claim to custody rights (in the absence of *de jure* parental responsibility on his part) see *Re C (Child Abduction) (Unmarried Father: Rights of Custody)* [2002] EWHC 2219, at [43] *per* Munby J.

[90] Council of Europe, *Explanatory Report to the Convention on Contact Concerning Children* (Strasbourg: Council of Europe, 2002) para 1.

[91] The final text of the Convention was formally adopted on 15 May 2003.

improve contact between children and their parents and other persons having family ties with children'. It is clear that the second and third of these objectives have in mind the promotion of cross-border contact. But so too – albeit less obviously – does the first. As the Explanatory Report states:

> The general principles in letter a of Article 1 . . . which are to be implemented by States Parties and to be applied by the judicial authority taking the decision . . . will not only assist judicial authorities, at a national level, to follow certain standards but will also ensure that any foreign decisions to be implemented from other States Parties . . . have been based on similar reliable standards.[92]

In short, since the Convention lays down certain common principles and substantive rules of law that shall be applied in contact decisions among all States Parties, there will be less scope for refusing to recognise the final judgments reached.

As regards scope, the Convention adopts a very broad and progressive concept of contact. It is wide enough to embrace not just the obvious case of actual contact in the form of staying visits and so on,[93] but also any form of communication between the child, on the one hand, and his or her parents, and (in some circumstances) others with family ties, on the other.[94] It even stretches, somewhat innovatively, to 'the provision of information to such a person *about the child* or to the chid *about such a person*'.[95] Furthermore, in adopting the term 'contact' in preference to what has hitherto been the ecumenically accepted term in Europe, 'access', the Convention endeavours to inculcate the modern notion that contact rights exist as much for the benefit of children as their parents and certain relatives.[96]

In step with this is the correspondingly broad meaning attributed to the term 'contact order'. For such orders include not just those awarded in the context of contested court proceedings, but also those that have been privately agreed *so long as* they have been confirmed subsequently by a competent judicial authority.[97]

A similarly flexible meaning is ascribed to the children to whom this Convention applies. According to Article 2(c), a child is 'a person under 18 years of age *in respect of whom a contact order may be made or enforced*'.[98] The emphasised words clearly serve to exclude the operation of the Convention in relation to children who, by the domestic laws of Member States,

[92] *Explanatory Report*, *op cit* n 90, para 17.

[93] Contact Convention, Art 2(a)(i).

[94] *Ibid*, Art 2(a)(ii). 'Family ties' are defined progressively as connoting 'a close relationship such as between a child and his or her grandparents or siblings, based on law or on a *de facto* family relationship': *ibid*, Art 2(d).

[95] *Ibid*, Art 2(a)(iii) (emphasis added).

[96] See *Explanatory Report*, *op cit* n 90, paras 6, 22–24.

[97] Contact Convention, Art 2(b).

[98] Emphasis added.

attain majority at an earlier age, or at least acquire the capacity to make their own decisions with respect to residence and contact before they reach eighteen. This approach obviously reflects compromise in that it allows for national differences that may in turn cause difficulties in the context of recognition and enforcement. Only time will tell – but with an ever-growing history of close co-operation between European States on private international law matters, combined with an emphasis on inter-State co-operation within the Convention, it is difficult to envisage that these potential difficulties will prove very problematic in practice.

Mechanics of the Convention

The general principles according to which the Convention will operate are set out at length in Chapter II. These are complemented by a number of specific duties in Chapter III aimed at promoting and improving cross-border contact that are to be fulfilled by the familiar media in such Conventions – specially designated Central Authorities. The provisions of both Chapters warrant closer analysis, and each is considered in turn.

The starting point is the legislative obligation imposed on all States Parties 'to ensure that the principles contained in [Chapter II] are applied by judicial authorities when making, amending, suspending or revoking contact orders'.[99] And broadly speaking, these principles can be summarised thus. Parents and children will be granted an automatic right to enjoy regular contact with one another that may only be restricted or excluded in the best interests of the child (and even then only with the possibility of supervised contact being considered first).[100] By contrast, no such automatic right to contact will be conferred upon a child and his or her other family members. But those others enjoying family ties with the child will be granted the right to establish formal contact rights subject to the child's best interests.[101] The reason for the distinction drawn between the right afforded to parents, and the lesser right that is attributed to more distant persons, has been officially explained in terms of European Human Rights principles:

> [T]he parents' right to bring up their children is . . . protected by Article 8 of the ECHR[102] . . . [By contrast] [p]ersons other than parents, having family ties with a child may have a right to apply for contact. However, this right is not on an equal footing with the right of a child and his or her parents to contact

[99] Contact Convention, Art 3. For the purposes of the Convention, the term 'judicial authorities' includes administrative authorities having powers equivalent to those of a court of law: *ibid*, Art 2(e).

[100] *Ibid*, Art 4.

[101] *Ibid*, Art 5(1). Individual States will be at liberty to extend this right to establish contact to others who do not possess family ties: *ibid*, Art 5(2).

[102] The European Convention on Human Rights.

because there is a presumption of contact for legally recognised parents and their children.[103]

Beyond these foundational principles, the Convention seeks to respect the incremental accretion of autonomy rights on the part of mature and adolescent minors,[104] and to ensure that contact disputes are solved, where possible, upon fully informed and perhaps even amicable bases, both in and out of court.[105] Where an amicable solution is not possible, and a formal contact order is necessary, each State must take all appropriate measures to secure the enjoyment of the specific contact rights contained in them.[106] In addition, and more specifically, with a view to ensuring that contact orders are carried into effect and that children are properly returned after a period of contact to their usual place of residence, the Convention requires States Parties to adopt two compulsory forms of safeguard *plus* a minimum of three further safeguards that may (but need not) be selected from a menu contained in the Convention[107] to ensure that contact orders are carried into effect.

As already noted, Chapter III of the Convention deals with the functions of Central Authorities in promoting and improving cross-border contact. There is a general obligation to appoint a Central Authority under Article 11. Yet as Nigel Lowe and his co-authors have shrewdly noted, 'since the 2003 Convention is intended to complement the two 1980 [Abduction] Conventions as well as the 1996 Convention, it seems advisable to designate the same Authority as under these Conventions'.[108] This seems an eminently sensible suggestion.

As is common for such Authorities, the duties incumbent upon them under this Convention fall into two broad classes. The first concerns the gathering and transfer of information about particular children (including their whereabouts) and about aspects of domestic law on parental responsibility and contact rights.[109] The second concerns the promotion of inter-State

[103] *Explanatory Report*, *op cit* n 90, paras 48–49.

[104] Contact Convention, Art 6.

[105] *Ibid*, Arts 7–8.

[106] *Ibid*, Art 9.

[107] *Ibid*, Art 10(1), (2). The compulsory safeguards are (i) that there be supervised contact in cases where supervision is desirable in the best interests of the child, and (ii) that there be a procedure established for the recognition and enforcement of custody and contact orders made in other States Parties. The menu of optional safeguards (set out in Art 10(2)) is very lengthy. It is divided into two parts: the first containing safeguards for carrying into effect a contact order; the second containing safeguards associated with correcting and preventing improper removals of children. For more detailed discussion see *Explanatory Report*, *op cit* n 90, paras 73–88. Whichever of the additional safeguards is adopted is immaterial; but details of them must be communicated to the Secretary General of the Council of Europe: *ibid*, Art 10(1).

[108] Lowe *et al*, *op cit* n 6, p 601.

[109] Contact Convention Art 12(c)–(e).

co-operation not just between the Central Authorities, but also between the judicial authorities of each State Party.[110] There are the usual requirements to fulfil these functions with 'all necessary despatch' and with a view to removing obstacles in the way of the Convention's smooth operation.[111] In addition, however, Central Authorities are also charged with the obligation to 'assist children, parents and other persons having family ties with the child . . . in instituting proceedings regarding transfrontier contact'.[112] It is something of a pity, bearing in mind the very limited assistance available under the two Abduction Conventions in this regard,[113] that the present Convention is not more explicit on the nature of the of assistance that must be provided. Indeed, as the Official Guidance points out:

> In cases concerning transfrontier contact, the assistance of Central Authorities to institute proceedings is *essential* and *more vital than in national cases*, because normally two different legal systems are implicated and quite often the applicant does not know even the language of the State where he or she wishes to lodge an application.[114]

Given the centrality of this provision it would have been helpful if some of the measures suggested in the *Explanatory Report* – for example, the provision of a list of lawyers and legal aid[115] – had been included in the Convention as concrete forms of assistance that ought to be provided.

Recognition and enforcement of transfrontier contact orders

The recognition and enforcement provisions of this Convention are designed 'to facilitate the exercise of contact and custody rights in the case of transfrontier contact orders'.[116] To this end, States Parties are required to establish a system specifically designed to achieve such recognition and enforcement[117] as well as a procedure whereby foreign contact orders 'may be recognised and declared enforceable in advance of contact being exercised within the State addressed'.[118] Recognition and enforcement are not rigid matters, however. Thus, Article 15 allows States Parties to modify or fix the

[110] *Ibid*, Art 12(a)–(b); Art 13.
[111] *Ibid*, Art 12(a) and (e), respectively.
[112] *Ibid*, Art 13(3).
[113] See ch 8.
[114] *Explanatory Report*, *op cit* n 90, para 107 (emphasis added).
[115] *Loc cit*.
[116] *Loc cit*, para 108.
[117] Contact Convention, Art 14(1)(a).
[118] *Ibid*, Art 14(1)(b). This provision complements the previous one in that it both discourages a parent with whom the child normally lives from hampering the transfrontier contact rights of the other parent and helps to ensure the prompt return of a child after a period of visitation: see *Explanatory Report*, *op cit* n 90, para 111.

conditions associated with the implementation of a contact order as changes in circumstances or the arrangements agreed by the persons concerned may from time to time dictate. What Article 15 forbids, however, is any is any such modifications that would undermine the essential elements of the order.[119]

Importantly, the duty to recognise and enforce cross-border contact orders is not explained, but is stated in the *Explanatory Report* not to extend to the situation in which an order granted in State A is at odds with the rules on majority in State B (in which State recognition is sought).[120] Nonetheless, State B's exoneration from the duty to afford recognition is implicit in the several definitions laid down in Article 2. It will be recalled that a 'contact order' is defined in terms of 'contact' which has been judicially sanctioned, and that contact invariably refers to a child. It therefore follows – though this is not stated in the Convention – that if the domestic law of State B does not recognise the existence of a 'child', there cannot logically be a meaningful contact order to which recognition could be afforded.

Two final matters

In recognition of the fact that cross-border contacts do not always end with the prompt and proper return of children, the Convention provides a facility whereby, at the request of the aggrieved person, the competent authorities in the State of visitation may engage the machinery of the Abduction Conventions in order to secure the swift return of the child.[121]

In addition, Article 17 of the Contact Convention contains a rather mixed provision with respect to costs in the context of transfrontier contact cases. This provision is far from immediately transparent since it entails what has been described as 'a difficult inter-relationship with the . . . [European Abduction] Convention'.[122] Nonetheless, the gist of this article is that 'while court costs for recognition and enforcement will be covered . . . this will not be the case insofar as they relate to that part of the hearing concerned with modification [of the contact conditions]'.[123]

[119] Article 15 of the Convention will replace Art 11(2) of European Abduction Convention 1980 (Contact Convention, Art 19) in order (supposedly) to remove the problems of interpretation associated with that provision, and in particular the question of whether the courts in State B are entitled to change the place of contact. For the suggestion that it may fail in this regard, see Lowe *et al*, *op cit* n 6, p 603.

[120] *Explanatory Report*, *op cit* n 90, para 109.

[121] Contact Convention, Art 16. It is specifically provided that this Convention is intended to affect the operation of neither of the two Abduction Conventions considered in this book, nor the Child Protection Convention 1996: *ibid*, Art 20.

[122] Lowe *et al*, *op cit* n 6, p 604.

[123] *Loc cit*.

Critique

The 1996 Child Protection Convention

Despite there being at one time a possible technical obstacle in the way of EU States ratifying the Hague Child Protection Convention,[124] it is at last clear, on the authority of the Council of the European Union, that they are now free to ratify. One can only hope that that the United Kingdom will formally do so in the very near future. For, all things considered, the Convention constitutes an important, innovative[125] and pluralistic instrument.[126] On the positive side of things, its chief achievement is arguably the extent to which it eliminates the scope for conflicts of jurisdiction and conflicts between various child protection orders obtained in different Contracting States.[127] Another significant feature is the novel approach it embodies with respect to securing cross-border parental access rights. In this respect, it goes beyond the assistance available under both the Hague Child Abduction Convention and the European Child Abduction Convention.[128] Also, in relation to its provisions facilitating the retention of parental responsibility following a change in habitual residence by those who would not automatically possess such responsibility in the new State, the Convention promotes both stability and continuity while affording great respect to the expectations of the parents and older children concerned. Finally, as Clive puts it, 'in relation to public law measures of child protection there is little doubt that the provisions on co-operation are potentially among the most valuable and important in the whole Convention'.[129] And while one may quibble over the primary status he ascribes to these measures, it is difficult to disagree with his general assertion that they have the potential to 'succeed in bringing about an improved climate of co-operation between the authorities in different Contracting States'.

On the negative side of things, the Convention bears a number of telling deficiencies. To begin with, it does not provide any definition of the pivotal

[124] For details, see Lowe *et al*, *op cit* n 6, pp 556–557.

[125] One of the chief shortcomings in the Hague Intercountry Adoption Convention is its inability to deal adequately with the problem of non-adoptable refugee children (for details see ch 7). Art 6 of this Convention, by contrast, allows for a special jurisdiction to take protective measures in respect of such children.

[126] Art 3 of the Child Protection Convention specifically includes *kafala* among the kinds of protective measures to which it applies.

[127] Such conflicts, as we noted at the start of this chapter, were the primary reason why the 1961 Convention which this Convention replaces proved to be so unpopular.

[128] Child Protection Convention, Art 35. On the other hand, it does not go as far as the not-yet-in-force European Convention on Contact Concerning Children 2003. This matter is considered below.

[129] Clive, *op cit* n 14, at 186.

concept of habitual residence.[130] And this could prove to be a critical omission since jurisdiction is predominantly founded on habitual residence while the equally important questions of applicable law and recognition and enforcement are closely associated with jurisdiction. From a domestic perspective, we might hope and expect in this context that the courts of this country will be guided by the wealth of authority on the concept of habitual residence that has been produced under the Hague Child Abduction Convention. Quite deliberately the two Conventions are closely inter-related. They share a number of common concepts and it would seem, therefore, inappropriate to develop a separate meaning of habitual residence for the purposes only of the Child Protection Convention.[131]

A second possible criticism of the Convention centres on the fact that, despite the second paragraph of the Preamble stating explicitly the aim of avoiding conflicts of jurisdiction and protective measures, not all such potential conflicts have been eliminated. We noted in passing two possible situations in which such remaining conflicts may well give rise to problems. They were, it will be recalled, the situation in which a court in the State of habitual residence makes an order 'trumping' an order by a court of refuge following an abduction, and the situation in which a change of residence occurs while proceedings for protective measures are still pending in the first State but the second State also proposes to take protective measures. Happily, the factual circumstances in which these problems may occur are heavily circumscribed and for this reason only likely to arise very infrequently. As such, they do not present serious potential problems for the operation of the Convention.

Finally, there is a certain, regrettable vagueness associated with the Article 26(2) requirement that each Contracting State must establish a 'simple and rapid' procedure for securing the enforcement in one Contracting State of measures promulgated in another such State. Given the importance within the Convention of the recognition and enforcement provisions, it is a pity that more rigid stipulations were not made with respect to this procedure. Again, however, the principle of co-operation may go a long way to reducing any potential problems that might arise in consequence of the obscurity of this provision.

[130] Apparently, attempts to introduce a partial definition failed: see *Lagarde Report*, *op cit* n 9, para 40. On the other hand, it is arguably implicit in Art 7 that either a sustained period of actual residence is required or that there be acquiescence in the change of habitual residence on the part of all those holding parental responsibility.

[131] For analysis of various possible connotations of the notion, see E. Clive, 'The Concept of Habitual Residence' [1997] *Juridical Review* 137.

The 2003 Contact Convention

This is another progressive Convention that adopts[132] a refreshingly open, non-marriage-centred definition of family ties (Article 2(d)) in order to promote the bilateral contact rights of a child and all those with whom he or she shares a close familial bond. Equally, and in contrast to the Child Protection Convention and the two Abduction Conventions, the new Contact Convention is premised on a flexible notion of who should be regarded as a child. This approach – though not entirely beyond criticism – respects differences among Member States as to the point at which majority and the capacity for minors to make their own residence decisions occurs. Furthermore, it takes pragmatic steps to ensure that contact, once it has been formally sanctioned, should be made enforceable even across national frontiers.

There are, inevitably, a number of minor criticisms that may be noted in relation to the Contact Convention. One is that it fails to make clear the extent to which States Parties are at liberty to alter the terms and conditions according to which cross-border contact may be exercised. The Convention itself allows for such amendments, but in the same breath imposes as a proviso the requirement that 'the essential elements of the contact order are [to be] respected'.[133] Without further clarification, it is thus left to individual States to work out where conditions for implementation end, and changes to the essential elements of an order begin. Any such scope for differential State practice in applying a supposedly common set of rules is always likely to be a matter of at least some regret. But in the present context this might be kept to a minimum given the clear political will on the part of the States of the European Union to move closer towards a harmonised set of family law rules.[134]

A second criticism, as hinted earlier, arises from the fact that the Contact Convention allows considerable scope for differences in approach among States Parties on the matter of which children are covered by the Convention in terms of their acquisition of majority and their acquisition of a right to self-determination in matters of contact. As such, this in turn provides the basis for potential refusals to recognise or enforce transfrontier contact orders obtained in one State where the second State would not treat the 'child' in question as being capable of forming the subject of such an order. Again, however, it is to be hoped that the principle of co-operation so central to the operation of this Convention will provide the framework within which any such problems may be resolved.

All things considered, the Contact Convention of 2003 represents a well-intentioned addition to the burgeoning array of international instruments

[132] Contact Convention, Art 2(d). For details see n 94, *supra*.
[133] *Ibid*, Art 15.
[134] C. McGlynn, 'The Europeanisation of Family Law' [2001] *Child and Family Law Quarterly* 35.

concerning children. But rather like its sibling, the seldom used European Abduction Convention 1980, it is open to the objection that it adds only a little to the existing Conventions and regulations in this area, and that it might therefore be considered largely otiose. In particular, the fact that its provisions on cross-border contact are a marked improvement on those contained in either of the two Abduction Conventions or the Child Protection Convention is danger of losing its significance in the wake of Brussels IIA[135] which, in cases of wrongful retention, will allow jurisdiction to be retained by the State of origin so that custody and access decisions taken there will be entitled to automatic recognition in accordance with Chapter III of the Regulation.[136] Put bluntly, the most significant feature of the 2003 Convention may already have been superseded.

[135] Council Regulation (EC) No 2201/2003.

[136] Brussels IIA, Art 40(2) provides that '[a] judgment given in a Member State shall be recognised and enforceable in another Member State without the need for a declaration of enforceability and without any possibility of opposing its recognition if the judgment has been certified in the Member State of origin'.

Part V

Conclusions

11

Concluding reflections

Domestic family law is intimately linked to social norms. It often reflects or supports them, but it sometimes serves to weaken or undermine them.[1] It is precisely because of this close relationship between family law and social norms that legal scholars have generally considered family law to be ill-suited to comparative analysis,[2] and to be a subject best studied on a jurisdictionally specific basis. But the legal landscape has now changed. So, whereas once we may have considered marriage and legitimacy to be the main organising concepts within the subject, and while, later, we may have viewed the law relating to children and parenthood to have come to the fore, we must now fully recognise the modern significance of a range of international dimensions. Some of these international dimensions have existed for a long time, but they were not really central to family law for reasons of limited practical importance. The conflicts of law rules on the recognition of foreign marriages and divorces are obvious examples. However, the dramatic increase in international migration (especially within Europe) combined with the advent abroad of same-sex marriage and intercountry adoption make it clear that these branches of the law have acquired a new significance.

In addition, there has occurred a virtual explosion in recent decades in terms of international endeavours to introduce harmonisation of, and co-operation over, family law matters. These initiatives are, of course, most evident in the various international instruments considered in this book.[3] And while the majority of these instruments have been designed primarily to

[1] See J. Eekelaar, 'Uncovering Social Obligations: Family Law and the Responsible Citizen' in M. Maclean (ed), *Making Law for Families* (Oxford: Hart Publishing, 2000).

[2] See D. Bradley, 'Comparative Law, Family Law and Common Law' (2003) 23 *Oxford Journal of Legal Studies* 127.

[3] But others exist also, such as the periodic international judicial conferences that now take place.

achieve inter-State co-operation and to establish certain common principles of private international law,[4] there are others, such as the highly successful Hague Abduction Convention, which lay down common rules of substantive law and still others, such as the United Nations Convention on the Rights of the Child, that make admirable attempts to lay down international norms and standards that fall short of precise rules of law.

In short, what has begun to occur is the progressive internationalisation of family law.[5] At the forefront of this process is the European Union which, having now harmonised a good deal of the private international family law rules, looks next destined to begin a more ambitious programme aimed at achieving a greater degree of commonality in terms of *substantive law*, too.[6] What seems clear, then, is that domestic family lawyers – whether judges, practitioners, academics or students – must now come to terms with this new legal order. It has been the aim of this book to chart what appear to be the principal strands to this process of internationalisation. But equally important has been the endeavour to bring a critical dimension to the discussion. In this respect several recurrent themes and concerns have emerged. At this point it seems appropriate to revisit these issues and to offer some concluding reflections of a general nature.

Looking backwards

The need for greater pluralism

In looking to the past, one of our major regrets must be the degree to which our family law rules of private international law developed, in the nineteenth century and early twentieth century, in a far from pluralistic fashion. Even more troubling is the fact that, although we can now see the errors of our ways, the law relating to the recognition of foreign marriages still plays host to a number of xenophobic and chauvinistic rules.[7] It is difficult to

[4] Their focus is generally on jurisdiction rules and those relating to the recognition and enforcement of foreign judgements. See, eg, the European Convention on Recognition and Enforcement of Decisions Concerning Custody of Children and on Restoration of Custody of Children 1980; Council Regulation (EC) No 2201/2003 ('Brussels IIA'); the Hague Child Protection Convention 1996; and the European Convention on Contact Concerning Children 2003. As regards the co-operation ideal, see also the Hague Intercountry Adoption Convention 1993.

[5] For a fuller account of the various ways in which this has occurred, see ch 1.

[6] See C.M.V. Clarkson, 'Brussels III – Matrimonial Property European Style' [2002] *Family Law* 683. See also C. McGlynn, 'The Europeanisation of Family Law' [2001] *Child and Family Law Quarterly* 35.

[7] See ch 3 and J. Murphy, 'Rationality and Cultural Pluralism in the Non-Recognition of Foreign Marriages' (2000) 49 *International and Comparative Law Quarterly* 643.

understand why, when the Law Commission was so critical of these rules,[8] no remedial action was taken. It is to be hoped that when the inevitable challenges for these rules posed by various forms of same-sex families finally emerge, the English courts will take the opportunity to revisit some of them and make the necessary changes. There can be no doubt that the relevant judicial will exists at the highest level.[9]

Unfortunately, similar criticisms can be made in relation to certain aspects of the law relating to the recognition of overseas divorces. For example, as Mayss has written:

> the discretionary grounds for refusing recognition to certain overseas divorces call . . . for radical revision if not wholesale removal from the statute book. [For] [a]s things stand, the legislation bears all too often deep shades of unwarrantable ethnocentrism.[10]

It seems wholly inappropriate that a body of conflicts rules should be susceptible to such criticisms in the twenty-first century. And this is particularly the case when one considers that the relevant rules in this context are in statutory form, and that the relevant legislation was produced as recently as 1986.

The need for greater pluralism in relation to international aspects of family law is not confined to English private international law rules. For example, the jurisdiction provisions of the Hague Convention Concerning the Powers of Authorities and the Law Applicable in Respect of the Protection of Infants 1961 was drafted in a manner that made little to no accommodation for common law jurisdictions. Its replacement, the Child Protection Convention 1996 is great improvement in this respect; and it was even specifically drafted so as to make it more attractive to Muslim States.[11]

On the other hand, the most widely ratified Convention considered in this book – the United Nations Convention on the Rights of the Child – is still open to criticism on the basis that it is dominated by concepts and concerns associated with States in the West. As Sonia Harris-Short has noted in relation to the drafting of that Convention:

> [t]here are certainly many . . . examples of the concerns of states from the developing world being effectively ignored . . . [Thus] a great deal more work still needs to be done to improve both the quantity and effectiveness of non-Western participation in the drafting process of international conventions if

[8] Law Commission, Working Paper No 89, *Private International Law: Choice of Law Rules in Marriage* (London: HMSO, 1985) para 3.17.

[9] *Ghaidan v Godin-Mendoza* [2004] UKHL 30.

[10] A. Mayss, 'Recognition of Foreign Divorces: Unwarrantable Ethnocentrism' in J. Murphy (ed), *Ethnic Minorities, Their Families and the Law* (Oxford: Hart Publishing, 2000) p 70.

[11] See ch 10.

the ideals of a fully inclusive, cross-cultural human rights regime are to be realised.[12]

Simplicity and consistency

Given the point made above – that there exist pockets of xenophobia and chauvinism within our system of private international law – a further issue that naturally arises is whether we ought not to rationalise and simplify our common law and statutory rules in relation to the recognition of foreign marriages and divorces. Take, for example, the public policy ground on which foreign divorces may be denied recognition under the Family Law Act 1986 and which hardly ever succeeds when raised in litigation. This may be criticised on two alternative grounds. First, where it does succeed, it has the capacity to appear xenophobic. And, secondly, where it is raised but does not succeed, it can arguably be seen as a waste of time and resources. Further, its anti-pluralist underpinnings would support the contention that it should never have been considered a legitimate line of argument in the first place.

There is even more scope for simplification in relation the common law rules on the recognition of foreign marriages. These, as we saw in chapter 3, are incredibly complex and specious. We also considered at that juncture the various advantages to be gained by codifying these rules. For this reason they need not be replicated here. Instead, it suffices to note that codification – perhaps along the Australian lines[13] – would provide the single best opportunity for eliminating those anomalous rules, referred to earlier, that are inescapably chauvinistic and xenophobic in nature.

Finally, in this context it should be noted that there exists enormous complexity within the range of international family law instruments. In particular, there is a troubling overlap between Brussels IIA, the Hague Abduction Convention, the European Abduction Convention, the Child Protection Convention and the European Convention on Contact Concerning Children. And while it is currently possible – albeit only just – to describe the various inter-relationships between these instruments, one wonders whether it might not make more sense for some of these instruments to be formally

[12] See S. Harris-Short, 'Listening to "The Other"? The Convention on the Rights of the Child' (2001) 2 *Melbourne Journal of International Law* 305, 332. See also R.L. Barsh, 'The Draft Convention on the Rights of the Child: A Case of Eurocentrism in Standard-Setting' (1989) 58 *Nordic Journal of International Law* 24 and P Schwab, 'Human Rights: A Western Construct with Limited Applicability' in A. Pollis and P. Schwab (eds), *Human Rights: Cultural and Ideological Perspectives* (New York: Praeger, 1979).

[13] See M. Neave, 'The New Rules on Recognition of Foreign Marriages – Insomnia for Lawyers' [1990] *Australian Journal of Family Law* 190. See also P.E. Nygh, *Conflict of Laws in Australia* (Sydney: Butterworths, 1995) ch 24; E.I. Sykes & M.C. Pryles, *Australian Private International Law* (Sydney: Law Book Co, 1991) ch 11.

abandoned. One candidate for such abandonment might well be the European Contact Convention 2003. For much as its content may be applauded when taken *in isolation*, it nonetheless looks somewhat unnecessary when read alongside the various other instruments that already operate among the various European States to which it would apply. The European Abduction Convention also now bears a distinctly redundant look. It has been largely superseded by Brussels IIA, but in any case, it was generally overlooked by the majority of States in which it applied in favour of the Hague Abduction Convention.

Positive implementation of international instruments

Another concern that emerges from the preceding chapters is the lack, hitherto, of a positive approach to the implementation of international family law instruments in this country. Reaction to the original version of Brussels IIA was mixed, but in the main was characterised by scepticism and hostility.[14] This negativity is also evident in the fact that the United Kingdom has yet to incorporate into municipal law the United Nations Convention on the Rights of the Child; and this is in spite of a specific call from the Committee on the Rights of the Child to do so.[15] Similarly, despite the green light given by the Council of the European Union for EU States to ratify the Child Protection Convention 1996, the UK has yet to do that, as well. In short, there is a history of this country being both dilatory and half-hearted when it comes to welcoming international family law initiatives. Even the European Convention on Human Rights – which has a significant bearing on family law – did not get transcribed into English domestic law until 1998.

Looking to the future

Closer involvement in further initiatives

For two main reasons, there ought in the future to be greater involvement and input on the part of English family lawyers in the exploratory and preparatory stages of future international instruments. First, there ought to be more input from the common law world generally so that the terminology adopted is universally meaningful. It is clearly unacceptable that, in the sphere

[14] See, eg, D. Truex, 'Brussels II – Beware!' [2001] *Family Law* 233; N. Mostyn, 'Brussels II – The Impact on Forum Disputes' [2001] *Family Law* 359, 363–365; I. Karsten, 'Brussels II – An English Perspective' [1998] *International Family Law* 75.

[15] Committee on the Rights of the Child, *Concluding Observations of the Committee on the Rights of the Child: United Kingdom of Great Britain and Northern Ireland* CRC/C/15 188 (Geneva: Centre for Human Rights, 2002) para 56(b). These observations are available at www.crights.org.uk/pdfs/UNCRC_conc_obs_2002.pdf.

of legal practice, '[f]or many, Brussels II . . . came as a bolt out of the blue'.[16] But even beyond this concern, and more centrally still, it is crucial that a family lawyer's perspective is brought to bear on the drafting of these instruments. As we begin an era in which certain substantive family law rules look set to be harmonised throughout the European Union, there is still a discernible tendency at that level according to which 'family rights are granted in pursuit of the economic ends of the single market, and not for the protection of family life *per se*'.[17] The impending regulations, Brussels III and IV, constitute the most immediate cases in which family lawyers from this country ought to involve themselves.

Implementation strategies

Given the dualist tradition of this country according to which international Conventions do not, upon mere ratification, create rights that can be enforced before the domestic courts, it is clear that a change in attitude is required in relation to taking positive steps towards the implementation of international instruments. But implementation strategies need to go beyond simply exhibiting greater willingness to incorporate multilateral Conventions. They must also, in many cases, be supplemented in some way so as to make them more workable and meaningful. In relation to nearly all the instruments considered in this book, there were criticisms associated with the vagueness of the language in which they were framed. Often, the instruments in question were deliberately drafted in this way in order to maximise the number of Contracting Parties.[18] For where Conventions eschew the use of clear, prescriptive language, they are less likely to be perceived as off-putting by developing nations that might otherwise struggle to fulfil their obligations. Prime examples are the United Nations Convention on the Rights of the Child and the Hague Intercountry Adoption Convention 1993.[19]

But in recognising this, and in recognising, also, the relative ease with which this country ought to be able to meet the requirements of these Conventions, it would seem strategically appropriate to accompany their incorporation with whatever supplementary regulations are needed in order to make the Convention in question properly meaningful. This, of course, has been done in large measure with respect to the Hague Intercountry Adoption Convention.[20] And it is a model of incorporation that ought to be replicated in the future.

[16] N. Lowe, 'New International Conventions Affecting the Law Relating to Children – A Cause for Concern?' [2001] *International Family Law* 171, 171.

[17] See McGlynn, *op cit* n 6, at 37.

[18] See, eg, C.P. Cohen, 'Elasticity of Obligation and the Drafting of the Convention on the Rights of the Child' (1987) 3 *Connecticut Journal of International Law* 71.

[19] See ch 7.

[20] Intercountry Adoption (Hague Convention) Regulations 2003 (SI 2003, No 118).

Index